AF846173

OXFORD MONOGRAPHS IN INTERNATIONAL LAW

General Editors

PROFESSOR CATHERINE REDGWELL

Chichele Professor of Public International Law at the University of Oxford and Fellow of All Souls College, Oxford

PROFESSOR ROGER O'KEEFE

Professor of International Law at Bocconi University, Milan

Statehood and the State-Like in International Law

OXFORD MONOGRAPHS IN INTERNATIONAL LAW

The aim of this series is to publish important and original pieces of research on all aspects of international law. Topics that are given particular prominence are those which, while of interest to the academic lawyer, also have important bearing on issues which touch the actual conduct of international relations. Nonetheless the series is wide in scope and includes monographs on the history and philosophical foundations of international law.

RECENT TITLES IN THE SERIES

Confronting the Shadow State
An International Law Perspective on State Organized Crime
Henri Decoeur

Irresolvable Norm Conflicts in International Law
The Concept of a Legal Dilemma
Valentin Jeutner

Institutionalizing State Responsibility
Global Security and UN Organs
Vincent-Joël Proulx

The Power of Process
The Value of Due Process in Security Council Sanctions Decision-Making
Devika Hovell

Statehood and the State-Like in International Law

ROWAN NICHOLSON

OXFORD
UNIVERSITY PRESS

OXFORD
UNIVERSITY PRESS

Great Clarendon Street, Oxford, OX2 6DP,
United Kingdom

Oxford University Press is a department of the University of Oxford.
It furthers the University's objective of excellence in research, scholarship,
and education by publishing worldwide. Oxford is a registered trade mark of
Oxford University Press in the UK and in certain other countries

© Rowan Nicholson 2019

The moral rights of the author have been asserted

First Edition published in 2019

Impression: 1

All rights reserved. No part of this publication may be reproduced, stored in
a retrieval system, or transmitted, in any form or by any means, without the
prior permission in writing of Oxford University Press, or as expressly permitted
by law, by licence or under terms agreed with the appropriate reprographics
rights organization. Enquiries concerning reproduction outside the scope of the
above should be sent to the Rights Department, Oxford University Press, at the
address above

You must not circulate this work in any other form
and you must impose this same condition on any acquirer

Crown copyright material is reproduced under Class Licence
Number C01P0000148 with the permission of OPSI
and the Queen's Printer for Scotland

Published in the United States of America by Oxford University Press
198 Madison Avenue, New York, NY 10016, United States of America

British Library Cataloguing in Publication Data
Data available

Library of Congress Control Number: 2019941568

ISBN 978–0–19–885121–9

Printed and bound by
CPI Group (UK) Ltd, Croydon, CR0 4YY

Statehood and the State-Like in International Law. Rowan Nicholson,
Oxford University Press (2019). © Rowan Nicholson
DOI: 10.1093/oso/9780198851219.001.0001

Links to third party websites are provided by Oxford in good faith and
for information only. Oxford disclaims any responsibility for the materials
contained in any third party website referenced in this work.

General Editors' Preface

Such are the sheer scope and the diversity of today's international law, with its proliferation of subject-matters and specialist fields, and such are the incentives for scholars to find a research 'niche' that canonical topics of international law—a denomination itself contested or considered quaint—can be passed over or crowded out. Additionally, there is something of a tendency in contemporary international legal scholarship to think of 'theorizing' solely in terms of the application to international law of other theoretical branches of the social sciences, such as political theory, philosophy, hermeneutics, linguistics or semiotics, and not in terms of legal theory, at least in the sense of formalist legal theory. An allied tendency is to treat 'theory' as coterminous with critical or ideal theory, when theory can equally be explanatory.

Rowan Nicholson's *Statehood and the State-like in International Law* bucks all three trends. It posits what in effect is an explanatory theory, founded on legal doctrinal analysis and analytical jurisprudence, in relation to two core topics of international law in the form of international legal personality and statehood. This should not, however, be mistaken as subscription to orthodoxy. While by no means heretical, the theory propounded is avowedly revisionist.

Dr Nicholson's book is ambitious. Not only does it address a question off the beaten track, namely which 'state-like entities' enjoy international legal personality. It also set outs to answer this via an inventive and intellectually dense doctrinal-cum-jurisprudential route which aims 'to provide insights into the nature of international law as a system'. Not content with the bald reply 'Those state-like entities which states treat as having such personality', Dr Nicholson grounds his conclusions in an original theory, premised on the putative implications of the work of WN Hohfeld for the definition of international legal personality, which challenges what he casts as the received wisdom on the international legal basis of statehood while traversing on the way nineteenth-century international legal history, the declaratory and constitutive accounts of statehood, the right to self-determination, the principle *ex injuria jus non oritur*, and the respective international legal positions of Hong Kong, Taiwan, and Niue, to name just a few. The result is a thoughtful, erudite, and fascinating work which offers a mildly controversial 'thick' rationale for historical and contemporary state practice not only in relation to the enjoyment of international legal personality by various non-state political-territorial entities but also as regards statehood itself. It is bound to stimulate and provoke.

RO'K, CR

Milan and Oxford
August 2019

Statehood and the State-Like in International Law. Rowan Nicholson, Oxford University Press (2019).
© Rowan Nicholson
DOI: 10.1093/oso/9780198851219.001.0001

Acknowledgements

This book is a revised version of a doctoral thesis that I completed at the University of Cambridge in October 2017; the thesis was called *A Theory of Statehood and Personality in International Law*. It was made possible by a Cambridge Australia WongCalthorpe Scholarship from the Cambridge Trust: thank you to the Trust and the benefactors. Thank you also to my college, Sidney Sussex. My ideas were shaped by valuable conversations with my supervisor, Lorand Bartels, and by work I did for James Crawford before beginning the doctorate. Among helpful friends and colleagues Tom Grant merits particular thanks. In revising the text for publication, I have had the additional benefit of advice from the examiners, who were Eyal Benvenisti and Roger O'Keefe, and from the anonymous peer reviewers. Finally, I am grateful to my family and most of all to my wife, Rachael White: I could not have done this without her.

Translations from French are mine unless otherwise indicated. So are any errors.

Statehood and the State-Like in International Law. Rowan Nicholson, Oxford University Press (2019).
© Rowan Nicholson
DOI: 10.1093/oso/9780198851219.001.0001

Contents

Statehood and the State-Like in International Law. Rowan Nicholson, Oxford University Press (2019).
© Rowan Nicholson
DOI: 10.1093/oso/9780198851219.001.0001

Table of Cases

Statehood and the State-Like in International Law. Rowan Nicholson, Oxford University Press (2019).
© Rowan Nicholson
DOI: 10.1093/oso/9780198851219.001.0001

Table of Instruments

Statehood and the State-Like in International Law. Rowan Nicholson, Oxford University Press (2019).

© Rowan Nicholson

DOI: 10.1093/oso/9780198851219.001.0001

List of Abbreviations

AC	Law Reports Appeal Cases (England and Wales)
AJIL	American Journal of International Law
AJIL Supp	American Journal of International Law Supplement
Annuaire IDI	Annuaire de l'Institut de droit international
ASIL Proc	American Society of International Law Proceedings
BFSP	British and Foreign State Papers
BYIL	British Yearbook of International Law
CLR	Commonwealth Law Reports (Australia)
CTS	Consolidated Treaty Series
CUP	Cambridge University Press
DLR 2d	Dominion Law Reports, 2nd series (Canada)
E Africa PLR	East Africa Protectorate Law Reports
ECHR	European Court of Human Rights
EJIL	European Journal of International Law
ER	English Reports
F 3d	Federal Reporter, 3rd series (United States)
F Supp 2d	Federal Supplement, 2nd series (United States)
GA	United Nations General Assembly
ICJ	International Court of Justice
ICJ Rep	International Court of Justice Reports of Judgments, Advisory Opinions and Orders
ICLQ	International and Comparative Law Quarterly
ICTY	International Criminal Tribunal for the former Yugoslavia
ILC Ybk	International Law Commission Yearbook
ILM	International Legal Materials
ILR	International Law Reports
JORF	Journal officiel de la République Française
KB	Law Reports King's Bench (England and Wales)
LN	League of Nations
LNOJ Sp Supp	League of Nations Official Journal Special Supplement
LNTS	League of Nations Treaty Series
LR Ind App	Law Reports Indian Appeals
MPEPIL	*Max Planck Encyclopedia of Public International Law* (first published 1991, OUP) <http://opil.ouplaw.com/home/epil>
NE	North Eastern Reporter (United States)
OJEC	Official Journal of the European Communities
OUP	Oxford University Press
PCIJ	Permanent Court of International Justice
Recueil des cours	Collected Courses of the Hague Academy of International Law

Statehood and the State-Like in International Law. Rowan Nicholson, Oxford University Press (2019).
© Rowan Nicholson
DOI: 10.1093/oso/9780198851219.001.0001

Recueil TAM	Recueil des décisions des tribunaux arbitraux mixtes institués par les traités de paix
SATS	South African Treaty Series
SC	United Nations Security Council
Stat	United States Statutes at Large
UK	United Kingdom of Great Britain and Ireland (1801–1927) *or* United Kingdom of Great Britain and Northern Ireland (from 1927 but reflecting the creation of the Irish Free State in 1922)
UKTS	United Kingdom Treaty Series
UN	United Nations
Unesco	United Nations Educational, Scientific and Cultural Organization
UNRIAA	United Nations Reports of International Arbitral Awards
UNTS	United Nations Treaty Series
UP	University Press
US	United States of America *or* United States Reports
USC	United States Code
US GPO	United States Government Printing Office
WTO	World Trade Organization

Introduction

Law between nations or states?

International law is law that exists between nations—or, at least, that is what the term implies if it is read literally.[1] But the word 'nation' does not have a clear meaning among international lawyers. They use it, when they use it at all, rhetorically or in old-fashioned fixed phrases such as 'most-favoured-nation treatment'.[2] They are more likely to reach for the technical legal term 'state', which on one view refers to entities with a government, a population, a territory, and independence. The pattern is similar in languages other than English.[3]

So what is a nation for the purpose of the term 'international law'?

Some clues can be found in a series of meetings that took place in February 1919 at the Hôtel de Crillon in Paris. The chair was President Woodrow Wilson of the United States; the other delegates were from Brazil, China, Japan, and six European states. Their task was to design an organization that would aim, among other things, to entrench international law as a 'rule of conduct'.[4] The organization was to be called the League of Nations, but the Portuguese and Brazilian delegates proposed an alternative name: the Society or League of States.[5] In dismissing this alternative, the French delegate explained that he 'understood that the word "Nations" was employed in the sense of "States" '.[6] The British delegate remarked that 'the difference between the words "Nations" and "States" was a very small one'.[7] But the difference, however small, must still have been significant for the British,

[1] The English term 'international law', replacing the earlier 'law of nations', first appeared in Jeremy Bentham, *Introduction to the Principles of Morals and Legislation* (first published 1789, OUP 1996).

[2] See, among other treaties, General Agreement on Tariffs and Trade (30 October 1947) 55 UNTS 194, art 1. Another occurrence of the word 'nation' in international law is the reference to 'civilized nations' in Statute of the International Court of Justice (26 June 1945) art 38(1)(c), on which see this book ss 2.2, 2.6.

[3] Eg, the Latin *ius gentium* (from *gens*, which is closer to 'people' than to 'state'), the French *droit international* and the earlier *droit des gens*, and cognates in other languages. Further on the history of these terms, see Jörg Fisch, 'Peoples and nations' in Bardo Fassbender and Anne Peters (eds), *The Oxford Handbook of the History of International Law* (OUP 2012) 27, 28–30. On the history of Chinese translations of these originally Western terms, see Rune Svarverud, *International Law as World Order in Late Imperial China: Translation, Reception and Discourse, 1847–1911* (Brill 2007), especially 107–8, 179–81.

[4] Covenant of the League of Nations (28 June 1919) preamble.

[5] Jaime Batalha Reis, Portugal (3 February 1919) and Epitácio Pessoa, Brazil (4 February 1919) in David Hunter Miller, *The Drafting of the Covenant* (GP Putnam's Sons 1928) vol 1, 135, 141–2.

[6] Ferdinand Larnaude, France (4 February 1919) in ibid, vol 1, 142.

[7] Robert Cecil, British Empire (3 February 1919) in ibid, vol 1, 135.

Statehood and the State-Like in International Law. Rowan Nicholson, Oxford University Press (2019).
© Rowan Nicholson
DOI: 10.1093/oso/9780198851219.001.0001

because they went on to insist that the Covenant of the League refer to 'Members' rather than more specifically to 'States'.[8] And they had a motive for avoiding references to statehood: 'to enable the British Dominions to become members of the League', on the view that the dominions—Australia, Canada, New Zealand, and South Africa—were not yet independent enough to qualify as states.[9] The British also foresaw separate membership for India, which was a non-self-governing colony and as such even further from statehood. Wilson had proposed a rule that new members at least be self-governing; he hesitated over India, but 'no one else seemed to care'.[10] The outcome was that the name of the organization referred to 'Nations', the Covenant generally referred to 'Members', and the dominions and India were allowed in.

The reference to nations was retained in the name of the League's successor, the United Nations. Although its Charter, unlike the Covenant, generally refers to its members as 'States', the United Nations still began life in 1945 with a few members that did not yet have statehood: India again, plus the Philippines (which was about to become independent of the United States) and the Soviet constituent republics of Belarus and Ukraine.[11]

The choice of the word 'nations' to allude to the members of these organizations suggests that it essentially denotes states but that it has, or had in the past, some elasticity.

Another interpretation of the word 'nations' is that it denotes the groups of men and women that states and nationalist movements claim to represent. This would fit with usage in politics and history, where nations have been described as 'imagined communities'.[12] Nations in this sense are more akin to what international lawyers call 'peoples'—nebulously defined groups that may aspire to create states in future—than to the formal institutions that belong to the United Nations, with their parliaments and armies. The term 'international law', on this interpretation, 'emphasizes not the reality but the ideal of international law'.[13]

[8] Ibid, vol 1, 477–92.

[9] Antonio Cassese, *Self-Determination of Peoples: A Legal Reappraisal* (CUP 1995) 27 n 45; this book s 3.1.1. Newfoundland was also a dominion but did not become a separate member of the League.

[10] Miller (n 5) vol 1, 157– 8, referring to the meeting on 5 February 1919; further 492–3. Covenant, art 1(2) allowed a 'fully self-governing State, Dominion or Colony' to seek to become a new member, but strictly the requirement to be self-governing did not apply to *original* members such as India.

[11] At the time these were the Byelorussian Soviet Socialist Republic and the Ukrainian Soviet Socialist Republic. There was also some doubt in 1945 about the status of Lebanon and Syria: Ulrich Fastenrath, 'Article 3' in Bruno Simma and others (eds), *The Charter of the United Nations: A Commentary* (3rd edn, OUP 2012) 335, para 6. On the relationship between statehood and UN membership, see further this book s 3.4.2. The word 'nation' also appears in the names of a few other international organizations, including the Association of Southeast Asian Nations and the (formerly British) Commonwealth of Nations.

[12] Benedict Anderson, *Imagined Communities: Reflections on the Origin and Spread of Nationalism* (first published 1983, rev edn, Verso 2006).

[13] Fisch (n 3) 30. On peoples, see this book s 4.2.

But the best explanation for the persistence of the 'nation' element in the term 'international law' may be that it is conveniently vague. Sometimes it is used as a straightforward synonym for the term 'state'; sometimes it can be stretched further to encompass a few other entities; sometimes it refers to a hazy ideal and, in that way, avoids saying anything much about the states and similar entities between which international law really exists.

My aim in this book is to identify those entities, the entities that the 'nation' element in 'international law' might loosely be taken to represent. To put the question in more precise terms: which state-like entities have personality in international law? This is a topic that has been debated for a long time and that is mixed up with other long-running debates in international law—about universality, validity, and recognition.

I will explain three things here at the outset: what the initial question I have posed is intended to cover, broadly how I am going to answer it, and why I am asking it at all.

The first explanation is needed because it may be surprising that I have chosen state-like entities as the initial category for analysis, not states alone, and that I have begun by pointing out that the term 'international law' refers to nations rather than states. Since states are by far the most important entities within the scope of the question, the theory to be presented in this book will be a theory mainly about statehood. But framing the question solely in terms of statehood might embed an assumption in it: that the primacy of states in their current form is a stable, integral feature of international law. This is open to doubt. It is true that the non-state 'nations' that joined the League or the United Nations were seen as anomalous even at the time; colonial India was 'an anomaly among anomalies'.[14] But in the course of this book I will encounter a great variety of past and present state-like entities other than states of the familiar sort: precolonial African chiefdoms, protectorates, what I will call 'states-in-context', and many more. Moreover, it cannot be taken for granted that states themselves form a legally distinct and homogenous class. I will find that until the twentieth century the word 'state' was barely more precise in meaning than 'nation'. I will also find that the view I adverted to in the opening paragraph—that states have a government, a population, a territory, and independence—is only partly correct: recognition provides a second, coexisting method of qualifying for statehood; and the two methods of acquiring statehood can be seen as instances of two generic methods by which other state-like entities can acquire personality.

If these points are not to be obscured, statehood must be considered in a broader context. Using state-like entities as the initial category for analysis is a way to achieve this.

14 Miller (n 5) vol 1, 493.

I will not use this term in any strict or technical way, just as a loose working term for entities that look at least a little like the entities typically described as states and that might, in that sense, be represented by the 'nation' element in the term 'international law'. The connotations of the term 'state-like entities' are not far from what scholars of politics mean when they speak about 'polities': 'collectivities with a significant measure of identity and institutionalization, a degree of hierarchy in their organization, and the capacity to mobilize persons and groups for political purposes'.[15] State-like entities include polities as diverse as precolonial chiefdoms, colonial India, and of course states themselves. But even a loose working term has limits. Polities are sometimes defined to encompass international organizations such as the United Nations along with major non-governmental organizations and companies.[16] Entities of at least one of these types—international organizations—have personality in international law. But with rare exceptions, notably the European Union,[17] entities of these types are not in any clear way 'state-like'. They also tend to raise questions of law quite different from those raised by state-like entities. The same is true of individual women and men, another possible class of persons. All these non-state-like entities fall outside the scope of this book, except insofar as they are relevant indirectly.

Another term used in my initial question also needs to be clarified: 'personality'. But this requires more detailed consideration, which I will give to it in Chapter 1 of the book. Drawing on concepts developed by WN Hohfeld, along with other ideas, I will define an international legal person as an entity that is constructed as a fact by norms of international law and to which such norms give at least one right or duty in Hohfeld's sense. This departs from definitions that treat personality as a 'capacity'. My definition emphasizes instead that it is about *conduct*: international law regulates conduct by persons towards other persons—an echo of the description of international law as a 'rule of conduct' in the League Covenant.[18]

The next thing to be explained here at the outset is broadly how I am going to answer the question of which state-like entities have personality in international law.

[15] Yale H Ferguson, 'Governance, global' in Bertrand Badie, Dirk Berg-Schlosser, and Leonardo Morlino (eds), *International Encyclopedia of Political Science* (SAGE 2011) vol 4, 1010, 1014. See further Yale H Ferguson and Richard W Mansbach, *Polities: Authority, Identities and Change* (South Carolina Press 1996); KJ Holsti, *Taming the Sovereigns: Institutional Change in International Politics* (CUP 2004) 28–31.

[16] Ferguson (n 15) 1014.

[17] The European Union has many state-like features—a flag, a parliament, a currency, and so on. But despite its peculiarities, and whatever else it may also be, in international law it is an international organization established and empowered by treaties between its member states; since international organizations generally fall outside the scope of this book, the European Union is excluded too. On some of the past and present complexities raised by its personality in international law, see Aurel Sari, 'The conclusion of international agreements by the European Union in the context of the ESDP' (2008) 57 ICLQ 53; Frank Hoffmeister, 'Litigating against the European Union and its Member States—who responds under the ILC's Draft Articles on international responsibility of international organizations?' (2010) 21 EJIL 723.

[18] Covenant, preamble.

Once I have clarified what I mean by personality, I will use the remaining four chapters of the book to look in turn at the personality of entities of different types: state-like entities in past eras of international law, then states, and then certain non-states that exist today.

In Chapter 2, I will look at state-like entities in eras before international law became an unquestionably global system—before, roughly, the early twentieth century. I will focus on differences between Western and non-Western entities in the immediately preceding century or so, which present a number of intertwined complications. One of these is that Western ideas about international law were not familiar to or not accepted by state-like entities in Africa, Asia, and elsewhere, many of which had their own, incompatible ideas. Another complication is that nineteenth-century Westerners dismissed these entities as insufficiently 'civilized' to participate in international law to the same extent as Western states. These complications will take some untangling. Although non-Western state-like entities have always had a degree of personality, I will conclude that it cannot be explained purely in terms of statehood; in the past, the state-like entities with personality have been very diverse.

Not until the early twentieth century can one confidently speak about statehood in a clear technical legal sense. Statehood in this sense entails, among other features, certain rights and duties and therefore personality. The next two chapters will primarily concern states in this sense: one of them deals with the general rules about statehood, the other with exceptions.

Chapter 3 is about the general rules and is where I will make the case that there are two coexisting methods of acquiring statehood. The debate about statehood is traditionally conducted between adherents of the 'declaratory' theory, who say that it depends on criteria of effectiveness such as government, population, territory, and independence, and adherents of the 'constitutive' theory, who argue that it depends on recognition. But if effectiveness and recognition are the potentially decisive factors, that leaves open not two but four possibilities: that effectiveness is necessary; that recognition is necessary; that both are necessary; and that *either* effectiveness *or* recognition can suffice for statehood. I will argue for a version of this last possibility, the 'effectiveness-or-recognition' view. An entity that meets the effectiveness criteria is generally a state (the effectiveness norm). Equally, an entity that is recognized by other states, even if not effective, generally has the attributes of a state relative to recognizing states (I will call this proposition the recognition norm). In many cases, calling such an entity a 'state' would be misleading, because it does not have statehood relative to non-recognizing states; in those cases I will use the term 'state-in-context'. But if an entity is recognized universally, it may for virtually all purposes be as much a state as it would be if it met the effectiveness criteria. This can explain how some entities, such as Somalia after it collapsed into anarchy in the 1990s, retain their statehood despite meeting the criteria only on a very generous interpretation. The idea that recognition provides a second, coexisting method of acquiring statehood is not new, but it is seldom seen for what it is: a departure from both the traditional theories of statehood. It also has complex implications that have seldom been considered in detail.

Two principles that are often invoked in debates about statehood I will leave aside until Chapter 4: self-determination and the principle that no law arises from unlawfulness (*ex iniuria ius non oritur*). The aim of this chapter is to identify exceptions to the general rules about effectiveness and recognition. Since there are two paths to statehood, the constraints on the creation of states that are usually said to exist, including where an entity is created by an unlawful use of force, must be looked at with fresh eyes. The exceptions that I will identify all reflect the principle that no law arises from unlawfulness. Among them is an exception to the recognition norm that partly aligns it with the effectiveness norm: a unilateral secessionist entity cannot be recognized in derogation from an existing state's territorial integrity. I will express doubt that inconsistency with the principle of self-determination creates a free-standing exception to the general rules, but I will postulate an exception to the exceptions: the existence of a right to external self-determination may enable states or states-in-context to emerge in circumstances that would otherwise render their creation invalid.

In Chapter 5, I will zoom out from my discussion of statehood and look at the personality of other state-like entities today, including subentities of states such as Hong Kong. So great is the dominance of states in international law today that this will be a brief exercise. But it will demonstrate that international law continues to allow personality to take diverse forms and will corroborate my finding that there are two methods of acquiring statehood.

I will draw the threads of the book together in the conclusion. From the outline I have just given it may be evident what type of conclusion this will be: I am setting out to formulate a direct answer to the question I have posed, not an intellectual history or a comparison of answers that have been given before (such a huge variety of answers have been given before that it might be unfeasible to consider them all anyway, though I will use major contributions to the debate, notably the work of James Crawford, as starting points for discussion[19]).

Over the course of the book, in order to formulate a conclusion of this type, I will have to make arguments of two kinds: doctrinal and jurisprudential. The question of which state-like entities have personality *in international law* is essentially doctrinal in form, in that it asks what the norms of international law say about a topic within their own internal logical framework. I will make doctrinal arguments based on evidence of what the law is and on 'judicial decisions and the teachings of the most highly qualified publicists'.[20] But the question spills over so quickly into the realm of theory that it becomes impossible to separate doctrinal

[19] James Crawford, *The Creation of States in International Law* (2nd edn, OUP 2006).

[20] Statute of the International Court, art 38(1)(d).

arguments from philosophical or jurisprudential ones. The doctrinal form of the question influences what sort of jurisprudential arguments are needed. Arguments are needed, first, to distinguish the internal framework of international law from other, extralegal perspectives and, second, to understand concepts that exist within that internal framework, such as rights or personality. The result is that my jurisprudential arguments will mostly be of the analytical sort—the tradition that focuses on the logical structure of law, exemplified by Hans Kelsen and HLA Hart (though I will not adopt their specific ideas about international law, such as Kelsen's views about its relationship with domestic law[21]).

The idea that international law has a discrete internal framework within which doctrinal questions can be answered, distinct from extralegal perspectives such as the study of power politics, is not universally accepted. In observing this distinction my approach contrasts with a great variety of other approaches to the topic that shift more freely between legal and extralegal perspectives. Examples that I will discuss are the actor conception of personality, approaches to the nineteenth-century notion of 'civilization', and the Hegelian view of the recognition of states.[22] Ultimately, my more formalist approach can be defended only by actually conducting the investigation and showing that it really is possible to answer the question from an internal legal perspective, consistent with the distinction.

The last thing I need to explain here is why I am investigating this topic at all. I have two purposes, which parallel the kinds of arguments I will make—doctrinal and jurisprudential.

The doctrinal purpose is to clarify legal rights and duties in specific practical situations. Among the many diverse situations that have raised issues of statehood are the inception of the Panama Canal and Russia's annexation of Crimea, not to mention such major disputes as those about Palestine and Taiwan. Even issues that seem to be of purely historical interest, such as the status of precolonial entities, may be relevant to ongoing territorial disputes.[23]

But an underlying reason for seeking to understand the personality of state-like entities is that it promises to provide insights into the nature of international law as a system. I began by pointing out that the term 'international law', read literally, seems to relate to nations. The term has two other literal implications: that international law is *law* and that it exists *between* (inter-) certain entities. These issues will also come up in the discussion. Among other things, I will consider how norms that create states can logically exist, given that it seems to be states themselves that render norms valid. I will argue that a norm that custom creates states and a norm that states create custom both form part of a basic, self-reproducing circle of norms

[21] This book s 1.1.3.

[22] This book ss 1.2, 2.1, 3.2; on this distinction generally see also s 1.1.3.

[23] Eg, *Western Sahara (Advisory Opinion)* [1975] ICJ Rep 12; *Land and Maritime Boundary between Cameroon and Nigeria (Cameroon v Nigeria: Equatorial Guinea Intervening)* [2002] ICJ Rep 303.

from which other norms are derived, and that this is what sustains international law as a legal system with a single, meaningful test of which potential norms are valid and which invalid.[24] This will help to demonstrate that international law is an intellectually coherent and robust system, a characterization that has often been contested in the context of statehood.

24 See this book s 3.1.3.

1
Personality

This first chapter will serve primarily to present my definition of personality. It will begin with a discussion of some other foundational concepts that will inform that definition: first, norms of international law, especially norms that regulate conduct; second, rights, duties, and other legal relations, which I will define by drawing on the ideas of WN Hohfeld; and, third, facts constructed by norms. Combining these three concepts, I will define a person as an entity that is constructed as a fact by norms of international law and to which such norms give at least one right or duty in Hohfeld's sense. This definition emphasizes that personality is at heart about conduct: persons are entities that international law has singled out from a mass of facts as potential perpetrators or victims of unlawful actions or omissions. It also links personality with the idea, implicit in the term 'international law', that international law exists between (inter-) certain entities: those entities are persons. The arguments that I will make throughout the rest of this book will rely explicitly or implicitly on the conceptual approach to norms, relations, facts, and personality from this chapter.

1.1 Elements of personality

1.1.1 Conduct norms

The first element of my definition of personality is the concept of norms of international law. In discussing such a well-worn concept, I am not seeking not to challenge how it is ordinarily understood, just to find a theoretically precise language that reflects how lawyers intuitively think about it and that will help to make sense of the concept of personality.

The 'signal of the normative' is traditionally said to be the word 'ought', as distinct from the word 'is'.[1] The norm prohibiting the use of force, for example, is in essence an ought-statement: it is the same as saying that, according to the law, states ought not to use force.[2] This traditional understanding of norms is often dismissed as inadequate; not everything that is commonly referred to as a norm is an ought-statement, at least not when considered in isolation from other

[1] Neil MacCormick, *Institutions of Law: An Essay in Legal Theory* (OUP 2007) 101, further ch 2.
[2] The norm and its exceptions are in Charter of the United Nations (26 June 1945) arts 2(4), 42, 51.

Statehood and the State-Like in International Law. Rowan Nicholson, Oxford University Press (2019).
© Rowan Nicholson
DOI: 10.1093/oso/9780198851219.001.0001

norms. Consider the norm that a treaty that has been procured by the use of force is invalid.[3] This cannot be expressed using the word 'ought'. It is an is-statement about whether or not certain other statements—the statements that appear in the treaty—form part of the system of norms known as international law. It does not say what ought to be done except in the indirect sense that, insofar as the statements in the treaty include ought-statements, it says whether or not those ought-statements are 'true' according to international law. Taxonomies that differentiate between norms of various types, some of which are not solely or not directly ought-statements, have been proposed by John Searle and HLA Hart.[4] Nonetheless, norms that say directly what ought to be done are of primary significance for my purposes, because they can be expressed in terms of rights and duties and therefore give rise to personality as I will define it. I will refer to them as 'conduct norms'. Conduct may embrace both what an entity does (its actions) and does not do (its omissions).

A useful way of thinking about conduct norms is as conditional statements that apply a particular binary distinction. The distinction is between lawfulness and unlawfulness. Any conduct that comes to the attention of the system of legal norms—any given action or omission—can be placed on one side of the distinction or the other: it is either lawful or unlawful.[5] Conduct norms can thus be defined as statements that follow the formula 'if a certain entity performs certain conduct, then that conduct is unlawful' or, alternatively, 'that conduct is lawful'. For instance, 'if a state performs the action of using force, then that action is unlawful'. Saying that certain conduct, if performed, would be unlawful is equivalent to saying that according to the law the conduct ought not to be performed.

This language of lawfulness and unlawfulness resonates with how lawyers usually speak. Note, however, that in systems of domestic law, although the underlying distinction is still between what is lawful and what is unlawful, different types of

[3] Vienna Convention on the Law of Treaties (23 May 1969) 1155 UNTS 331, art 52.

[4] John R Searle, *Speech Acts: An Essay in the Philosophy of Language* (CUP 1969) 33–42('constitutive' and 'regulative'); HLA Hart, *The Concept of Law* (first published 1961, 3rd edn, OUP 2012) ch 5 ('primary' and 'secondary').

[5] This interpretation of conduct norms is inspired by social systems theory, which refers to the binary distinction as a 'code': see Niklas Luhmann, *Law as a Social System* (first published 1993, Klaus Ziegert tr, OUP 2004), especially ch 4 and the editors' introduction; Michael King and Chris Thornhill, *Niklas Luhmann's Theory of Politics and Law* (Palgrave Macmillan 2003) ch 2. But social systems theorists take this idea much further than I do. Among other things, they assert that *all* legal norms, not just conduct norms, are conditional statements that apply an underlying binary 'code' involving law and its negation, of which the distinction between lawful and unlawful conduct is just one manifestation. On this view, a norm that a treaty is invalid also applies the 'code', but here it takes the form of a distinction between being and not being part of the law and can better be expressed using the terms 'law' and 'non-law' rather than 'lawful' and 'unlawful'. For my purposes, it is enough to establish the more straightforward point that conduct norms have a binary structure. Compare MacCormick (n 1) ch 7, who interprets legal norms in binary terms of 'wrong' and 'not wrong' without fully embracing social systems theory. On one element of a broader definition of valid norms of international law, whether conduct norms or not, see this book s 3.1.3.

unlawful conduct are often referred to by quite different terms—crimes, breaches of contract, and so on. These terms reflect, among other differences, the specific type of norms that make the conduct unlawful and what remedies or other legal consequences tend to flow from the unlawfulness. In international law, the differences between types of norms are less marked.[6] I will use the generic language of lawfulness and unlawfulness regardless of whether conduct norms derive from customary international law, from a treaty, or from elsewhere, and regardless of what remedies may exist.

The language is important because it is part of what differentiates a system of *legal* norms from systems of other types. The system is made up of conduct norms that apply the particular distinction between lawfulness and unlawfulness, along with other norms that are systematically linked to those conduct norms. If norms applied a different distinction, such as a distinction between what conduct is moral and immoral or a distinction between what conduct is politic and impolitic, they would be norms of morality or politics or something else rather than legal norms. This has a corollary. Since the functioning of a system of legal norms is premised on the existence of a distinction between lawfulness and unlawfulness, the norms themselves take that distinction for granted. Within the system, lawfulness and unlawfulness are irreducible basic concepts; they cannot be broken down into more-basic concepts or given any meaning except in relation to each other. Unlawfulness is just the negation of lawfulness; lawfulness is just the negation of unlawfulness. One can, of course, debate what the word 'lawfulness' ultimately represents or why this particular system of norms is called 'law' whereas another system is called 'morality', but those debates must be conducted from a perspective that is external to the system of legal norms.[7]

In summary, then, conduct norms are traditionally understood as ought-statements but can also be thought about in another way: as conditional statements that apply an irreducible binary distinction—the distinction between lawfulness and unlawfulness—to conduct. This way of thinking about conduct norms will underpin the other elements of my definition of personality. Facts are connected with the 'if' part of the conditional formula ('if a certain entity performs certain conduct'). Rights, duties, and other legal relations, which I turn to next, are a way of expressing the 'then' part of the formula ('then that conduct is unlawful' or 'lawful'): they provide a language for describing how conduct norms apply the binary distinction.

[6] Articles on Responsibility of States for Internationally Wrongful Acts [2001] 2(2) ILC Ybk 26, commentary to art 2, para 7: the 'terminology of breach of an international obligation of the State is long established and is used to cover both treaty and non-treaty obligations'. The Articles mostly refer to 'wrongful acts'.

[7] Compare Richard Nobles and David Schiff, 'Introduction' in Niklas Luhmann, *Law as a Social System* (first published 1993, Klaus Ziegert tr, OUP 2004) 1, 19–20.

1.1.2 Rights, duties, and other legal relations

Terms such as 'rights' and 'obligations' can have a variety of meanings, which are often ambiguous or contested. I am going to adopt Hohfeld's view that they can be analysed—in principle, if not always easily in practice—as aggregations of four precisely definable legal relations: duties, rights, freedoms, and 'no-rights'.[8] These relations are necessarily correlative; if one entity has a duty, there must be another entity with a correlative right. The significance of this for my definition of personality is that it reveals that lawful or unlawful conduct is always perceived by norms of international law as being performed *by* one entity and *towards* another entity, and in this sense international law can be said to exist *between* entities. I will introduce each of the four relations, elaborate on the idea of correlativity, and respond to doubts that might be raised about it. I will then introduce some additional relations that complete Hohfeld's scheme, of which the most important is a power.

Hohfeld thought that the four relations could each be expressed as a function of any of the others but were otherwise 'the lowest common denominators of the law' and '*sui generis*'.[9] Another way to look at them is to treat lawfulness and unlawfulness as the irreducible basic concepts, as I have suggested, and to treat the four relations as functions or applications of those concepts. Take the first relation: a 'duty'. Hohfeld defined this as 'that which one ought or ought not to do'.[10] Since this is a legal ought-statement, expressing it in terms of unlawfulness is straightforward. If an entity has a duty to perform certain conduct, then that is the same as saying that it would be unlawful for the entity *not* to perform the conduct. I emphasize that, though I will sometimes say in this book that a norm 'gives' an entity a duty (or other relation), the norm and the duty are not separate things; speaking in terms of a duty is a convenient language for describing how the norm applies the distinction between lawfulness and unlawfulness to conduct by the duty-bearing entity. I will define Hohfeld's other relations as functions of duties and therefore also of that binary distinction.

The correlate of a duty is a 'right' in a strict, Hohfeldian sense (this is sometimes called a 'claim-right' to distinguish it from a 'right' in a looser or non-Hohfeldian sense;[11] I will mostly call it simply a right, clarifying where necessary). If one entity has a duty towards another entity to perform certain conduct, then that other entity has a right that the conduct be performed. There can never be a right without a duty or a duty without a right: they correlate exactly. So this is another case in

[8] WN Hohfeld, 'Some fundamental legal conceptions as applied in judicial reasoning [part 1]' (1913) 23 Yale Law Journal 16; WN Hohfeld, 'Some fundamental legal conceptions as applied in judicial reasoning [part 2]' (1917) 26 Yale Law Journal 710. Hohfeld used the term 'privilege' instead of 'freedom'; others have used 'liberty'.

[9] Hohfeld, 'Conceptions [part 1]' (n 8) 30, 58.

[10] Ibid, 32, quoting *Lake Shore & MS Railway Co v Kurtz*, 37 NE 303 (Indiana, 1894) 304.

[11] Eg, William A Edmundson, *Introduction to Rights* (CUP 2004) ch 5.

which different terms are used for convenience to express the same idea: the idea that failing to perform certain conduct would be unlawful.

Some examples of correlative rights and duties in international law can be taken from the *Wimbledon* case. This concerned a provision of the Treaty of Versailles of 1919:

> The Kiel Canal and its approaches shall be maintained free and open to the vessels of commerce and of war of all nations at peace with Germany on terms of entire equality.[12]

Germany had a duty not to interfere with navigation of the Kiel Canal by 'vessels of commerce and of war of all nations at peace with Germany'. This might be called a 'substantive' duty. On a Hohfeldian interpretation of the provision, other parties to the treaty, among them France, had a correlative right against Germany that it not interfere with navigation. By refusing passage to a steamship chartered by a French company, on grounds that were rejected by the Permanent Court of International Justice, Germany breached the substantive duty; it acted unlawfully. As a result of this breach, Germany acquired another duty, which might be called a 'remedial' duty: 'to make good the prejudice sustained by the vessel and her charterers'.[13] The International Law Commission has acknowledged the difference between substantive and remedial duties by commenting that a new legal relationship 'arises upon the commission by a State of an internationally wrongful act'.[14] As is common in international law, and like the substantive duty, Germany's remedial duty was owed not to an individual or to the company that chartered the ship but to another state, France. The Court ordered Germany to pay France a sum of money.[15] Germany thereby acquired a duty to comply with the judgment, a 'judgment' duty, which was binding under the Court's statute.[16] Each of these three duties—the substantive duty, the remedial duty, and the judgment duty[17]—was analytically separate, and each of them correlated with a separate right of France.

This provides an illustration of Hohfeld's first two relations, rights and duties, but it does not exhaust all the relevant legal relations between Germany and France.

The Permanent Court in *Wimbledon* spoke about a 'right of free passage' through the canal.[18] But the 'right' to which it was referring can be analysed as an aggregation of *two* of Hohfeld's legal relations. France had the Hohfeldian right correlating

[12] Treaty of Peace between the Allied and Associated Powers and Germany, Versailles (28 June 1919) 225 CTS 188, art 380.

[13] *SS Wimbledon (UK, France, Italy, and Japan v Germany)* (1923) PCIJ ser A 1, 33.

[14] Articles on Responsibility of States, commentary to part 2, para 1.

[15] *Wimbledon* (1923) PCIJ ser A 1, 33.

[16] Statute of the Permanent Court of International Justice (16 December 1920) 6 LNTS 389, art 59.

[17] Duties of these three types are distinguished in WN Hohfeld, 'Nature of stockholders' individual liability for corporation debts' (1909) 9 Columbia Law Review 285, 293–5.

[18] *Wimbledon* (1923) PCIJ ser A 1, 21.

with Germany's duty not to interfere with navigation. It also had something of a different nature, which concerned its own conduct rather than Germany's. France (and other states) had a Hohfeldian 'freedom' to navigate the canal. This is equivalent to saying that France lacked a duty *not* to navigate the canal: a freedom is just the absence of a duty. This freedom was an integral part of the canal regime. If France had not been granted this specific freedom to navigate the canal, navigating a German internal waterway without Germany's consent might have breached its general duty to respect Germany's sovereignty over the territory.

The correlate of a freedom is a 'no-right': the absence of a right. In this case, Germany lacked a right (or 'possessed' a no-right) that France refrain from navigating the canal.

It is so common for freedoms to be accompanied by rights that the two relations can be hard to disentangle. But Hohfeldian rights and freedoms are analytically distinct and sometimes exist independently. This can be illustrated by contrasting the Kiel Canal regime with another regime. Before 1856, states had a freedom of navigation on the high seas—meaning that it was not unlawful for states to navigate the high seas—but during this period the freedom was *not* accompanied by a Hohfeldian right against interference with navigation to the extent that, during wartime, it was lawful for other states to authorize privateers to attack foreign ships.[19] On the high seas today, as in the former Kiel Canal regime, states have both a freedom *and* a right. The distinction between these two relations can be seen in the Convention on the Law of the Sea. Article 87(1) makes clear that navigating the high seas is not unlawful: it affirms that all states have 'freedom of navigation' on the high seas. Article 87(2) makes clear that each state also has a Hohfeldian right that each other state not interfere with that freedom: the freedom 'shall be exercised by all States with due regard for the interests of other States in their exercise of the freedom of the high seas'.[20]

This illustrates that terms such as 'right' are not always used in the same strict sense: a 'right' may, in Hohfeldian terms, really be a freedom, an aggregation of rights and freedoms, or another legal relation entirely (such as a power in the sense I will introduce shortly). But the scheme implies, in principle, that 'rights' and 'obligations' in a looser sense can be disaggregated into Hohfeldian relations, each of which correlates with a relation of another entity—a right with another entity's duty, a freedom with another entity's no-right.

[19] Privateering was abolished by Declaration Respecting Maritime Law, Paris (16 April 1856) 115 CTS 1, art 1. See further Francis R Stark, *The Abolition of Privateering and the Declaration of Paris* (Columbia University 1897).

[20] United Nations Convention on the Law of the Sea (10 December 1982) 1833 UNTS 3. Under art 87(2), states must 'refrain from any acts that might adversely affect the use of the high seas by nationals of other States': Myron Nordquist, Satya N Nandan, and Shabtai Rosenne (eds), *United Nations Convention on the Law of the Sea, 1982: A Commentary* (first published 1985, Brill 2013) pt 87.9(l), quoting the International Law Commission.

Hohfeld made a clarification about this idea of correlativity. Lawyers sometimes speak about rights in things, *in rem*, which operate 'against the world' rather than against a specific entity. In domestic law, property works like this; so does territory in international law. These rights may sound as if they are not correlative, but they are quite consistent with the idea of correlativity. Hohfeld would have described one state's right to exclude a particular other state from its territory as 'one of a large class of fundamentally similar yet separate rights, actual and potential, residing in a single person' (the state whose territory it is) 'but availing respectively against persons constituting a very large and indefinite class' (every entity that has a duty to respect that state's territory).[21] A state's right to exclude other states from its territory is thus still correlative. The difference is that the potential bearers of the correlative relations cannot be comprehensively enumerated but must instead be defined as a class. *Wimbledon* again provides an example. An alternative interpretation of the Treaty of Versailles was that Germany's duty to keep the Kiel Canal open did not correlate solely with rights of the other treaty parties but rather created a 'servitude'.[22] Servitudes were said at the time to be 'inherent to the object with which they are connected (rights *in rem*)'.[23] But, like territory, a servitude would still have been correlative: it would have entailed granting rights to an indefinite class of 'interested' states, which may not have been parties to the treaty.[24]

In international law, the idea that relations correlate with relations of other entities has been around in some form since the seventeenth century.[25] It was influential during the drafting of the Articles on the Responsibility of States by the International Law Commission (though the drafters refrained from endorsing the idea explicitly in the final Articles and commentary). Roberto Ago, in his capacity as the Commission's special rapporteur, remarked in 1970 that

> it seems perfectly legitimate, in international law, to regard the idea of the breach of an obligation as the exact equivalent of the idea of the impairment of the

[21] Hohfeld, 'Conceptions [part 2]' (n 8) 718 (emphasis removed).

[22] *Wimbledon* (1923) PCIJ ser A 1, 24. The Court refrained from choosing between these two interpretations, because they would both have led to the same result.

[23] LFL Oppenheim, *International Law* (3rd edn, Ronald F Roxburgh ed, Longmans, Green, & Co 1920) vol 1, pt 207.

[24] Compare the finding in Report of the International Committee of Jurists upon the Legal Aspects of the Aaland Islands Question (1920) 3 LNOJ Sp Supp 3, 16–19: a treaty in which Russia agreed to demilitarize the Aaland Islands gave the islands 'a special international status' that bound Russia's successor in title, Finland, and with which 'every State interested' had 'the right to insist upon compliance'. The Committee expressed doubt that a concept of 'servitudes' really existed, but its finding was to an effect similar to that which servitudes were said to have: Philip Marshall Brown, 'The Aaland Islands question' (1921) 15 AJIL 268, 271.

[25] Hugo Grotius, *The Rights of War and Peace* (first published 1625, Richard Tuck ed, Liberty Fund 2005) pt I.I.V (italics removed): 'a Right properly, and strictly taken' embraces the 'Faculty of demanding what is due, and to this answers the Obligation of rendering what is owing'. Further on the history and theory of correlativity in international law, see Bart L Smit Duijzentkunst, *The Concept of Rights in International Law* (doctoral thesis, University of Cambridge 2015) ch 2.

> subjective rights of others. . . . The correlation between a legal obligation on the one hand and a subjective right on the other admits of no exception; . . . there are certainly no obligations incumbent on a subject which are not matched by an international subjective right of another subject or subjects, or even . . . of the totality of the other subjects of the law of nations.[26]

The reference to 'the totality of the other subjects of the law' is an allusion to communitarian duties. These are typically duties of states that reflect principles that are considered especially important, such as the duties not to commit genocide or to use force; they are said to be duties *erga omnes* (towards all) or 'towards the international community as a whole'.[27]

The concept of communitarian duties may give rise to doubts about whether *all* the duties that exist in international law correlate with rights in a Hohfeldian sense.[28] Such doubts will have only limited relevance to my argument (most of which will relate to rights and duties that are plainly correlative) but in any event are misplaced. Whatever view is taken of the meaning of the 'international community', it is consistent with correlativity. The key is to distinguish between the substantive and remedial aspects of the concept. By the substantive aspect I mean, for example, the substantive communitarian duty not to use force; the remedial aspect means the consequences of a breach of that duty or another communitarian duty.

The main practical significance of the concept is remedial. A breach of an ordinary duty entitles the 'injured State' to invoke responsibility; that is to say, that particular state acquires a full suite of remedial rights, including a right to reparation and a right that the wrongdoer cease the 'wrongful act' (along with other legal relations such as powers).[29] A breach of a communitarian duty likewise creates remedial rights, though with a difference. As with an ordinary breach, only an injured state can claim reparation on its own behalf; but *any* state, injured or not, 'is entitled to invoke the responsibility' of the wrongdoing state and may claim 'cessation of the wrongful act' and 'performance of the obligation of reparation . . . in the interest of the injured State or of the beneficiaries of the obligation breached'.[30] Remedial rights thus vest in a 'large and indefinite class' of entities.[31] As I explained in discussing rights *in rem*, that is quite consistent with correlativity. Moreover, all these remedial rights correlate with duties of the wrongdoing state in

[26] Roberto Ago, Second Report on State Responsibility [1970] 2 ILC Ybk 177, para 46. This observation is noted in Articles on Responsibility of States, commentary to art 2, para 8.

[27] *Barcelona Traction, Light and Power Company, Limited (Belgium v Spain) (New Application: 1962) (Second Phase)* [1970] ICJ Rep 3, para 33. See further Articles on Responsibility of States, art 48 and commentary; Christian J Tams, *Enforcing Obligations Erga Omnes in International Law* (CUP 2005).

[28] See further John R Morss, 'The legal relations of collectives: belated insights from Hohfeld' (2009) 22 Leiden Journal of International Law 289, 292; Smit Duijzentkunst (n 25) ch 3.

[29] Articles on Responsibility of States, arts 28, 30–1, 42. An example of a remedial power that an injured state might acquire in some cases is a power to initiate proceedings before a court or tribunal.

[30] Ibid, art 48(1)(b), (2).

[31] Hohfeld, 'Conceptions [part 2]' (n 8) 718.

a straightforward way. So the remedial aspect of communitarian duties does not in any way challenge the idea of correlativity.

As for the substantive duty, it is notable that the language used is explicitly correlative: a communitarian duty is not a duty *tout court*, a duty without further qualification, but a duty explicitly 'towards' something—'towards the international community as a whole'.[32] There is controversy about what that thing is. Is the 'international community' a nebulously defined but discrete entity with 'rights' of its own (a person, on the definition I will adopt, albeit of an attenuated kind that seems to be unable to act on its own behalf)?[33] Or is the 'international community' shorthand for the class of all states or perhaps even 'the totality of the . . . subjects of the law',[34] each of which has a separate correlative right?[35] For my purposes, what matters is that on either interpretation the communitarian duty is still correlative; a breach of such a duty, like a breach of an ordinary duty, is conduct 'towards' something.

The idea of correlativity is therefore not challenged either by the substantive or by the remedial aspect of the concept of communitarian duties, on either view of the 'international community'. Bart Smit Duijzentkunst draws the same conclusion: the 'notion of correlativity is perfectly compatible with the idea that an international claim-right is held by, or an international obligation is owed to, a large number of entities including the "international community as a whole" '; an assumption that rights correlate with duties actually 'underpins' the '*erga omnes* effect of international claim-rights and obligations'.[36]

This analysis of communitarian duties illustrates a general point about Hohfeld's scheme. Although it is a much more detailed and adaptable way of describing conduct norms than the irreducible binary distinction between lawfulness and unlawfulness, it still describes only the skeletal structure of conduct norms. In particular, it has no implications for which entities may possess legal relations or what remedies may arise from a breach; that depends on specific norms. Thus, the two aspects of communitarian duties raise two discrete questions: the question of which entities have rights correlating with a *substantive* communitarian duty does not necessarily determine which entities have rights correlating with the *remedial* duties that arise from its breach. This point is also made by Smit Duijzentkunst. He interprets communitarian duties as shorthand for 'bilateral legal relations' between

[32] *Barcelona Traction (Second Phase)* [1970] ICJ Rep 3, para 33.

[33] Contrast *Legal Consequences for States of the Continued Presence of South Africa in Namibia (South West Africa) notwithstanding Security Council Resolution 276 (1970) (Advisory Opinion)* [1971] ICJ Rep 16, 241 (Judge Fitzmaurice dissenting). See further Claudia Annacker, 'The legal régime of *erga omnes* obligations in international law' (1994) 46 Austrian Journal of Public and International Law 131, 138–40.

[34] Ago (n 26) para 46.

[35] *East Timor (Portugal v Australia)* [1995] ICJ Rep 90, 172 (Judge Weeramantry dissenting): an '*erga omnes* right is, needless to say, a series of separate rights *erga singulum*'.

[36] Smit Duijzentkunst (n 25) ch 3.

many pairs of entities, but he observes that the 'consequences of a violation' do not depend on that 'situation of correlativity'; instead they depend 'on whether the right-holder is injured'.[37]

To complete this discussion of legal relations, I need to fill in the rest of Hohfeld's scheme. In addition to duties, rights, freedoms, and no-rights, he identified a set of four higher-order relations that can similarly be expressed as functions of other legal relations. The most important one for my purposes is a 'power'. This means specifically an ability 'to effect [a] particular change' to legal relations, which might involve creating or terminating relations as well as modifying existing ones.[38] An example is a state's power to consent to a deployment of another state's troops on its territory: an exercise of that power gives the other state a freedom to deploy the troops, without which the deployment would be an unlawful invasion. The contractual powers of states to create treaty relations are Hohfeldian powers of a special sort to which I will return later.[39] The remaining higher-order relations can be expressed as functions of powers. If an entity has a power to change relations of another entity, that is exactly equivalent to saying that the other entity has a 'susceptibility'.[40] The absence of a power over another entity is a 'disability'; that other entity has an 'immunity'. So powers correlate with susceptibilities; disabilities correlate with immunities.[41]

There is a crucial difference here. Norms that give entities lower-order relations—duties and rights, freedoms and no-rights—are conduct norms as I have defined them: conditional statements that apply the distinction between what is lawful and unlawful to conduct by one entity towards another entity. An exercise of a power is also a sort of conduct. But the norms that give entities powers and other higher-order relations are not conduct norms; they do not say directly whether the conduct that constitutes an exercise of a power is lawful or unlawful. Instead, they are statements about whether or not certain other norms, including conduct norms, *exist* within the international legal system—whether those norms are valid. I mentioned a norm of this type earlier: the norm that a treaty that has been procured by the use of force is invalid. This norm, for example, can be said to give entities a disability (the absence of a power to make a treaty procured by the use of force).

I am not assuming here that the exercise of a power is the only way to create norms or relations in international law. Hohfeld observed that if a relation does not result from the exercise of powers, it must result 'from some superadded fact or group of facts not under the volitional control' of any entity.[42] Perhaps the purest

37 Ibid.
38 Hohfeld, 'Conceptions [part 1]' (n 8) 44.
39 See this book s 3.2.
40 Hohfeld used the term 'liability' instead of 'susceptibility'.
41 MacCormick (n 1) 172 observes that '[a]ll legal powers . . . are relational in the sense that any person's exercise of a power involves a change in the normative position of some other person'.
42 Hohfeld, 'Conceptions [part 1]' (n 8) 44.

case of this in an international legal context is natural law, which in the past was believed to exist regardless of the will of any particular entity.[43] Hans Kelsen argued that customary international law may also be non-volitional, in contrast with 'consciously and intentionally' enacted domestic statutes: he wrote that the authors of a customary norm 'do not necessarily know that they are creating legal norms and they do not necessarily have the intention of creating any', and that the creation of a customary norm is 'the effect and not the purpose of their activity'.[44] In any case, since customary norms depend on an indefinite and variable number of actions and opinions by many states, it would be awkward to use the language of Hohfeldian powers to analyse their creation.[45] In Chapter 5, a distinction between powers and custom will form the framework for a discussion about different methods of acquiring personality.

Earlier I established that conduct norms are conditional statements that apply a distinction between lawfulness and unlawfulness to conduct. I have now introduced a way to describe in more detail how this distinction is applied: the language of legal relations, which necessarily correlate with relations of other entities. Rights and duties, which will form part of my definition of personality, make up one pair of correlative relations. Since the lawfulness or unlawfulness of conduct can be expressed in terms of relations between entities, the conduct is always perceived by norms of international law as being performed *by* one entity and *towards* another entity, and international law can be said to exist between those entities. This leaves still to be addressed the questions of what 'entities' and 'conduct' actually are.

1.1.3 Facts constructed by norms

The last element of my definition of personality is the concept of a fact. In order to be a person, something must exist in some sense as a matter of fact. When I refer to an 'entity', I do not mean anything essentially different from a fact; this is just a more natural way to speak about facts when the question under discussion is whether those facts are persons.

So what is a fact?

It has long been a commonplace among scholars that at least some of the facts that legal systems deal with are not facts of physical reality but are facts that are in some way selected or constructed by legal norms. FH Lawson, writing about domestic law, observed:

[43] See this book s 2.2.

[44] Hans Kelsen, 'Théorie du droit international public' (1953) 84 Recueil des cours 1, 123 (translation).

[45] These propositions assume that custom operates on the basis of the prevailing legislative view of custom (see this book s 2.3) and the effectiveness norm (ss 3.1.1–3.1.4).

> We must first note and emphasize the separateness and completeness of what we may call the legal plane. . . . Legal personality is not the same as human personality, an estate in fee simple does not exist physically in the same way as the land over which it exists, nor is a contract the same as the agreement of which it is the legal manifestation. Legal personality, estates, and contracts are parts of a world of their own . . .[46]

Neil MacCormick distinguishes between 'sheer physical facts and realities' and 'institutional facts', which 'depend on the interpretation of things, events, and pieces of behaviour by reference to some normative framework'.[47] In domestic law, a contract might be described as an 'institutional' fact because its existence as a contract depends on legal norms about its validity. An individual woman or man has some 'non-institutional' features ('age, sex, or mental competence') but also has some 'institutional' features ('citizenship, legitimacy, matrimonial status, or solvency').[48] In international law, a similar distinction is suggested by James Crawford when he writes that a state

> is not a fact in the sense that a chair is a fact; it is a fact in the sense in which it may be said a treaty is a fact: that is, a legal status attaching to a certain state of affairs by virtue of certain rules or practices.[49]

Distinctions of this kind are, however, potentially misleading. It is true that some facts are imbued with meaning by legal norms more or less *explicitly*. The Vienna Convention on the Law of Treaties contains an explicit definition of a treaty between states ('an international agreement concluded between States in written form and governed by international law'); its other provisions add to this definition by detailing circumstances in which an ostensible agreement does or does not count as a valid treaty.[50] But some apparently 'sheer physical facts' are also explicitly defined in this way. International law actually does provide an explicit definition of chairs. Chairs appear in the Harmonized Commodity Description and Coding System, which may be used to interpret legally binding tariff commitments within the World Trade Organization; this distinguishes between, among several other types of chairs, 'Seats other than garden seats or camping equipment, convertible into beds' and 'Dentists', barbers' or similar chairs'.[51] Moreover, different

[46] FH Lawson, 'The creative use of legal concepts' (1957) 32 New York University Law Review 909, 913.

[47] MacCormick (n 1) 11.

[48] Ibid, 90.

[49] James Crawford, *The Creation of States in International Law* (2nd edn, OUP 2006) 5.

[50] Vienna Convention on Treaties, art 2(a).

[51] International Convention on the Harmonized Commodity Description and Coding System (14 June 1983) 1503 UNTS 167, annex: Harmonized System Nomenclature, codes 940110–940190, 940210. On the relevance of the system to interpreting tariff commitments, see *European*

legal norms may define apparently 'sheer physical facts' differently for particular purposes. For example, in the Convention on the Prevention of Pollution from Ships, a ship means 'a vessel of any type whatsoever operating in the marine environment', whereas in the Convention on the Law of the Sea, its meaning is not fixed and 'will depend on the circumstances'.[52] Already, then, the apparent distinction between 'sheer physical' and 'institutional' facts becomes muddied and difficult to apply.

But one can go further than this. Within the framework of a system of legal norms, there is really no such thing as a 'sheer physical fact'; legal norms must construct *all* the facts with which they deal. If there is no legal norm explicitly defining a fact, norms must at least construct that fact impliedly before they can say anything about it. This is evident from the conditional formula followed by conduct norms: 'if a certain entity performs certain conduct, then that conduct is unlawful' or 'lawful'. The words of the 'if' part of this formula explicitly or impliedly identify the entity as a fact and likewise identify the conduct as a fact; they must also identify any circumstances surrounding the conduct or other facts that are relevant to whether or not it is lawful. To some extent MacCormick acknowledges this, despite the distinction he draws: although he describes an individual's 'age, sex, or mental competence' as 'non-institutional features', he nonetheless also describes them as 'legally determined'.[53] The law itself determines what counts as 'mental competence' for the purposes of its own norms. Such features must be constructed in the sense of being perceived by norms, of being selected from among an indefinite number of features that might be perceived.

It is significant for how entities and conduct are constructed as facts that, where a norm gives entities a Hohfeldian right and a correlative duty, that norm applies to conduct by the *duty-bearer*; the norm makes certain conduct by the duty-bearer unlawful.[54] This means that the duty-bearer must be constructed in a lot of detail—at least enough detail to indicate when actions or omissions have been performed by it. States, for instance, are constructed as performing actions or omissions in part by explicit customary norms of attribution, such as the norm that the 'conduct of any State organ shall be considered an act of that State . . . whether the organ exercises legislative, executive, judicial or any other functions'.[55] But it is different with a *right-bearer*. A conduct norm creating a right is not as such concerned with conduct by the right-bearer, only with conduct *towards* it. The legal system

Communities—Customs Classification of Frozen Boneless Chicken Cuts (WTO case WT/DS269/AB/R, 12 September 2005) paras 192–9.

[52] International Convention for the Prevention of Pollution from Ships (2 November 1973) 1340 UNTS 184, art 2(4); Nordquist, Nandan, and Rosenne (n 20) pt 1.28.

[53] MacCormick (n 1) 90.

[54] Compare Matthew H Kramer, 'Rights without trimmings' in Matthew H Kramer, NE Simmonds, and Hillel Steiner, *A Debate over Rights: Philosophical Enquiries* (Clarendon 1998) 7, 13–14.

[55] Articles on Responsibility of States, art 4.

can therefore afford to be vague about the characteristics of a right-bearer towards which others must perform certain conduct but which has no duties of its own. A possible example of this has arisen already: the nebulously defined 'international community'. Another will come up later: a right to self-determination is said to vest in 'peoples', entities which are defined in very loose terms and which may lack representatives through which they can act; but the correlative duties fall on states, whose characteristics and modes of acting are well-known.[56]

As this illustrates, the thrust of the view that I have adopted is that norms of international law must construct all their own facts to the extent norms have anything to say about those facts.

Although this leaves no room for sharp distinctions among the facts that are dealt with by international law, there is another distinction that must be drawn instead. This is between two distinct levels of analysis: the internal framework of international legal norms, which constructs facts as I have described, and perspectives that are external to international law.

By perspectives that are 'external' to international law, I do not necessarily mean the physical world of flesh-and-blood women and men. External perspectives include other social or legal perspectives that construct reality in a different way from how international law perceives it. For instance, it is possible to talk about 'persons' in the language of philosophy or politics. It is possible to talk about what counts as a 'person' within a system of *domestic* law. Similarly, an entity may be described as a 'state' from any of these perspectives or may be thought of as a 'nation' in the collective imagination of a group of individuals. These statements are not necessarily relevant to questions about what is lawful or unlawful according to international legal norms; they may construct reality in a different way from how international law constructs facts and may apply different concepts or distinctions to those facts, instead of the distinction between lawfulness and unlawfulness.

The other level of analysis, the internal one, is what Lawson called 'the legal plane':[57] the world as it is constructed *internally* by norms of international law. Bear in mind that this world is composed of facts of many different kinds: not just facts about such things as treaties, which international law brings into being more or less explicitly, and not just facts about physically real things such as chairs, but also information about how reality is constructed from other social or legal perspectives.[58] For example, within the internal framework

[56] This book s 4.2.

[57] Lawson (n 46) 913–14.

[58] Compare the views of social systems theorists. Systems such as law construct 'internal models of the outside world with which they are able to interact internally'; law then 'formulates rules and decisions with reference to an internal legal representation of social reality': Gunther Teubner, 'Autopoiesis in law and society: a rejoinder to Blankenburg' (1984) 18 Law and Society Review 291, 297. This outside world—the 'environment' of law—may embrace 'the physical world, society as a whole, human consciousness', and 'other social subsystems', such as politics: Richard Nobles and David Schiff, *Observing Law through Systems Theory* (Hart 2013) 16.

of international law, norms of domestic legal systems are facts that must be constructed by norms of international law in the same way as facts of any other kind.

This can be illustrated by considering an argument made by Kelsen that does not observe the distinction between levels of analysis. The argument is about the nature of actions and omissions—conduct—as facts. Kelsen thought that it could not 'be seriously denied that actions and forbearances can only be actions and forbearances of a human being':[59]

> Obligations and rights of the State do not mean that some being, existing apart from human individuals, 'has' these obligations and rights. We speak of such obligations and rights when we impute to the State, to the personified unity of the legal order, those human acts which form the contents of these obligations and rights. The latter are obligations and rights of individuals who . . . have the capacity of State organs.[60]

From an extra-legal perspective, it is uncontroversial to say that conduct imputed to the state is really conduct by individuals acting in their capacity as state officials or agents. But this is at best a misleading way to speak about the facts as they are constructed from the internal perspective of international law. Within international law, it is a fact that conduct is performed *by* the state, even if physically it is done by an individual. That is what is achieved by norms of attribution, such as the norm that the 'conduct of any State organ shall be considered an act of that State'.[61] Moreover, the state itself is constructed as the bearer of rights and duties, not the individuals whose actions or omissions are imputed to it.

Kelsen might have answered this by saying that the work of specifying the individuals who ultimately bear these rights and duties is not done by international law but is delegated to systems of domestic law:

> When international law imposes upon a State the obligation to behave a certain way *vis-à-vis* another State . . . it is determined only what ought to be done in the name of one State . . . but it is not determined who, that is to say, which individual as organ of the State, has to fulfil the obligation stipulated by international law. . . The determination of the individuals whose behaviour forms the contents of international obligations and rights is left to the legal order of the State obligated and authorized by international law.[62]

[59] Hans Kelsen, *General Theory of Law and State* (Anders Wedberg tr, Harvard UP 1949) 97.
[60] Ibid, 199.
[61] Articles on Responsibility of States, art 4.
[62] Kelsen, *General Theory* (n 59) 342–3.

Kelsen thought that international law and domestic law were parts of a single system of legal norms, in which international law was supreme.[63] But this does not reflect how the boundaries of the system of international law are drawn by the system itself, and to that extent it blurs together the two levels of analysis. There are certainly situations in which domestic legal norms are relevant in international law; for instance, domestic nationality law is relevant to whether or not a state may exercise diplomatic protection over an individual.[64] But domestic law is relevant only insofar as specific norms of international law—such as the international law of diplomatic protection—*make* it relevant. The general rule, articulated by the Permanent Court, is that from 'the standpoint of International Law . . . municipal laws are merely facts which express the will and constitute the activities of States'.[65]

I have concluded that a distinction must be drawn between perspectives that are external to international law (including, contrary to Kelsen, the perspectives of domestic legal systems) and the internal framework of international law itself. I have also concluded that, within that internal framework, no sharp distinctions can be drawn among facts: international legal norms must construct *all* the facts with which they deal. 'Person' is a technical legal term for legally constructed facts of a particular type. The question that I now need to consider is what distinguishes those facts from other facts.

1.2 A definition of personality

Although a term of art, 'personality' (or 'legal' or 'international personality') is not a term with a universally accepted definition. There is no definition that is 'correct' in the sense that it is consistent with every use of the term by lawyers, courts, or scholars. Some of the ways in which the concept has been understood historically in international law—some of which are contradictory or out of date—have been discussed in works by Roland Portmann, Janne Nijman, and others.[66] My aim here is not to find a definition of personality that encapsulates all this intellectual history. It is to produce a definition that is broadly consistent with usage, that holds together theoretically, and that can reveal useful information about the entities that

[63] Jochen von Bernstorff, *The Public International Law Theory of Hans Kelsen* (CUP 2010) 93–103; Jean L Cohen, 'Sovereignty in the context of globalization: a constitutional pluralist perspective' in Samantha Besson and John Tasioulas (eds), *The Philosophy of International Law* (OUP 2010) 261, 265–8.

[64] Articles on Diplomatic Protection [2006] 2(2) ILC Ybk 24, art 4.

[65] *Certain German Interests in Polish Upper Silesia (Germany v Poland)* (1926) PCIJ ser A 7, 19.

[66] Roland Portmann, *Legal Personality in International Law* (CUP 2010); Janne Elisabeth Nijman, *The Concept of International Legal Personality: an Inquiry into the History and Theory of International Law* (Asser 2004); Catherine Brölmann and Janne Elisabeth Nijman, 'Personality' in Jean d'Aspremont and Sahib Singh (eds), *Concepts for International Law: Contributions to Disciplinary Thought* (Elgar 2019) 678. See further the works discussed in Rose Parfitt, 'Theorizing recognition and international personality' in Florian Hoffmann and Anne Orford (eds), *The Oxford Handbook of the Theory of International Law* (OUP 2016) 583.

are to be discussed in this book. I will summarize the main potential approaches to personality and then develop my own definition, making use of the concepts that I have introduced: norms, Hohfeldian legal relations, and legally constructed facts.

Portmann identifies five competing approaches to personality in international law: the states-only, recognition, individualistic, actor, and formal conceptions.[67]

The states-only conception treats personality in international law as synonymous with the concept of statehood; the recognition conception begins with that proposition but accepts that states can create 'derivative' persons by recognizing them.[68] Some of the ideas that underlie these conceptions, in particular recognition and the idea that international law emanates from the free will of states, will be discussed in Chapter 3.[69] But they are of no use at this stage because they are not purely definitions of personality in the abstract; they make claims about which entities *have* personality and from where it is derived. It is similar with the individualistic conception, which asserts that individuals are persons 'in the field of so-called fundamental norms of international law'.[70] Portmann acknowledges that this is, at least partly, a claim about who *has* personality when he argues that the individualistic and formal conceptions complement each other and adopts a synthesis of them.[71] Moreover, since my focus is on state-like entities rather than individuals, the individualistic conception is not of direct relevance.

The actor conception, which is often associated with Rosalyn Higgins, a former judge and president of the International Court of Justice, tends to replace the language of personality with terms such as 'actor' and 'participant'. An entity's status as a participant depends not 'on legal rules or specific acts of recognition, but on effective power to participate'.[72] For example, Higgins argues that individual men and women are 'participants' because, among other things, they participate in international human rights bodies and in domestic courts that 'respond to international law claims advanced by individuals', perhaps by interpreting a treaty to resolve a dispute about preventive custody, extradition, or foreign property.[73]

The actor conception of personality or 'participation' is underpinned by an analysis of international law not as an abstract system of norms but rather as an observable, practical decision-making process that takes account of wider political and economic considerations as well as legal rules and principles.[74] International law is not collapsed completely into politics; as an authoritative decision-making

67 Portmann (n 66) 13–14. See further Kate Parlett, *The Individual in the International Legal System: Continuity and Change in International Law* (CUP 2011) chs 1, 6.

68 Portmann (n 66) 13, further chs 5, 6.

69 This book s 3.2.

70 Portmann (n 66) 13, further ch 7.

71 Ibid, ch 11.

72 Ibid, 213, further ch 9.

73 Rosalyn Higgins, 'Conceptual thinking about the individual in international law' (1978) 4 British Journal of International Studies 1, 8, further 6–10.

74 Portmann (n 66) 223.

process, it remains distinct from the exercise of raw power. But the view that an entity's status (at the level of international law) depends directly on its power to participate (in the wider world of politics) blurs together the two levels of analysis that I identified earlier. It may be compared with the earlier views of the German American realist Hans Morgenthau, who was one of the influences on the actor conception. He wrote that a rule of international law 'is valid when its violation is likely to be followed by an unfavourable reaction, that is, a sanction against its violator' but that an 'alleged rule, the violation of which is not followed by such a sanction, is a mere idea, a wish, a suggestion, but not a valid rule'.[75] If this were interpreted as a statement about what norms themselves say within their own internal framework, it would be straightforwardly wrong. Like the idea that an entity's status as an actor in international law depends on its power to participate, it declines to acknowledge a distinction between, on the one hand, what legal norms say on their own terms and, on the other, what connection those norms may have with an entity's actual behaviour, as observed from a perspective that is external to the system of norms.

Portmann doubts that the actor conception fits well with how lawyers and others think about international law: they do not generally conceive of it as 'a decision-making process in which policy considerations take precedence over legal rules and principles, nor is effective action directly relevant in normative terms'.[76] In any event, since the actor conception rejects or de-emphasizes the character of international law as a system of norms that is analytically separate from politics, instead beginning from dramatically different premises and using quite different terms and concepts, it cannot serve my purposes in this book.

That leaves the last approach to personality identified by Portmann: the formal conception. This is the view that 'every entity is an international person that according to general principles of interpretation is the addressee of the norms of international law'.[77] This is close to how personality is usually defined by theorists of domestic law. For example, John Salmond, writing from the perspective of a common-law system, argued that

[75] Hans Morgenthau, 'Positivism, functionalism, and international law' (1940) 34 AJIL 260, 276. He accepted that 'to deny that international law exists at all as a system of binding legal rules flies in the face of all the evidence' in that it governs such matters as 'the limits of territorial jurisdiction, the rights of vessels in foreign waters, and the status of diplomatic representatives', but he argued that it had little effect on 'high' politics: Hans Morgenthau, *Politics among Nations: The Struggle for Power and Peace* (2nd edn, Knopf 1954) 251. On whether norms of international law really are as toothless in the realm of 'high' politics as has been claimed by realists such as Morgenthau, see James Crawford and Rowan Nicholson, 'The continued relevance of established rules and institutions relating to the use of force' in Marc Weller (ed), *The Oxford Handbook of the Use of Force in International Law* (OUP 2015) 96.

[76] Portmann (n 66) 269.

[77] Ibid, 13, further ch 8. Portmann adds an additional characteristic that I will reject—that personality entails 'the capacity to invoke international responsibility and to be held internationally responsible': at 275.

> a person is any being whom the law regards as capable of rights and duties. Any being that is so capable is a person, whether a human being or not, and no being that is not so capable is a person, even though he be a man. Persons are the substances of which rights and duties are the attributes. It is only in this respect that persons present juridical significance, and this is the exclusive point of view from which personality receives legal recognition.[78]

This is the only approach to personality that is independent of the question of which particular entities have personality and that accords with the existence of separate levels of analysis.

Domestic lawyers sometimes refer to individual men and women as 'natural' persons and to companies and other institutions as 'artificial' persons. This distinction between types of personality appears to evoke the idea (which I rejected) that legal norms distinguish between 'sheer physical' and 'institutional' facts. But adherents of the formal conception understand that even ostensibly 'natural' persons must be legally constructed as facts before legal norms can say anything about them; they must be selected from among an indefinite number of features that might be perceived by legal norms. This is exemplified by the denial of domestic legal personality to women and slaves in certain times and places and by debates about whether unborn children are persons.[79] The law must make choices about which entities to construct as 'natural' persons. In Bryant Smith's words, 'artificial' personality is 'just as real as and no more real than the legal personality of a normal human being. . . . it is an abstraction, one of the major abstractions of legal science, like title, possession, right and duty'.[80] Ngaire Naffine writes that personality according to this conception does not formally 'depend on the physical human form of the entity' or its 'mental attributes' but 'reflects the earliest meaning of the term person: that of a "mask" worn by an actor who plays a part'.[81]

I will take an essentially formal approach to personality in international law, though I will not define it in exactly the same way as Portmann or theorists of domestic law.

A starting point for developing a definition that is consistent with usage—the nearest thing international lawyers have to an authoritative statement on the topic—is the *Reparation for Injuries* advisory opinion, in which the International Court discussed the personality of the United Nations. The Court remarked that to say that something is an 'international person'

[78] John Salmond, *Jurisprudence* (7th edn, Sweet & Maxwell 1924) pt 108.

[79] On the theory of personality in domestic law, see Richard Tur, 'The "person" in law' in Arthur Peacocke and Grant Gillett (eds), *Persons and Personality: A Contemporary Inquiry* (Blackwell 1987) 116; Ngaire Naffine, 'Who are law's persons? From Cheshire Cats to responsible subjects' (2003) 66 Modern Law Review 346.

[80] Bryant Smith, 'Legal personality' (1928) 37 Yale Law Journal 283, 293.

[81] Naffine (n 79) 366.

> is not the same thing as saying that it is a State . . . or that its legal personality and rights and duties are the same as those of a State. . . . What it does mean is that it is a subject of international law and capable of possessing international rights and duties, and that it has capacity to maintain its rights by bringing international claims.[82]

I will consider each element of the Court's description of personality in turn: the reference to being 'capable' of possessing rights and duties; the meaning of 'rights and duties' in this context; the reference to 'international claims'; and the reference to being a 'subject'.

The description of persons as being 'capable' of possessing rights and duties implies that in international law an entity may have a capability or capacity to possess rights and duties without actually possessing any.[83] It is difficult to know where to look for such an entity: it has been pointed out that 'the main way of determining whether the relevant capacity exists in case of doubt is to inquire whether it is in fact exercised'.[84] It is not clear anyway how such an entity would differ from facts that are not said to be persons in international law, such as chairs and ships. There is nothing inherent in a ship that makes it theoretically *incapable* of being given rights and duties in international law; in domestic legal systems, rights and duties sometimes have been given to ships.[85] And domestic law furnishes more peculiar examples of personality. In 1925, the Privy Council held that a Hindu idol was a 'juristic entity' which had 'the power of suing and being sued' and was managed by an agent, like an infant heir's estate.[86] Personality, on the formal approach, has been called 'an empty slot'; it can be filled in whatever way legal norms choose to fill it.[87] So defining a person as anything 'capable' of possessing rights and duties in international law could potentially embrace almost anything that international law constructs as a fact. The category of 'persons' might become so large and open-ended as to be practically useless. This will be reinforced in Chapters 3 and 5, where I will

[82] *Reparation for Injuries Suffered in the Service of the United Nations (Advisory Opinion)* [1949] ICJ Rep 174, 179. Further on the Court's approach to personality in this case, in particular its description of the United Nations as having 'objective international personality' (at 185), see this book s 5.2.

[83] Compare Smith (n 80) 283–4. In some systems of domestic law, there may be an established distinction between 'personality' and 'capacity': Andreas Heldrich and Anton F Steiner, 'Legal personality' in Alex Chloros, Max Rheinstein, and Mary Ann Glendon (eds), *International Encyclopedia of Comparative Law*, vol 4: *Persons and Family* (Mohr 2007) 3. But 'capacity' does not have a clear technical meaning in international law. For one interpretation of it, see Daragh Murray, *Human Rights Obligations of Non-State Armed Groups* (Hart 2016) 79–81.

[84] James Crawford, *Brownlie's Principles of Public International Law* (8th edn, OUP 2012) 115.

[85] *Tucker v Alexandroff*, 183 US 424 (1901) 438: in 'the baptism of launching', a ship 'acquires a personality of her own; becomes competent to contract, and is individually liable for her obligations, upon which she may sue in the name of her owner, and be sued in her own name'. English courts used to take a similar view, though this was deprecated as a fiction in *Republic of India v India Steamship Co Ltd (No 2)* [1998] AC 878, 906–9, 913.

[86] *Mullick v Mullick* (1925) 52 LR Ind App 245, 250.

[87] Tur (n 79) 121.

conclude that the class of entities that have a susceptibility to be granted rights and duties by states is in principle open-ended.[88] Persons can only be sharply and unambiguously distinguished from other legally constructed facts if they are defined as *actually possessing* rights and duties. I will therefore leave the word 'capable' out of my definition.

The next question is the meaning of 'rights and duties' in this context.

Consider a very wide interpretation: any Hohfeldian right, duty, freedom, or no-right, or any aggregation of those things. This creates a problem similar to that created by including the word 'capable' in the definition of personality: the resulting definition embraces a meaninglessly large category of entities. Explaining this problem requires a digression.

I have established that rights, duties, freedoms, and no-rights are created by conduct norms, which are conditional statements that apply a binary distinction between lawfulness and unlawfulness. This binary structure is uncompromisingly rigid. Any fact that legal norms construct as conduct by one entity towards another entity, in principle, must be deemed *either* lawful *or* unlawful, because the two concepts are the direct negations of each other. There is no third or intermediate possibility within the normative framework of international law. If Germany interferes with navigation in the Kiel Canal, that is either unlawful or it is not. When the United States and its allies bombed Serbia-Montenegro[89] in 1999 to end the persecution of Kosovars, their conduct was described by some scholars as 'illegal but legitimate' or 'justified'.[90] Statements such as this are best interpreted as being made in part outside the framework of international law: they imply that a use of force can be unlawful (according to international law) and yet still be politically or morally justified on humanitarian grounds (from an extra-legal perspective). *Within* international law, any given use of force, like any other conduct, must in principle be either lawful or unlawful.

A clarification is provided by Michael King and Chris Thornhill:

> In legal argument it is not possible for both prosecution and accused, plaintiff and defendant to be right. They can agree not to dispute issues..., but only by accepting that one side of the distinction or the other should be applied to the conduct in question. Moreover, the fact that in some legal cases a clear-cut winner . . . fails to emerge, because some issues are decided in favour of one party and some in favour of the other, does not in any way undermine the validity of [the distinction].

[88] This book ss 3.4.2 and 5.1.1.

[89] At the time officially the Federal Republic of Yugoslavia.

[90] Independent International Commission on Kosovo, *The Kosovo Report: Conflict, International Response, Lessons Learned* (OUP 2000) 4. See also Bruno Simma, 'NATO, the UN and the use of force: legal aspects' (1999) 10 EJIL 1. This differs from Simma's later proposal for a third possibility (to be discussed momentarily): that conduct might be 'tolerated'. It is also different from the argument, made by some, that the bombing was actually *lawful* on the ground of humanitarian intervention, on which see Christine Gray, *International Law and the Use of Force* (3rd edn, OUP 2008) 39–51.

> Each of these sub-issues will require a decision between the positive and the negative side of [the distinction].[91]

In addition, since conduct in international law is always understood as conduct performed *by* a particular entity and *towards* a particular entity, the same action may be unlawful towards one entity but lawful towards another. An action that breaches a treaty, for instance, is generally unlawful only towards other treaty parties; it may still be lawful towards another entity that is not a party to the treaty.[92] But applied to any specific question about the application of conduct norms, the distinction is rigid. Either particular conduct is unlawful towards a particular entity or it must be lawful towards that particular entity.

There are some scholars, such as Ronald Dworkin, who speculate that there really is a single correct answer to every legal question—that law is a formally complete system of norms with no gaps.[93] Note that this is not quite the same as the point that I am making here. My point is that the internal structure of legal norms is *premised on an assumption* that there is a correct, binary answer to every conceivable question about whether conduct is lawful or unlawful, whether or not that assumption is 'true' in some wider sense, and even though it is sometimes difficult for lawyers to say with certainty what the answer to a question is.[94]

This assumption—that there is an answer to every question about whether or not conduct is lawful—has an importance consequence. This is that the system must contain a *default* conduct norm, in order to answer questions that are not answered by a more specific conduct norm: either lawfulness or unlawfulness must be the residual category. The more intuitive view is that this category is lawfulness: the default conduct norm is that any conduct that is not specifically made unlawful is by default lawful. This may be a condition of any realistic system of legal norms. The alternative—a world in which every conceivable action or omission, no matter how trivial, is unlawful unless specifically permitted—sounds like a totalitarian dystopia. The correctness of the more intuitive view can be illustrated by the approach that the International Court took in *Kosovo*. The question was whether a declaration that Kosovo was independent (the conduct) was not 'in accordance with international law', which the Court took to mean 'in violation of international law' (unlawful).[95] (Note that, on the Court's interpretation, this was a discrete question about whether certain conduct was lawful or unlawful; it was not the same as the much more complex question of whether that conduct had the

[91] King and Thornhill (n 5) 57; on the existence of default norms, see further 56.

[92] Vienna Convention on Treaties, arts 34–8.

[93] Ronald Dworkin, *Law's Empire* (Hart 1986) ch 7.

[94] Compare Luhmann (n 5) 428–9. Compare also the idea that legal norms have an 'open texture' that allows them to be adapted to answer every question, even one the drafters did not anticipate: Hart (n 4) ch 7.

[95] *Accordance with International Law of the Unilateral Declaration of Independence in Respect of Kosovo (Advisory Opinion)* [2010] ICJ Rep 403, para 56.

result of actually transforming Kosovo into an independent state.[96]) The Court remarked that the lawfulness of the conduct depended 'on whether or not the applicable international law prohibited the declaration of independence' and that it was not required 'to take a position on whether international law conferred a positive entitlement on Kosovo unilaterally to declare independence'.[97] It proceeded to look for an applicable prohibition and, not finding one, concluded that the declaration was therefore not a violation of the law.[98] Thus the Court assumed that anything that was not specifically prohibited was lawful by default.

There was some criticism of this approach. Judge Simma argued that, in addition to conduct being specifically prohibited or made lawful, there are 'possible degrees of non-prohibition, ranging from "tolerated" to "permissible" to "desirable" '; the possibility that 'an act might be "tolerated" would not necessarily mean that it is "legal", but rather that it is "not illegal" ' and that 'there are areas where international law has not yet come to regulate'.[99] This is to some extent a disagreement about the use of language.[100] Saying that conduct is lawful, as I am using that term, essentially is a negative statement that the law has not specifically 'come to regulate' the conduct. In this context, it means that an entity lacked a duty *not* to declare independence (which is equivalent to saying that it had a freedom) and nothing more than that. It does not mean that the entity had positive permission or a positive Hohfeldian right of any kind. This does not seem very far from Simma's idea of acts that international law does not regulate and hence that are 'tolerated'. In any case, the plurality of the Court took the orthodox approach: if conduct is not unlawful, it is lawful by default.

In Hohfeldian terms, then, the default answer to any question about whether conduct is lawful is that every entity has an absolute freedom and a blanket no-right relative to every other entity (which is equivalent to saying it has no duties or rights). This is true not only of, say, states, but of anyone or anything about which the question can be asked. There was a debate in *Kosovo* about whom the declaration was conduct *by*. The Court decided that it was not conduct by the legislature of Kosovo acting in its official capacity but rather by members of the legislature acting in a capacity 'outside the framework of the interim administration'.[101] But the Court's decision that the conduct was by a group of individuals acting unofficially did not stop it from answering the question. Consider other questions the Court might conceivably have been asked. Is it unlawful for a private company to declare Kosovo independent? Was it unlawful for James Crawford to declare South Australia independent, which, as counsel, he did during the hearing in order to

[96] On whether Kosovo is a state see this book s 4.3.
[97] *Kosovo* [2010] ICJ Rep 403, para 56.
[98] Ibid, para 84.
[99] Ibid, 479–81 (Judge Simma).
[100] Simma's more far-reaching criticism was that the Court interpreted the question too narrowly.
[101] *Kosovo* [2010] ICJ Rep 403, para 109.

illustrate a point?[102] These, too, are questions that the Court could answer by applying the default conduct norm, and the answer would be 'no': international law does not prohibit that conduct. In principle, if something is legally constructed as a fact to which conduct can be attributed, the norms of international law can provide answers to questions about whether that conduct is lawful or unlawful. And the default answer is that everyone and everything have the freedom to do as they please.

How, then, is this digression relevant to the hypothesis I am considering—that, for the purpose of defining personality, 'rights and duties' may include any right, duty, freedom, or no-right?

Persons cannot be defined to include every entity with a freedom or a correlative no-right. That would embrace anything at all that is legally constructed as a fact that can perform conduct: the legislature of Kosovo; the members of that legislature acting unofficially; a private company; perhaps even a ship or a Hindu idol, insofar as conduct can plausibly be attributed to them. All these entities can be said to have freedoms and correlative no-rights under the default conduct norm, which is the same as saying that they have not specifically been given duties and rights by international law—it means no more than that. The concept of personality must therefore be defined more narrowly, to include only entities to which more specific conduct norms give rights or duties in the Hohfeldian sense.

This does not mean that norms creating freedoms and no-rights, including the default conduct norm, are doing something essentially different from norms creating rights and duties. Hohfeld insisted that a freedom was a 'true legal relation' and that this was confirmed by the fact that conduct that is *permitted* by the law 'would ordinarily be pronounced "lawful"', just as forbidden conduct is pronounced unlawful (notably, Hohfeld used the same terms that I am using to describe the binary distinction).[103] The significance of defining personality by reference solely to rights and duties is this: personality becomes a way to describe entities that have been singled out from the mass of facts constructed by international law and have been identified as potential perpetrators or victims of unlawful conduct. They have lost their condition of absolute freedom, in the Hohfeldian sense as well as in the sense of Thomas Hobbes, who argued that absolute freedom is the natural position of individuals and states in the absence of an authority established over them.[104] International law regulates conduct *between persons*. This is consistent with the thrust of other formal definitions of personality, but it has the advantage of greater theoretical precision.

[102] James Crawford, Oral Statement for the UK (10 December 2009) ICJ Pleadings: *Accordance with International Law of the Unilateral Declaration of Independence in Respect of Kosovo*, CR 2009/32, 46, 47.

[103] Hohfeld, 'Conceptions [part 1]' (n 8) 42 n 59. See further Pierre Schlag, 'How to do things with Hohfeld' (2015) 78 Law and Contemporary Problems 185, 212–16.

[104] Thomas Hobbes, *Leviathan* (first published 1651, Richard Tuck ed, CUP 1996) chs 13, 14.

I turn to the next element of International Court's description of a person in *Reparation for Injuries*: 'capacity to maintain its rights by bringing international claims'.[105]

This is a reference to 'the customary methods recognized by international law for the establishment, the presentation and the settlement of claims', including 'protest, request for an enquiry, negotiation', and, subject to consent, submission to a tribunal.[106] In its request to the Court for an advisory opinion, the General Assembly had specifically asked about the capacity of the United Nations to bring claims. The Court may have been highlighting a specific attribute of the United Nations.[107] But if it meant that such capacity is an essential element of personality *in general*, then the consequences of that are not straightforward. Customary norms generally entitle injured states to invoke responsibility for unlawful conduct; it is similar with international organizations.[108] But I noted earlier that the nature of such remedies can vary, in particular where a communitarian duty is breached. In any event, the customary norms of responsibility are just default rules; they may be overridden by an agreed *lex specialis*.[109] In the World Trade Organization, for instance, there is a different regime.[110] Nor are entities prevented from bringing claims if the customary norms do not apply to them. The commentary to the Articles on Responsibility of States observes:

> In cases where the primary obligation is owed to a non-State entity, it may be that some procedure is available whereby that entity can invoke the responsibility on its own account and without the intermediation of any State. This is true, for example, under human rights treaties which provide a right of petition [and under] investment protection agreements. . . . It will be a matter for the particular primary rule to determine whether and to what extent persons other than States are entitled to invoke responsibility on their own account.[111]

In summary, 'capacity to maintain . . . rights by bringing international claims' could refer to a variety of remedial rights and other legal relations that the bearers of substantive rights can invoke sometimes under general custom, sometimes under

[105] *Reparation for Injuries* [1949] ICJ Rep 174, 179.
[106] Ibid, 177.
[107] Definitions of personality in international law that otherwise accord with the Court's description in *Reparation for Injuries* often omit any reference to a capacity to bring international claims. Eg, it is defined simply as 'capacity to be a bearer of rights and duties under international law' in Georg Schwarzenberger and ED Brown, *A Manual of International Law* (6th edn, Professional Books 1976) 42.
[108] Articles on Responsibility of States, arts 42, 48; Articles on Responsibility of International Organizations [2011] 2(2) ILC Ybk 40, arts 43, 49.
[109] Articles on Responsibility of States, art 55; Articles on Responsibility of International Organizations, art 64.
[110] Marrakesh Agreement Establishing the World Trade Organization (15 April 1994) 1867 UNTS 154, annex 2.
[111] Articles on Responsibility of States, commentary to art 33, para 4.

specific customary norms or treaties, and sometimes not at all. In a system of domestic law in which most or all right-bearing entities can sue or be sued in court (meaning that they have specific remedial rights and powers), it may be straightforward to define persons as entities with remedial rights or other relations. But in international law it is difficult to do this without arbitrariness.

Leaving aside for a moment this practical complication, the idea that personality requires an entity to have at least some remedial rights or other relations might be defended on theoretical grounds. According to some theories of rights, a 'right' without a remedy is not genuinely a right at all.[112] But it has been argued that such theories are inapt in international law. Most obviously, they ignore the language used by international human rights law, which treats entities as right-bearers in a substantive sense even though the entities may lack remedies. Ignoring this language is an inflexible approach that 'neither fits practice, nor appeals to the normative cause' of relevant fields of international law.[113] This inflexible approach is certainly inapt for the purposes of this book, because it makes *a priori* theoretical assumptions about what types of entities exist or are worthy of consideration. It will be better to start with an open mind by persisting with Hohfeld's distinction between substantive and remedial rights. This approach acknowledges that entities whose rights are purely substantive (not remedial) are still constructed as potential victims of unlawful conduct, even if they do not have 'rights' in a narrower theoretical sense: international law can still broadly be said to exist between them and other entities.[114] The view that entities with purely substantive rights can be 'subjects of the law' has been taken by, among others, Hersch Lauterpacht:

> The fact that the beneficiary of rights is not authorised to take independent steps in his own name to enforce them does not signify that he is not a subject of the law . . . [An international] instrument may make [individuals] subjects of the law without conferring upon them procedural capacity; it may do both these things.[115]

To avoid the practical complication of determining, probably arbitrarily, what counts as a 'capacity to maintain . . . rights by bringing international claims', and

[112] Eg, Tom Campbell, *Rights: A Critical Introduction* (Routledge 2006) 88–91. In international law, compare Robert Jennings and Arthur Watts, *Oppenheim's International Law* (9th edn, Longman 1996) vol 1, pt 375: 'rights *stricto sensu*' are rights that entities 'can enforce in their own name before international tribunals'.

[113] Smit Duijzentkunst (n 25) conclusion, further ch 4.

[114] Hohfeld's scheme on its own does not provide an explanation of who the right-bearer *is* in cases where that is in doubt. In international law such cases often involve the apparent rights of individuals rather than those of the state-like entities that are the topic of this book. For a discussion of the problem, see ibid.

[115] Hersch Lauterpacht, 'The subjects of the law of nations [part 2]' (1948) 64 Law Quarterly Review 97, 97. See also Hersch Lauterpacht, 'The subjects of the law of nations [part 1]' (1947) 63 Law Quarterly Review 438.

also in order to keep an open mind about what types of entities exist or are important in international law, I will leave aside the reference to 'international claims' in *Reparation for Injuries*. Instead, I will reserve the term 'persons' for the wider category of entities that possess *any* Hohfeldian right or duty. If it is relevant whether or not entities can bring claims of a particular kind or under a particular instrument, that distinction can be drawn within the wider category.

Similar reasoning can be applied to any suggestion that the term 'person' be confined to entities that possess a specific right or other legal relation. There is speculation in the commentary to the Articles on Responsibility of States that it 'may be that the notion of responsibility for wrongful conduct is a basic element in the possession of international personality'.[116] Another suggestion that has been made is that a treaty-making power is necessary for personality.[117] As with remedies, a distinction could be drawn between entities with and without these additional characteristics if needed, but there is nothing to be gained by ignoring any entities that lack them by excluding such entities from the definition of personality. This is not to imply that personality in my sense is more important than, say, treaty-making powers: that may depend on the context. On the contrary, it once again avoids embedding *a priori* assumptions about the existence or importance of entities in the definition of a basic concept. As Crawford writes, 'the extent of the powers, rights and responsibilities of any entity is to be determined only by examination of its actual position'.[118]

The final relevant remark made by the Court is that a person is 'a subject of international law'.[119] It is not obvious what this adds, if anything. In the past, some international lawyers drew a distinction between 'persons' and 'subjects'.[120] One scholar who maintains that there is a distinction is David Raič: for him, 'a subject of international law is *any* entity which bears rights and/or duties under international law'; a 'person' must additionally have 'the capacity or right to make an international claim'.[121] If I were to take a similar approach, I would have to use the term 'subject' for the wide, analytically robust category of entities that I have

[116] Articles on Responsibility of States, commentary to art 1, para 7.

[117] Hersch Lauterpacht, Report on the Law of Treaties [1953] 2 ILC Ybk 90, 100 called treaty-making capacity 'a corollary of international personality'. See further Anne Peters, 'Treaty making power' (last updated 2009) MPEPIL. One ground for this is a belief that 'the minimum requirement for the attribution of personality' is the capacity to do a legal *act*: Jean Combacau, *Le Droit des traités* (Presses Universitaires de France 1991) 12 (translation). This may be a requirement of bearing duties, which concern conduct by the duty-bearer, but it is not necessarily a requirement of bearing rights, which concern conduct by someone or something else. I pointed out earlier that some entities, such as peoples, may have rights but not duties.

[118] Crawford, *Creation* (n 49) 30.

[119] *Reparation for Injuries* [1949] ICJ Rep 174, 179.

[120] On the historical distinction and rare later examples of it, see Parlett (n 67) 29–30, 356–7.

[121] David Raič, *Statehood and the Law of Self-Determination* (Kluwer 2002) 13–14 (emphasis from original).

identified; since I have rejected a capacity to bring claims as an inapt and probably arbitrary basis on which to categorize entities in international law, I would not have much use for the term 'person'. But in fact the terms are not ordinarily or consistently distinguished. Portmann points out that in textbook chapters 'on international personality or on the subjects of international law', the two expressions are 'mostly used as synonyms'; he, too, uses them interchangeably, as do other writers on the topic of personality.[122] It is largely a matter of terminological preference, and an attempt to maintain a sharp distinction might even cause confusion. I will therefore continue to use what may be the more common term: 'person'.[123] I will use it for the analytically robust category of entities that I have identified.

In identifying that category, I have whittled down the description of persons from *Reparation for Injuries* to this: a person in international law is an entity that is constructed as a fact by norms of international law and to which such norms give at least one Hohfeldian right or duty; personality means the possession of rights and duties by such a legally constructed entity.[124] The concept is at heart about whether an entity has been singled out from the mass of facts constructed by international law as a potential perpetrator or victim of unlawful conduct; in international law, conduct norms operate *between persons*. An implication of this definition is that, since every right or duty is borne by an entity relative to another entity (which bears the correlative duty or right), and since personality is a function of rights and duties, personality always exists relative to certain other entities.

1.3 The question clarified

In the introduction to this book, I described the term 'state-like entity' as a loose, working term for entities that look at least a little like states, including states themselves. This term has no necessary implications for whether an entity has rights or duties in international law and therefore for whether it is a person on my definition

[122] Portmann (n 66) 1. Compare Murray (n 83) 25: after alluding to attempts to distinguish between the two concepts, he concludes that they 'may be legitimately treated as synonymous' for his purposes and proceeds to use them in that manner.

[123] This is also the less likely of the two terms to be used in other ways. The term 'subject' may be used, for instance, to describe a state 'subject to the authority' of another state: *Customs Régime between Germany and Austria (Advisory Opinion)* (1931) PCIJ ser A/B 41, 57 (Judge Anzilotti). See further this book s 5.1.2.

[124] Kelsen, *General Theory* (n 59) 94 wrote, similarly, that in law a 'person exists only insofar as' that person '"has" duties and rights; apart from them the person has no existence whatsoever'. This is true in the sense that if a person's rights and duties were all stripped away it would no longer exist *as a person*, but the same entity could still exist as a legally constructed fact that might be relevant to the rights and duties of others.

(an entity that is constructed as a fact by norms of international law and to which such norms give at least one Hohfeldian right or duty). Investigating which state-like entities have personality is the task to which I now turn. I will begin with entities before roughly the early twentieth century, when international law was transformed from a Western system into an unquestionably global one.

2
State-like entities in past eras of international law

In the late nineteenth century, Western scholars argued that international law (or most of it, at any rate) was the preserve of a 'family of nations'. Membership of this exclusive club was said to depend on meeting a standard of 'civilization'. In 1894, for example, the British international lawyer John Westlake gave the following list of states 'having European civilisation', which he described as forming the 'international society to which we belong, and of which what we know as international law is the body of rules':

> *First*, all European states. . . . *Secondly*, all [North and South] American states. These, on becoming independent, inherited the international law of Europe . . . *Thirdly*, a few Christian states in other parts of the world, as the Hawaiian Islands, Liberia and the Orange Free State. The same cannot be said for all Christian states, not for instance of Abyssinia [Ethiopia].[1]

Hawaii was at that time (though only ephemerally[2]) controlled by men of European descent who had overthrown the indigenous monarchy; Liberia was governed by descendants of freed African American slaves; the Orange Free State had been founded by Boers, settlers of Dutch descent, alongside another Boer republic in the Transvaal. These entities fit the pattern of the list in that, like states in Europe and the Americas, they had Western-style governments. In contrast, the wholly *non-*Western state-like entities that Europeans had encountered during their centuries of exploration and expansion—the Ottoman Empire, imperial China, the chiefdoms of Africa, and many others—were dismissed as less than 'civilized'.

Having explained in Chapter 1 what I mean by personality in international law, I now turn to the question of which state-like entities had personality before the early twentieth century. The supposed distinction between the 'civilized' West and the rest of the world, which greatly complicates any attempt to answer this question,

[1] John Westlake, *Chapters on the Principles of International Law* (CUP 1894) 78, 81–2 (emphasis from original). Maps of the 'civilized' world as defined by Westlake, TE Holland, and Lassa Oppenheim between 1882 and 1949 can be found in Arnulf Becker Lorca, *Mestizo International Law: A Global Intellectual History 1842–1933* (CUP 2014) 362.

[2] The overthrow occurred in 1893; a republic was declared in 1894; Hawaii was annexed to the United States in 1898. See *Larsen v Hawaiian Kingdom* (PCA case 1999-01, 5 February 2001) annexures 1, 2.

Statehood and the State-Like in International Law. Rowan Nicholson, Oxford University Press (2019).
© Rowan Nicholson
DOI: 10.1093/oso/9780198851219.001.0001

will be the focus of the chapter. Not only does this supposed distinction imply that the personality of Western states was somehow different from that of non-Western entities, it is connected with a host of other complex matters—among them, the question of what *counts* as international law for the purpose of discussing past eras. My analysis of these matters will prepare the ground for my later analysis of statehood. In particular, I will conclude here that it was not possible to speak about statehood as a concept with a stable technical meaning before, roughly, the early twentieth century; the emergence of statehood in the current technical sense was the result of the globalization of international law and of the homogenization of state-like entities in all parts of the world.

This chapter will deal in turn with three matters. First, I will untangle the question that I am primarily investigating from other legal and extra-legal approaches that might be taken to the supposed distinction between Western and non-Western entities. Second, I will discuss which state-like entities had personality during the period when theories of natural law held sway. This discussion will be brief, because its relevance to personality in the present day is comparatively limited. Third—and this will form the majority of the chapter—I will consider which state-like entities had personality during the subsequent period, the era of the turn to positivism that culminated in the late nineteenth century with the standard of 'civilization'. I will look separately at Western states and then at non-Western state-like entities of different types.

My conclusion about the personality of Western and non-Western entities during this period will be that there *was* a difference, though it was not 'civilization'. When Western international law determined whether or not a particular customary norm applied to an entity, a non-Western entity—which may not have been familiar with Western international law—was more likely to be subjected to a requirement that it consent specifically to that norm; a Western state was more likely not to be subjected to such a requirement. But this must be seen in the context of the instability that affected both practice and doctrine during the period.

2.1 Perspectives other than Western international law

Like the broader question I am seeking to answer in this book, the question of which entities had personality before the early twentieth century is a question asked from within the internal framework of international law. The topic could be approached from the perspective of politics rather than law; it could also be approached from a legal perspective other than the one in which I am primarily interested. Some of the uncertainty about the personality of Western and non-Western entities in the past results from confusion among these various perspectives. My first task in this chapter is to resolve this confusion.

2.1.1 Political perspectives

References to the family of nations and the standard of 'civilization' frequently have more to do with politics than with international law as such. In particular, the family of nations has been equated with the idea of an 'international society' developed by the English School of international relations. As Hedley Bull defined it, an international society 'exists when a group of states, conscious of certain common interests and common values, form a society in the sense that they conceive themselves to be bound by a common set of rules in their relations with one another, and share in the working of common institutions'.[3] International law has been called the 'most essential evidence for the existence of an international society'.[4] Past international societies include China in the Warring States Period and the world of classical Greece and Rome.[5] On the English School account, the family of nations was initially an international society confined to European states that shared the same conception of international law. Emer de Vattel called them 'a sort of republic, of which the members—each independent, but all linked together by the ties of common interests—unite for the maintenance of order and liberty'.[6] This then began to expand into a global international society. Gerrit Gong argues that what 'demarcated countries which were full members of the "civilized" international society' was the standard of 'civilization'.[7] At first merely implicit, this standard was eventually formulated explicitly, partly in response to Japan's embrace of Western 'civilization' after the transfer of political power to the court of the Meiji Emperor in 1868.[8]

From a political perspective, 'civilization' was a determinant of the status of entities in the realm of global politics. When international lawyers wrote about 'civilization', this is at least sometimes what they seem to have had in mind. Lassa Oppenheim, in observing that Japan had met the standard of 'civilization', remarked that since 'her war with China in 1895, she must be considered one of the Great Powers that lead the Family of Nations'.[9]

[3] Hedley Bull, *The Anarchical Society: A Study of Order in World Politics* (4th edn, Palgrave Macmillan 2012) 13.

[4] Martin Wight, *Power Politics* (2nd edn, Penguin 1979) 107.

[5] Martin Wight, *Systems of States* (Leicester UP 1977); Victoria Tin-bor Hui, *War and State Formation in Ancient China and Early Modern Europe* (CUP 2005); Barry Buzan, *An Introduction to the English School of International Relations* (Polity 2014).

[6] Emer de Vattel, *The Law of Nations* (first published 1758, Béla Kapossy and Richard Whatmore eds, Liberty Fund 2008) pt III.47.

[7] Gerrit W Gong, *The Standard of 'Civilization' in International Society* (Clarendon 1984) 10.

[8] Ibid, 240–1, further ch 6; Susumu Yamauchi, 'Civilization and international law in Japan during the Meiji era (1868–1912)' (1994) 24 Hitotsubashi Journal of Law and Politics 1; Kinji Akashi, 'Japan–Europe' in Bardo Fassbender and Anne Peters (eds), *The Oxford Handbook of the History of International Law* (OUP 2012) 724.

[9] LFL Oppenheim, *International Law* (Longmans, Green, & Co 1905–6) vol 1, pt 28.

This chapter is not concerned with the family of nations or with 'civilization' in an extra-legal, political sense, which does not distinguish rigorously between an entity's political status and its personality according to norms of international law. These ideas will be relevant only insofar as they shaped personality as I defined it in Chapter 1 (the possession, by an entity that is constructed as a fact by norms of international law, of Hohfeldian rights or duties given to it by such norms). An entity that was outside Western 'international society' might still have had a degree of personality in the relevant, legal sense.

2.1.2 Other conceptions of international law

The distinction between international law and politics is a familiar one; the other source of confusion in dealing with periods before the twentieth century is the existence of *multiple conceptions* of international law, and this confusion is much more difficult to resolve.

Today, most scholars recoil from the idea of a standard of 'civilization' on the ground that it was imperialist, racist, or at best ignorantly and parochially Western. It came into fashion at a time when European colonialism in Africa, Asia, and the Pacific was intensifying and when Charles Darwin's theory of natural selection was being distorted to explain alleged differences between human groups.[10] More persistent is the belief that international law is something uniquely European that was imparted to Africans, Asians, and others during the colonial period. In recent times, historians of international law have tried to correct this notion.[11] Treaties were already being made in Mesopotamia more than four millennia ago and in later periods appeared almost everywhere; Islamic and east Asian cultures had rules about war, diplomacy, and so on that were as sophisticated as anything produced by contemporaneous Europeans; and interaction between peoples was regulated by shared principles on all continents, including in Aboriginal Australia.[12] The idea that international law in this wide sense has ever been uniquely European must be abandoned before the discussion can begin.

[10] Martti Koskenniemi, *The Gentle Civilizer of Nations: The Rise and Fall of International Law 1870–1960* (CUP 2001), especially 70–6. For an overview of the literature, see Liliana Obregón Tarazona, 'The civilized and the uncivilized' in Bardo Fassbender and Anne Peters (eds), *The Oxford Handbook of the History of International Law* (OUP 2012) 917.

[11] This was a goal of Bardo Fassbender and Anne Peters (eds), *The Oxford Handbook of the History of International Law* (OUP 2012). See further Ignacio de la Rasilla del Moral, 'The shifting origins of international law' (2015) 28 Leiden Journal of International Law 419.

[12] Fassbender and Peters (n 11), especially chs 16–21, 29–33, 43; Stephen C Neff, *Justice among Nations: A History of International Law* (Harvard UP 2014). On Mesopotamia, see Raymond Cohen and Raymond Westbrook (eds), *Amarna Diplomacy: The Beginnings of International Relations* (Johns Hopkins UP 2000). On Australia, see Gerald C Wheeler, *The Tribe, and Intertribal Relations in Australia* (J Murray 1910), especially ch 10; Henry Reynolds, *Aboriginal Sovereignty: Reflections on Race, State and Nation* (Allen & Unwin 1996).

This is not, however, the same as saying that all these rules, principles, and interactions, whether Western or non-Western, cohered into a single system of international legal norms.

This can be illustrated by the conclusions of CH Alexandrowicz—a pioneer of efforts to correct the Eurocentrism of international law—about state-like entities in the regions around the Indian Ocean in the sixteenth and seventeenth centuries. These entities formed what has been described as a 'well-developed international society' in the English School sense.[13] It encompassed parts of Africa, such as Zanzibar; Arabia, where it stretched into the area dominated by the Ottoman Empire; Iran; south Asia; and southeast Asia.[14] Not all the members of this society were considered equals or exercised forms of sovereignty that would have been familiar to Europeans. The Mughal Empire, for example, commanded a complex and extensive network of vassals.[15] And their rulers and scholars had a variety of conceptions of international law, some influenced by Hindu jurists such as Kautilya, others by the Islamic notion of the *Ummah* (the community of believers transcending borders).[16] When Europeans entered the area in significant numbers, following Vasco da Gama's voyage to Calicut in 1498, they brought with them yet another conception of international law. Initially, the Europeans were in the less influential position. Dutch, English, and French chartered trading companies exercised elements of authority on behalf of their states. They had expected to discover and occupy new lands; instead they found that they had to join the pre-existing club of Asian and African entities through treaties and diplomacy, sometimes even by becoming vassals themselves.[17]

Alexandrowicz observed that neither the European trading companies nor all the Asian and African entities fitted neatly into the legal categories familiar to the other side. Despite that difficulty, 'it was not impossible for sovereigns from various parts of the world to find some common language, to *classify* each other in terms of *de jure* status and *de facto* power, to negotiate and to reach agreement with or without the use of force'.[18] Their interaction was a 'repository for the experience of European–Asian State practice which had its impact on the formation of certain principles of the law of nations'.[19] For example, the Indian Ocean was subject

[13] Buzan (n 5) ch 5.

[14] CH Alexandrowicz, 'The Afro-Asian world and the law of nations (historical aspects)' (1968) 123 Recueil des cours 117, especially 124–5, 129.

[15] Ibid, 136–7.

[16] CH Alexandrowicz, 'Treaty and diplomatic relations between European and South Asian powers in the seventeenth and eighteenth centuries' (1960) 100 Recueil des cours 203, 310–12; Yasuaki Onuma, 'When was the law of international society born? An inquiry of the history of international law from an intercivilizational perspective' (2000) 2 Journal of the History of International Law 1; Bimal N Patel, 'India' in Bardo Fassbender and Anne Peters (eds), *The Oxford Handbook of the History of International Law* (OUP 2012) 500.

[17] Alexandrowicz, 'Afro-Asian world' (n 14) 134–5.

[18] Ibid, 136.

[19] Alexandrowicz, 'Treaty' (n 16) 312.

to a principle of the freedom of the sea that may have influenced the Dutch jurist Hugo Grotius to challenge the closed regime then prevailing among European states.[20] Yet Alexandrowicz did not think that one could speak of 'a public law of Europe and Asia in the sense of a coherent and operating legal system'.[21] The Indian Ocean was a forum for clashes and compromises between *different* conceptions of international law. Europeans constructed Asian and African entities in one way; Muslim rulers and scholars saw non-Muslims according to their own view of the world; and so on. They merely had enough in common that they could muddle along in practice.

Some of the non-Westerners involved in this interaction may have applied the binary distinction between lawfulness and unlawfulness in a different way from how Westerners applied it; some may have used different distinctions and concepts (Islamic law, for example, classifies conduct as obligatory, recommended, neutral, abominable, or sinful[22]); some non-Westerners may not have sharply separated international law from domestic law, morality, or other social practices. The point is that these various versions or conceptions of international law cannot be conflated. Efforts to correct Eurocentrism must not lead one to imagine an idealized, cosmopolitan system that provided answers to legal questions with which, say, Europeans, Arabs, and Pacific islanders would all have agreed. The particular conception of international law that was eventually globalized was Western in origin—and, for the most part, it was spread not through a process of compromise and synthesis with non-Western ideas, but rather by colonization, military force, and economic and cultural pressure.

There are different ways of dealing with the existence of multiple 'international laws'.

Rose Parfitt suggests that international lawyers could stage encounters between different conceptions of law: *Western* international law (as I will call it when speaking about the past) is not the only perspective from which, say, the colonization of Australia could be assessed.[23]

Alternatively, even if the perspective taken is generally that of Western international law, other legal perspectives might displace or complement that of Western international law in certain contexts. This possibility was raised directly before the International Court of Justice in *Western Sahara*. The question was whether Western Sahara had been *terra nullius* (land belonging to no one) in the 1880s. The suggestion that went the furthest was made by Mohammed Bedjaoui on behalf of Algeria. He described the problem as one 'of conflict between different legal

[20] Alexandrowicz, 'Afro-Asian world' (n 14) 162.

[21] Alexandrowicz, 'Treaty' (n 16) 312. Compare the discussion in Onuma (n 16) 39–40 n 98 about relations 'on an *ad hoc* basis' between Europeans and Africans before the twentieth century.

[22] Ralf Michaels, 'What is non-state law? A primer' in Michael A Helfand (ed), *Negotiating State and Non-State Law: The Challenge of Global and Local Legal Pluralism* (CUP 2015) 41, 54.

[23] Rose Parfitt, 'The spectre of sources' (2014) 25 EJIL 297, 303.

systems in the same period, that is, of conflict between European international law and Islamic international law' and speculated that one answer to it might be to find that the territory could not have been *terra nullius* because it was part of the *Dar al-Islam* (the House of Islam).[24] The Court did not adopt this pluralist view—and even Bedjaoui did not press it but went on to make arguments from Western international law. A hazard of taking the pluralist view was articulated on behalf of Spain, the former colonizer of Western Sahara: 'if the idea that general [Western] international law is unique were abandoned . . . legal reasoning would be unable to produce a minimum of agreement, because fundamentally different basic categories would be used'.[25] The test of *terra nullius* that the Court applied (which I will look at later) was a test from Western international law.

Another alternative is simply to refuse to take historical Western international law seriously as a system of norms that can be separated from its ideology. As many have pointed out, the rhetoric of 'civilization' was used to justify the dispossession of colonized peoples.[26] But it is doubtful that law is ever unblemished by ideology. And if one takes the international law of the present seriously, why treat that of the past differently? It is part of the same conversation among international lawyers and others that has continued over the centuries without interruption. Moreover, as illustrated by *Western Sahara*, questions about what international law historically said on a point may still be relevant to legal disputes today.

I will start from the premise that historical Western international law was a more or less coherent system of norms that can be analysed much like international law today (though it will be seen that its norms were not always stable or free from contradiction). This does not imply that it was a *just* system. On the contrary, evidence that historical international law discriminated explicitly against non-Westerners might lead one to reflect on the justice of international law today, including the norms that accord personality to some entities but deny it to others. Nor does this approach assume that other conceptions of international law are irrelevant. The Court in *Western Sahara*, though it did not adopt the pluralist view suggested by Bedjaoui, accepted that 'the legal régime of Western Sahara, including its legal relations with neighbouring territories, cannot properly be appreciated without reference to . . . special characteristics' that 'largely determined the way of life and social and political organization of the peoples inhabiting it'.[27] These

[24] Mohammed Bedjaoui, Oral Statement for Algeria (15 July 1975) ICJ Pleadings: *Western Sahara*, vol 4, 467, 489–90 (translation). See further Malcolm N Shaw, *Title to Territory in Africa: International Legal Issues* (Clarendon 1986) 55–8.

[25] Fernando Arias-Salgado, Oral Statement for Spain (18 July 1975) ICJ Pleadings: *Western Sahara*, vol 5, 51, 58 (translation).

[26] Georg Schwarzenberger, 'The standard of civilisation in international law' (1955) 8 Current Legal Problems 212, 220; Antony Anghie, *Imperialism, Sovereignty and the Making of International Law* (CUP 2004); Brett Bowden, 'The colonial origins of international law: European expansion and the classical standard of civilization' (2005) 7 Journal of the History of International Law 1; Brett Bowden, *The Empire of Civilization: The Evolution of an Imperial Idea* (University of Chicago Press 2009).

[27] *Western Sahara (Advisory Opinion)* [1975] ICJ Rep 12, para 87.

non-Western practices were relevant, however, only because Western international law *made them relevant* within its own internal framework.

Interaction between different conceptions of international law will be a recurring theme in this chapter. I turn next to an especially striking illustration of it: the disjunction between the Western notion of universalist natural law and an incompatible non-Western perspective. This will serve to introduce the next question that I need to discuss now that I have untangled my approach from other legal and extra-legal perspectives. This is the question of which state-like entities had personality in Western international law during what I will refer to—extremely loosely, but for the sake of convenience—as the era of natural law.

2.2 The era of natural law

In 1245, Pope Innocent IV sent multiple diplomatic missions to the Great Khan (*Khagan*) of the Mongols.[28] At this time the Pope, as 'the vicar of Jesus Christ', claimed 'power not only over Christians but also over all infidels, for Christ had power over all men'.[29] One of the missions never made it. After reaching the camp of a Mongol commander, one of its leaders, the Dominican friar Ascelin, insisted that the commander be baptized—and narrowly escaped execution. But another mission, led by the Franciscan friar Giovanni da Pianô Carpine, reached its destination in time to witness the election and coronation of Güyük Khan, to whom it delivered the Pope's letters. In the letters, after urging the Khan to acknowledge Jesus as God's son, the Pope chastised the Mongols for invading 'many countries belonging both to Christians and to others' in breach of natural law, 'the very elements which go to make up the world machine'.[30] In response, Güyük Khan contested the Pope's authority: 'How dost thou know that such words as thou speakest are with God's sanction?' And he challenged the Pope's assertions about the grounds on which it was unlawful for the Mongols to make war:

> Other words which thou hast sent me: 'I am surprised that thou hast seized all the lands of the Magyar and the Christians. Tell us what their fault is.' . . . The eternal God has slain and annihilated these lands and peoples, because they have neither adhered to Chingis [Genghis] Khan, nor to the Khagan, both of whom have been sent to make known God's command, nor to the command of God.

[28] Bowden, 'Colonial origins' (n 26).

[29] Innocent IV, 'Commentaria doctissima in quinque libros decretalium' (c 1250) in James Muldoon (ed), *The Expansion of Europe: The First Phase* (University of Pennsylvania Press 1977) 191.

[30] Innocent IV, Two Bulls Addressed to the Emperor of the Tartars (1245) in Christopher Dawson (ed), *The Mongol Mission: Narratives and Letters of the Franciscan Missionaries in Mongolia and China in the Thirteenth and Fourteenth Centuries* (Sheed & Ward 1955) 73.

> Like thy words, they also were impudent, they were proud and they slew our messenger-emissaries.[31]

This clash illustrates two things. First, the Pope and other Europeans of the period had a conception of international law that was universalist in that non-Christians as well as Christians had rights and duties—and hence personality. It was universalist because it was a conception of natural law; it was said to be derived from nature. Regardless of whether this claim was 'true' in some extra-legal sense, it was part of how the facts of the world were constructed within the internal logical framework of international law.[32] Second, since this conception of international law purported to exist naturally, it had no regard at all to whether or not the Mongols or anyone else accepted it as binding. It was irrelevant that Güyük Khan had a *different* conception of law (on a very loose definition of 'law': his arguments were framed in terms of 'God's command'). As Gong remarks, 'the universal Family of Nations hypothesized under classical [Western] natural law was based more on the conceptions of European theorists, than on the realities of sustained contact among the countries of the world'.[33]

Western international law remained primarily naturalist and largely universalist for a long time. This is too long and too diverse an era to consider in depth here. But one important change over the course of it was to the way in which the ostensible universality of the law was explained.[34] In the sixteenth century, the Spanish scholar Francisco de Vitoria began to unshackle natural law from the universal authority attributed to the Pope and the Holy Roman Emperor on the basis of Christian beliefs. Vitoria thought there was a *secular* order that 'natural reason has established among all nations'.[35] He called this *ius gentium*. It applied not only to states such as Spain but also to the indigenous peoples the Spanish had encountered in the Americas, on the ground that they 'are not of unsound mind, but have, according to their kind, the use of reason . . . for they have polities which are orderly arranged and they have definite marriages and magistrates, overlords, laws and workshops, and a system of exchange, all of which call for the use of reason'.[36] The idea that natural law was based on secular, natural reason rather than on Christian principles was developed further by Grotius, Christian Wolff, and others. Grotius defined it as 'the Rule and Dictate

[31] Güyük Khan, Letter to Pope Innocent IV (1246) in Dawson (n 30) 85. Güyük Khan was a grandson of Genghis Khan.

[32] Compare Richard Nobles and David Schiff, *A Sociology of Jurisprudence* (Hart 2006) 70, further ch 3.

[33] Gong (n 7) 44.

[34] Neff, *Justice among Nations* (n 12), especially chs 3–5.

[35] Francisco de Vitoria, *De Indis et de jure belli* (first published 1557, John Pawley Bate tr, Carnegie Institution of Washington 1917) 151. See further Bowden, 'Colonial origins' (n 26) 4; Anghie (n 26) ch 1.

[36] Vitoria (n 35) 127.

of Right Reason' and asserted that it 'is so unalterable, that God himself cannot change it'.[37]

Grotius further argued, influenced by earlier work by Francisco Suárez, that international law was composed not only of natural law but also of voluntary law, which arose from agreement between its subjects and could modify natural law.[38] This *positive* international law was said to exist only insofar as entities consented to it. The introduction of a notion of positive international law did not at first greatly affect the rules about which state-like entities had personality. According to Ian Brownlie, international law still did not emphasize a formal standard of statehood and did not impose any 'regional or cultural limitation' on which entities could bear rights and duties.[39] According to Alexandrowicz, 'all *de facto* independent State entities' continued to be treated 'as existing *de jure* in the international field'.[40]

Jennifer Pitts warns that these assessments of historical international law must be viewed with caution: even 'earlier so-called natural law theories relied on the practice of nations for the content of that law, and often specified that they meant "civilized nations"', and Alexandrowicz 'overstated the consensus in seventeenth- and eighteenth-century Europe that Asian states were fellow members of an international legal community'.[41] Partly for this reason, there is no sharp dividing line, for my purposes, between what I have been calling the era of natural law and the ensuing era of more dogmatic positivism. What did happen was that, from around the end of the eighteenth century, international lawyers began to articulate doubts about the personality of non-Western state-like entities in more explicit and categorical terms. Alexandrowicz observed that by the time of the Congress of Vienna in 1815,

> the existence of international persons . . . became dependent on the consent of the existing States. The European powers (with an extension to the USA) assumed the authority of an 'international agency' which could issue, or deny, a certificate of birth to States . . . irrespective of their *de facto* existence. The consequence was that Asian powers found themselves in the nineteenth century in the position of candidates for recognition.[42]

[37] Hugo Grotius, *The Rights of War and Peace* (first published 1625, Richard Tuck ed, Liberty Fund 2005) pts I.I.X.1, I.I.X.5.

[38] Neff, *Justice among Nations* (n 12) ch 4, especially 160–1, referring to Francisco Suárez, *De legibus ac Deo legislatore* (1612).

[39] Ian Brownlie, 'The expansion of international society: The consequences for the law of nations' in Hedley Bull and Adam Watson (eds), *The Expansion of International Society* (Clarendon 1984) 357, 361.

[40] Alexandrowicz, 'Treaty' (n 16) 309.

[41] Jennifer Pitts, 'Empire and legal universalisms in the eighteenth century' (2012) 117 American Historical Review 92, 100.

[42] Alexandrowicz, 'Treaty' (n 16) 309–10.

Before analysing the results of this change, I need to complete this brief discussion of natural law by considering what relevance the naturalist view of personality continued to have.

First, does it follow from the premise that non-Western state-like entities had personality in the era of natural law that they necessarily retained that personality in the subsequent era, despite the turn to positivism? Alexandrowicz thought the 'family of nations could not have been reduced from universality to a regional framework by a change of doctrine'.[43] He argued:

> the admission of Turkey, Persia [Iran], Siam [Thailand], China and Japan into the Family of Nations in the nineteenth or twentieth centuries can hardly mean admission sensu stricto but constitutes at most an *inter-temporal* adjustment caused by the differences between the pre-nineteenth century law of nations and the nineteenth or twentieth century conceptions of international law.[44]

Nineteenth-century international law certainly does not determine which entities had personality in the earlier, universalist period. That would breach the 'intertemporal' principle from *Island of Palmas*: 'a juridical fact must be appreciated in light of the law contemporary with it, and not of the law in force at the time when a dispute in regard to it arises or falls to be settled'.[45] But this might cut both ways: *pre*-nineteenth-century international law might not be able to determine which entities had personality in a *later* period. That is suggested by a caveat to the principle made by the arbitrator in *Island of Palmas*, Max Huber:

> As regards . . . the so-called intertemporal law . . . a distinction must be made between the creation of rights and the existence of rights. The same principle which subjects the act creative of a right to the law in force at the time the right arises, demands that the existence of the right, in other words its continued manifestation, shall follow the conditions required by the evolution of law.[46]

An entity's personality (as I have defined it) is a function of rights and duties, at least some of which must continue in existence in order for the entity to continue to count as a person. So perhaps Huber's reasoning might apply here: the 'continued manifestation' of personality might have to 'follow the conditions required by the evolution' of international law.

[43] CH Alexandrowicz, 'Doctrinal aspects of the universality of the law of nations' (1961) 37 BYIL 506, 515.
[44] Alexandrowicz, 'Treaty' (n 16) 316.
[45] *Island of Palmas (US/Netherlands)* (1928) 2 UNRIAA 829, 845.
[46] Ibid. The International Court seemed to lend support to this caveat to the intertemporal principle in *Minquiers and Ecrehos (France/UK)* [1953] ICJ Rep 47, 56.

What was at issue in *Island of Palmas* was not personality generally but a package of rights and other relations of a distinct type: territorial sovereignty (I will have more to say shortly about what this package contains). The caveat to the intertemporal principle was relevant only if a particular hypothesis was correct: that in sixteenth-century international law 'discovery' was a sufficient basis for territorial sovereignty but that by 1898 international law had evolved such that 'discovery' alone, without effective occupation, was not sufficient. The question was whether, on that hypothesis, Spain could have maintained territorial sovereignty over an island up to 1898 solely on the basis that it had 'discovered' the island back in the sixteenth century. Huber, applying the caveat to the intertemporal principle, held that it could not. This has been criticized. Philip Jessup worried that, if Huber were correct, every state would have to be constantly 'examining its title to each portion of its territory in order to determine whether a change in the law had necessitated, as it were, a reacquisition'; he added that if the same view were taken of titles in domestic law 'the result would be chaos'.[47] Jessup's remarks might be interpreted not as a criticism of the caveat as a general matter of principle but rather as a warning specifically about applying it to territory: there is an impetus in international law to preserve territorial arrangements even when other arrangements are destabilized.[48] But if Jessup was justified in worrying that chaos would result from applying the caveat to territory, there may be even more reason to worry where what is at stake is an entity's entire existence as an international legal person. Perhaps international law could avoid this chaos by treating the acquisition of personality as a once-and-for-all event occurring at a certain point in time and whose continuing validity depends on the law of that point in time.

On the other hand, the fact that a doctrine might cause chaos does not make it wrong. As will be seen, claims that non-Western entities lacked personality in the nineteenth century, despite having enjoyed it throughout previous centuries, actually did seem to throw international law into a kind of chaos. So the possibility must be left open that the caveat to Huber's intertemporal principle *can* apply to norms that affect an entity's personality: the mere fact that a particular non-Western entity had personality in the era of natural law is not enough to establish conclusively that it retained that personality in a later period. All that can be said for certain is that it would be very surprising if international law had evolved in such a way as to extinguish utterly the personality attributed to entities in the era of natural law.

There is a second, more direct way in which universalist natural law could have remained relevant up to the nineteenth century (and hence could have alleviated

[47] Philip C Jessup, 'The Palmas Island arbitration' (1928) 22 AJIL 735, 740.

[48] Eg, *Territorial Dispute (Libya/Chad)* [1994] ICJ Rep 6, paras 72–3: the establishment of a boundary by treaty 'is a fact which, from the outset, has . . . a legal life of its own'; the boundary stands even if the treaty ceases to be in force. See also Vienna Convention on the Law of Treaties (23 May 1969) 1155 UNTS 331, art 62(2)(a) on fundamental changes of circumstances; this book s 4.1.1 on territorial integrity.

the risk of chaos): insofar as a bedrock of natural law survived beneath positive international law. This possibility goes back at least as far as Grotius. Grotius has been described as presenting a 'dual or concentric conception of international society' composed of 'an outer circle that embraces all mankind, under natural law, and an inner circle, the *corpus Christianorum*'.[49] Despite the turn towards positive international law, for a long time Westerners continued to refer to natural law in their dealings in other parts of the world. For instance, in 1786, the *de facto* governor-general of British India, Warren Hastings, was indicted before the British parliament. He had deposed the Rajah of Benares (Varanasi) for resisting payment of an exorbitant sum in tribute. Edmund Burke, who conducted the case against the governor-general, defended the Rajah's rights by citing a principle from Emer de Vattel that he described as 'the law of India as well as Europe because it is the law of reason and the law of nature'.[50] More generally, as Martti Koskenniemi points out, even the nineteenth-century proponents of the ideas of a family of nations and 'civilization' were 'not "positivists" in any clear sense but made constant use of arguments about morality or natural law'.[51] I will cite examples later in the chapter.

The explanatory power of natural law diminishes with the passage of time. By the twentieth century, it had been relegated to a historical or minor role. The Statute of the Permanent Court of International Justice was drafted in 1920; the Statute of its later incarnation, the International Court of Justice, is substantially identical. Article 38(1) states that the Court shall apply (a) treaties, (b) custom, and (c) 'general principles of law recognized by civilized nations'.[52] It does not mention natural law as an extra category of norms. Some have interpreted 'general principles' as a vestige of natural law. For example, in his dissent in *South West Africa*, Judge Tanaka argued that 'some natural law elements are inherent' in them.[53] Others disagree; yet others argue that general principles are not a discrete category of norms at all but are always a manifestation of either treaty or custom.[54] Whatever they are, they are of comparatively minor importance next to the other categories.

[49] Wight, *Systems* (n 5) 128.

[50] Alexandrowicz, 'Afro-Asian world' (n 14) 137–8. See further Pitts (n 41) 109–14.

[51] Koskenniemi (n 10) 130–1.

[52] Statute of the Permanent Court of International Justice (16 December 1920) 6 LNTS 389; Statute of the International Court of Justice (26 June 1945) art 38(1). Art 38(1)(d) adds: 'subject to the provisions of Article 59, judicial decisions and the teachings of the most highly qualified publicists of the various nations, as subsidiary means for the determination of rules of law'. But it is apparent from the words 'subsidiary means' and from art 59 (a 'decision of the Court has no binding force except between the parties and in respect of that particular case') that this is evidence of what norms say rather than an additional category of norms: James Crawford, *Brownlie's Principles of Public International Law* (8th edn, OUP 2012) 37–43.

[53] *South West Africa (Ethiopia v South Africa; Liberia v South Africa) (Second Phase)* [1966] ICJ Rep 6, 298 (Judge Tanaka dissenting).

[54] Eg, Hans Kelsen, *Principles of International Law* (Rinehart 1952) 393–4. See further Malcolm N Shaw, *International Law* (7th edn, CUP 2014) 70–1; Hugh Thirlway, *The Sources of International Law* (OUP 2014) ch 4.

I have observed that the Western international law of the naturalist era had a tendency to attribute rights, duties, and hence personality to both Western and non-Western entities. Although this does not necessarily determine the position in later eras of international law, it at least hints that entities of both types probably retained some personality.

2.3 The positivist era in the West

Some preliminary matters have been dealt with: I have distinguished the internal framework of Western international law from other legal and extra-legal perspectives, and I have briefly discussed which state-like entities had personality within that framework in the era of natural law. I can move on to the issue that will take up the rest of this chapter: which state-like entities had personality during what I will refer to—again, very loosely, but for convenience—as the positivist era. For my purposes, this period began when international lawyers began to raise more explicit doubts about the personality of non-Western entities based on positivist ideas; it ended in the early twentieth century in a manner that I will discuss in due course. I will highlight some relevant features of the personality of Western states during the positivist era; then I will look separately at two categories of non-Western entities.

The features of Western states I will highlight are their sovereignty and the applicability to them of customary norms that gave them additional rights and other relations. These features will be relevant to the comparison with non-Western entities. I leave aside until the next chapter the question of what might have underpinned their possession of these features if not natural law, including the role of recognition. At this stage, the term 'Western state' is not intended to commit me to a position on that question or on what the word 'state' means on its own. It simply refers to a group of entities that clearly had these two features: entities in Europe that were described as 'states' and similar entities with Western-style governments in the Americas or elsewhere.[55]

'Sovereignty' is a term with any number of meanings.[56] I will use it, consistent with common usage in international law, to mean a particular package of rights and other relations that an entity possesses relative to other entities that also possess sovereignty in this sense. A judicial definition of it that is often cited is Huber's from *Island of Palmas*: '[s]overeignty in the relations between States signifies independence', and '[i]ndependence in regard to a portion of the globe is the right

[55] See the list at the beginning of this chapter.

[56] Samantha Besson, 'Sovereignty' (last updated 2011) MPEPIL; James Crawford, 'Chance, order, change: The course of international law' (2013) 365 Recueil des cours 9, ch 3, especially paras 118–21.

to exercise therein, to the exclusion of any other State, the functions of a State'.[57] According to a recent textbook definition, sovereignty entails 'a jurisdiction, prima facie exclusive, over a territory and the permanent population living there' and 'a duty of non-intervention in the area of exclusive jurisdiction of other states'; in this context 'jurisdiction' refers to an entity's 'competence under international law' to make its own domestic laws and 'to take executive or judicial action in pursuance of or consequent on' those laws.[58]

Since sovereignty mostly consists of rights and other relations whose operation depends on the extent of an entity's territory—*territorial* sovereignty—it can be hard to untangle from norms that define territory (land, internal waters, territorial sea, and airspace). There also exist some more-specifically formulated norms that may be seen as aspects of sovereignty, such as those about territorial integrity, intervention, and immunity. And sovereignty is by no means absolute: the rights and other relations that it comprises are qualified by countless other norms of international law. For all these reasons, it is hard to say where the category of sovereign rights ends and an entity's other rights begin; in the next chapter I will argue that—nowadays, at least—there is no sharp analytical distinction between sovereignty and the various other relations that states have under customary international law.[59]

Still, despite this haziness at the edges of the concept, it is clear that sovereignty embraces at least one particular Hohfeldian freedom and one particular right. A sovereign entity must have a freedom to exercise jurisdiction in its territory, which correlates with the absence of a right of other such entities to insist that it *not* exercise that jurisdiction. I observed in Chapter 1 that unless norms say otherwise, every entity has an absolute freedom by default (though all that this means is that its conduct is not unlawful, not that others owe it any duties or that its conduct has any particular consequence: that is part of the point of distinguishing freedoms from rights).[60] This freedom by itself is not enough to mark an entity out as an international legal person. But consider the two definitions of sovereignty that I quoted a moment ago: Huber referred to exercising functions 'to the exclusion' of other entities; the textbook definition alludes to 'a duty of non-intervention in the area of exclusive jurisdiction of other states'. These definitions make clear that a sovereign entity also has a Hohfeldian *right* that other sovereign entities not intervene in its exercise of jurisdiction in its territory, which correlates with a duty of those other entities. Since I have defined personality in terms of Hohfeldian rights and duties, this aspect of sovereignty necessarily entails personality. It is this aspect that I will

[57] *Island of Palmas* (1928) 2 UNRIAA 829, 838. I will not follow Huber in using the word 'independence' as a synonym for sovereignty or any aspect of it, for reasons that will be evident from this book s 3.1.1.

[58] Crawford, *Brownlie's* (n 52) 447, 456.

[59] This book s 3.1.2.

[60] This book s 1.2.

primarily have in mind when I refer to sovereignty throughout this chapter and the rest of this book.

Another key feature of Western states in the period under discussion was the applicability to them of customary norms that gave them additional rights and other relations.

Until around 1850, the norms of customary international law (as distinct from norms derived from treaties) did not go very far beyond the relations that might be considered aspects of sovereignty. Custom dealt with 'the definition of the state and its appendages, such as the territorial sea', 'the mechanism of establishing and maintaining diplomatic relations', 'the forms of treaty-making', and 'the law of war and neutrality'.[61] International law was generally not concerned with matters such as individual criminal responsibility or human rights; such principles as self-determination had yet to emerge. There was 'no mechanism for law enforcement, except for war', the use of force not generally being prohibited.[62] It will be useful to bear the very limited scope of customary international law in mind when I come to discuss the personality of *non*-Western state-like entities. There is no reason to imagine that if African and Asian entities had enjoyed all the same rights as Western states then that would have protected them from imperialism. As Fukuzawa Yukichi of Japan put it, a 'hundred volumes of universal law of nations' could not defeat 'several cannons'.[63]

Today, customary norms are said to require state practice accompanied by *opinio iuris sive necessitatis* ('a belief that this practice is rendered obligatory by the existence of a rule of law requiring it'[64]). A practice, 'including that of states whose interests are specially affected, should have been both extensive and virtually uniform . . . and should moreover have occurred in such a way as to show a general recognition that a rule of law or legal obligation is involved'.[65] As the International Law Commission has observed, 'it is not necessary to show that all States have participated in the practice in question'; nor is it 'necessary to establish that all States have recognized (accepted as law) the alleged rule as a rule of customary international law' but merely to establish 'broad and representative acceptance, together with no or little objection'.[66] Moreover—and this is the significant point for present

[61] Brownlie (n 39) 359.

[62] Antonio Cassese, 'States: Rise and decline of the primary subjects of the international community' in Bardo Fassbender and Anne Peters (eds), *The Oxford Handbook of the History of International Law* (OUP 2012) 49, 54–5.

[63] Onuma (n 16) 65, quoting in translation Fukuzawa Yukichi, *Fukuzawa Yukichi zenshu* [*The Complete Works of Fukuzawa Yukichi*] (Iwanami shoten 1959) vol 4, 637.

[64] *North Sea Continental Shelf (Federal Republic of Germany/Denmark; Federal Republic of Germany/Netherlands)* [1969] ICJ Rep 3, para 77. This formulation was repeated in *Military and Paramilitary Activities in and against Nicaragua (Nicaragua v US)* [1986] ICJ Rep 14, para 207.

[65] *North Sea Continental Shelf* [1969] ICJ Rep 3, para 74.

[66] Conclusions on Identification of Customary International Law [2018] 2(2) ILC Ybk, UN doc A/73/10, commentary to conclusion 8, para 3; commentary to conclusion 9, para 5. Compare Robert Jennings and Arthur Watts, *Oppenheim's International Law* (9th edn, Longman 1996) vol 1, pt 10; Thirlway (n 54) ch 3.

purposes—once a norm is formed in this way, it is generally binding on *every state*, whether or not that state contributed to its formation or has otherwise consented specifically to the norm. The International Court affirmed in *North Sea Continental Shelf* that customary norms 'by their very nature, must have equal force for all members of the international community'.[67] Roland Portmann extracts some further corroboration of the point from the same case. The question was whether West Germany was bound by a norm under which its continental shelf would be delimited by the equidistance method. The Court found that it was not a party to a treaty that incorporated the norm and had not 'by conduct, by public statements and proclamations, [or] in other ways' recognized the norm as applicable.[68] In other words, West Germany had not consented specifically to the norm. But Denmark and the Netherlands argued that

> the use of this method . . . is, or must now be regarded as involving, a rule that is part of the *corpus* of general international law;—and, like other rules of general or customary international law, is binding on the Federal Republic [West Germany] automatically and independently of any specific assent, direct or indirect, given by the latter.[69]

The Court impliedly accepted this: despite its finding that West Germany had not consented specifically to the norm, it went on to consider whether a customary norm existed that was binding on West Germany (though in the event it found that none existed).[70] Note that a state may sometimes be deemed to have accepted a practice as law *tacitly* by failing to react to the practice in circumstances where a reaction is called for.[71] The point that I am making goes further than this in that no specific consent is required at all, not even tacit consent.

This general rule that a customary norm binds every state even if it has not consented specifically to that norm is reinforced by the existence of an exception that serves, in narrow circumstances, to excuse states from being bound: the persistent-objector rule. In the Commission's formulation, '[w]here a State has objected to a rule of customary international law while that rule was in the process of formation, the rule is not opposable to the State concerned for so long as it maintains its objection'; the 'objection must be clearly expressed, made known to other States, and

[67] *North Sea Continental Shelf* [1969] ICJ Rep 3, para 63. The Court added that norms 'cannot therefore be the subject of any right of unilateral exclusion exercisable at will by any one of them in its own favour', although there is a narrower exception to be introduced momentarily, the persistent-objector rule.

[68] Ibid, paras 26–7, 32. The treaty was Geneva Convention on the Continental Shelf (29 April 1958) 499 UNTS 311, art 6(2).

[69] *North Sea Continental Shelf* [1969] ICJ Rep 3, para 37.

[70] Roland Portmann, *Legal Personality in International Law* (CUP 2010) 259–60.

[71] Conclusions on Identification of Customary International Law, conclusion 10(3). See further *Fisheries (UK v Norway)* [1951] ICJ Rep 116, 139: 'the attitude of governments', including their 'general toleration' of a method of maritime delimitation followed by Norway over a long period, 'bears witness to the fact that they did not consider [the Norwegian method] to be contrary to international law'.

maintained persistently'.[72] This narrow exception would be unnecessary if the state would not generally be bound by the norm anyway.

That is the prevailing view today (though in comments on the Commission's work on the topic some states supported a wider exception; for example, the Netherlands, while agreeing that the general rule is that states will be bound by a norm unless they object to it during its formation, doubted that an objection must then be 'maintained persistently'[73]). The view that every state is generally bound by a customary norm even if it has not consented specifically to that norm is called by Stephen Neff the 'legislative' view of custom.[74] Even though specific consent to each norm is not required, a possible positivist justification for this view is that states consent—or can be deemed or presumed to consent when they come into being as states—to the institution of customary international law as a whole.[75]

In the nineteenth century, there was scholarly support for a rival approach to custom, which Neff calls the 'contractual' view. Some schools of positivism argued that no customary norm could apply to a state unless that specific state had consented to that specific norm.[76] This meant there could be 'no such thing as *universal* international law' except in the 'unrealistic scenarios' of 'a treaty to which literally every state in the world was a party, or a customary practice in which every single state participated'.[77] Neff suggests that in 'the nineteenth century, this contractual outlook was the dominant one' among scholars.[78]

Despite this, it may not be inexcusably anachronistic to project the legislative view of custom back into the past. First, the legislative view fits better with the apparent continuity of international law from the preceding era of natural law to the positivist nineteenth century up to the present. Although the theoretical justification was radically different, the impact of the belief that norms derive from natural law was, in an essential respect, similar to that of the legislative view of custom: a body of general norms bound every Western state even if it had not consented specifically to each norm. Taking a contractual view of nineteenth-century international law requires one to postulate that this body of general norms once existed, then temporarily ceased to exist (except insofar as states specifically consented to

[72] Conclusions on Identification of Customary International Law, conclusion 15. See further *Fisheries (UK v Norway)* [1951] ICJ Rep 116, 131. Some scholars have raised doubts about the rule, and there is only limited practice that unambiguously supports it, but most accept its existence: Thirlway (n 54) 86–7. On one way in which the persistent-objector rule may be relevant to statehood, see this book s 5.2.

[73] Identification of Customary Law: Comments and Observations Received from Governments (14 February 2018) UN doc A/CN.4/716, 54, further 51–5.

[74] Stephen C Neff, 'The dormancy, rise and decline of fundamental liberties of states' (2015) 4 Cambridge Journal of International and Comparative Law 482, 491.

[75] This justification may be less convincing today than in the past, for two reasons. First, one possible basis for it was the recognition-only view of statehood, which has gone out of fashion and which I will reject: this book s 3.2. Second, it is arguable that today states cannot opt out of the legislative view: s 3.1.1.

[76] Neff, *Justice among Nations* (n 12) 247–9.

[77] Ibid, 248.

[78] Neff, 'The dormancy, rise and decline' (n 74) 492.

each component of it), and later re-emerged when the legislative view took hold. The view that a body of general norms existed the entire time, even if its theoretical justification changed, can more elegantly explain the fact that such dramatic shifts are hard to discern in practice. Second, one can find support for the legislative view—at least insofar as it applied to Western states—even from late-nineteenth-century scholars who were among the strictest of positivists. For instance, Westlake (whose description of the family of nations was given at the beginning of this chapter and who will feature again later, as an exemplar of a positivist approach to non-Western entities) accepted that when a rule 'is invoked against a state, it is not necessary to show that the state in question has assented to the rule' but merely 'that the general *consensus* of opinion within the limits of European civilisation is in favour of the rule'.[79]

This is one respect, among several that I will discuss, in which the transition from natural law to positivism destabilized international law. I will compare the position of Western states with that of non-Western entities on the premise that the legislative view applied to Western states but also on the alternative premise that the contractual view applied to them.

2.4 The positivist era in the Ottoman Empire, Asia, and parts of Africa

I now turn to the personality of *non*-Western state-like entities in the positivist era, in particular to whether their personality differed from that of Western states.

There is still an active debate about this—especially in respect of the late nineteenth century, when international lawyers articulated the standard of 'civilization' in explicit terms.[80] These proponents of the standard of 'civilization' did not take as extreme a position as might be imagined. True, sometimes they seemed to imply that all non-Western state-like entities utterly lacked rights and duties in international law. The Treaty of Paris of 1856 declared the Ottoman Empire to be 'admitted to participate in the advantages of the public law and concert of Europe'.[81]

[79] Westlake (n 1) 78. Neff, *Justice among Nations* (n 12) 229 describes Westlake as an exponent of the 'empirical variant of positivism'.

[80] Georg Schwarzenberger and ED Brown, *A Manual of International Law* (6th edn, Professional Books 1976) 84 argued that it 'crystallised into a rule of international customary law' from the mid-nineteenth century. Gong (n 7) 14 concludes that it had emerged by 1905 at the latest. See further Wilhelm G Grewe, *The Epochs of the Law of Nations* (first published 1984, Michael Byers tr, de Gruyter 2000) 445–58.

[81] General Treaty for the Re-establishment of Peace, Paris (30 March 1856) 114 CTS 409, art 7 (translation). It has been argued that treaties of 1799 and 1840 were more significant for the Ottoman Empire's 'admission': Thomas Naff, 'The Ottoman Empire and the European states system' in Hedley Bull and Adam Watson (eds), *The Expansion of International Society* (Clarendon 1984) 143. In any case its 'admission' occurred before the standard of 'civilization' had been expressly articulated. Gong (n 7) 110 explains this by saying that an implied standard existed earlier in the nineteenth century.

Oppenheim wrote that from this moment, 'International Law ceased to be a law between Christian States solely'.[82] But the context makes clear that he did not mean that all non-Christian entities had previously lacked rights and duties. That position would have been indefensible: not only had the Ottoman Empire made numerous treaties earlier in the same century, Western states had applied customary norms to it as well. For instance, by proclaiming neutrality during the Greek rebellion of 1821, the United Kingdom indicated that it considered the law of neutrality to apply in Ottoman territory.[83]

The standard of 'civilization' was a more complex idea. State-like entities were classified by their alleged *degree* of 'civilization'. Some nineteenth-century international lawyers—among them Henri Bonfils, James Lorimer, and Ernest Nys—adopted from an American anthropologist, Lewis Henry Morgan, the idea of dividing humanity into three concentric spheres.[84] In the inner sphere were the 'civilized' Western states (echoing the older notion of the *corpus Christianorum*, but substituting 'civilization' for Christianity); in the intermediate sphere was 'barbarous humanity'; and in the outer sphere was 'savage humanity'.[85] As Lorimer put it, 'civilised nations' owed entities in these different spheres

> three stages of recognition—plenary political recognition [for fellow civilised nations], partial political recognition [for barbarians], and natural or mere human recognition [for savages]. . . . [T]he international jurist . . . is not bound to apply the positive law of nations to savages, or even to barbarians, as such; but he is bound to ascertain the points at which, and the directions in which, barbarians or savages come within the scope of partial recognition.[86]

The intermediate sphere of supposedly 'barbarous' entities is the first group of non-Western entities I will look at; I postpone discussion of the outer sphere. Entities in this intermediate category included the Ottoman Empire, Japan, China, Thailand, and Iran.[87] Occasionally also included were Ethiopia, the state-like entities of north Africa (most of which were politically linked in various degrees to the Ottomans[88]), and those of central Asia. Other entities that might have been put in this category had by Lorimer's time come under European colonial control, such as the precolonial entities subsumed into or subordinated to British India.

[82] Oppenheim (n 9) vol 1, pt 28.
[83] Herbert Arthur Smith (ed), *Great Britain and the Law of Nations*, vol 1: *States* (PS King & Son 1932) 16–17.
[84] Neff, *Justice among Nations* (n 12) 311.
[85] James Lorimer, *The Institutes of the Law of Nations: A Treatise of the Jural Relations of Separate Political Communities* (William Blackwood & Sons 1883–84) vol 1, 101–2.
[86] Ibid (emphasis from original).
[87] Ibid, vol 1, 102.
[88] Fatiha Sahli and Abdelmalek El Ouazzani, 'Africa north of the Sahara and Arab countries' in Bardo Fassbender and Anne Peters (eds), *The Oxford Handbook of the History of International Law* (OUP 2012) 385, 388–9.

Oppenheim, articulating a view shared by others, wrote that these entities were 'for some parts within' and 'for other parts outside' the family of nations: 'their civilisation has not yet reached that condition which is necessary to enable their Governments and their population in every respect to understand and to carry out the command of the rules of International Law'.[89] Westlake put it like this: 'international society exercises the right of admitting outside states to parts of its international law without necessarily admitting them to the whole of it'.[90] He thought these intermediate entities 'must be recognised as being civilised, though with other civilisations'.[91] Franz von Liszt called them 'semi-civilized'.[92] Although only partial members of the club, they were considered future candidates for full admission. Lorimer hoped that Japan might be admitted in another twenty years, though he bemoaned the 'bitter experience of the consequences of extending rights of civilisation' to the Ottomans, 'barbarians who have proved to be incapable of performing its duties'.[93]

These nineteenth-century proponents of the standard of 'civilization' occupy one extreme of the debate; at the other are scholars today who deny that any such standard ever existed. Alexander Orakhelashvili claims that Westerners and non-Westerners effectively shared 'one single system of international law'.[94] From the fifteenth century onward, he writes,

> on the basis of the classical concept of universality . . . the history of international law witnessed the irreversible affirmation of universality and secularity of international law, realized through extensive treaty and diplomatic practice between European and non-European powers. This process affirmed that universality in clear practice and in the attitudes of states.[95]

Orakhelashvili may not be talking about the Western international legal system in the strict sense that I have defined it; much of the evidence he cites, such as practice in antiquity and treaties made by China between the eighth and thirteenth centuries, could be seen as manifestations of what I have characterized as other conceptions of international law. I have noted that international law in this wide sense has never been unique to the West. Even so, Orakhelashvili's claims are ambitious. He challenges not only suggestions that the nineteenth century 'witnessed . . . a shrinking of international law to a regional European system', but also suggestions of 'the emergence of an elite European subsystem'.[96] This seems to discount

89 Oppenheim (n 9) vol 1, pt 28. The Ottoman Empire and Japan were by then deemed to be 'civilized'.
90 Westlake (n 1) 82.
91 Ibid, 102.
92 Franz von Liszt, *Le droit international* (first published 1913, Gilbert Gidel tr, Pédone 1927) 5–6 (translation). WE Hall, *A Treatise on International Law* (4th edn, Clarendon 1895) used the same term.
93 Lorimer (n 85) vol 1, 102–3. Compare Hall (n 92) 42–3.
94 Alexander Orakhelashvili, 'The idea of European international law' (2006) 17 EJIL 315, 339.
95 Ibid, 336.
96 Ibid.

the possibility that there were *any* differences between the personality of Western states and that of non-Western state-like entities such as China.

My conclusions will fall somewhere between these extremes: there were differences, but they were not based on 'civilization'. I will look at two factors relevant to the personality of supposedly 'barbarous' or 'semi-civilized' entities: first, the significance of explicitly unequal legal regimes; then the applicability of customary norms generally. After that I will consider some possible explanations of apparent differences between their personality and that of Western states.

2.4.1 Personality under unequal regimes

Some definitions of 'civilization' were too vague to be easily translated into a legal test. Carlos Calvo defined it as 'the result of the reciprocal action of industry, art, science, literature, morals and religion'.[97] But later scholars have argued that it also had a more concrete meaning: whether an entity 'was sufficiently stable to undertake binding commitments under international law and whether it was able and willing to protect adequately the life, liberty and property of foreigners'.[98] So it makes sense to begin with legal regimes devised to remedy the alleged inability of the Ottoman Empire, China, and other non-Western entities to protect foreigners—notably, regimes of consular jurisdiction. International lawyers pointed to these as evidence of legal inequality.[99]

They undoubtedly *were* evidence of legal inequality, in that privileges were accorded to Western states without reciprocal privileges being given to their non-Western counterparts.[100] Westerners were subject to jurisdiction exercised by the consuls of their home states rather than to that of the local authorities. This legal inequality was primarily the product of unequal terms in particular treaties. Francis Piggott, for example, explained in 1907 that

> the sovereignty of the potentates of these oriental States, as well as of barbarous chieftains, is recognized to as full an extent as that of the Sovereigns of what was formerly called 'Christendom.' The basis of . . . 'foreign jurisdiction' is treaty: and although 'other lawful means' are recognized as a sound foundation for the

[97] Carlos Calvo, *Dictionnaire de droit international public et privé* (Puttkammer & Muhlbrecht 1885) vol 1, 148 (translation).

[98] Schwarzenberger (n 26) 220. Five criteria for 'civilization' are identified by Gong (n 7) 14–15: an entity had to guarantee basic rights, especially for foreigners; had to exist as an organized political bureaucracy; had to adhere to international law and to have a just domestic law, especially for foreigners; had to fulfil obligations of the international system; and had to conform to 'civilized' norms and practices. Compare Edwin DeWitt Dickinson, *The Equality of States in International Law* (Harvard UP 1920) 223–4.

[99] Eg, Lorimer (n 85) vol 1, 216–19; Dickinson (n 98) 223–9. See further Becker Lorca (n 1) 43–4.

[100] Becker Lorca (n 1) 43–4.

> exercise of the jurisdiction, and indeed have occasionally to justify it, treaty is resorted to wherever possible . . . They are concluded by the British Sovereign as with an equal Sovereign Prince.[101]

Orakhelashvili argues that since consular jurisdiction and other unequal regimes derived from treaties or from local domestic law, they had 'absolutely nothing to do with the ambit of international law'.[102] States are always capable of granting non-reciprocal privileges to other states by treaty.[103] So unequal treaties are not evidence of a distinction between discrete legal categories of 'civilized' and 'semi-civilized' entities. Corroboration of this is that some entities that were acknowledged to be 'civilized' states were in a similar position. Arnulf Becker Lora writes that Latin American states were subjected to treaties with European states and the United States that were functionally equivalent to unequal treaties and that the aggressive use of diplomatic protection in Latin America served a function similar to consular jurisdiction.[104] So insofar as the legal inequality of entities in the intermediate sphere was based on particular treaties, Orakhelashvili's view is correct.

But note the reference, in Piggot's explanation of consular jurisdiction, to 'other lawful means' of justifying it. Was there a customary element in consular jurisdiction?

In the case of one non-Western entity, the Ottoman Empire, the regime had been shaped over centuries by compromises between different conceptions of international law. An early event that set the pattern—said to be the first time a major modern Western state addressed a non-Western ruler as an equal—was the Franco-Ottoman alliance of 1536.[105] Under related arrangements, France acquired certain trade concessions and other privileges in Ottoman territory. The alliance scandalized the rest of Christendom; Europeans saw the Ottomans as culturally alien and inferior.[106] But equally the Ottomans, as the heirs to the universalist tradition of the earlier Islamic caliphates, saw the West as inferior.[107] From their perspective, France belonged to the *Dar al-Harb* (the House of War) and a formal military alliance with it would have breached Islamic law. So whereas the French thought that they had made a treaty in a Western sense, all that the Ottomans

[101] Francis Piggott, *Extraterritoriality: The Law Relating to Consular Jurisdiction* (Butterworth 1907) 4.

[102] Orakhelashvili (n 94) 327.

[103] Vattel (n 6) pt II.89, quoted in Orakhelashvili (n 94) 327.

[104] Becker Lorca (n 1) 88–90.

[105] Traité de paix, d'amitié et de commerce (18 February 1536) in Ignace de Testa (ed), *Recueil des traités de la Porte ottomane avec les puissances étrangères* (Amyot 1864) vol 1, 15; Becker Lorca (n 1) 83. The parties made secret plans, never executed, to attack the Habsburg territories: Naff (n 81) 146–8.

[106] Alexandrowicz, 'Afro-Asian world' (n 14) 127–8. King François I of France, for his part, argued that it 'would have evil effects if the ties of blood and nationhood would estrange particular societies from the universal society of nations': quoted in Ernest Nys, *Les origines du droit international* (Castaigne 1894) 162 (translation from Alexandrowicz, 'Afro-Asian world' (n 14) 127–8).

[107] Naff (n 81).

thought had occurred was that an individual sultan, Süleyman I, had granted the French unilateral concessions as a measure of policy (an *ahdname* or capitulation, so named after its *capitula*—chapters).[108] This pattern was repeated in following centuries. Documents were sometimes described in Turkish as unilateral concessions but in Latin, French, or Italian translation as treaties.[109]

It was similar with the consular jurisdiction regime. Although Westerners would later see it as evidence that the Ottomans lacked 'civilization', the Ottomans at first established it for the opposite reason: because they did not consider Christians capable of understanding Islamic religious law.[110] They retained their own, Islamic conception of international law for a long time. After 1699, they kept records of their commitments to Western states and experimented with reciprocal diplomacy, though Gong argues that during this period the Ottomans still 'shared few of Europe's interests, principles, or norms'.[111]

Whether consular jurisdiction had a customary element depends on how norms of Western international law constructed the facts of this history of compromise.

In a study in 1916, Edwin Borchard argued that in the Ottoman Empire (and certain other entities with which the West had a long history of interaction, such as Morocco), 'so-called extraterritorial rights, resting in their origin upon treaty, have in the course of time . . . gathered around themselves by custom an accretion of further encroachments on the local jurisdiction, so as to constitute in some countries a veritable *imperium in imperio*' (loosely: a state within a state).[112] John Bassett Moore likewise thought that the regime in the Ottoman Empire rested 'upon ancient custom as well as upon the provisions of treaties'.[113] He cited a letter from 1892 in which the US secretary of state indicated explicitly that the regime rested on custom in the relevant sense—norms from which the Ottomans could not resile:

> The status of foreigners in Turkey depending . . . on ancient usage . . . is to a certain extent determined by the capitulations or treaties between the Porte [the Ottoman Empire] and various nations. . . . As these various capitulations acted rather to recognize and confirm existing rights than to create especial privileges, it was inevitable that in the course of centuries . . . rights and privileges, born of inherent prerogatives of non-Mussulmans and acquiesced in by long and continuous usage, should become vested rights, sanctioned by the Ottoman power and indefeasible by any act of the Turkish sovereign.[114]

108 Ibid, 146–8; Umut Özsu, 'The Ottoman Empire' in Bardo Fassbender and Anne Peters (eds), *The Oxford Handbook of the History of International Law* (OUP 2012) 429, 430.
109 Becker Lorca (n 1) 82–3.
110 Gong (n 7) 107.
111 Ibid, 108–9.
112 Edwin M Borchard, *The Diplomatic Protection of Citizens Abroad* (Banks Law 1916) 431.
113 John Bassett Moore, *A Digest of International Law* (US GPO 1906) vol 2, 596.
114 John W Foster, Letter to David P Thompson (29 November 1892) in ibid, vol 2, 739.

One aspect of the regime was singled out on the basis that it could have derived only from custom, not treaties. Consuls of treaty states could 'exercise jurisdiction and grant protection to nationals of other treaty powers or even of non-treaty powers, which in other extraterritorial countries they [could not] do.'[115] For example, Switzerland did not have a consular jurisdiction treaty with the Ottomans, but Swiss nationals could seek protection from France, Germany, or the United States.[116] In 1853, the US secretary of state observed that by 'the laws of Turkey and other eastern nations', Western consulates could receive strangers who 'become thereby invested with the nationality of the protecting consulate' and that '[i]nternational law recognizes and sanctions the rights [acquired] by this connection.'[117]

The view that consular jurisdiction had a customary element is supported by the Treaty of Sèvres, which the Ottomans signed after the First World War. This provided for the re-establishment and extension of the 'capitulatory regime resulting from treaties, conventions *or usage*'.[118] Turkey (the legal continuation of the Ottoman Empire) never ratified the treaty and maintained that the capitulations were unilateral concessions that it was free to revoke.[119] But Western states did not accept that view; the capitulations were eventually abolished not unilaterally but by another multilateral treaty, the Treaty of Lausanne.[120]

In an 1868 case, the argument that consular jurisdiction had a customary element was extended beyond the Ottoman Empire. After a British ship and an American ship collided off the Japanese coast, the US consular court in Japan held both parties liable for damages. The British party applied to the US Department of State to declare the judgment void on the ground that the treaty granting the court consular jurisdiction was limited to disputes between Americans and Japanese. The US official examining the claim accepted that 'in the Levant' (Ottoman territory) 'treaties rather recognized than conferred' consular jurisdiction; he added that when China and Japan opened up to Westerners, Western states imported

> the views and practices in respect of extraterritoriality which had been matured through ages in the Levant. These were recognized in part by express convention, in part by tacit acquiescence. It was a necessary consequence of the extraterritoriality which each western power asserted on behalf of its own subjects, that it excluded the jurisdiction of Japan to administer justice to the subject of one Christian power against the subject of another.[121]

[115] Borchard (n 112) 103.
[116] Moore (n 113) vol 2, 722, 736.
[117] William L Marcy, Letter to Edwin De Leon (26 September 1853) in ibid, vol 2, 728.
[118] Treaty of Peace between the Allied Powers and Turkey, Sèvres (10 August 1920, never in force) 15 AJIL Supp 179, art 261 (emphasis added).
[119] Özsu (n 108) 443–4.
[120] Treaty of Peace with Turkey, Lausanne (24 July 1923) [1923] UKTS 16, art 28.
[121] E Peshine Smith, quoted in Moore (n 113) vol 2, 601. Compare the argument of GW Keeton, *The Development of Extraterritoriality in China* (Longmans, Green, & Co 1928) vol 2, 93–104: Western

This implies that extraterritoriality in Japan was not based solely on treaties. But there is less to support the argument here than in the Ottoman case. Consular jurisdiction in disputes *between nationals of Western treaty states* in Japan has been explained as 'a logical deduction from local jurisdiction expressly secured by treaties', meaning that it still rested ultimately on treaties.[122] In Japan, unlike in the Ottoman Empire, there was no consular jurisdiction in disputes *involving non-treaty states* (which would have required an explanation not based on treaties). This is evidenced by the *Maria Luz* arbitration in 1875. Japan had enquired into the condition of mistreated workers on a Peruvian ship and released some workers. The outcome was that Peru, in the absence of a treaty granting it extraterritorial rights in Japan, could not object to measures taken in accordance with Japan's own legislation.[123] Moore concluded that in Japan and similarly in China the regime 'began with and rested upon the treaties, and did not originate in custom, as it did in the Ottoman dominions'.[124]

In summary, unequal treaties do not point to any basic differences of personality between Western and non-Western entities; any treaty between any two entities can have unequal terms. But it appears that the Ottoman Empire, at least, also had limited *customary* duties under unequal regimes that differed from the duties that existed among Western states.

2.4.2 Personality under custom generally

Did any other customary norms apply differently in the West and in the intermediate sphere of non-Western state-like entities? If so, that might result in differences of personality. I will look first at Western views and then at evidence from non-Westerners themselves.

In 1795, Robert Ward observed that the 'Laws of Nations' are '*not* the Laws of the World' but that 'no one has yet examined, how far they obtain with particular Nations; or how far attention ought to be paid to the circumstance of their obeying another Code'.[125] One might have hoped for this to be rectified when, in 1875, the

states had already been exercising consular jurisdiction in China before the treaties, and to 'regard extraterritoriality in China as derived solely from the treaties is equivalent to regarding English law as comprising statutes alone'.

---

[122] Moore (n 113) vol 2, 602.

[123] *Maria Luz (Japan/Peru)* (arbitration, 29 May 1875) in John Bassett Moore, *History and Digest of the International Arbitrations to Which the United States Has Been a Party* (US GPO 1898) vol 5, 5034.

[124] Moore (n 113) vol 2, 602. Further practice is cited and discussed at vol 2, 593–755. The same view was taken by the Japanese lawyer Tsurutaro Senga, discussed in Becker Lorca (n 1) 57, 64–5.

[125] Robert Ward, *An Enquiry into the Foundation and History of the Law of Nations in Europe from the Time of the Greeks and Romans to the Age of Grotius* (first published 1795, Garland 1973) vol 1, 168–9. He argued, foreshadowing some of the scholarly views I will cite later, that 'the law was not obligatory upon persons who had never been called upon to decide upon its ramifications; who might widely differ as to its application, and even to its general and fundamental principles': at vol 1, xi–xii.

Institut de Droit International began a project on the question 'in what conditions and up to what point the customary law of nations of Europe is applicable to Oriental nations'.[126] A questionnaire was sent to European experts and Asian diplomats.[127] The chair, Travers Twiss, reported that 'the notions of Oriental peoples concerning the obligation to observe the stipulations of treaties were not different at heart from those of Christian peoples' and that any difficulties Western states had encountered with, say, China were practical rather than theoretical; in its advance into the Western-dominated world, China walked 'grandiosely, but slowly, at an elephant's pace'.[128] In contrast, NJ Saripolos argued that for the Ottomans the Qur'an was not only their moral code, 'but also their code of international law, their defence against entering into relations with infidels', with whom it did not permit treaties.[129] But since so few conclusions could be drawn, the Institut essentially gave up trying to answer the question.[130]

It is no easier today than it was for the Institut to find evidence of *particular* differences. Proponents of the standard of 'civilization' asserted in general terms that differences existed, but they seldom gave detail outside the context of unequal regimes (as just discussed) and of specific treaties (which are not evidence of any underlying differences of personality, because any two treaty-making entities can contract unique or unequal relations in that manner).[131] Still, some cases and official opinions in which particular differences were identified can be found in practice. The few clearly relevant examples I will cite are British.[132]

One legal opinion, whose authors included the attorney-general and the solicitor-general of England and Wales, differentiated between prizes (captured ships and their cargo) taken by the British East India Company based on their origin. When prize was made of a French ship, 'a condemnation in the High Court of Admiralty is necessary; but . . . in case of an Indian ship so taken, no condemnation is necessary, neither treaties nor usage between the Indians and their enemies requiring it'.[133] The opinion is notable for its date: 1757, long before the notion of

[126] Documents relatifs à la session de La Haye, 25–31 Août 1875 (1877) 1 Annuaire IDI 36, 51 (translation).

[127] Applicabilité du droit des gens européen aux nations orientales—questionnaire (1877) 1 Annuaire IDI 141.

[128] Quatrième commission d'étude – application aux nations orientales du droit des gens coutumier de l'Europe (1879) 3–4(1) Annuaire IDI 298, 302 (translation).

[129] Ibid, 308 (translation).

[130] Ibid, 311. See further Koskenniemi (n 10) 132–3.

[131] In the nineteenth century the British law officers gave a number of opinions on treaties between the United Kingdom and non-Western entities. For a discussion of some of these (and of their approach to such entities generally) see Andrew Fitzmaurice, 'Equality of non-European nations in international law' in Randall Lesaffer and Inge van Hulle (eds), *International Law in the Long Nineteenth Century* (Brill 2018).

[132] See further Smith (n 83) vol 1, 14–33; Arnold Duncan McNair (ed), *International Law Opinions* (CUP 1956) vol 1, 65–6.

[133] Charles Pratt, Charles Yorke, and John Browning, Opinion (13 November 1757) in William Burrell (ed), *Reports of Cases Determined by the High Court of Admiralty and Upon Appeal Therefrom* (William Clowes & Sons 1885) 392.

degrees of 'civilization' had entrenched itself in the literature. It suggests that there was already some flexibility in the application of customary norms to non-Western entities.

The admiralty judge William Scott, whom Pitts describes as 'Britain's foremost judicial authority on the law of nations at the turn of the nineteenth century', made a series of decisions on the applicability of international law to north African entities.[134] In *The Hurtige Hane*, in 1801, he articulated explicitly the idea that they could not necessarily be presumed to be familiar with or to practise customary norms. He remarked that the inhabitants of Morocco

> may, on some points of the law of nations, be entitled to a very relaxed application of the principles established by long usage between the states of Europe, holding an intimate and constant intercourse with each other. It is a law made up of a good deal of complex reasoning, though derived from very simple rules, and altogether composing a pretty artificial system, which is not familiar either to their knowledge or their observance.[135]

Scott cited an earlier case, *The Kinders Kinder*, in which he had noted that it was a practice of north African entities, 'under a law of nations now peculiar to themselves . . . to redress themselves for what they consider an unjust capture' of a ship 'by demanding compensation from the countrymen of the aggressors'.[136] He went on to indicate that whether a norm was given a relaxed application depended on the particular norm. The norm in *The Hurtige Hane*—'that persons are not to carry into the blockaded port supplies of any kind'—was 'not a new operation of war' but 'one of the most universal and simple operations of war, in all ages and countries, excepting such as were merely savage'. The 'subjects of the Barbary States could not be ignorant' of it; 'no indulgence' could be shown to them.[137] The following year, in *The Madonna del Burso*, Scott remarked that since the inhabitants of the Ottoman Empire 'are not professors of exactly the same law of nations with ourselves', the court had 'repeatedly expressed a disposition, not to hold them bound to the utmost rigour of that system of public laws, on which European States have so long acted' and that it never entertained such cases 'without notice given to the Ottoman Minister, and to the Turkish Company'.[138]

A later opinion by the British law officers concerned a conflict in Japan in 1869, in the aftermath of the transfer of political power from the Tokugawa shogun to the

[134] Pitts (n 41) 117, further 114–17. Scott is sometimes referred to by his later title, Lord Stowell.

[135] *The Hurtige Hane* (1801) 3 C Rob 324, 165 ER 480, 481.

[136] *The Kinders Kinder* (1799) 2 C Rob 88, 165 ER 248, 248. See also the related case *The Fortune* (1800) 2 C Rob 92, 165 ER 250, 252, in which Scott affirmed that he did not 'mean to apply' to the Algerian claimants 'the exact rigour of the law of nations as understood and practised amongst the civilised states of Europe; it would be to try them by a law not familiar to any law or practice of theirs'.

[137] *The Hurtige Hane* (1801) 3 C Rob 324, 165 ER 480, 481–2.

[138] *The Madonna del Burso* (1802) 4 C Rob 169, 165 ER 574, 575.

court of the Meiji Emperor. Rebels loyal to the deposed shogun had declared an independent 'Republic of Ezo' on the island now known as Hokkaido.[139] The British law officers wrote that whether civil war existed was 'a question of pure fact' and that in Europe civil war meant 'such a substantial suspension of the powers of the central Government, as to prevent its arm being felt, or its law administered by the ordinary Tribunals'. But they thought that this definition was 'essentially European' and could not 'be strictly applied with exactness or rigour to communities where the action of the central Government is different, probably more irregular'; instead, 'the question of civil war or not is a question to be decided with special reference to local circumstances'. They concluded that Japan's refusal of belligerent rights to the rebels implied that in a legal sense 'no war in fact exists' and that 'the Japanese Government have no more than the [rebels] the right as against neutrals, like [the United Kingdom], to assume the exceptional rights of belligerents; but must confine their action, as far as [British] shipping and commerce are concerned, to their rights in time of peace'.[140]

The fact remains that it is not easy to find clear discussions of particular differences between the customary norms applicable among Western states and in the intermediate sphere of non-Western entities. Nor are the examples I have cited free from ambiguity. Scott's remarks in *The Hurtige Hane* could be taken to indicate merely that 'he permitted himself to exercise a somewhat wider measure of judicial discretion in dealing with the subjects of non-Christian or uncivilised states'.[141] On that view, his decisions might not point to any real difference between their rights and duties and those of Western states, just to a difference in the degree to which a British court was willing to overlook unlawful conduct. But it is notable that in the other instances I have cited, a similar explanation was given: a norm did not apply to an entity that had not consented to or was not familiar with the norm. This can be juxtaposed with evidence about the attitudes of non-Westerners themselves, which confirms that they often did not consent to or were not familiar with Western norms and suggests that the cases and opinions I have cited cannot lightly be set aside.

Among the major non-Western entities, probably the least receptive to Western international law was imperial China. Although a few earlier treaties can be found, such as the Treaty of Nerchinsk of 1689 with Russia,[142] China was mostly in self-imposed isolation from Europeans until the nineteenth century. It thus provides

[139] Romulus Hillsborough, *Samurai Revolution: The Dawn of Modern Japan Seen through the Eyes of the Shogun's Last Samurai* (Tuttle 2014) 820–2.

[140] RP Collier, JD Coleridge, and Travers Twiss, Opinion (19 April 1869) in Hersch Lauterpacht, *Recognition in International Law* (first published 1947, CUP 2013) 213, 214.

[141] Smith (n 83) 15.

[142] Treaty of Nerchinsk, China–Russia (7 September 1689) 18 CTS 503; Chi-Hua Tang, 'China–Europe' in Bardo Fassbender and Anne Peters (eds), *The Oxford Handbook of the History of International Law* (OUP 2012) 701, 704.

the starkest illustration of the relevance of non-Western perspectives to the applicability of Western norms.

China's unreceptiveness is illustrated by an incident that echoes, half a millennium later, the clash between the competing universalisms of Pope Innocent IV and Güyük Khan. In 1792, Lord Macartney led a British embassy to the court of Qing China to open diplomatic relations on the Western model.[143] That proposal did not make sense to the Chinese. China was at the centre of a tribute system that stretched into parts of central, east, and southeast Asia and that in theory was as universal as the Western conception of natural law had ever purported to be.[144] China acknowledged only legal inferiors, not legal equals; it maintained a department of foreign tribute, not one of foreign affairs as such.[145] The Qianlong Emperor's response to the embassy was disdainful. 'O King', he wrote (addressing George III), 'inclining your heart towards civilization, you have specially sent an envoy to present a state message' from which 'your sincere humility and obedience can clearly be seen'. Macartney's request that Great Britain be allowed to post an ambassador in Beijing was rejected on the ground that 'this does not conform to the Celestial Empire's ceremonial system'.[146]

Western international law seeped into the Chinese consciousness slowly. Chi-Hua Tang writes that there is nothing in any official Qing documents to verify that China accepted *any* of its norms before 1839.[147] A pivotal moment occurred in 1842, when China lost the First Opium War and signed the Treaty of Nanjing, which opened some of its ports to Western trade.[148] Becker Lorca suggests that if international law has a history before this time, 'it is the history of different—geographically and culturally disconnected—regional level orders'.[149] In 1864, China 'received international law as text', when Henry Wheaton's *Elements of International Law* was translated by the head teacher of a school founded to train interpreters for diplomacy with the West.[150] The emperor's ministers at first objected that 'China had her own institutions and systems, and did not feel free to consult foreign books'.[151] But the text was soon put to use. The same year Prussia, which was at war with Denmark, captured some Danish ships in China's territorial waters in breach of its neutrality. Prince Gong, the regent, explained to the Qing court that it was necessary to protest to secure jurisdiction in the area. In

143 Alain Peyrefitte, *The Collision of Two Civilisations: The British Expedition to China in 1792–4* (Jon Rothschild tr, Harper Collins 1993).
144 Tang (n 142) 703.
145 Peyrefitte (n 143) 291 n ‡.
146 Qianlong Emperor, Letter to King George III (3 October 1793) in ibid, 288, 289.
147 Tang (n 142) 704.
148 Treaty of Peace, Friendship and Commerce, UK–China, Nanjing (29 August 1842) 93 CTS 465.
149 Becker Lorca (n 1) 10.
150 Tang (n 142) 705; Immanuel CY Hsü, *China's Entrance into the Family of Nations* (Harvard UP 1960) 121–31.
151 Hsü (n 150) 132, quoting in translation *Chouban yiwu shimo* [*Complete Account of the Management of Barbarian Affairs*] (1836–74) 27:25b–26.

protesting, he cited a treaty with Prussia that referred to what China called its 'inner ocean' (its territorial waters) and added that, '[a]s to the European law of war, China cannot be obliged to know all'.[152] Prussia duly released the ships and paid China compensation. Prince Gong concluded that Wheaton's text contained 'sporadic useful points'.[153] It would still be a few decades before China accepted Western norms unreservedly rather than merely selectively. Until the 1880s the treaty port regime served as a Qing device for 'accommodating the West and giving it a place within the Chinese world'.[154] Although China began to make treaties with Western states on a basis of legal equality, concurrently it maintained the tribute system with other Asian entities, such as Korea.[155]

I emphasize that what mattered, within the internal framework of Western international law, was not the Chinese perspective taken on its own terms but rather how Chinese practices and beliefs were constructed as facts and thereby given a particular significance *by Western international law*. I pointed out earlier that the Mongols were bound by the Pope's conception of natural law according to that conception, regardless of what the Great Khan thought. The same could have been true here to an extent: China might have been bound by Western norms according to those norms, regardless of what the Chinese thought. Sometimes Westerners assumed that customary norms that applied to Western states also applied to China. In 1840, during the First Opium War (and thus after Macartney's mission but before the Treaty of Nanjing), the United Kingdom complained that a Chinese imperial commissioner had acted 'in violation of the Law of Nations' by imprisoning the British government's agent in Guangzhou and demanding that he give 'orders' to private traders to surrender contraband opium. The United Kingdom demanded 'satisfaction', including repayment of the value of the seized opium, and that in future its agent 'be treated . . . in a manner consistent with the usages of civilized Nations'.[156] The British also implied that China was in breach of a duty to enforce its domestic law impartially as between its own subjects and foreigners.

Despite episodes such as this, concerns were voiced in the West about whether China was able and willing to comply with Western norms. For instance, WE Hall, in the 1890s, thought that it could not 'be hoped that China, for a considerable time to come, would be able, if she tried, to secure obedience by her officers and soldiers even to the elementary European rules of war'.[157] Such concerns resonate with the

[152] Ibid, 133, quoting in translation *Choúban yiwu shimo* (1836–74) 26:33; further 132–8. See also Neff, *Justice among Nations* (n 12) 313.

[153] Hsü (n 150) 134, quoting in translation *Chouban yiwu shimo* (1836–74) 26:33.

[154] JK Fairbank, 'The early treaty system in the Chinese world order' in JK Fairbank and Ta-tuan Ch'en (eds), *The Chinese World Order: Traditional China's Foreign Relations* (Harvard UP 1968) 257, 258; Becker Lorca (n 1) 87; Tang (n 142) 703.

[155] Onuma (n 16) 30; Tang (n 142) 722.

[156] Lord Palmerston, Dispatch to the Minister of the Emperor of China (20 February 1840) in Frederick Whyte, *China and Foreign Powers: An Historical Review of their Relations* (OUP 1927) 40, 40–1. See further Smith (n 83) 17–18.

[157] Hall (n 92) 44. Compare TE Holland, *Studies in International Law* (Clarendon 1898) 128–9.

cases and opinions I cited earlier about north African and Asian entities, which exhibited a concern with whether particular Western norms were 'familiar either to their knowledge or their observance'.[158]

2.4.3 Explaining differences of personality

I have not found evidence of a test of personality based on 'civilization', whether defined in vague terms or in terms of protecting the life, liberty, and property of foreigners. As Orakhelashvili correctly points out, doctrines 'emphasizing the European character of international law' relied on 'cultural, ethnographic, psychological and sociological, that is extra-legal, considerations'.[159] But this is not a sufficient reason to take the position at the opposite extreme: that there were *no* differences between the personality of state-like entities in the inner and intermediate spheres identified by theorists of 'civilization'. I have found indications of limited differences. At least one custom that applied between the Ottoman Empire and Western states, an element of the regime of consular jurisdiction, differed from the norms applicable among Western states. And some Western judges and other officials raised doubts about whether Western customary norms could be applied to Asian and north African entities—not in every case, and not unambiguously, but consistent with evidence that non-Western entities could not plausibly be said to have consented to those norms.

So how might these apparent differences be explained?

I will consider four possible explanations, all of which relate to the manner in which customary norms applied and which will reveal some fault lines that contributed to the instability of international law in this period. I will then draw a tentative conclusion and consider it in light of some relevant observations by the International Court.

The first possible explanation is that, consistent with what Neff calls 'the dominant' outlook among nineteenth-century international lawyers,[160] the contractual view of custom was correct (meaning that an entity was bound by a customary norm only if it had consented specifically to that norm) and applied both among Western states and to the intermediate sphere of non-Western entities. Differences between the two groups can be readily explained by the fact that non-Western entities tended to consent to fewer components of customary international law than did Western states. This has the virtue of simplicity. Against this explanation are the arguments I made against the contractual view earlier: that many scholars did not support it even at the time and that, since the legislative view has now

[158] *The Hurtige Hane* (1801) 3 C Rob 324, 165 ER 480, 481.
[159] Orakhelashvili (n 94) 317.
[160] Neff, 'The dormancy, rise and decline' (n 74) 492.

triumphed, a more elegant interpretation of the history of Western international law is that it was wrong all along.

On the second possible explanation, the legislative view applied both among Western states and to the intermediate sphere of non-Western entities (meaning that an entity was generally bound by a customary norm even if it had not consented specifically to that norm), though some entities were additionally bound by 'local' or 'particular' customs.

This reflects how international law works today. In *Asylum (Colombia/Peru)*, Colombia argued that a local custom about the granting of asylum existed among Latin American states. The International Court concluded that even if 'a custom of this kind' existed among certain other Latin American states, 'it could not be invoked against Peru which, far from having by its attitude adhered to it', had repudiated the ostensible local custom by refraining from ratifying treaties that contained it.[161] This has been interpreted as imposing a stricter standard of consent than that applicable to 'general' custom (which I will mostly continue to call plain 'custom'). Whereas general custom is governed by the legislative view and applies unless states opt out by persistently objecting, a norm of local custom is always, at least in a loose sense, contractual: it requires each affected state to opt in. In the words of the International Law Commission, '[e]ach of these States must have accepted the practice as law among themselves'.[162]

James Crawford suggests this as an explanation of the norms applicable to non-Western entities. Although the same rules were not necessarily applied to or by them 'as were applied by European States between themselves . . . that is to be explained not by any distinction between "civilized" and "barbarous" States but because many of those rules were what would now be called regional or local customs rather than general international law'.[163]

This might be a persuasive explanation of the customary element of consular jurisdiction in the Ottoman Empire—if that were all that required explanation. It could also incorporate into Western international law some of the rules that local groups of non-Western entities had developed among themselves. But the idea of local custom is that it is exceptional; according to the Court, local custom 'must prevail over any general rules'.[164] The flipside of this is that in the absence of a local custom to which both parties have specifically consented, one party can insist on the general rules, which still apply by default. So if this is the sole explanation of the apparent differences of personality under discussion, then the extent to which general custom applied in interaction with non-Western entities would have depended on the willingness of Western states to indulge their different conceptions

[161] *Asylum (Colombia/Peru)* [1950] ICJ Rep 266, 276–8. Compare Shaw, *International Law* (n 54) 66.

[162] Conclusions on Identification of Customary International Law, commentary to conclusion 16, para 7.

[163] James Crawford, *The Creation of States in International Law* (2nd edn, OUP 2006) 260–1.

[164] *Right of Passage over Indian Territory (Portugal v India)* [1960] ICJ Rep 6, 44.

of international law. It does nothing about the artificiality of treating Western and non-Western entities alike; nor does it reflect the reluctance of some Western judges and officials to treat them in that way. Although that does not mean that this explanation is wrong, it exposes international law in the positivist era to an accusation of hypocrisy: positivism trumpeted consent as the theoretical basis of law, which may have been plausible in the case of Western states that (on the legislative view) could be seen as having consented to customary international law as a whole; but this reasoning cannot plausibly be extended beyond the West. If it was Eurocentric or racist to exclude non-Western entities from international law as not 'civilized' enough, then applying Western norms to them unreservedly was also Eurocentric.

The third explanation is that, although the legislative view applied among Western states, a contractual view applied to the intermediate sphere of non-Western entities—not just in the supplementary sense of local customs, but in the sense that the *only* customary norms that bound these entities were norms to which they had specifically consented.

Support can be found for this explanation in Scott's decisions in the High Court of Admiralty. In *The Helena*, in 1801, he remarked that north Africans conceive 'that there is no other law of nations, but that which is derived from positive compact and convention.'[165] Twiss (the English jurist I quoted earlier as chair of the 'Oriental nations' project and co-author of the opinion on Japan) cited this case, along with *The Hurtige Hane*, in postulating that no 'Common Law of Nations' was 'observed between European and African States', though there could be treaties or an 'established usage'.[166]

The idea that the legislative view of custom applied exclusively among Western states also accords broadly with other scholarly explanations that were offered at the time, by both English-speaking and continental European writers (insofar as it is possible to ignore how the language of 'civilization' was invoked to bolster these explanations ideologically). Liszt, for example, thought that the only parts of positive international law that applied to relations with non-Western entities were those codified in treaties with 'civilized' states to which the entities consented.[167] It seems logical to extend this reasoning to any customary norms to which they gave their specific consent, expressly or tacitly. Huber argued that Western states had passed beyond the purely contractual stage of international law and now recognized legal propositions by common conviction, but that this community could continue to

[165] *The Helena* (1801) 4 C Rob 3, 165 ER 515, 516.

[166] Travers Twiss, 'Applicability of the European Law of Nations to African Slave States' (1876) 1 Law Magazine and Review 409, especially 412–13, 423–4. Twiss argued for the existence of 'an established usage . . . between the Nations of Europe and of Africa' under which Western ships could protect fugitive slaves.

[167] Liszt (n 92) 5–6.

conduct purely *contractual* relations with entities that remained outside it.[168] And an argument made by Hall similarly implied that what defined the family of nations was the fact that its members had accepted customary international law as a whole rather than selectively. He argued that 'differently civilised' entities, in order to shed their intermediate status,

> must formally enter into the circle of law-governed countries. They must do something with the acquiescence of the latter, or of some of them, which amounts to an acceptance of the law in its entirety beyond all possibility of misconstruction. It is not enough consequently that they shall enter into arrangements by treaty identical with arrangements made by law-governed powers, nor that they shall do acts, like sending and receiving permanent embassies, which are compatible with ignorance or rejection of law.[169]

This explanation is strengthened by its consistency with the positivist emphasis on consent as the theoretical basis of law. Gong calls it 'the orthodox positivist doctrine'.[170]

There was a variant of this explanation that retained elements of natural law, which is the fourth possibility I will consider. Once again, the legislative view of custom applied to Western states and the contractual view applied to non-Western entities, but additionally, on this view, there remained a bedrock of natural law that applied to both groups.

This possibility was propounded by DHL von Ompteda in 1785. Alexandrowicz described Ompteda as attempting 'to secure the idea of continuity of the universal family of nations' against the danger that positivism would leave non-Western entities 'in a legal vacuum being neither in the orbit of European positive law . . . nor even covered by the rules of the declining universal natural law which tended to be displaced by the former'.[171] Ompteda acknowledged a category of treaty and customary norms that derived from the specific consent of their subjects. He also postulated two categories of general norms. One was *ius gentium voluntarium*, which was based not necessarily on agreement or express acceptance by its subjects but on their *consensus praesumptus* (a presumption of consent, similar in effect to the legislative view): this applied to 'civilized' nations and included, for example, systematic privileges and immunities of diplomats and the prohibition of poisoned weapons. The other category was *ius gentium naturale*, which applied to *all* nations, 'civilized' or not, and entailed their natural freedom, independence, and

168 Becker Lorca (n 1) 196, discussing Max Huber, 'Die Gleichheit der Staaten' in Fritz Berolzheimer (ed), *Juristische Festgabe des Auslandes zu Josef Kohlers 60. Geburtstag* (Enke 1909) 88.
169 Hall (n 92) 42–3.
170 Gong (n 7) 56.
171 Alexandrowicz, 'Doctrinal aspects' (n 43) 508.

equality.[172] Similarly, in the nineteenth and early twentieth centuries, scholars such as Georg Friedrich von Martens argued that if there were 'a society subsisting between states, nations, etc, as between individuals, that society is natural, and not positive, and regulates itself only by natural laws'.[173] The applicable norms of natural law would have included elements of sovereignty.

The last two explanations I have given are the most elegant, in that they acknowledge that Western states already formed a community of the sort that exists in international law today—of which one manifestation is the legislative view of custom—and at the same time the apparent differences in the norms applicable to non-Western entities can be explained in a manner consistent with the positivist emphasis on consent and with contemporary doctrine.

Nonetheless, because of the instability revealed by practice and by the existence of these four possibilities, my conclusion cannot be expressed in these elegant terms. There were three major fault lines: whether the legislative or the contractual view of custom applied to Western states; which of those views applied to the intermediate sphere of non-Western entities; and the continuing role of natural law. What created the fault lines was the transition from a system based primarily on natural law to one justified by reference to the positivist principle of consent. That principle was in tension with the fact that many non-Western entities, which under universalist natural law would have had similar rights and duties to Western states, could not plausibly be said to consent to norms with which they were unfamiliar. Moreover, over the course of the lengthy period under discussion, opinions on these points shifted and a further source of instability emerged (to be discussed later in this chapter): doubts about when entities such as the Ottoman Empire or Japan 'graduated' from the intermediate into the inner sphere to sit alongside Western states—perhaps, to use Hall's phrase, on the basis that they had accepted custom 'in its entirety beyond all possibility of misconstruction'.[174]

What *can* be concluded is this: when Western international law determined whether or not a particular customary norm applied to an entity, the legislative view was more likely to be applied to a Western state, whereas the contractual view was more likely to be applied to a non-Western entity.

This is not the same as saying that international law in this era was a hopeless mess. The customary norms applicable among Western states, on any view, were comparatively stable. In consequence, the boundary with the intermediate sphere of non-Western entities was a real, meaningful boundary: it marked the edge of a zone of significantly greater instability, within which it was often unclear which

[172] Ibid, 507, discussing DHL von Ompteda, *Literatur des gesammten sowohl natürlichen als positiven Völkerrecht* (Regensburg 1785).

[173] Georg Friedrich von Martens, *Précis du droit des gens moderne de l'Europe* (new edn, Aillaud 1831) vol 1, 49 (translation). See also Henri Bonfils and Paul Fauchille, *Manuel de droit international public* (4th edn, Rousseau 1905) 17–18, quoted in this book s 2.5.2.

[174] Hall (n 92) 42–3.

norms were applicable. Moreover, in practical terms, this is not very far from the more elegant conclusion that the legislative view applied to Western states and the contractual view applied in the intermediate sphere. Imagine that an international lawyer is trying to establish with certainty that a customary norm applied to an entity in the normatively unstable intermediate sphere. The investigation that the lawyer will undertake is in practice similar to what it would be if the contractual view definitely applied in this sphere. What will most interest the lawyer is evidence that the entity specifically consented to a relevant norm: if it consented to a general Western norm, then that norm would have been applicable on any possible view; if it consented to a local custom accepted by the other entities involved, then that would have superseded any generally applicable norm on any possible view. The lawyer will look for evidence of this kind, which is capable of answering the question with certainty; the lawyer will hesitate to rely on the mere fact that a norm applied among Western states, because it is not certain that that fact is relevant.

This conclusion—that there was a meaningful boundary of a sort between the inner and intermediate spheres of entities—can be tested against the approach that has actually been taken by the International Court. Although it has not dealt with the point directly, the Court has made some relevant observations about the historical rights and duties of entities that nineteenth-century scholars would have placed in the intermediate sphere.

In *Right of Passage*, decided in 1960, Portugal claimed a right of passage across Indian territory between enclaves that were under Portuguese sovereignty. Among the grounds on which Portugal defended its sovereignty over the enclaves and the right of passage was the Treaty of Poona of 1779 between it and the Maratha Confederacy, along with certain *sanads* (decrees) issued by the Maratha ruler in the 1780s.[175] The territory across which the right was claimed had since come under British administration and then that of independent India. India contested the validity and interpretation of the treaty, which existed in divergent Marathi and Portuguese texts not accepted as authentic by the opposing party. The Court held:

> the validity of a treaty concluded as long ago as the last quarter of the eighteenth century, in the conditions then prevailing in the Indian Peninsula, should not be judged upon the basis of practices and procedures which have since developed only gradually. The Marathas themselves regarded the Treaty of 1779 as valid and binding upon them, and gave effect to its provisions. . . . The Marathas did not at any time cast any doubt upon the validity or binding character of the Treaty.[176]

Nothing can be inferred from this definitively; it appears that the Court was speaking at least in part about the differences between eighteenth- and twentieth-century

[175] *Right of Passage* [1960] ICJ Rep 6, 37.
[176] Ibid.

international law rather than differences between state-like entities from different regions or legal spheres. Still, the Court was hesitant to presume that norms applied to the Marathas. It did not analyse practice and *opinio iuris* from the West (or from other parts of the world) and conclude that the same norms must also have applied in this case. It drew its conclusions only after taking account of circumstances that were specific to the Marathas: the 'conditions then prevailing in the Indian Peninsula' and the fact that the Marathas themselves regarded the treaty 'as valid and binding'.[177] The Court also took account of a local notion of tenure: in considering at which date Portugal had acquired territorial sovereignty over the enclaves, it found that, when the Marathas intended to transfer sovereignty, they usually used expressions such as cession 'in perpetuity', whereas here 'what was granted to the Portuguese was only a revenue tenure called a *jagir* or *saranjam*', a common form of grant in south Asia.[178]

The Court went on to decide the case on the ground of a norm to which the relevant entities tacitly consented—a local custom. The local custom that it identified is not directly relevant to the historical personality of non-Western state-like entities, because the custom was established only after 1818, when the territory came under British administration.[179] But the Court also remarked on the wider significance, during this period of south Asian history, of practices to which entities gave their specific consent, expressly or tacitly:

> Historically the case goes back to a period when, and relates to a region in which, the relations between neighbouring States were not regulated by precisely formulated rules but were governed largely by practice. Where therefore the Court finds a practice clearly established between two States which was accepted by the Parties as governing the relations between them, the Court must attribute decisive effect to that practice for the purpose of determining their specific rights and obligations.[180]

This description might be applied to other parts of Asia and Africa as well.

Judge Spender made some comments to similar effect in *Temple of Preah Vihear*, in 1962. The question was whether adverse inferences could be drawn from Thailand's silence and lack of protest when the French presented maps of disputed territory to it in 1908. He said:

> In determining what inferences may or should be drawn from Thailand's silence and absence of protest regard must . . . be had to the period of time when the

[177] Ibid.
[178] Ibid, 38.
[179] Ibid, 40: 'there existed during the British and post-British periods a constant and uniform practice allowing free passage' to the Portuguese for certain civil and private purposes that was 'accepted as law by the Parties and has given rise to a right and a correlative obligation'.
[180] Ibid, 44.

> events we are concerned with took place, to the region of the world to which they related, to the general political conditions existing in Asia at this period, to political and other activities of Western countries in Asia at the time and to the fact that of the two States concerned one was Asian, the other European. It would not . . . be just to apply to the conduct of Siam in this period objective standards comparable to those which reasonably might today be or might then have been applied to highly developed European States.[181]

Spender, then, was reluctant to apply Western customary norms to Thailand. His approach, like the Court's in *Right of Passage*, is broadly consistent with the idea that such norms cannot simply be presumed to have applied to a non-Western entity unless there is evidence that the non-Western entity had specifically accepted them. Note that Spender was writing in dissent: the plurality of the Court held that Thailand had accepted the maps, without commenting on the basis on which custom applied.[182] So this also serves as a reminder about the instability of the law. Still, in keeping with my conclusion, the International Court sometimes seems to apply a stricter requirement of consent to historical non-Western entities.

My conclusion remains that there *were* differences between the inner sphere of Western states and the intermediate sphere of non-Western state-like entities, though they depended on the manner in which entities became bound by customary norms rather than on 'civilization'. Both doctrine and practice were unstable. But when Western international law determined whether or not a particular customary norm applied to an entity, a non-Western entity was more likely to be subjected to a requirement that it consent specifically to that norm (the contractual view), whereas a Western state was more likely not to be subjected to such a requirement (the legislative view). As well as being more likely, each of these approaches was also the more theoretically coherent way to deal with entities of the relevant type. The result was the potential existence of state-like entities with different customary rights, duties, and degrees of personality.

2.5 The positivist era in the Americas, most of Africa, and the Pacific

Still to be discussed is the personality of non-Western state-like entities falling into the remaining group: the allegedly 'savage' or least 'civilized' outer sphere in the three-sphere scheme.[183] This was the category to which scholars relegated the indigenous peoples of the Americas and the Pacific (including Australia and some of

[181] *Temple of Preah Vihear (Cambodia v Thailand)* [1962] ICJ Rep 6, 128 (Judge Spender dissenting).
[182] Ibid, 23–5.
[183] Lorimer (n 85) vol 1, 101–2.

the islands of southeast Asia) and most Africans. Some scholars argued that, because these entities allegedly had 'civilization' only in the lowest degree, they were *wholly* outside the family of nations. Liszt wrote that 'in the entirety of its relations with uncivilized communities, the international community can avail itself of its factual power; it is bound only by principles of moral order connected with Christian sentiment and sentiment of humanity'.[184] Oppenheim argued that the treatment of state-like entities outside the family of nations *ought* 'to be regulated by the principles of Christian morality', but that ultimately it was in accordance with 'discretion, and not International Law' that members of the family of nations dealt with them.[185]

What has attracted the most attention here is an argument related to the belief that these entities were wholly outside international law: that the land on which they lived was *terra nullius* and thus open to territorial acquisition by Western states by means of occupation alone. This was distinguished from acquisition under a treaty of cession, by conquest in war, or by prescription (which is where territory remains under 'continuous and undisturbed dominion during a period sufficient to justify the assumption that the position has become part of the established international order').[186] This argument was always doubted by many international lawyers.[187] In *Western Sahara*, the International Court essentially rejected it by endorsing an approach to *terra nullius* that had more regard to the people living on the land:

> Whatever differences of opinion there may have been among jurists, the State practice of the relevant period indicates that territories inhabited by tribes or peoples having a social and political organization were not regarded as *terrae nullius*. It shows that in the case of such territories the acquisition of sovereignty was not generally considered as effected unilaterally through 'occupation' of *terra nullius* by original title but through agreements concluded with local rulers. . . . In the present instance . . . at the time of colonization Western Sahara was inhabited by peoples which, if nomadic, were socially and politically organized in tribes and under chiefs competent to represent them.[188]

As this indicates, there was still a threshold. An entity had to be 'socially and politically organized'. This reflects earlier formulations of the test. In the 1920s MF

[184] Liszt (n 92) 6 (translation).

[185] Oppenheim (n 9) vol 1, pt 29. He referred to 'such States as are outside that circle', but he may not have meant 'States' in any technical legal sense. Presumably he meant entities that were wholly outside the family of nations along with supposedly 'semi-civilized' entities insofar as they were outside it.

[186] MF Lindley, *The Acquisition and Government of Backward Territory in International Law* (Longmans, Green, & Co 1926) 2.

[187] On scholarship from the era of natural law to the present, see ibid, 10–23; Crawford, *Creation* (n 163) 260–74.

[188] *Western Sahara* [1975] ICJ Rep 12, paras 80–1, compare para 92.

Lindley wrote that although the 'proper distinction is not between civilization and no civilization', territory was *terra nullius* unless its inhabitants were 'united permanently for political action'.[189]

Yet it is hard to identify a precolonial community anywhere in the world that failed this test. Aboriginal Australians and the Fuegians of the tip of South America were sometimes suggested.[190] But even these alleged exceptions look dubious once incorrect colonialist assumptions that they were not 'socially and politically organized' are abandoned. The colonization of Australia, almost uniquely among the inhabited parts of the world, was defended for a long time on the basis of *terra nullius*.[191] In 1889 the Privy Council held that when the first British colony, New South Wales, was founded in 1788, it had 'consisted of a tract of territory practically unoccupied, without settled inhabitants or settled law'.[192] But in *Mabo v Queensland*, in 1992, the High Court of Australia held that Australia had never been *terra nullius*. The High Court's decision concerned property rights in Australian domestic law, not territorial sovereignty in international law, but it was based in part on the international legal test articulated by the International Court in *Western Sahara*.[193]

The main function of the test of *terra nullius* was to determine whether a colonial territory could have been validly acquired by a Western state. Lindley wrote that most norms of international law were 'inapplicable to the conditions of backward peoples', but it was 'one of the admitted functions of International Law to lay down rules' about how territory could be acquired by Western states.[194] He added that the law 'should and does recognize the rights of independent backward races to the extent of distinguishing those territories to which a title may be acquired by . . . Occupation from those which, in the absence of consent on the part of the inhabitants, can be obtained only by Conquest—or through Prescription'.[195] These are 'rights' in at least a loose sense. In theory, they protected interests of non-Western entities (though in reality they did not protect people from being subjugated, exploited, or killed: Western states had the ability to take territory by force anyway). But it may not follow incontrovertibly that these entities actually had any

[189] Lindley (n 186) 20–4.

[190] DP O'Connell, 'International law and boundary disputes' (1960) 54 ASIL Proc 77, 81; Brownlie (n 39) 361–2.

[191] For other possible examples see Lindley (n 186) 42 (on the South Island of New Zealand); Stuart Banner, *Possessing the Pacific: Land, Settlers, and Indigenous People from Australia to Alaska* (Harvard UP 2009), especially ch 5 (on California) and ch 6 (on British Columbia). Compare *Legal Status of Eastern Greenland (Denmark v Norway)* (1933) PCIJ ser A/B 53, in which Norway made a *terra nullius* argument. Before the early twentieth century, the term *territorium nullius* (territory belonging to no one) was sometimes used: Andrew Fitzmaurice, 'Discovery, conquest, and occupation of territory' in Bardo Fassbender and Anne Peters (eds), *The Oxford Handbook of the History of International Law* (OUP 2012) 840, 856–60.

[192] *Cooper v Stuart* (1886) 14 AC 286, 291. See further Lindley (n 186) 40–1.

[193] *Mabo v Queensland (No 2)* (1992) 175 CLR 1, paras 40–1 (Brennan J).

[194] Lindley (n 186) 46.

[195] Ibid, 47.

rights in the Hohfeldian sense—in the sense that certain conduct by Western states was unlawful *towards them*. It could be that their 'consent' was merely a fact that was relevant to whether or not Western states validly acquired rights *relative to other Western states*.

I will conclude that these entities did have certain Hohfeldian rights of their own and therefore personality. Lindley was apparently of that view too: he wrote that '[m]any of the so-called "savage" races . . . possess organized institutions of government, and it cannot be truly said that the territory inhabited by such races is not under any sovereignty'.[196] But since this conclusion may not follow incontrovertibly from the test in *Western Sahara*, it requires further discussion. I will look at treaty rights and duties and then at rights and duties not derived from treaties, in particular sovereignty.

2.5.1 Personality under agreements

The ubiquity of treaties between these entities and Western states is the greatest obstacle to the view that they were wholly outside international law. The Americas had mostly been colonized earlier, during what I called the era of natural law; but in the nineteenth century Western states, including the United States, were still making treaties with indigenous peoples in the Americas—for example, in western North America.[197] And in Africa and the Pacific, Western explorers and colonizers made treaties virtually everywhere they went.[198]

Many of these were treaties ceding territory. That, and occasionally conquest, were the usual legal grounds on which Western states colonized territory in Africa.[199] Often ceding territory was the sole act that an African state-like entity ever performed in Western international law, as if it stepped on to the stage and walked off again in one movement. Some treaties merely created colonial protectorates.[200] Western states did not necessarily acquire sovereignty from these treaties of 'protection',[201] though in practice they often administered the territory as their own and sooner or later acquired sovereignty on other grounds.[202] Treaties could

[196] Ibid, 20.

[197] Ken Coates, 'North American Indigenous peoples' encounters' in Bardo Fassbender and Anne Peters (eds), *The Oxford Handbook of the History of International Law* (OUP 2012) 787.

[198] A list of British treaty partners from 1750 to 1850 appears in Brownlie (n 39) 360, with the comment that it is representative of 'the more important powers'. This was compiled from Clive Parry and Charity Hopkins (eds), *Index to British Treaties 1101–1968* (Her Majesty's Stationery Office 1970).

[199] Alexandrowicz, 'Afro-Asian world' (n 14) 172.

[200] 'Colonial' protectorates is what Crawford, *Creation* (n 163) 307 calls these arrangements to distinguish them from true 'international' protectorates. On the international kind, see this book s 5.1.2.

[201] Mamadou Hébié, 'The role of the agreements concluded with local political entities in the course of French colonial expansion in West Africa' (2015) 85 BYIL 21, 56–72.

[202] *Land and Maritime Boundary between Cameroon and Nigeria (Cameroon v Nigeria: Equatorial Guinea Intervening)* [2002] ICJ Rep 303, paras 207–9.

have other purposes too. In his study of French practice in west Africa, Mamadou Hébié cites treaties that guaranteed or regulated freedom of commerce; attempted to suppress the slave trade; formed alliances, sometimes military ones; declared friendship and peace; recognized spheres of influence at the expense of other African entities; returned territory that France had earlier acquired by cession or conquest; or demarcated boundaries.[203] On the premise that these were valid treaties in international law, they could have given rights, duties, and hence personality to their non-Western parties.

The notion that they were valid treaties has, however, been questioned.

In *Western Sahara*, the Court equivocated on the issue. All it said was that 'agreements with local rulers, whether or not considered as an actual "cession" of the territory, were regarded as derivative roots of title, and not original titles obtained by occupation of *terrae nullius*'.[204] This suggests two possibilities: either agreements of this sort were genuine treaties that effected an actual cession, or Western states derived sovereignty from them in a less direct manner. What that less direct manner may have been was suggested by Huber as arbitrator in *Island of Palmas*. Between 1677 and 1899, the Netherlands (or the Dutch East India Company on its authority) had made a number of agreements with rulers based on the island of Sangir (now in Indonesia), who also ruled certain other islands. The Netherlands argued that these agreements established its sovereignty over the island of Palmas or Miangas. Huber held that they were not treaties binding in international law but instead were *contracts*, 'a form of internal organisation of a colonial territory, on the basis of autonomy for the natives'.[205] Although they could not effect a cession as such, they were *facts* of which international law

> must in certain circumstances take account. . . . [S]uzerainty over the native State becomes the basis of territorial sovereignty as towards other members of the community of nations. It is the sum-total of functions thus allotted either to the native authorities or to those of the colonial Power which decides the question whether at any certain period the conditions required for the existence of sovereignty are fulfilled.[206]

Another possibility is that an agreement of this sort was neither a treaty in international law nor a form of organization in domestic law but had some even-less-concrete status. In 1958, a Canadian judge held that if a treaty had been made with the indigenous Mi'kmaq people then it was not a treaty in the international legal

[203] Hébié (n 201) 56–86.
[204] *Western Sahara* [1975] ICJ Rep 12, para 80.
[205] *Island of Palmas* (1928) 2 UNRIAA 829, 858 (emphasis removed).
[206] Ibid, 858–9.

sense but 'in the nature of a special agreement based on goodwill and expediency made by the Crown with a body of inhabitants'.[207]

Some treaties, whether or not governed by domestic law to begin with, certainly came to be treated as instruments in domestic law with the passage of time. For example, in 1831, the US Supreme Court held that indigenous North American peoples who had previously made treaties with the United States were now 'domestic dependent nations'.[208] A special rapporteur of the United Nations deprecated this process as 'domestication'.[209] From the time they were 'domesticated', treaties of this sort can be put aside, along with instruments that were clearly always governed by domestic law.[210]

But that still leaves treaties that, at the time of their conclusion, appeared to be governed by international law. For one thing, many treaties used the *language* of international law: 'treaty', 'sovereignty', 'territory'. The Congo Declarations of 1885 referred to treaties 'concluded with the legitimate sovereigns in the basin of the Congo'.[211] Some scholars who denied that international law applied seemed to pass this language by without notice.[212] But the problem was tackled head-on by Westlake. He pointed to collateral purposes that might motivate Western states to use the language of international law in agreements with 'uncivilised tribes'.[213] Such agreements could buttress claims to territory that primarily rested on other grounds. They could also serve as instruments of political practicality: 'no men are so savage as to be incapable of coming to some understanding with other men', and 'some understanding, however incomplete it may be, is a better basis for their mutual relations than force'.[214] Yet whatever language Westerners used in documents, Westlake argued that there was an insurmountable barrier to making genuine treaties, certainly treaties directly ceding territory. This was the ability to consent. Westlake thought it was 'possible that a right of property may be derived from

[207] *Warman v Francis* (1958) 20 DLR 2d 627, para 8.

[208] *Cherokee Nation v Georgia*, 30 US 1 (1831) 17. Compare *Worcester v Georgia*, 31 US 515 (1832). The US Congress later legislated that 'hereafter no Indian nation or tribe within the territory of the United States shall be acknowledged or recognized as an independent nation, tribe, or power with whom the United States may contract by treaty': Act of 3 March 1871, ch 120 s 1, 16 Stat 566, 25 USC s 71.

[209] Miguel Alfonso Martínez, Final Report on Treaties, Agreements and Other Constructive Arrangements between States and Indigenous Populations (22 June 1999) UN doc E/CN.4/Sub.2/1999/20, paras 168–244. See further Gudmundur Alfredsson, 'Indigenous peoples, treaties with' (last updated 2011) MPEPIL.

[210] See also CH Alexandrowicz, *The European-African Confrontation: A Study in Treaty Making* (Sijthoff 1973) 97–103, on agreements with African entities 'which are obviously not treaties in international law' but concern 'rights in private law'.

[211] Declarations Exchanged between the Belgian Congo and the International Association of the Congo, Berlin (23 February 1885) in Edward Hertslet (ed), *The Map of Africa by Treaty* (3rd edn, Routledge 1909) vol 2, 544. See further Alexandrowicz, 'Afro-Asian world' (n 14) 176.

[212] Onuma (n 16) 49.

[213] Westlake (n 1) 143–5.

[214] Ibid, 143.

treaties with natives' who understood the concept.[215] But 'natives in the rudimentary condition' had 'no rights under international law', and

> it follows that no document in which such natives are made to cede the sovereignty over any territory can be exhibited as an international title ... [T]he right to establish the full system of civilised government, which in these cases is the essence of sovereignty, cannot be based on the consent of those who at the utmost know but a few of the needs which such a government is intended to meet. ... [N]o form of cession by them can confer any title to what they do not understand.[216]

This was plainly inconsistent. Lindley thought it was 'difficult to see why, if the natives are to be regarded as capable of possessing and transferring property, they should not also be considered competent to hold and transfer the sovereignty which they actually exercise.'[217] DP O'Connell described the idea that these agreements were a nullity as 'not only a typical piece of late 19th-century arrogance' but as leading 'to the absurd and morally reprehensible conclusion that the colonial authorities, having gone through the motions of good faith, could then without a pang of conscience tear up their solemn legal acts as being void.'[218]

There is also the critical fact that the Western officials who actually dealt with these entities *did not* assume that they were categorically incapable of consenting to treaties, either as a general matter or to cede territory. Western officials actively took steps to establish consent by employing witnesses and interpreters in their dealings with Africans.[219]

This is not to say that negotiations were always politically equal. They obviously were not. A notorious example is Henry Morton Stanley's voyage up the Congo River in 1878 on behalf of a private association organized by Leopold II, the King of the Belgians. This would lead to the establishment of the Congo Free State, in which millions of people were worked to death. Stanley claimed to have made more than two hundred treaties with African chiefs.[220] Some had terms so disproportionate that it is hard to credit that the African parties understood what was going on.[221] Koskenniemi highlights a treaty of 1884 in which the chiefs of Ngombi and Mafela gave away 'sovereignty and all sovereign and governing rights to all their territories' and agreed to provide their labour to the association; this was in exchange for 'one piece of cloth per month to each of the under-signed

215 Ibid, 144–5. Compare TE Holland, *Lectures on International Law* (Sweet & Maxwell 1933) 117.
216 Westlake (n 1) 144–5.
217 Lindley (n 186) 21, further 169–77.
218 O'Connell (n 190) 81.
219 Alexandrowicz, 'Afro-Asian world' (n 14) 76–81.
220 Koskenniemi (n 10) 136–43.
221 Lindley (n 186) 172–4; Alexandrowicz, 'Afro-Asian world' (n 14) 179.

chiefs, besides present cloth in hand'.[222] Not all treaties of this sort would have met the requirements of international law (though bear in mind that the requirements were laxer in the nineteenth century than today: duress did not always vitiate consent[223]). In fact, Western states sometimes challenged the validity of treaties that rival colonial powers made with African state-like entities. Grounds for such challenges included whether the individual acting on behalf of the entity had authority to transfer territory; whether a treaty complied with the entity's own rules; and whether a treaty expressed a ruler's genuine will, especially in cases of coercion or fraud.[224]

And yet, as Yasuaki Onuma observes, 'hardly any European state seemed to attack other European states for concluding an agreement with an African ruler on the ground that African tribes were uncivilized and therefore not entitled to conclude a treaty'.[225] *In principle*, it was possible for treaties of this sort to be valid, even if the requirement of consent was not always met (note that this is a statement about how validity and consent were constructed within the framework of Western international law, as distinct from an African world view). There is thus every reason to take the position, propounded by scholars in more recent times, that a treaty between a Western state and another state-like entity 'must be presumed to involve an acceptance of the capacity of the other Party to enter into such an agreement'.[226] The treaties created rights and duties in international law and to that extent personality.

2.5.2 Personality under other norms

Did entities in the outer sphere also have sovereignty? I suggested earlier that this does not follow incontrovertibly from the *terra nullius* test. Still, *terra nullius* means land belonging to no one, and land inhabited by even the supposedly least 'civilized' state-like entities was not *terra nullius*: this implies that it belonged to *someone*. Moreover, I have found that agreements made by these entities were treaties that could cede sovereignty to Western states: that strongly suggests that they previously had sovereignty themselves (*nemo dat quod non habet*: one cannot give what one does not have).[227] Lindley described the treaties of cession

222 Koskenniemi (n 10) 136; Adam Hochschild, *King Leopold's Ghost: A Story of Greed, Terror, and Heroism in Colonial Africa* (Houghton Mifflin 1998) 72.

223 Lindley (n 186) 174–5. Despite this, the United States argued at the Berlin Conference of 1884–85 for 'a principle looking to the voluntary consent of the natives of whose country possession is taken in all cases when they may not have provoked the act of aggression': Alexandrowicz, *Confrontation* (n 210) 47; Alexandrowicz, 'Afro-Asian world' (n 14) 179.

224 Onuma (n 16) 48–9; Alexandrowicz, *Confrontation* (n 210) 36–41.

225 Onuma (n 16) 49.

226 Brownlie (n 39) 360.

227 Lindley (n 186) 44 also cites this maxim.

made with them as 'abundant evidence . . . that advanced Governments do recognize sovereign rights in less advanced peoples with whom they come into contact'.[228]

This is corroborated by some further evidence from Western practice.

A colonial court, the Court of Appeal for Eastern Africa, dealt with the issue of sovereignty obliquely in *Ol Le Njogo*, in 1913. Members of a Maasai tribe had brought proceedings against the British government for breach of agreements under which part of the tribe had been removed to a reserve in exchange for land rights and other inducements. The irony of this case is that the colonialists were in the position of arguing that the agreements were treaties, while the people being colonized had to argue that the agreements were *not* treaties and that the tribe no longer exercised any sovereignty. This is because the British colonialists were seeking to deny the Maasai a remedy by pleading the doctrine of act of state, according to which treaties were not justiciable before a domestic court. The Court accepted this: the Maasai were 'foreigners in a foreign country', and the agreements 'could only be enforced by diplomatic representations, or in the last resort, by war'.[229]

In reaching this decision, the leading judge paid lip-service to the view that 'an agreement between a civilised State and an uncivilised community is not governed by International law' (which he attributed to Hall and Westlake), but for all practical purposes he held that such agreements *were* treaties: they must 'be taken to be governed by some rules analogous to International law and to have similar force and effect to that held by a treaty, and must be regarded by Municipal Courts in a similar manner'.[230] The question was whether the Maasai had retained any sovereignty after the British established the East Africa Protectorate. The judge held that a protecting state must exercise elements of sovereignty 'in uncivilised countries where no means exists for their exercise otherwise', but 'it is competent to the protecting State to permit some vestige of sovereignty to remain in the native authority'.[231] Under the law of the colonial protectorate, the Maasai retained 'concurrent jurisdiction . . . over native cases', and it was 'at least arguable' that this was 'a remnant of sovereignty still remaining' in them.[232] Given the capriciousness of this decision—the Maasai had lost their sovereignty in virtually every respect except insofar as it suited their colonizers—it must be approached with caution. But by suggesting that the tribe had retained 'some

[228] Ibid, 46.

[229] *Ol Le Njogo v Attorney-General* (1913) 5 E Africa PLR 70, 110, 114 (King Farlow J). Further on this case see James Thuo Gathii, 'Imperialism, colonialism, and international law' (2007) 54 Buffalo Law Review 1013.

[230] *Ol Le Njogo* (1913) 5 E Africa PLR 70, 91–2 (Morris Carter CJ). Compare King Farlow J at 112: 'a treaty is none the less a treaty because it is entered into with a tribe or community, which, by reason of their being uncivilised, may not be recognised as coming strictly within the Rules of International Law'.

[231] Ibid, 92–3 (Morris Carter CJ).

[232] Ibid, 93 (Morris Carter CJ).

vestige of sovereignty', the Court impliedly accepted that *before* the establishment of the British protectorate the tribe had had *exclusive* sovereignty over its own subjects.

In another British colonial case, *Re Southern Rhodesia*, the Privy Council discussed the status of Lobengula, the king of Mashonaland and Matabeleland (now in Zimbabwe). It found that the United Kingdom had 'recognized Lobengula as sovereign of both peoples': in 1888, the British had described him to the Portuguese government as an 'independent king' who had not parted with his sovereignty, and in 1889 the colonial secretary had assured Lobengula that he was 'king of the country' and that 'no one can exercise jurisdiction in it without his permission'.[233] This explicitly acknowledged that an African entity had—to quote from Huber's definition of sovereignty—'in regard to a portion of the globe . . . the right to exercise therein, to the exclusion of any other State', certain functions associated with statehood.[234] It also implied that Western states had a correlative duty of non-intervention. One might further infer that if Western states owed this duty to an entity in the outer sphere, then that entity probably had a reciprocal duty to respect the sovereignty of Western states.

Beyond the basic elements of sovereignty, there are very limited indications that these entities had further customary rights and duties. There is a hint in *Ol Le Ngojo* that sovereign immunity applied to African chiefs: the judge speculated that although the Maasai as a whole were subject to the jurisdiction of the lower court of the British protectorate, if they had 'a sovereign ruler . . . he might claim to be exempt from the jurisdiction'.[235] A memorandum of the Colonial Office in 1840 referred to the recognition by the United Kingdom 'of New Zealand as a substantive and independent state',[236] and the norms that the British considered to be at least potentially applicable to relations with the Maori of New Zealand included norms of diplomatic law. Instructions given to the governor of New South Wales, Richard Bourke, read: '[y]ou . . . will claim the protection and privileges which you will tell them are accorded in Europe and America to British Subjects holding in Foreign states situations similar to yours'.[237] The law of war and neutrality was sometimes applied, too. In 1870, Twiss advised the British government that 'a state of hostilities exists, and has been recognized in the correspondence of Her Majesty's Government to exist, in the Bonny River [now in Nigeria], which would invest the

[233] *Re Southern Rhodesia* [1919] AC 211, 214. The case concerned the consequences for domestic property rights of the United Kingdom's later acquisition of the territory by conquest. Since Lobengula had 'a regular government in which the actual rule was his', the Privy Council thought acquisition by occupation alone was out of the question: at 214–16.

[234] *Island of Palmas* (1928) 2 UNRIAA 829, 838.

[235] *Ol Le Njogo* (1913) 5 E Africa PLR 70, 96 (Morris Carter CJ).

[236] Memorandum Enclosed in Letter from the Colonial Office to Lord Palmerston (18 March 1840), quoted in Smith (n 83) 31. See also Treaty of Waitangi, UK–New Zealand (5–6 February 1840) 89 CTS 473.

[237] Lord Aberdeen, Dispatch to Richard Bourke (21 December 1834), quoted in Smith (n 83) 33.

rival Chiefs with the rights of belligerents'.[238] In addition, as has been seen, at least some rules of treaty-making were evidently applied to these entities.

But clear examples of customary norms being applied are exceptional. Alexandrowicz observed that formal diplomatic relations between Western states and precolonial African entities were rare.[239] And Antony Anghie writes that the degree of personality attributed to entities in the outer sphere was decided 'on an almost completely ad hoc basis'.[240]

The largely *ad hoc* nature of the practice suggests a conclusion that the personality of state-like entities in the outer sphere was not essentially different from that of entities in the intermediate sphere, even if its manifestations were less visible and less varied. At least some of them had sovereignty. As in the intermediate sphere, one possible theoretical justification for this was the survival of a bedrock of natural law. According to a leading French international law text by Henri Bonfils and Paul Fauchille, '*positive* International Law was formed in Europe' and was 'applied to the relations of all States that have attained that degree of civilization', but '*natural* or *rational* International Law' applied 'to all States, to all peoples . . . even to the barbarian tribes that still exist in Africa'.[241] Another possible justification was customary international law, applicable on the basis of either the contractual or the legislative view, which might also have underpinned the other rights and duties that some entities appeared to have in addition to sovereignty and treaty relations. Once again, it seems more theoretically coherent to apply the contractual than the legislative view, given that many of these entities had no familiarity with Western customary norms whatsoever. But my earlier caveats about instability and ambiguity apply here as well, perhaps with even greater strength.

I conclude that there was no sharp boundary between entities in the intermediate and outer spheres: entities of both types could make treaties and were subjected to other norms on an unstable basis. The clearest difference was one of degree: the likes of the Ottoman Empire and China interacted with Western states more frequently and in more complex ways, with the result that their personality tended to be greater in extent and less often questioned.

2.6 Implications for statehood

In the earliest period I have discussed in this chapter (the era of natural law, which for the purposes of this discussion of personality can be extended into the initial, Grotian phase of positivism), Western international law had a tendency to attribute

[238] Travers Twiss, Opinion (29 September 1870) in Lauterpacht, *Recognition* (n 140) 205.
[239] Alexandrowicz, 'Afro-Asian world' (n 14) 181.
[240] Anghie (n 26) 81.
[241] Bonfils and Fauchille (n 173) 17–18 (translation with emphasis from original).

rights, duties, and hence personality to non-Western as well as Western entities. This was despite the fact that many non-Western entities did not accept or even know about Western norms. Malcolm Shaw draws a conclusion similar to mine about how international law was 'transformed by positivism and European colonization': in the nineteenth century, it had

> a three-level structure . . . as it related to the issue of international personality. States within the European-defined 'family of nations' were full and complete subjects of international law, States outside this 'family' had only a limited impact upon the development of the law and not all of it applied to them, while certain non-State entities or communities possessed only a limited personality in international law, although this certainly included the capacity to hold title to territory and territorial sovereignty.[242]

More precisely, I have concluded that a body of general norms was likely to be applied in full to Western states (the legislative view) but that these norms were likely to be applied to non-Western entities more selectively, depending on whether an entity had consented specifically to each norm (the contractual view). This could create differences of personality. The word 'likely' is an acknowledgment of the instability of both practice and doctrine.

Shaw describes entities in the inner and intermediate spheres, but not the outer sphere, as 'States'. He is far from alone in using the term in this way. Compare how the International Court used it in *Cameroon v Nigeria*. It was discussing an ostensible treaty of protection of 1884 between the United Kingdom and the Kings and Chiefs of Old Calabar. The Court observed that in some parts of Africa, Western states made treaties of protection 'with entities which retained thereunder a previously existing sovereignty under international law', such as Morocco, Tunisia, and Madagascar.[243] But elsewhere in Africa, 'treaties termed "treaties of protection" were entered into not with States, but rather with important indigenous rulers exercising local rule over identifiable areas of territory'; the ostensible treaty in this case 'was one of a multitude in a region where the local Rulers were not regarded as States'.[244]

I will finish this chapter by considering the meaning of the term 'state' in light of the diversity of the state-like entities that I have concluded had personality in past eras.

Its meaning was not explained in *Cameroon v Nigeria*. The Court might be interpreted as having implied that statehood was a precondition for a treaty-making power or sovereignty. It described the fact that Old Calabar was not a state as one

[242] Shaw, *Title to Territory* (n 24) 44–5.
[243] *Cameroon v Nigeria* [2002] ICJ Rep 303, para 205.
[244] Ibid, paras 205–7.

of 'many factors point[ing] to the 1884 Treaty . . . as not establishing a protectorate'; and it quoted from Huber's argument (discussed earlier) that some ostensible treaties were really a form of internal colonial organization.[245] At the same time, the Court emphasized that 'apart from the parallel declarations of various lesser Chiefs agreeing to be bound' by the treaty, there was 'not even convincing evidence of a central federal power' in Old Calabar but merely 'individual townships, headed by Chiefs, who regarded themselves as owing a general allegiance to more important Kings and Chiefs'.[246] So the problem in Old Calabar may have been the lack of any identifiable entity at all rather than a lack of statehood. Similarly, in *Western Sahara*, the Court found that a precolonial 'Mauritanian entity', which had been described as a 'nation' or 'people' rather than a state, 'did not have the character of a personality or corporate entity distinct from the several emirates and tribes which composed it'.[247]

Imagine that the term 'states' is defined, consistent with Shaw's usage and with that in *Cameroon v Nigeria*, to include both Western states and entities in the intermediate sphere, such as Morocco and Tunisia, but to exclude entities in the outer sphere. I have concluded that no sharp line can be drawn between the intermediate and outer spheres; the clearest difference between them was in the degree of their interaction with Western states. On this definition 'statehood', although useful as a shorthand term for comparatively complex entities, is not an analytically robust legal category that necessarily reflects the extent of their personality. On the other hand, it would clash with ordinary usage to widen the term 'states' to include entities of other types, such as chiefdoms and nomadic communities: Westerners occasionally used the term in dealings with, for instance, west African entities, but not consistently or in any strict sense.[248] It would be equally contrary to ordinary usage to restrict the term to Western states: the likes of the Ottoman Empire and China were almost always described as states.

It follows that during the period when international law was reshaped by positivism, from roughly the late eighteenth century to the early twentieth, the term 'states' cannot be given a clear technical legal meaning. The personality of non-Western entities was too unstable, and usage of the term did not correlate with an analytically robust category. And to this can be added the complication that it was not even completely certain in what manner *Western* states bore customary rights and duties (whether on the temporarily fashionable contractual view or the eventually prevailing legislative view)—a further cause of instability.

245 Ibid.

246 Ibid, para 207.

247 *Western Sahara* [1975] ICJ Rep 12, paras 138, 149.

248 Hébié (n 201) 50–1. Further on the fluidity of the concept in this period, see JA Andrews, 'The concept of statehood and the acquisition of territory in the nineteenth century' (1978) 94 Law Quarterly Review 408.

What changed was that by the early twentieth century virtually all non-Western state-like entities had been colonized or otherwise politically subordinated by 'civilized' states. Only six survived with their independence more or less intact.[249] These were all entities from the intermediate sphere that were deemed to have met the standard of 'civilization' by the early twentieth century: the Ottoman Empire, Japan, China, Thailand, Iran, and Ethiopia. This was a haphazard and gradual process. Koskenniemi argues that, although the idea of a 'standard' gave 'the appearance of fair treatment and regular administration' to admission into the family of nations, in fact every 'concession was a matter of negotiation, every status dependent on agreement, quid pro quo'.[250] What was legally significant was not 'civilization' as such but that it ceased to be doubted that custom applied to these entities in the same manner and to the same extent as to Western states. This process was accompanied and clarified by two developments I have already mentioned: the triumph of the legislative view of custom and the diminution of the role of natural law to nothing or almost nothing.

The transformation was also aided by extra-legal developments. In the West, the idea of degrees of 'civilization' fell out of favour. It became embarrassing after the First World War, in which Westerners proved to be experts at barbarity and savagery.[251] The allusion to 'civilized nations' in article 38(1) of the Court's Statute, drafted after the war, is usually treated as redundant: the drafters apparently considered all 'nations' then existing to be 'civilized'.[252] In 1937, Hersch Lauterpacht argued that the idea of 'civilization' had been wrong all along.[253] At the same time, in other parts of the world, Western ideas were internalized by officials and jurists. Becker Lorca argues that 'a particular European discourse, the international legal discourse of the nineteenth century, was appropriated and then transformed by non-Western states and their lawyers', including the Ottomans and the Japanese.[254] Other conceptions of international law were abandoned or partially assimilated. This process was alluded to in the *Eritrea/Yemen* arbitration in 1998. In considering an argument about historic title to islands, the tribunal referred to 'a *res communis* that has existed for centuries for the benefit of the populations on both sides of the Red Sea . . . permitting the African as well as the Yemeni fishermen to

[249] Entities such as Oman, Afghanistan, Nepal, and Bhutan were not formally colonized but in practice still lost much of their independence, such as control of foreign affairs. A few entities were colonized by other non-Western entities, such as Korea by Japan. See Crawford, *Creation* (n 163) ch 7, appendix 1.

[250] Koskenniemi (n 10) 134–5.

[251] Schwarzenberger (n 26); Rose Parfitt, 'Theorizing recognition and international personality' in Florian Hoffmann and Anne Orford (eds), *The Oxford Handbook of the Theory of International Law* (OUP 2016) 583.

[252] Alain Pellet, 'Article 38' in Andreas Zimmermann and others (eds), *The Statute of the International Court of Justice: A Commentary* (OUP 2012) 731, para 261. Compare *North Sea Continental Shelf* [1969] ICJ Rep 3, 134 (Judge Ammoun): the term must have 'a universal scope involving no discrimination between the members of a single community based on sovereign equality'.

[253] Hersch Lauterpacht, 'Règles générales du droit de la paix' (1937) 62 Recueil des cours 95, 256.

[254] Becker Lorca (n 1) 7.

operate with no limitation throughout the entire area'.[255] This accorded with an Islamic conception of law, 'which practically ignored the principle of "territorial sovereignty" as it developed among the European powers and became a basic feature of nineteenth century western international law'; but the Ottoman Empire, which came to govern the area,

> started after the end of the Crimean War in 1856 to abandon the communal aspects of the Islamic system of international law and to adopt the modern rules prevailing among the European concert of nations to which the Sublime Porte became a fully integrated party. . . . According to this new modern international law, the legal concept of 'territorial sovereignty' became a cornerstone for most of the state powers, and the situation in the Red Sea could no longer escape the juridical consequences of that new reality.[256]

Parfitt argues that a process like this was still going on as late as the 1920s in Ethiopia. After Ethiopia joined the League of Nations, its leaders continued to speak a 'semi-Abyssinian international legal "dialect" '.[257] They conceived of both their own culture and the culture of the League as springing from Christian principles they shared with the West.

The process of homogenization would be reinforced when Western states decolonized most of Africa, Asia, and the Pacific in the second half of the twentieth century. In terms of international law, this generally did not mean that state-like entities that had existed before colonization regained their independence.[258] Instead, new states were founded on the Western model: where the Maratha Confederacy, the Mughal Empire, and other entities had once been, India and Pakistan; in the lands of the Maasai and other groups, Kenya. Some of these new states criticized international law as 'a product of relations among imperialist States and of relations of an imperial character between imperialist States and colonial peoples' and challenged the scope of particular customary norms, such as diplomatic protection, that had been 'established during a period when . . . it was "enough to show that the general consensus of opinion within the limits of European civilisation is in favour of the rule" '.[259] But these challenges to certain customary norms were made within

[255] *Eritrea/Yemen (Territorial Sovereignty and Scope of the Dispute)* (1998) 33 UNRIAA 209, paras 126–8.

[256] Ibid, paras 130–1.

[257] Rose Parfitt, '*Empire des nègres blancs*: The hybridity of international personality and the Abyssinia crisis of 1935–36' (2011) 24 Leiden Journal of International Law 849, 870.

[258] Alexandrowicz, 'Afro-Asian world' (n 14) 165–7; Crawford, *Creation* (n 163) 697–9.

[259] S Prakash Sinha, 'Perspective of the newly independent states on the binding quality of international law' (1965) 14 ICLQ 121, 121–2, quoting Westlake (n 1) 78. See further *Barcelona Traction, Light and Power Company, Limited (Belgium v Spain) (New Application: 1962) (Second Phase)* [1970] ICJ Rep 3, 307–13 (Judge Ammoun).

the existing internal framework of Western international law; they took its general binding force for granted.

The intermediate and outer spheres of entities that I have discussed have thus ceased to exist. That just leaves entities of the kind that I have so far called Western states, including assimilated or newly created non-Western entities. Essentially these are what, elsewhere in this book, I will call plain 'states'. But the diversity of the state-like entities that I have discussed in this chapter offers a warning that questions about personality cannot be reduced to a dichotomy between states and non-states. This will be borne out in the next chapter, where I will find that the process of homogenization has not been absolute: there is still diversity in the form of 'states-in-context' and of two coexisting legal underpinnings for statehood.

3

States

The effectiveness and recognition norms

I have reached the point at which, as a result of the globalization of international law and of a process of homogenization, the question of which state-like entities have international legal personality comes down primarily to the question of which entities have statehood. In this chapter and the next I will consider statehood—a central concept of the book—against the theoretical and historical background provided by the preceding chapters.

International lawyers tend to agree that the acquisition of statehood hinges on the roles of two potentially decisive factors: whether an entity complies with criteria of effectiveness (including at least territory, population, and government) and whether the entity is recognized as a state by other states. Any agreement ends there; although the debate about statehood is less intense than it once was, it has never been totally resolved. It is traditionally presented as a debate between two theoretical traditions into which the various competing views can be fitted: the 'declaratory' and the 'constitutive'. But this traditional way of categorizing the possibilities is misleading. If there are two potentially decisive factors, logically that leaves room for not two but four views about what how statehood is acquired: that effectiveness alone is necessary; that recognition alone is necessary; that both effectiveness and recognition are necessary; and that *either* effectiveness *or* recognition can be sufficient. After considering each of these four views, I will adopt a version of the last: international law contains two coexisting rules, the effectiveness norm and the recognition norm, either of which can suffice to create statehood. I postpone until the next chapter consideration of the exceptions to these rules, which will bring in factors such as the use of force and self-determination; the present chapter is concerned only with the general rules about statehood.

A caveat to my conclusion that either effectiveness or recognition can be sufficient for statehood will be this: if an entity acquires statehood solely under the recognition norm and if the entity is recognized universally, the term 'state' can be used without further qualification; but if the entity is recognized by just one or several states, it is better to use the term 'state-in-context'. States-in-context can be thought of as another category of state-like entities (in addition to states properly so called) that have personality in international law.

In the course of the chapter, I will have to consider another question that is important for statehood and for international law overall: how norms that create

Statehood and the State-Like in International Law. Rowan Nicholson, Oxford University Press (2019).
© Rowan Nicholson
DOI: 10.1093/oso/9780198851219.001.0001

states can even exist, given that it is states themselves that render norms valid. I will suggest that validity in international law rests not on a single basic norm but rather on a self-reproducing basic circle of norms.

3.1 The view that only effectiveness is necessary

The currently dominant view about statehood is what I will call the 'effectiveness-only' view. This is what international lawyers usually mean when they refer to the declaratory theory. An authority often cited for it is *Deutsche Continental Gas-Gesellschaft v Polish State*, in which a tribunal examined the new Polish entity that had emerged at the end of the First World War. After the armistice in November 1918, the Polish National Committee had installed itself as an effective government. Germany had recognized Poland as a state and ceded it territory under the Treaty of Versailles of June 1919.[1] But Russia had not ceded Poland the previously Russian territory that Poland controlled (which included its capital, Warsaw). The tribunal held that neither Germany's recognition nor Russia's apparent non-recognition determined whether or not Poland had the rights of a state over the territory that it controlled. What mattered was that it met certain criteria of effectiveness: 'the condition of possessing a territory, a collectivity of people inhabiting that territory, [and] a public power exercised over that territory and that collectivity'.[2] The tribunal added:

> According to the opinion rightly admitted by the great majority of writers on international law, the recognition of a State is not constitutive but merely declaratory. The State exists by itself and the recognition is nothing else than a declaration of this existence, recognised by the States from which it emanates.[3]

This view was also taken by a body established by the European Community to provide advice on the collapse of Yugoslavia, the Badinter Commission: the existence of a state 'is a question of fact', and 'the effects of recognition by other States are purely declaratory'.[4]

I will begin by drawing out the implications of the declaratory or effectiveness-only view for what statehood *is*. This is the standard against which I will assess the other possible views of statehood, each of which has somewhat different implications for what statehood is. The effectiveness-only view implies that states

[1] Treaty of Peace between the Allied and Associated Powers and Germany, Versailles (28 June 1919) 225 CTS 188, art 87.
[2] *Deutsche Continental Gas-Gesellschaft v Polish State* (1929) 9 Recueil TAM 336, 344 (translation).
[3] Ibid (translation from the summary of the decision at 5 ILR 11, 13).
[4] *Opinion No 1* (Badinter Commission) (1991) 92 ILR 162, 164–5. See also *Restatement of the Law: The Foreign Relations Law of the United States* (3rd edn, American Law Institute 1987) pts 201, 202.

have three main attributes in common: first, they comprise a class of facts that meet effectiveness criteria; second, customary norms grant them a package of rights, duties, and other relations; and third, they contribute to the formation of customary norms. These attributes are causally linked: an entity that meets the effectiveness criteria thereby acquires the other two attributes. Although I am introducing these attributes in the context of the effectiveness-only view, later in this chapter I will incorporate them, with some qualifications, into my own view. Once I have introduced them I will go on to assess the evidence for the claims made by the effectiveness-only view.

3.1.1 States are facts that meet effectiveness criteria

In Chapter 1, I concluded that norms of international law must construct all their own facts (not just 'institutional' facts) to the extent that norms have anything to say about those facts, including for the purpose of giving an entity rights, duties, and personality. I also clarified that when I refer to an 'entity' I do not mean anything essentially different from a fact. States, like anything else, must be legally constructed as facts. They certainly exist outside international law insofar as a number of their characteristics are part of the physical world (land, sea, buildings, inhabitants) and in the sense that they can be spoken about from other perspectives, like domestic law or politics; but these characteristics must be apprehended or selected by norms of international law before such norms can deal with them.

If a number of facts necessarily share a characteristic, they might be called a 'class' of facts. Not every international legal person can be fitted neatly into a class; in Chapter 5, I will discuss some state-like entities whose personality is unique. But on the effectiveness-only view, states form a class of facts; the characteristic that they share is that they meet certain criteria that are determined by custom. This view postulates a customary norm 'entities that meet effectiveness criteria are defined as states'. What are these criteria? The three from *Deutsche Continental Gas-Gesellschaft*—'the condition of possessing a territory, a collectivity of people inhabiting that territory, [and] a public power exercised over that territory and that collectivity'[5]—are usually referred to as territory, population, and government. They were identified by Georg Jellinek in 1900.[6] These are the criteria most often alluded to by states and are widely accepted in the literature.[7] I am not setting out

[5] *Deutsche Continental* (1929) 9 Recueil TAM 336, 344 (translation).

[6] Stefan Talmon, 'The constitutive versus the declaratory theory of recognition: *Tertium non datur*?' (2005) 75 BYIL 101, 109–10, discussing George Jellinek, *Allgemeine Staatslehre* (O Häring 1900) 355–93. On Jellinek's approach to international law generally see Martti Koskenniemi, *The Gentle Civilizer of Nations: The Rise and Fall of International Law 1870–1960* (CUP 2001) 198–206.

[7] On a fourth criterion that is often cited, capacity to enter into relations with other states, see this book s 3.3.

to add to that literature by examining in detail how they apply in every scenario (on the contrary, it will become evident that on my view there is much less evidence on which to base such an examination than might be thought). One clarification is important, however. Although the likes of Uttar Pradesh, South Australia, and Wales have territories, populations, and governments, and although the first two are referred to as 'states' and the third as a 'country', they are obviously not states in an international legal sense; they are subentities of states, whose potential personality I will discuss in Chapter 5.[8] The explanation is that an entity can meet the criteria only if it is *independent*. James Crawford, in his comprehensive treatment of the criteria, describes independence as the 'central criterion for statehood'.[9]

I am following Crawford in referring to the criteria cumulatively as 'effectiveness'.[10] This highlights the essential point that, whatever the precise relationship may be between the four criteria of territory, population, government, and independence, they relate to whether or not an entity can *effectively* perform functions that are associated with statehood.

Two observations can be made about the idea that statehood depends on effectiveness.

First, the effectiveness criteria do not—and as a matter of principle cannot—require that an entity already possess a particular Hohfeldian right or duty before it can acquire statehood; they relate purely to how the entity's factual characteristics are legally constructed.

This can be illustrated by contrasting different meanings of 'independence'. In the last chapter, I quoted a remark from *Island of Palmas* that '[i]ndependence in regard to a portion of the globe is the right to exercise therein, to the exclusion of any other State, the functions of a State'.[11] I interpreted this as entailing a Hohfeldian right that other entities not intervene in an entity's exercise of jurisdiction in its territory, a basic element of sovereignty. Imagine that the criteria for statehood include independence in this sense: before an entity can become a state, it must already have this basic sovereign right. On this hypothesis, in order to explain how an entity acquires statehood, one must first identify the norm under

[8] Compare Vaughan Lowe, *International Law* (OUP 2007) 157.

[9] James Crawford, *The Creation of States in International Law* (2nd edn, OUP 2006) 62, further 63–89. One of several situations that are not considered to derogate from a state's independence is the 'exercise of governmental competence by another international person on behalf of and by delegation from a State', for example, by the European Union on behalf of its member states: at 70. But see this book s 5.1.2 on what happens when a state delegates so much as to call its independence into question. Further on the criterion of independence, see James Crawford, 'Chance, order, change: The course of international law' (2013) 365 Recueil des cours 9, 147. Compare Tiqiang Chen, *The International Law of Recognition with Special Reference to Practice in Great Britain and the United States* (Praeger 1951) 58–9.

[10] Crawford, *Creation* (n 9) ch 2.

[11] *Island of Palmas (US/Netherlands)* (1928) 2 UNRIAA 829, 838, quoted in this book s 2.3. Sovereignty is also equated with independence in *Customs Régime between Germany and Austria (Advisory Opinion)* (1931) PCIJ ser A/B 41, 47 (Judge Anzilotti), on which see this book s 5.1.2.

which it acquires this right.[12] If the way it acquires the right is by meeting a set of factual criteria, the problem is revealed to be illusory: the criteria for statehood are factual after all, though the list of criteria must be expanded to include the criteria for acquiring the right to exclusive jurisdiction. Otherwise, one will be compelled to adopt a different explanation of how an entity acquires the right, such as recognition by other states: that amounts to abandoning the effectiveness criteria as an explanation of statehood, or at least hybridizing them with something else.

So the effectiveness criteria can explain which entities are states only if, in the last analysis, the criteria do not include prior possession of the right to exclusive jurisdiction; by the same reasoning, the criteria cannot include prior possession of *any* right or duty.

It might appear that some international lawyers interpret the criterion of independence as, at least in part, a right. Crawford distinguishes between 'actual' and 'formal' aspects of independence: 'independence for the purposes of statehood should be presumed where an entity is formally independent', but 'where formal independence masks a lack of any actual independence at all, the entity should be regarded as not independent'.[13] Actual independence is 'the minimum degree of real governmental power at the disposal of the authorities of the putative State'.[14] This is clearly a factual characteristic rather than a Hohfeldian right or other legal relation. But formal independence, in contrast, is 'where the powers of government of a territory (in internal and external affairs) are vested in the separate authorities of the putative State'.[15] Stefan Talmon also emphasizes this aspect of independence: '[i]ndependence of other States' as a criterion for statehood 'refers to *legal* independence; that is, the State must only be subject to international law, not to the laws of any other State'.[16] 'Formal' or 'legal' independence, as an aspect of the effectiveness criteria, sounds like it might be a right.

But when I discussed how norms of international law construct facts, I emphasized that these legally constructed facts include information about how reality is constructed from other social or legal perspectives; in particular, within the framework of international law, rights, duties, and other relations *from domestic law* are facts. The main way Crawford says formal independence is manifested is under the domestic law in force in a territory, usually a constitution. From the perspective of

[12] If this, in turn, depended on prior possession of yet another right or duty, the problem would recur; one would have to drill down until one found an explanation that did not depend on possession of a prior right or duty. The problem does not arise with Hohfeldian freedoms or no-rights, because they are given to entities by the default conduct norm and so do not require any further explanation: see this book s 1.2.

[13] Crawford, *Creation* (n 9) 88–9. He attaches another condition to this presumption: that the entity's 'creation was not attended by serious illegality'. On this see this book s 4.1.3.

[14] Ibid, 72.

[15] Ibid, 67.

[16] Talmon, 'Constitutive' (n 6) 110.

international law that is a legally constructed fact; it does not necessarily translate into a right *in international law*. Similarly, the Badinter Commission observed that for the purpose of applying the effectiveness criteria 'the form of internal political organization and the constitutional provisions are mere facts'.[17] Crawford adds that formal independence may instead result from 'a grant of full power from the previous sovereign' or 'may be established, or recognized, by bilateral or multilateral treaty'.[18] Although this may sound like a direct grant of rights, in this context it might just serve as part of the background to the creation, as a matter of fact, of domestic constitutional authorities. It is that factual result that is important. 'Formal' or 'legal' independence is thus still a fact, albeit one of a special kind, not a right in the international legal sense.[19]

It is sometimes suggested that self-determination is 'an additional criterion of statehood', for example, by Malcolm Shaw.[20] Although the existence of a right to self-determination is certainly relevant to the emergence of states, when I discuss it in Chapter 4 I will not conclude that it is a criterion for statehood in the sense that prior possession of such a right is *necessary* to acquire statehood by the effectiveness method.[21] And even if that changed—even if a customary norm emerged that prior possession of a right to self-determination were necessary—then the criteria for statehood would remain purely factual. This is because possession of a right to self-determination itself depends on a factual test: the list of the criteria for statehood would merely have to be expanded to include compliance with that factual test.

The second observation to be made about effectiveness is that it is an 'automatic' test. By this I mean that the test does not depend primarily on the exercise of a Hohfeldian power by an entity[22] (recall that a Hohfeldian power means an entity's ability to create or change legal relations, such as a power to enter into a treaty[23]). Instead, when the test is met, rights, duties, and other legal relations come into being by automatic operation of customary international law. I will discuss what these relations are under the next heading. But for present purposes note that relations are received, on one side, by the effective entity that becomes a new state and also, on the other side, by existing states—each of which receives duties correlating with the new state's rights, rights correlating with its duties, and so on. Relations are received automatically by *both sides*. And neither side is required to exercise a power.

17 *Opinion No 1* (1991) 92 ILR 162, 165.
18 Crawford, *Creation* (n 9) 67.
19 Compare Hans Kelsen, 'The draft Declaration on Rights and Duties of States: Critical remarks' (1950) 44 AJIL 259, 267: '[i]ndependence is not a right, it is an essential characteristic of the state'.
20 Malcolm N Shaw, *International Law* (7th edn, CUP 2014) 150.
21 This book s 4.2.
22 Further on this concept, including the significance of the word 'primarily', see this book s 5.2.
23 WN Hohfeld, 'Some fundamental legal conceptions as applied in judicial reasoning [part 1]' (1913) 23 Yale Law Journal 16, 44.

It is plain enough that the existing states are not required to exercise a power: that is the whole point of saying that recognition by other states is not necessary for statehood. But it may seem less obvious that the effective entity *itself* does not need to exercise a power in order to become a state. Apparent suggestions to the contrary are often heard. For instance, there is the island of Taiwan. Although autonomous in fact, the Taiwanese government does not clearly take the view that Taiwan is a separate state from mainland China. Its official position still appears to be that there is a single Chinese state, encompassing both Taiwan and the mainland, but that the Taiwanese government is the true government of that single state (being the continuation of the government of the Republic of China, which was based on the mainland until 1949).[24] In concluding that Taiwan is not a separate state 'but part of a larger China', Crawford observes that '[s]tatehood is a claim of right' and that 'in the apparent absence of any claim to secede the status of Taiwan can only be that of a part of the State of China under separate administration'.[25] This seems to imply that an entity must 'claim' statehood in order to acquire it. But a somewhat fine distinction must be drawn here between two types of 'claim': an assertion that an entity is not formally dependent on any other entity; and an assertion that it has the rights, duties, and other legal attributes of a state.

In order for an entity within the territory of an existing state to secede and become a new state, it may need to make an assertion that it is no longer formally dependent on its parent state. I noted in the introduction that Australia and other British dominions were not considered states before 1919. Yet before 1919 the dominions, being self-governing, already met the effectiveness criteria in many respects in their domestic affairs. Why were they not states? The reason was that they took the official position that they were ultimately still subordinate to the legislative and executive authority of the United Kingdom (a position that shifted gradually over the years—a decisive change was evident by 1926[26]). Their lack of statehood was a consequence of the effectiveness criteria as already described: absent an assertion that they were formally independent, the dominions could not meet the criterion of independence.[27] Crawford's argument that Taiwan would have to make a 'claim of right' to secede from China must be read in a similar light: Taiwan would have to assert that it and mainland China are two separate, formally independent states. It cannot be read to mean that Taiwan must 'claim' to be a state in the very

[24] For a detailed discussion see Frank Chiang, *The One-China Policy: State, Sovereignty, and Taiwan's International Legal Status* (Elsevier 2018). See also on Taiwan this book s 5.1.1.

[25] Crawford, *Creation* (n 9) 211, further 198–219. Compare *Restatement: Foreign Relations* (n 4) pt 201 comment *f*.

[26] Crawford, *Creation* (n 9) 365–6 concludes that 'the critical date of the independence of the Dominions' was that of the Report of the Inter-Imperial Relations Committee of the Imperial Conference [Balfour Report] (18 November 1926) 21 AJIL Supp 21. But he adds that their status was uncertain between their participation at the Versailles conference in 1919 and that date in 1926.

[27] A self-governing entity existing today that may lack statehood for a similar reason is Iraqi Kurdistan.

different sense of consenting to have the rights, duties, and other legal attributes of a state, because the Taiwanese government actually does claim that; it is just that the claim appears to made on behalf of a single Chinese state.[28]

Suggesting that an effective entity must 'claim' to be a state in the sense of consenting to have the rights, duties, and other legal attributes of a state would have radical consequences. It would amount to saying that an entity that meets the effectiveness criteria, including independence (assuming it is not tainted by the exceptions to be discussed later), could refuse to shoulder the duties of a state. This was close to the position of some of the non-Western entities I discussed in Chapter 2, such as Qing China, in that they did not acknowledge all the norms of Western international law. But since the early twentieth century, virtually no state-like entity has challenged the bindingness of international law in this way. An exception is the armed group calling itself the 'Islamic State', which at various times in the 2010s held territory in Iraq, Syria, and Libya. Despite its self-description as a state, it showed no interest in international law; on the contrary, it aspired to create a potentially universal theocracy. If it had met the effectiveness criteria then it might have offered evidence on the present point, but probably it did not meet the criteria and hence was not a state on any view anyway.[29]

For limited evidence one must reach back to Russia after the Bolshevik revolution of 1917. Leon Trotsky, on entering the former tsarist foreign ministry, announced that he would 'publish the secret treaties and then shut up the shop'.[30] Russia no longer needed a foreign ministry, because 'revolutions were expected to sweep the world and replace interstate relations with fraternal relations between working men everywhere'.[31] Scholars such as Evgeny Korovin would go on to dispute the bindingness of much of international law in relations between entities with social structures as different as those of capitalist Western states and Russia (from 1922, the Soviet Union) and to deny that Russia had a duty to pay sovereign debt inherited from the tsars.[32] But in practice the Bolsheviks were compelled to

[28] In 2005, it asserted that 'based on the Montevideo Convention' (the effectiveness criteria) 'it is undeniable that the Republic of China is a sovereign and independent state': Republic of China (Taiwan) Mainland Affairs Council, 'The official position of the Republic of China (Taiwan) on the People's Republic of China's Anti-Secession (Anti-Separation) Law' (press release, 29 March 2005) pt III.1.

[29] Compare Marco Longobardo, 'The self-proclaimed statehood of the Islamic State between 2014 and 2017 and international law' (2017) 33 Anuario Español de Derecho Internacional 205, 215–18. A unilateral secessionist entity usually cannot become effective while its parent state is still carrying on the struggle for supremacy: see this book s 4.1.1. There are allegations of genocide: SC res 2379 (21 September 2017, Islamic State in Iraq and the Levant). So the discussion of genocide in s 4.1.3 may also be relevant.

[30] Victor Serge and Natalia Sedova-Trotsky, *The Life and Death of Leon Trotsky* (Arnold J Pomerans tr, Wildwood House 1975) 72.

[31] John N Hazard, 'Socialism and international public law' (1985) 23 Columbia Journal of Transnational Law 251, 252; further John N Hazard, 'Cleansing Soviet international law of anti-Marxist theories' (1938) 32 AJIL 244.

[32] Rudolf Schlesinger, *Soviet Legal Theory* (2nd edn, Routledge 1951) 273–93. See further Evgeny Korovin, 'La République des Soviets et le droit international' [1925] Revue générale de droit

participate in international law from the start—notably, by signing a peace treaty with Germany in 1918—and eventually even Korovin acknowledged, faced with the practice, that some of his theories had been wrong.[33]

Consistent with the limited evidence provided by Russia, the idea that entities can qualify for statehood by meeting the effectiveness criteria and yet can refuse the duties of statehood is generally not taken to be part of the effectiveness-only view.[34] As Tiqiang Chen made the point:

> it cannot be imagined that a State can voluntarily withdraw or be expelled from the international community. . . . So long as a State remains a State, it must be subject to international law. Neither itself nor any other State can alter the situation.[35]

In Chapter 2, I introduced the now-prevailing 'legislative' view of custom (the view that a state is generally bound by a customary norm even if it has not consented specifically to that norm), and I observed that one possible positivist justification for this view is that states can be presumed to consent to the institution of custom as a whole when they come into being as states.[36] Russia's experience and Chen's remark suggest that any such presumption is today irrebuttable: a state does not need to exercise a power to render custom applicable to itself on the basis of the legislative view, nor does it have a power to opt out completely.[37]

So the effectiveness criteria amount not only to a purely factual test for statehood (they do not include possession of a Hohfeldian right or duty) but also to an automatic test (they do not require a power to be exercised by the new state or by any other particular entity).

international public 292; Lauri Mälksoo, 'Russia–Europe' in Bardo Fassbender and Anne Peters (eds), *The Oxford Handbook of the History of International Law* (OUP 2012) 764, 781–5. On the possibility of Russia in some sense exiting international law, compare *Luther v Sagor* [1921] 3 KB 532, 556: Scrutton LJ opined that if an entity 'appropriates other people's property without compensation, the remedy appears to be to refuse to recognize it as a sovereign state'. See further Georg Schwarzenberger, 'The standard of civilisation in international law' (1955) 8 Current Legal Problems 212, 225.

---

[33] Hazard, 'Socialism and international public law' (n 31) 254; Schlesinger (n 32) 279.

[34] In any case, when I come to the recognition-only view—which implies that this *is* possible—it will become clear that this idea is incompatible with the existence of non-derogable peremptory norms.

[35] Chen (n 9) 37.

[36] This book s 2.3.

[37] Note that this is a statement about *customary* norms. Whether a new state is bound by *treaties* made by its parent state depends on the law of state succession. If a new state is not bound by a treaty made by its parent, that does not impair any parallel duties that it may have under customary norms: Vienna Convention on Succession of States in Respect of Treaties (23 August 1978) 1946 UNTS 3, art 5.

3.1.2 States have customary rights and other relations

This leads me to the second main attribute that states share: the package of customary rights and other relations that apply to them on the basis of the legislative view of custom.

I have said that the effectiveness-only view postulates a customary norm 'entities that meet effectiveness criteria are defined as states'. But this norm just defines states as a class of facts; alone, it does not grant the entities so defined any legal relations. That result is achieved in combination with the countless norms in the form 'any entity that is defined as a state has a particular right or other relation'. It is as if the term 'state', whenever it appears in a customary norm, serves as a cross-reference back to the definition setting out the effectiveness criteria. Together, these norms give rights, duties, and other relations to every entity that meets the criteria—which means that the entity acquires personality as I have defined it (the possession, by an entity that is constructed as a fact by norms of international law, of Hohfeldian rights or duties given to the entity by such norms).[38]

It is sometimes suggested that that certain 'fundamental' rights and duties of states are integral to the definition of statehood. For example, the Montevideo Convention of 1933 says that a state has 'the right to defend its integrity and independence, to provide for its conservation and prosperity, and consequently to organize itself as it sees fit, to legislate upon its interests, administer its services, and to define the jurisdiction and competence of its courts'.[39] The Friendly Relations Declaration of 1970 is to similar effect.[40] But merely by virtue of being defined as a state, a state has more than the rights and duties in these short lists. It has legal relations in every area of customary international law: customary rights to the inviolability of diplomatic missions,[41] customary duties concerning transboundary environmental harm,[42] customary duties not to mistreat prisoners of war,[43] and so on. These relations can never be exhaustively listed; they are in flux. An entity

[38] Compare David Raič, *Statehood and the Law of Self-Determination* (Kluwer 2002) 38.

[39] Convention on the Rights and Duties of States, Montevideo (26 December 1933) 165 LNTS 19, art 3.

[40] Declaration on Principles of International Law Concerning Friendly Relations and Co-operation Among States in Accordance with the Charter of the United Nations, annex to GA res 2625 (XXV) (24 October 1970). Compare the 'core of the concept of statehood' according to Crawford, *Creation* (n 9) 211, 40–2.

[41] Vienna Convention on Diplomatic Relations (18 April 1961) 500 UNTS 95, art 22, which was said to reflect custom in *US Diplomatic and Consular Staff in Tehran (US v Iran)* [1980] ICJ Rep 3, para 62, and which has customary roots predating Hugo Grotius, *The Rights of War and Peace* (first published 1625, Richard Tuck ed, Liberty Fund 2005) pt II.XVIII.

[42] Rio Declaration on Environment and Development (3–14 June 1992) annex to UN doc A/CONF.151/26, principle 2, which was indicated in general terms to reflect custom in *Legality of the Threat or Use of Nuclear Weapons (Advisory Opinion Requested by the General Assembly)* [1996] ICJ Rep 226, paras 27–9.

[43] Geneva Convention [III] Relative to the Treatment of Prisoners of War (12 August 1949) 75 UNTS 135, which was said substantially to reflect custom in *Prisoners of War—Ethiopia's Claim 4 (Partial Award)* (Eritrea–Ethiopia Claims Commission) (2003) 26 UNRIAA 73, paras 30–2.

that meets the effectiveness criteria is subject to any current or future customary norm that applies to all states in the circumstances of that particular state. If it is landlocked but later acquires a coast, it acquires the rights and duties of a coastal state under the law of the sea; if a new norm that applies to all states crystallizes into custom, it is bound by that (unless, perhaps, it has persistently objected).

So what can be made of the idea that certain rights and duties of states are fundamental?

In Chapter 2, I found indications that sovereignty—a package of relations that embraces some of the rights in the Montevideo Convention and Friendly Relations Declaration—has historically been attributed to a miscellany of state-like entities all over the world, even in the era when positivists doubted the extent of the other rights and duties of non-Western entities; sometimes, especially in earlier times, sovereignty was said to derive from natural law rather than custom. Sovereignty might in this historical sense be called 'fundamental'. But I observed that it is hard to say precisely what falls within the package of relations described by the term 'sovereignty' and what falls outside. And in any case, at least today, no robust analytical distinction can be drawn between sovereignty and other customary relations of states. Hans Kelsen thought that such a distinction had 'no basis in positive international law'.[44] This is because a state acquires both sovereignty and its other customary relations in the same manner: custom gives them to an entity that meets the effectiveness criteria. Sovereignty differs only in that it has been the most stable and enduring component of the relations of states, while their other relations have varied, multiplied, and changed.

For this reason, my definition of statehood, unlike some conventional definitions, will not include a list of fundamental rights and duties. I will continue to refer to the 'relations of states', which include whatever relations custom gives them from time to time.

3.1.3 States create custom, which creates states

Statehood is not just about personality; it also plays other roles in international law. The third main attribute that states share is that they contribute to custom. This, too, is a result of the norm defining states in combination with another customary norm: 'the practice and *opinio iuris* of all the entities that are defined as states contribute to customary norms'. States are thus not only persons but also lawmakers—an additional status that is not necessarily implied or required by my definition of personality. This double role of states as both persons and lawmakers leads to

[44] Kelsen, 'The draft Declaration on Rights and Duties of States: critical remarks' (n 19) 266–7. Compare Stephen C Neff, 'The dormancy, rise and decline of fundamental liberties of states' (2015) 4 Cambridge Journal of International and Comparative Law 482 and other articles in the same volume.

an apparent paradox. I have referred to the norm that defines certain entities as states as a customary norm; yet customary norms, or at least all other customary norms, depend on the practice and *opinio iuris* of states. If states are defined by a customary norm, how can that customary norm derive its validity from states? This is a manifestation of a problem that is common to every system of legal norms. Stated in general terms, the problem is that if norms derive their validity from other norms (for instance, from a constitution empowering legislators and judges to make law), then it is hard to see what makes *those other norms* valid. As with the other attributes of statehood, it is convenient to discuss this now, in the context of the effectiveness-only view, but the discussion will apply equally to my own approach to statehood when that approach is set out later.

There are a limited number of ways to answer epistemological questions in the form 'why is this proposition true?'. This includes the question of what makes it true that a norm is valid. Greek and Roman sceptics identified five possible solutions, none of which is intuitively satisfactory.[45]

The first is to accept that there is disagreement among observers—to suspend judgment. Lawyers and courts can get away with doing that most of the time. Clients seldom ask for advice on abstract questions such as what makes law valid in the first place; they are seldom put in issue in litigation. My aim in this book, however, is to explore questions of that kind.

The second solution is infinite regress. One might be led to think that the norm defining states is not an ordinary customary norm after all. The effectiveness criteria are sometimes described as grounded in natural law.[46] That was certainly true before the turn to positivism insofar as personality was attributed to all '*de facto* independent State entities'—which was already an effectiveness test of a sort, albeit not one articulated as explicitly or in as much detail as the criteria are today.[47] Could the answer be to revert to the idea that the definition of states is grounded in natural law? No. Even if one could convincingly trace the validity of norms back to 'nature', one would still not have an ultimate explanation (and the same problem would occur if one traced it back to some other extra-legal factor instead of nature). What makes *natural law* valid? If it is 'reason', as Vitoria and Grotius thought,[48] then where does reason come from? One will have to keep coming up with further explanations *ad infinitum*. At some point, lawyers will hand the question over to

45 Sextus Empiricus, *Outlines of Scepticism* (first published late 2nd century, Julia Annas and Jonathan Barnes trs, rev edn, CUP 2000) pts I.164–9.

46 Eg, Chen (n 9) 18–19.

47 CH Alexandrowicz, 'Treaty and diplomatic relations between European and South Asian powers in the seventeenth and eighteenth centuries' (1960) 100 Recueil des cours 203, 309 (but see Jennifer Pitts' warning about this cited in this book s 2.2). As this suggests, the idea that a state-like entity's personality depends on its effectiveness is not an innovation but has a long pedigree. Also compare the test of being 'socially and politically organized' from *Western Sahara (Advisory Opinion)* [1975] ICJ Rep 12, paras 80–1, 92.

48 Francisco de Vitoria, *De Indis et de jure belli* (first published 1557, John Pawley Bate tr, Carnegie Institution of Washington 1917) 151; Grotius (n 41) pt I.I.X.1. See further this book s 2.2.

philosophers, but in doing so they will have resorted to suspending judgment, as with the first solution.

The third solution is relativism. The sceptic Sextus Empiricus thought this led to the same dead end: something 'appears to be such-and-such relative to the subject judging and to the things observed together with it, but we suspend judgment on what it is like in its nature'.[49]

The fourth solution is an axiom beyond which one will not look. This is broadly the approach taken by positivists such as Kelsen and HLA Hart. Kelsen postulated a 'basic norm' (*Grundnorm*) 'the validity of which cannot be derived from a superior norm', but must instead be presupposed, and from which 'all the different norms of which an order consists' derive their validity.[50] Hart postulated a 'rule of recognition' that specifies 'some feature or features possession of which by a suggested rule is taken as a conclusive affirmative indication that it is a rule of the group to be supported by the social pressure it exerts'.[51] Kelsen's and Hart's theories both identify an axiom, a boundary beyond which one need not look in order to answer questions from within the system of norms. The main difficulty with this approach is identifying what the basic norm or rule of recognition of the system *is*. This has especially troubled international lawyers, who do not even have a written constitution with which to begin the search.[52] Kelsen thought that international law presupposed a basic norm that 'a State is legally obliged to comport itself in the manner in which other States habitually comport themselves' (the norm about the formation of custom through practice and *opinio iuris*).[53] Hart disparaged this as 'a mere useless reduplication of the fact that a set of rules are accepted by states as binding rules'; he thought international law lacked a rule of recognition altogether and hence was not truly a 'system' at all.[54] A further problem with Kelsen's postulated basic norm is that it leaves open the question of how to know what 'a State' is.

So an axiom beyond which one will not look, such as a rule of recognition or basic norm, offers a solution of a sort, but it requires one to hypothesize an extra component of the system whose existence and substance are in doubt. It is also not very different from pursuing the process of infinite regress back to a certain point and then suspending judgment.

[49] Sextus Empiricus (n 45) pt I.167, further pts I.135–40.

[50] Hans Kelsen, *General Theory of Law and State* (Anders Wedberg tr, Harvard UP 1949) 111.

[51] HLA Hart, *The Concept of Law* (first published 1961, 3rd edn, OUP 2012) 94. The term 'rule of recognition' is not to be confused with the term I will use for one of the rules about statehood, the 'recognition norm'.

[52] The International Law Commission has observed that 'fundamental principles of the international legal order are not based on any special source of law or specific law-making procedure, in contrast with rules of constitutional character in internal legal systems': Articles on Responsibility of States for Internationally Wrongful Acts [2001] 2(2) ILC Ybk 26, commentary to art 12, para 7.

[53] Hans Kelsen, 'Théorie du droit international public' (1953) 84 Recueil des cours 1, 129 (translation). See further Jochen von Bernstorff, *The Public International Law Theory of Hans Kelsen* (CUP 2010) 160–5.

[54] Hart (n 51) 236.

The remaining solution to what makes norms of international law valid is circularity. This embraces the apparent paradox at the root of the system of international legal norms. There are customary norms defining certain entities as states and giving them certain attributes; among those attributes is their role in forming state practice and *opinio iuris*, which—circularly—gives rise to customary norms. Custom creates states; states create custom. To call a norm 'valid' means that it is derived directly or indirectly from this self-reproducing circle of conditional statements. This concept of validity applies system-wide.

Like all the other possible solutions, this is not intuitively satisfactory. In other contexts logical circularity is deprecated.[55] But a legal system, as an intellectual structure with its own self-contained logical framework, has a certain circularity built into it. Its norms exist within this internal framework; they even construct their own internal version of the facts—'a world of their own'.[56] Their logic is their own internal logic, to be justified by reference only to itself rather than some extra-legal standard. In a way, accepting that validity is based on circular reasoning (like the other solutions) involves a suspension of judgment: it means refusing to say whether or not norms are 'valid' in any sense that is external to the self-contained logical framework of international law and insisting, instead, that questions about validity only make sense *within* that framework. Still, this is the least unsatisfactory solution to the problem. It reflects what international lawyers actually do: they answer questions about the validity of this or that particular norm on the basis of consistency with the rest of the system of norms, not by testing them against an extra-legal standard.

Moreover, this approach does not postulate an extra component of the system—a basic norm or rule of recognition—whose existence and substance are in doubt. It points to norms whose existence is already widely acknowledged or assumed and shows that they form a self-reproducing circle. In international law, instead of a single basic norm, there is thus a basic *circle* of norms from which other valid norms are derived, which includes a norm that custom creates states and a norm that states create custom. This approach to validity can be placed in the same broad tradition as Kelsen and Hart, because it shares the idea that a legal system decides for itself what counts as a valid norm within that system—either through a basic norm or rule of recognition or in a circular fashion—rather than relying on an extra-legal standard.[57] (A qualification here is that Hart's rule of recognition is a

[55] An image of logical circularity that is sometimes evoked is of Baron Münchhausen, as fictionalized in eighteenth-century tall tales, lifting himself out of the swamp by his own hair. The choice between infinite regress, an axiom, and circularity has been called the 'Münchhausen trilemma': Hans Albert, *Treatise on Critical Reason* (first published 1968, Mary Varney Rorty tr, Princeton UP 1985) 18.

[56] FH Lawson, 'The creative use of legal concepts' (1957) 32 New York University Law Review 909, 913; this book s 1.1.3.

[57] My approach is influenced by—though it is not strictly an application of—the view of social systems theorists that 'validity is circularity': Niklas Luhmann, 'The self-reproduction of law and its limits' in Gunther Teubner (ed), *Dilemmas of Law in the Welfare State* (de Gruyter 1988) 111, 115 (emphasis removed). On one formulation of the social systems view, a statute in domestic law may acquire

channel through which the concept of validity as it exists within the system is open to external social pressure.)

Although not an element of their personality, this attribute of states—that they contribute to custom and in that respect form part of a self-reproducing basic circle of norms—is critical to the existence of valid rights and duties in the first place and hence to the existence of personality. The perpetual motion of this circle is what keeps the system running.

3.1.4 Whether effectiveness is sufficient

The method by which effectiveness creates statehood can now be summarized as follows. One: there is a norm defining as a state any entity that meets effectiveness criteria, a purely factual and automatic test. Two: there are norms giving customary rights and other relations to every entity so defined, thereby according states personality. Three: there is a norm that the practice and *opinio iuris* of these entities contribute to customary norms, which, circularly, is how all these norms acquire their validity within the internal framework of international law.

The effectiveness-only view makes two claims about this method. These are encapsulated by a formulation of the view given by WE Hall: entities enter 'of right into the family of states' and must be treated in conformity with international law 'from the moment, and from the moment only, at which they acquire the marks of a state'.[58] The first claim made here is that entities become states 'from the moment' they become effective: effectiveness is *sufficient* for statehood. The second claim is that they become states from that moment 'only': effectiveness is also *necessary* for statehood. Having analysed what the effectiveness-only view implies about what statehood is, I now turn to the evidence for each of these claims, starting with the claim that effectiveness is sufficient for statehood.

State practice and *opinio iuris* consistent with this claim can be found even where they might not be expected: among Western states in the nineteenth century, when a competing view (the recognition-only view) was emerging. In 1822, President James Monroe proposed that the United States recognize Argentina, Chile, Gran Colombia, and Mexico, which had all purported to secede unilaterally

'validity only through the judge's act, the validity of which can in turn be established only by reference to a statute': Gunther Teubner, *Law as an Autopoietic System* (Anne Bankowska and Ruth Adler trs, Blackwell 1993) 42. This leaves no room for a hierarchy of norms, because their validity always depends on other norms, and so Kelsen's idea of a basic norm is rejected: Niklas Luhmann, *Law as a Social System* (first published 1993, Klaus Ziegert tr, OUP 2004) 103. But even the social systems view has basic parallels with Kelsen: Richard Nobles and David Schiff, *A Sociology of Jurisprudence* (Hart 2006) 128. See also Stefan Oeter, 'International law and general systems theory' (2001) 44 German Yearbook of International Law 72, 87.

[58] WE Hall, *A Treatise on International Law* (4th edn, Clarendon 1895) pt 2.

from Spain.[59] After Spain protested, the US secretary of state, John Quincy Adams, gave this defence of the policy of recognizing effective entities:

> the United States, far from consulting the dictates of a policy . . . yielded to an obligation of duty of the highest order, by recognizing as Independent States, Nations which, after deliberately asserting their right to that character, have maintained and established it against all the resistance which had been or could be brought to oppose it. This recognition . . . is the mere acknowledgment of existing facts . . .[60]

Mikulas Fabry argues that this policy of recognizing effective entities was '[c]rafted by early nineteenth-century American and British foreign policy-makers in response to unilateral secessions in Latin America' and 'was gradually adopted by other powers'.[61] He traces the spread of the practice to entities in Europe, where, for instance, recognition of Belgium 'entered the diplomatic agenda only with the strong prospect of its *de facto* independence' in 1830–31.[62] But caution is needed here. This might be taken to indicate that effectiveness, rather than dynastic legitimacy or consent by the parent state or something else, was a test that existing states applied when they decided *whether or not to grant recognition*. That is certainly consistent with the claim that effectiveness is sufficient for statehood. But it is not compelling evidence for that claim, because it may still be consistent with the possibility that effective entities did not acquire statehood until they were recognized.[63]

Finding compelling evidence that effectiveness is sufficient for statehood is not easy. Today, as among Western states in the nineteenth century, most states are clearly effective and are also universally recognized. Their statehood is consistent with all four of the views I will discuss: since both the potentially decisive factors are present, there is no way to tell whether either factor on its own is necessary or sufficient. Evidence for the claim that effectiveness is sufficient can, however, be found where an effective entity that is *not* recognized is in practice treated as having the rights and other relations of states.

For instance, during the Cold War there were a number of effective entities aligned with either the Soviet Union or the United States that were not recognized by states in the opposing bloc; states in the opposing bloc tended to treat these entities as states in practice. In 1968, the United States accused North Korea of

[59] Mikulas Fabry, *Recognizing States: International Society and the Establishment of New States since 1776* (OUP 2010) ch 2.

[60] John Quincy Adams, Letter to Joaquin de Andagua (6 April 1822) in William R Manning (ed), *Diplomatic Correspondence of the United States Concerning the Independence of the Latin American Nations* (OUP 1925) vol 1, 156, 157.

[61] Fabry (n 59) 49, 69.

[62] Ibid, 82.

[63] See further Thomas D Grant, *The Recognition of States: Law and Practice in Debate and Evolution* (Praeger 1999) ch 4 ('Criteria for recognition or criteria for statehood?').

committing an 'offence against international law' by attacking a US ship—implying that North Korea, which it did not recognize, nonetheless had the duties of a state.[64] In 1973, the constitutional court of West Germany made observations that explicitly confirmed that effectiveness is sufficient for statehood:

> In international law terms the GDR [East Germany] is a State and as such a subject of international law. This observation is independent of any recognition of the GDR, under international law, by the Federal Republic [West Germany]. Not only has the FRG [West Germany] not formally given such recognition but it has expressly withheld it.[65]

Despite this non-recognition, the Germanies had agreed to 'proceed on the principle that the sovereign jurisdiction of each of the two States is confined to its own territory' and to 'respect each other's independence and autonomy in their internal and external affairs'.[66]

Further evidence can be drawn from the violent collapse of Yugoslavia[67] in the early 1990s. Four of its subentities, the constituent republics of Slovenia, Croatia, Macedonia, and Bosnia,[68] declared independence as new states. An entity comprising the remaining constituent republics, which to avoid ambiguity I will call Serbia-Montenegro,[69] initially claimed to be the legal continuation of the old Yugoslavia; but this claim was rejected by other states and by the Badinter Commission[70] and in 2000 was abandoned.[71] The result, in sum, was that the old

64 Arthur J Goldberg, US, in SC 1388th mtg (26 January 1968) UN doc S/PV.1388, para 85. See further 'The crisis in Korea' (1968) 58 US Department of State Bulletin 188.

65 *Re Treaty on the Basis of Relations between the Federal Republic of Germany and the German Democratic Republic, 1972* (Federal Constitutional Court, Federal Republic of Germany) (1973) 73 ILR 149, 165–6.

66 Treaty on the Basis of Intra-German Relations (21 December 1972) 12 ILM 16, art 6. The court thought this at most amounted to '*de facto* recognition of a special kind': *Re Treaty on the Basis of Relations* (1973) 73 ILR 149, 166. See further Christian Tomuschat, 'Recognition of new States—the case of premature recognition' in Peter Hipold (ed), *Kosovo and International Law: the ICJ Advisory Opinion of 22 July 2010* (Nijhoff 2012) 31, 31–2. The situation in Germany between 1945 and 1990 raised a number of unique complications, on which see Crawford, *Creation* (n 9) 452–66, who concludes that there may have been *three* Germanies.

67 Known by various official names until 1963 and after that as the Socialist Federal Republic of Yugoslavia.

68 Officially Bosnia and Herzegovina. On the statehood of these entities, see this book s 4.1.1.

69 Officially the Federal Republic of Yugoslavia until 2003 and then the State Union of Serbia and Montenegro until 2006, when Montenegro became independent.

70 *Opinion No 8* (Badinter Commission) (1992) 92 ILR 199, para 4; *Opinion No 9* (Badinter Commission) (1992) 92 ILR 203; *Opinion No 11* (Badinter Commission) (1993) 96 ILR 719, paras 2, 7. See further Grant, *Recognition* (n 63) ch 6; Crawford, *Creation* (n 9) 186–9, 395–401. Since many states withheld recognition from Serbia-Montenegro during this dispute but nonetheless treated it as a state, it might be cited in support of the view that effectiveness is sufficient for statehood. But the complex dispute about continuity muddies its usefulness as evidence.

71 Application of the Federal Republic of Yugoslavia for Admission to Membership in the United Nations (30 October 2000) UN doc S/2000/1043: with this, Serbia-Montenegro accepted that it was a new state.

state ceased to exist in international law and was replaced by five new states. Of interest is the delayed recognition of Macedonia. It effectively became independent on 17 November 1991.[72] Most states withheld recognition from it until 1993 because of a dispute about its name, which it shared with the ancient Hellenistic kingdom and a region of modern Greece.[73] But in the meantime they still referred to it as a 'state': members of the European Community declared themselves 'willing to recognise *that State* as a sovereign and independent State, within its existing borders, and under a name that can be accepted by all parties concerned'.[74] Jure Vidmar comments that this 'use of the term "State" rather than, for example, "entity" clearly implies that Macedonia's attributes of statehood were not in dispute; it was simply that the EC did not want to enter into relations with Macedonia under its constitutional name'.[75] Matthew Craven writes that the alternative view (that Macedonia did not acquire statehood until it was recognized) 'is difficult to square with general State practice as regards Yugoslavia and would leave open the status of the territory after the dissolution of [the old Yugoslavia] and before [the Republic of Macedonia's] recognition'.[76]

Examples such as these support the claim, inherent in the effectiveness-only view and widely accepted, that effectiveness suffices for statehood even without recognition.

3.1.5 Whether effectiveness is necessary

Evidence that effectiveness is sufficient for statehood goes only halfway towards establishing the effectiveness-only view. The traditional name of this view—the 'declaratory' theory—emphasizes that recognition merely 'declares' a state to exist rather than directly determining whether one exists; by eliminating recognition as a means of acquiring statehood, this implies that effectiveness is the *only* such means—that effectiveness is *necessary* for statehood. This claim poses much greater

[72] *Opinion No 11* (1993) 96 ILR 719, para 5.

[73] Roland Rich, 'Recognition of states: The collapse of Yugoslavia and the Soviet Union' (1993) 4 EJIL 36, 51–3; *Application of the Interim Accord of 13 September 1995 (the former Yugoslav Republic of Macedonia v Greece)* [2011] ICJ Rep 644. Under a treaty with Greece it has now changed its name to 'North Macedonia': Final Agreement for the Settlement of the Differences as Described in the United Nations Security Council Resolutions 817 (1993) and 845 (1993), the Termination of the Interim Accord of 1995, and the Establishment of a Strategic Partnership between the Parties, Prespa (17 June 2018) art 1(3).

[74] European Community, Declaration on the former Yugoslav Republic of Macedonia (1–2 May 1992) in Christopher Hill and Karen Smith (eds), *European Foreign Policy: Key Documents* (Routledge 2000) 376 (emphasis added).

[75] Jure Vidmar, 'Explaining the legal effects of recognition' (2012) 61 ICLQ 361, 374. Compare Raič (n 38) 106; Christian Hillgruber, 'The admission of new states to the international community' (1998) 9 EJIL 491, 498–9.

[76] Matthew Craven, 'What's in a name? The former Yugoslav Republic of Macedonia and issues of statehood' (1995) 16 Australian Yearbook of International Law 199, 209 n 76.

evidential difficulty than the claim that effectiveness is sufficient. The difficulty is that some entities that are universally accepted as states meet the effectiveness criteria only on a very generous or apparently inconsistent interpretation.

Somalia in the 1990s has been described by Gérard Kreijen as 'a nail in the coffin of the declaratory theory', at odds with the assumption of the effectiveness-only view 'that a State ceases to exist if it loses the basic requirements of statehood'.[77] For much of the civil war that began in 1990–91, Somalia had no functional central government to speak of, maintained no embassies, did not present credentials at the United Nations, and was likewise absent from other international organizations.[78] One region (which I will discuss later[79]) purported to secede unilaterally under the name 'Republic of Somaliland'. In 1992, a British judge in *Somalia v Woodhouse Drake and Carey* concluded, on the basis of a letter written by the Foreign Office, that 'Her Majesty's Government does not consider that there is at present any effective government in Somalia'.[80] Yet although Somalia to all appearances failed the criterion of government, no other state ceased to recognize it as a state.[81]

Crawford argues that in Somalia 'the existence of territory and people have compensated for the virtual absence of a central government'.[82] But no one suggests that it is *generally* true that only a territory and population are necessary for statehood; that would be to abandon the criterion of government and would make the criteria impractically vague. So one must explain what special feature makes Somalia different.

The explanation heard most often is that there is a difference between an entity that is trying to establish itself as a new state and an *existing* state that is trying to survive. A state can survive 'even a period of anarchy and absence of government, provided that such period is temporary'.[83] In other words, there is a presumption that an existing state retains its effectiveness. That makes practical sense; international law might become chaotic if states legally ceased to exist as soon as they were engulfed by civil war. It might be compared to another circumstance in which a state may cease to have its own government and yet legally survive: where it falls under belligerent occupation by a foreign power.[84] But Somalia is not a case of belligerent occupation. And a period of ten or twenty or more years is hardly

77 Gerard Kreijen, *State Failure, Sovereignty and Effectiveness: Legal Lessons from the Decolonization of Sub-Saharan Africa* (Nijhoff 2004) 355.

78 Ibid, 71–2, further 66–73, 353–6; Anonymous, 'Government recognition in Somalia and regional political stability in the Horn of Africa' (2002) 40 Journal of Modern African Studies 247.

79 This book s 4.3. Along with Somaliland, another comparatively orderly region was Puntland.

80 *Somalia v Woodhouse Drake and Carey (Suisse) SA* (Queen's Bench, England) (1992) 94 ILR 609, 619.

81 John Dugard, 'The secession of states and their recognition in the wake of Kosovo' (2013) 357 Recueil des cours 9, 60.

82 Crawford, *Creation* (n 9) 223.

83 Krystyna Marek, *Identity and Continuity of States in Public International Law* (2nd edn, Librairie Droz 1968) 188. Compare Hall (n 58) pt 2.

84 Marek (n 83) 189, further 73–126.

'temporary'—or at least, it can be said to have been temporary only in hindsight, after the eventual re-establishment of a central government.[85]

Vaughan Lowe suggests that the 'road to Statehood is a one-way street'; once 'an entity has become a State it will remain one, no matter how useless and ineffectual its government might become'.[86] On this approach, existing states are not merely presumed to retain their effectiveness; the presumption is seemingly permanent. But states historically have ceased to exist. This sometimes happens by consent, as with Czechoslovakia at the beginning of 1993, but not always.[87] The Badinter Commission found that 'the existence *or disappearance* of the State is a question of fact' and that 'the demise of [Yugoslavia] . . . resulted not from an agreement between the parties but from a process of disintegration that lasted some time'.[88] Whether or not the Commission was correct that the old Yugoslavia ceased to exist in this way in 1992, there is support for its assertion that in principle the disappearance of a state is 'a question of fact'—of a lack of effectiveness. Talmon, for example, observes that statehood 'describes a state of affairs, not a one-off event; therefore, the criteria for statehood serve as a test for both the creation and the continued existence of the State'.[89] If this were wrong—if effectiveness were a test solely for *new* states—some other test would then be needed to explain why Somalia could continue to exist as a state but Yugoslavia could not.

Somalia, then, exemplifies the scenario where an existing state that previously met the effectiveness criteria apparently ceases to meet them and yet survives as a state.

Another scenario is where an entity that is treated as a state never meets the criteria in the first place, except on a very generous interpretation. This is exemplified by the Vatican City, the entity ruled by the Pope that was established in 1929 by the Lateran Pacts with Italy[90] (there is some uncertainty about its relationship with a pre-existing entity, the Holy See, but I will deal with that question later[91]). Ostensibly a state, the Vatican City has a territory of 44 hectares, composed of a few buildings in Rome; it has a population of a few hundred, composed almost solely of clergy, members of religious orders, and Swiss Guards; it relies on Italy for

[85] After a decade of transition, a new government was formed in 2012: SC res 2067 (18 September 2012, Somalia). Some months later it was announced 'that, for the first time since 1991, the United States recognizes the Government of Somalia': US Department of State, 'Somalia President Hassan Sheikh Mohamud's visit to Washington, DC' (press release, 17 January 2013).

[86] Lowe (n 8) 165.

[87] Czechoslovakia's two successor states treated the old state as ceasing to exist: Michael P Scharf, 'Musical chairs: The dissolution of States and membership in the United Nations' (1995) 28 Cornell International Law Journal 29, 65–7.

[88] *Opinion No 1* (1991) 92 ILR 162, 164–5 (emphasis added); *Opinion No 11* (1993) 96 ILR 719, 721.

[89] Talmon, 'Constitutive' (n 6) 124; he cites other authorities at 124 n 147.

[90] Kurt Martens, 'The position of the Holy See and Vatican City State in international relations' (2006) 83 University of Detroit Mercy Law Review 729, 740–2; John R Morss, 'The international legal status of the Vatican/Holy See complex' (2015) 26 EJIL 927, 941–5.

[91] This book s 5.2.

police, communications, water, and sanitation; and it exists mainly to serve purposes of the Roman Catholic Church rather than purposes usually associated with statehood, such as governing a permanent population.[92] Crawford observes that its status 'is peculiar and that the criteria for statehood in its case are only marginally (if at all) complied with' and proffers an explanation that is the converse of what he says about Somalia: 'the strength and influence of the government—the Holy See—have compensated for a tiny territory and the lack of a permanent population'.[93] The Vatican City is, in his parlance, an entity recognized as a state 'for special reasons'.[94] It is the most striking example from among a number of tiny states that appear to fall short of the criteria; another, which I will discuss later, is Monaco.

It does not follow from all this that the effectiveness-only view is incapable of explaining entities such as Somalia, the Vatican City, and Monaco. But possible explanations tend to burden this view with caveats such that it looks less like an automatically applicable general rule.

The explanations that I have mentioned so far might suggest that there is not a single, standardized test of effectiveness but a sort of sliding scale, applicable differently in different scenarios: there might be a special set of criteria, de-emphasizing government, for existing states such as Somalia that lose their effectiveness; there might be another set of criteria for the unique circumstances of the Vatican City; it is sometimes also argued that the criteria are less strict in cases involving self-determination and more strict in cases of unilateral secession (though I leave these scenarios aside for Chapter 4). Already a little vague, the effectiveness criteria become hard to apply to novel scenarios in a predictable manner.

A slightly different explanation might be that, even in ambiguous cases, recognition or non-recognition functions as state practice and *opinio iuris* and, as such, can provide evidence of whether an entity meets the customary criteria of effectiveness—or can even recalibrate the customary criteria to make the entity fit. For example, when states continued to recognize Somalia despite the ambiguity about whether it met the criterion of government, that could have resolved the ambiguity. Statehood still depends on the criteria, but recognition provides evidence of how the criteria are to be applied in novel situations.[95] This explanation accords with how custom ordinarily works and must be accepted up to a point. But *only* up to a point: there are two reasons it is not totally satisfactory. First, if it is used to explain very difficult cases such as Somalia, the result is that *in practice*, whenever statehood is genuinely in doubt, recognition becomes a much more useful guide

[92] Crawford, *Creation* (n 9) 222–5.
[93] Ibid, 223.
[94] Ibid, 221.
[95] Compare ibid, 93: recognition, 'while in principle declaratory', may be 'important evidence of legal status'. But Crawford adds that it 'may be constitutive of legal obligation for the recognizing or acquiescing State', so this could be read as a gesture towards the effectiveness-or-recognition view, as I will discuss.

than the criteria. This seems to defeat the point of having an automatically applicable general rule, because the rule is liable to be altered to suit each situation in an inconsistent and unpredictable way. Second, although acts of recognition may function as state practice and *opinio iuris* where they form a pattern evidencing a general rule, it must be doubted whether that remains true when they depart radically from the pattern that is usually observed. Ordinarily, practice must be 'of such a character as to make it possible to discern a virtually uniform usage'.[96] Some 'inconsistencies and contradictions'—terms that might describe recognitions at odds with the usual pattern—do not threaten the existence of a customary norm, but nor do they necessarily recalibrate the norm.[97] This is especially so when, as in the case of Somalia, there is an abundance of wider evidence indicating that effectiveness requires a government.

So these attempts to explain how the effectiveness criteria operate in difficult cases, though plausible, are somewhat self-defeating: they defend the existence of an effectiveness norm by undermining its practical usefulness as a predictor of statehood. I emphasize that I am not rejecting them outright. They are not inconsistent with the view that I will later adopt, which is that recognition sometimes *directly* creates statehood rather than merely evidencing it. But when I come to that later stage of the discussion, it will be seen that my view largely removes the need to make self-defeating arguments to defend the effectiveness norm. Perhaps counterintuitively, my view enables the effectiveness norm to be more predictable and stable: since recognition provides an alternative path to statehood, novel or difficult cases can be resolved without having to recalibrate the criteria sporadically to suit them.

For now, I draw the following conclusions about the claims made by the effectiveness-only view. There is evidence that meeting effectiveness criteria is sufficient for statehood. The claim that this is also necessary for statehood is not clearly wrong, but it has explanatory weaknesses that justify continuing the search for a more satisfactory approach.

3.2 The view that only recognition is necessary

The traditional competitor of the declaratory theory is usually called the constitutive theory. But it would be more accurate to describe the constitutive theory as a family of theories. The strictest version of it says that recognition is sufficient

[96] Conclusions on Identification of Customary International Law [2018] 2(2) ILC Ybk, UN doc A/73/10, commentary to conclusion 8, para 2, citing *North Sea Continental Shelf (Federal Republic of Germany/Denmark; Federal Republic of Germany/Netherlands)* [1969] ICJ Rep 3, paras 74, 77.

[97] Conclusions on Identification of Customary International Law, commentary to conclusion 8, para 7, citing *Military and Paramilitary Activities in and against Nicaragua (Nicaragua v US)* [1986] ICJ Rep 14, para 186.

and necessary for statehood and that effectiveness is irrelevant. This strict version is what I will call the 'recognition-only' view of statehood. It conflicts with a conclusion I have already drawn: that effectiveness, even in the absence of recognition, is sufficient for statehood. But I will still give this view a hearing, both because it was widely held for a long time and to highlight which of its features do or do not lead to theoretical problems. It will become evident that the problematic features are not shared by the very different approach to recognition that I will eventually adopt.

In the era of universalist natural law and the early phases of positivism, Western international lawyers did not theorize about recognition.[98] They tended to believe in dynastic legitimacy: monarchs had a hereditary authority to rule that was equated with ownership of land and that was unaffected by internal strife or external attack.[99] Samuel von Pufendorf, for example, wrote that a king 'need not obtain the consent and approval of other kings or states, before he may carry himself like a king and be regarded as such' and that for a foreigner to question his sovereignty 'would entail an injury'.[100] The positivist principle of consent 'was not yet allowed to extend to the field of recognition'.[101] But positivism eventually became more dogmatic, as I discussed in Chapter 2 in connection with non-Western state-like entities.[102] Dynastic legitimacy also came under challenge, both from liberal thinkers, such as John Locke, Montesquieu, and Immanuel Kant, and from France under the leadership of Napoleon, who founded new republics and monarchies—client entities—all over Europe.[103] These developments led rulers to seek guidance on changes to governments and states that the belief in dynastic legitimacy could no longer convincingly provide.[104]

The seed of the recognition-only view came from GWF Hegel.[105] He thought that an individual's 'personality' (which in this context does not necessarily mean legal personality in my sense) could be constituted only by being acknowledged by another formally equal 'personality'. Just as a community was composed of individuals, individuality required the existence of a community. Hegel applied similar reasoning to states, which were analogous to individuals in that legally they were formal equals. He distinguished their internal from their external aspects. The legitimacy of a state, including its authority to conduct foreign relations, was an

[98] CH Alexandrowicz, 'Theory of recognition *in fieri*' (1958) 34 BYIL 176, 176.

[99] Grant, *Recognition* (n 63) 8–9.

[100] Samuel von Pufendorf, *De jure naturae et gentium* (first published 1672, CH Oldfather tr, Clarendon 1934) pt VIII.III.9.

[101] Alexandrowicz, 'Theory' (n 98) 191.

[102] See further Fabry (n 59) 23–4.

[103] Alexandrowicz, 'Theory' (n 98) 196; Grant, *Recognition* (n 63) 8–9.

[104] Alexandrowicz, 'Theory' (n 98) 196.

[105] See further ibid, 195; Hersch Lauterpacht, *Recognition in International Law* (first published 1947, CUP 2013) 38; Rose Parfitt, 'Theorizing recognition and international personality' in Florian Hoffmann and Anne Orford (eds), *The Oxford Handbook of the Theory of International Law* (OUP 2016) 583, 585–6.

internal matter, presumably reflected in its domestic law. But it was 'equally essential that this legitimacy should be *supplemented* by recognition on the part of other states'.[106] It was only by external recognition that a state could be constituted on the international plane. Hegel concluded:

> Without relations with other states, the state can no more be an actual individual than an individual can be an actual person without a relationship with other persons. . . . When Napoleon said before the Peace of Campo Formio 'the French Republic is no more in need of recognition than the sun is', his words conveyed no more than that strength of existence which itself carries with it a guarantee of recognition . . .[107]

In other words, although some entities are strong or important enough that others have little practical choice but to recognize them, it is still by recognition that they are constituted as states.

Early debates about recognition did not always distinguish between new states and new *governments*. In the terms that international lawyers would use today, Hegel's anecdote about Napoleon was not about recognition of a new state; the French First Republic was legally the same France as that over which Louis XVI had reigned, just with a new form of government. International law treats a state as continuing to exist—as the same entity but with features that vary over time—despite changes of government as dramatic as Russia's transformation from a dynastic empire into the Soviet Union and later into a federation lacking a quarter of its former territory. Thus Russia retains the permanent seat on the Security Council that the text of the UN Charter describes as belonging to the Soviet Union.[108] Today, although states sometimes explicitly recognize new governments of other states, international lawyers mostly agree that all that a government requires is secure factual control of all or most of a state's territory; recognition of a government is 'declaratory' of an existing situation.[109]

DP O'Connell thought the distinction between changes of statehood and of government 'often wears thin to the point of disappearance' and that there was

[106] GWF Hegel, *Elements of the Philosophy of Right* (first published 1821, HB Nisbet tr, CUP 1991) 366–7.

[107] Ibid.

[108] Charter of the United Nations (26 June 1945) art 23(1); Ulrich Fastenrath, 'Article 3' in Bruno Simma and others (eds), *The Charter of the United Nations: A Commentary* (3rd edn, OUP 2012) 335, para 10. See further Scharf (n 87) 43–52.

[109] In the seminal case, which concerned a revolutionary government of Costa Rica, the arbitrator held that although non-recognition of a government 'is usually appropriate evidence that it has not attained the independence and control entitling it by international law to be classed as such', non-recognition could not outweigh evidence 'as to the *de facto* character of Tinoco's government, according to the standard set by international law': *Tinoco (UK/Costa Rica)* (1923) 1 UNRIAA 369, 381. See further Stefan Talmon, *Recognition of Governments in International Law with Particular Reference to Governments in Exile* (OUP 1998).

'pressure in the direction of assimilating these two categories of events'.[110] But the two questions are about different things and may have different answers. Whether a state exists is about whether international law accords an entity particular rights and other attributes. Who constitutes the government of a state affects which conduct counts as conduct by that state, including for the purposes of determining whether the state has acted unlawfully; for instance, it is relevant to which 'organs' count under the norm that the 'conduct of any State organ shall be considered an act of that State under international law'.[111] But norms about governments do not concern *whether or not* an entity is a state; they are only indirectly relevant to personality.

In its mature form, the recognition-only view concerns states, not governments. Henry Wheaton has been identified as the first to articulate the constitutive theory in this mature form, in 1846.[112] It is encapsulated in Lassa Oppenheim's assertion that a 'State is and becomes an International Person through recognition only and exclusively'.[113]

Some theories that are described as constitutive may forbid or require recognition depending on whether an entity meets the criteria of territory, population, government, and independence: Chen even describes this as one of the standard features of constitutivism.[114] But I will deal with that view under the next heading. What I am concerned with here is the purer view that recognition *alone* is sufficient and necessary for statehood. On this view, as Wheaton wrote, every 'State is at liberty to grant, or refuse . . . recognition, subject to the consequences of its own conduct in this respect'; and as James Lorimer remarked, each 'State is to say, not only whether or not a given community fulfils the requirements of international existence, but is, moreover, left to determine what these requirements are'.[115] Thus if states continued to recognize anarchic Somalia in the 1990s, that was a choice they were legally empowered to make or not to make. Equally, if states do not recognize an entity such as the one in Oregon that claimed to be 'God's Government on Earth', which issued its own driving licences to 'citizens of Heaven' and promoted tax fraud,[116] that is just because they choose not to: international law says that in principle they could grant recognition.

This means that on the recognition-only view states lack one of the attributes of statehood that I introduced earlier: they do not cohere into a class of facts. This is

[110] DP O'Connell, *State Succession in Municipal Law and International Law* (CUP 1967) vol 1, 6–7; Crawford, *Creation* (n 9) 34–5 criticizes this argument.

[111] Articles on Responsibility of States, art 4, further arts 5–11.

[112] Henry Wheaton, *Elements of International Law* (3rd edn, Lea & Blanchard 1846) pt I.II.6; Alexandrowicz, 'Theory' (n 98) 195; CH Alexandrowicz, 'The Afro-Asian world and the law of nations (historical aspects)' (1968) 123 Recueil des cours 117, 127.

[113] LFL Oppenheim, *International Law* (Longmans, Green, & Co 1905–6) pt 71.

[114] Chen (n 9) 54–5.

[115] Wheaton (n 112) pt I.II.6; James Lorimer, *The Institutes of the Law of Nations: A Treatise of the Jural Relations of Separate Political Communities* (William Blackwood & Sons 1883–84) 107.

[116] *US v Stoll* (US District Court WD Wash civ no C05-0262RSM, 7 June 2005).

not to deny that they *are* facts (they must still be legally constructed as facts, as with anything else), but unlike on the effectiveness-only view they do not necessarily have anything factual in common. States retain, though in a different way, the two other attributes: they possess a package of customary rights and other relations, and they contribute to custom.

So where do the relations of states—including the rights and duties that compose their personality—now come from? On this view they are created not by a norm defining a class of facts but by the exercise of a Hohfeldian power (an entity's ability to create or to change rights or other relations[117]). More precisely, they are created by the exercise of what might be called 'contractual' powers.

WN Hohfeld analysed the formation of a contract under a domestic common-law system as the exercise of powers.[118] This example of how contractual powers work can be adapted to the formation of a treaty between two states in international law. First, one state consents to the terms of a proposed treaty.[119] In a common-law system, this would be called an offer. It is the exercise of a power to grant to another state an unconditional power to bring into being the rights and other relations in the treaty. Second, the other state consents, which amounts to an exercise of that unconditional power to create the treaty relations. Although these events are easier to disaggregate when they are separated in time, it does not matter if both states consent practically simultaneously.[120] The point is that a state has a power to create relations whose force is conditional on the exercise of a power by another state.[121] This is a contractual power. Each side also has a correlative contractual susceptibility.

On the recognition-only view of statehood, international law *as a whole* is contractual. Its contractual foundations are emphasized, for example, by Robert Redslob:

> international law, which is contractual and which in consequence has the inherent freedom to extend itself to partners of its choice, encompasses certain States within its community and does not welcome certain others. . . . [R]ecognition . . . is defined as the extension of the community of international

[117] Hohfeld, 'Conceptions [part 1]' (n 23) 44.
[118] Ibid, 49.
[119] Vienna Convention on the Law of Treaties (23 May 1969) 1155 UNTS 331, arts 11–15.
[120] At common law, offer and acceptance are generally analysed as if they are separated in time. It has been noted that the formality of consenting to a treaty generally 'renders superfluous any enquiry into the steps by which its precise terms were arrived at', so 'the familiar common-law concepts of offer and acceptance . . . usually have no role', though they probably exist 'in the background': Hugh Thirlway, *The Law and Procedure of the International Court of Justice: Fifty Years of Jurisprudence* (first published 1989–2011, OUP 2013) 332, 1294. Compare Martins Paparinskis, 'Regulating treaties: A comparative perspective' in Christian J Tams, Antonios Tzanakopoulos, and Andreas Zimmermann (eds), *Research Handbook on the Law of Treaties* (Elgar 2014) 39, 62–3.
[121] Compare 'bilateral powers' as defined in Neil MacCormick, *Institutions of Law: An Essay in Legal Theory* (OUP 2007) 172.

law to a new State, not a member until then. . . . Recognition is thus an agreement between the parties involved, more precisely a fundamental pact that puts into force a system of law.[122]

Note that, despite their similar positivist origins and terminology, this contractual view of statehood is not necessarily tied to the contractual view of custom discussed in the previous chapter (the view that an entity is not bound by a customary norm unless it has consented specifically to that norm). It is compatible with the legislative view of custom that prevails today. An entity may make an overarching contract to 'join' international law—recognition—and under the terms of this contract the entity is generally bound by customary norms even if it has not contributed to their formation or otherwise specifically consented to them.

On this view, the acquisition of the customary rights and other relations of states by the exercise of contractual powers might be analysed as follows. First, an entity claims to be a state. That is a sort of offer. It amounts to claiming to have the customary rights and other relations of a state, and since these must correlate with the customary duties and so on of *other* states, it entails impliedly recognizing the statehood of one or more other entities. Second, one of those other entities recognizes the claimant entity. They have now exercised contractual powers to grant each other the customary relations of states. It is as if they have created a norm in the form 'these particular entities are defined as states relative to each other', which applies for the purposes of all customary norms concerning states.

This highlights an apparent problem with the recognition-only view: its extreme relativism.

Kelsen inferred from this view that a state's international legal personality (as distinct from its 'natural' existence and its existence in domestic law) was entirely relative. It could exist 'legally only in its relations to other states' that had recognized it as a state; there could be 'no such thing as absolute existence'.[123] Kelsen was sanguine about this. Since, in the age of Albert Einstein, 'we have to acknowledge the relativity of time and space —the general conditions of natural existence—relativity of legal existence is no longer paradoxical'.[124] In Hohfeldian terms, the rights and other relations that an entity acquires by being recognized correlate solely with duties and other relations of the entities that recognize it. Others have drawn the same inference with more reluctance, for example, Hersch Lauterpacht:

[122] Robert Redslob, 'La reconnaissance de l'état comme sujet de droit international' (1934) 13 Revue de droit international 429, 431–2 (translation). The idea that recognition is an agreement is not shared by all versions of constitutivism. Versions that treat it as a unilateral act are discussed in Przemysław Saganek, *Unilateral Acts of States in International Law* (Brill 2016) 547–51.

[123] Hans Kelsen, 'Recognition in international law: Theoretical observations' (1941) 35 AJIL 605, 608–9.

[124] Ibid, 609.

> The grotesque spectacle of a community being a State in relation to some but not to other States is a grave reflection upon international law. It cannot be explained away, amidst some complacency, by questionable analogies to private law or to philosophical relativism. That paradoxical phenomenon, which more than anything else signifies the negation of the unity of international law as a system of law, may be unavoidable pending the collectivization of the process of recognition.[125]

Scholars who emphasize effectiveness dismiss this relativity as incoherent. Crawford calls it a seeming 'violation of common sense' and adds that if 'a central feature of the constitutive position is open to such criticism the position itself must be flawed'.[126] Talmon calls it the 'most compelling argument against the constitutive theory'.[127] He cites Vice-President Ammoun's separate opinion in the International Court in *Namibia*.[128] This did not concern statehood but rather an allegedly analogous question: the continuing existence of South Africa's mandate to govern Namibia, which had been granted by the League of Nations. The General Assembly of the United Nations, in lieu of the defunct League, had revoked the mandate by majority vote; a minority of UN members had opposed the revocation. How could the mandate, asked Ammoun,

> having lapsed for the quasi-unanimity of States, survive in the eyes of some others? An institution is a creature of reason which either exists or does not: it cannot at one and the same time be and not be. That would be no less curious than if a State admitted by majority vote to the United Nations should be a member for some but not for others.[129]

But a state is not a monolithic 'creature of reason which either exists or does not': I have split it into a number of attributes, one of which is a package of rights and other relations. These could be further split into relations correlating with relations of *this* particular other state, with relations of *that* particular other state, and so on. Since Hohfeldian relations are always correlative, they must of necessity exist relative to *some* entity or other. On the effectiveness-only view (according to which statehood depends on a factual and automatic test), every state has rights and duties relative to every other state. I observed in Chapter 1 that personality is *always* relative in the sense that it is always relational; it is the product of Hohfeldian

[125] Lauterpacht, *Recognition* (n 105) 78. The allusion to 'analogies to private law' was directed at Dionisio Anzilotti, *Cours de droit international* (3rd edn, Gilbert Gidel tr, Recueil Sirey 1929) vol 1, 167–8.
[126] Crawford, *Creation* (n 9) 21–2.
[127] Talmon, 'Constitutive' (n 6) 102.
[128] Ibid.
[129] *Legal Consequences for States of the Continued Presence of South Africa in Namibia (South West Africa) notwithstanding Security Council Resolution 276 (1970) (Advisory Opinion)* [1971] ICJ Rep 16, 73 (Vice-President Ammoun).

relations between entities.[130] It is just that some persons have personality relative to more entities than do other persons. This is true no matter what view is taken of statehood.

Talmon also makes a different argument against the relativism of the recognition-only view: that the 'idea of one State deciding upon another State's personality in international law is at odds with the sovereign equality of States'.[131] But on the recognition-only view, every state is in principle *equally* able to refuse recognition to every other state. If, in practice, most states do not fear being refused recognition—like Napoleon in Hegel's anecdote—that is due to their political, economic, or military importance; it has nothing to do with their equality in international law. Furthermore, 'sovereign equality' generally means legal equality in the sense that all states have an identical package of customary rights and other relations; it is an attribute that depends on statehood.[132] On the recognition-only view, entities do not *have* statehood relative to non-recognizing states and so cannot be protected by the principle of sovereign equality relative to those states. This renders international law a potentially very harsh environment, but it was harsh anyway for most of its history: until the use of force was prohibited in the mid-twentieth century, states were able to destroy each other's legal existence by war. Lauterpacht compared that with the ability of states to refuse recognition: in both cases, what was at stake was 'the right to live as an international person'.[133] What the recognition-only view implies is that states can still achieve by non-recognition what they used to be able to do with violence. Although this seems to authorize arbitrary power politics[134]—which is one reason the recognition-only view has gone out of fashion—that does not as such make it incoherent as a legal theory.

The relativism of statehood on this view does, however, have a theoretically problematic implication. This relates to the other main attribute of states: that they contribute to custom, the flipside of which is that customary norms depend on their practice and *opinio iuris*.

Imagine a simple recognition-only world in which the entities of Athens and Boeotia recognize each other as states but, although each of them taken separately may recognize additional states, there is only one other state that they *both* recognize: Corinth. Since Athens and Boeotia recognize each other, the customary norms applicable to states apply between them. But how are those norms to be identified? When the entities exercise contractual powers to grant each other the

[130] This book s 1.2.

[131] Talmon, 'Constitutive' (n 6) 102.

[132] Friendly Relations Declaration, principle *f*.

[133] Hersch Lauterpacht, 'Règles générales du droit de la paix' (1937) 62 Recueil des cours 95, 245 (translation).

[134] Compare Jean L Cohen, 'Sovereignty in the context of globalization: A constitutional pluralist perspective' in Samantha Besson and John Tasioulas (eds), *The Philosophy of International Law* (OUP 2010) 261, 264.

rights and other customary relations of states, they must tacitly agree what to count as state practice and *opinio iuris* for the purpose of identifying the applicable relations. There are only three entities that Athens and Boeotia can agree to count as states: themselves plus Corinth. So the question of what customary norms apply between Athens and Boeotia depends on the practice and *opinio iuris* of those three states. Now imagine that Athens and Corinth, as well as recognizing each other and Boeotia, both recognize an additional state: Sparta. The question of what customary norms apply between Athens and Corinth depends on the practice and *opinio iuris* of not just three but four states, which might result in a slightly or even a radically different set of norms. And so on: a different set of customary norms might apply between each pair of states.

Although adherents of the recognition-only view do not tend to spell this consequence out, it follows logically. Any two entities that recognize each other as states occupy their own parallel universe of norms.[135] If this does not result in chaos, that is because, in practice, the entities in which international lawyers are interested almost all recognize each other, so that their parallel universes are the same in most respects and divergences are negligible.[136]

The contractual foundations of international law on the recognition-only approach reinforce the idea that there can never be factual criteria restricting what entities can grant and receive recognition. Perhaps state practice and *opinio iuris* may appear to provide evidence of certain factual criteria. But if a state recognizes and is recognized by an entity that does not meet those criteria, the two entities thereby create a new parallel universe of norms and, in order to do so, must tacitly agree that the criteria do not apply for the purpose of their bilateral relations. How can these entities ignore the apparent evidence of factual criteria restricting recognition? Because whatever the entities contract, including by recognition, is the sole determinant of validity within their parallel universe; there are no absolute, meta-universal preconditions for what they can decide is valid.

This approach to validity is a key feature of the recognition-only view. It reflects the positivist idea that international law must emanate solely and directly from the free will of the states between which it applies, which was traditionally invoked to justify the role of recognition.[137] This traditional idea seems to assume that the states that create international law must, before they create it, already exist in an extra-legal or even a metaphysical sense. That sits awkwardly with my conclusion that states must be legally constructed as facts before international law can say anything about them (and therefore before they can have any influence on the law).

[135] Some strands of nineteenth-century positivism had similarities with this interpretation of the recognition-only view: see Stephen C Neff, *Justice among Nations: A History of International Law* (Harvard UP 2014) 231–43.

[136] Today, almost all UN members recognize and are recognized by all other members as states; among the few exceptions are Cyprus (not recognized by Turkey), Israel, and the two Koreas.

[137] Roland Portmann, *Legal Personality in International Law* (CUP 2010) 59–64, 90–3.

Acceptance of the broad idea that states are legally constructed, in one form or another, has contributed to the decline of the recognition-only view; the debate has moved on to *how* states are 'received and constructed by international law'.[138] On the premise that states must be legally constructed as facts, the idea that their free will is the sole determinant of validity might instead be explained on the basis of circularity: the customary norms applicable to each pair of states derive their validity from a contract between that pair of states, whose powers to make that contract are—circularly—validated by one of those customary norms. This is very similar to my explanation of validity on the effectiveness-only view. The difference is that on the effectiveness-only view there was a single concept of validity, which connected norms together systematically, whereas on the recognition-only view each parallel universe of norms contains a *separate* and potentially unique concept of validity; norms can never be described as 'valid' or 'invalid' in absolute terms.

The recognition-only approach to validity, whether in its traditional form or reinterpreted on the basis of circularity, raises doubts about whether international law as a whole—the structure made up of all these parallel universes—can meaningfully be called a legal system. Krystyna Marek remarks that the constitutive theory denies the existence of 'an objective system of law'; she wonders 'what remains of international law *qua* law' if it lacks 'an objective character and validity'.[139]

Even if these doubts about the systematicity of international law could be resolved or ignored, the recognition-only approach to validity leads to a more direct problem.

In the mid-twentieth century, the principle crystallized into custom that certain customary norms, such as the norm prohibiting the use of force, are *ius cogens* (peremptory law). In 1969, the Vienna Convention defined 'a peremptory norm of general international law' as

> a norm accepted and recognized by the international community of States as a whole as a norm from which no derogation is permitted and which can be modified only by a subsequent norm of general international law having the same character.[140]

The Convention provides that a 'treaty is void if, at the time of its conclusion, it conflicts with a peremptory norm' (subject to a savings provision insofar as the treaty is unobjectionable).[141] As suggested by the phrase 'a norm from which no derogation is permitted', the customary principle that is in part codified in this provision is not confined to treaties but applies to the exercise of powers of any sort; for example, it

[138] Jean d'Aspremont, *Epistemic Forces in International Law: Foundational Doctrines and Techniques of International Legal Argumentation* (Elgar 2015) 37.

[139] Marek (n 83) 136.

[140] Vienna Convention on Treaties, art 53.

[141] Ibid.

also applies to a unilateral declaration.[142] A pair of states can never create rights or other relations that conflict with peremptory norms, not even just between themselves; peremptory norms are absolutely valid in the sense that their validity can never be contracted out of.

If the recognition-only view were correct, the idea of peremptory norms would make no sense. Since each pair of states would have a clean slate on which to write their own rules of validity, nothing could stop them from contracting out of whatever they liked. The two ideas are logically incompatible. There is also the practical difficulty that, in a harsh recognition-only world in which entities could deny each other's statehood, peremptory norms would be futile: for instance, all that an aggressive but law-abiding state would have to do to evade the peremptory norm prohibiting the use of force might be to refuse recognition to the victim of its attack.[143]

It is the emergence of peremptory norms, then, that has finally put the recognition-only view to rest. Although the idea that the personality of states exists relative to other states is not as such theoretically problematic, and even if doubts about the systematic nature of international law could be resolved or ignored, there is now a compelling reason to dismiss this view: it is incompatible with a principle that can clearly be observed to operate in international law. This corroborates the evidence I cited that effectiveness is sufficient for statehood by showing that statehood cannot depend solely on recognition.

3.3 The view that both effectiveness and recognition are necessary

This leaves open the possibility that recognition plays a more limited role. Some approaches claim that effectiveness is necessary for statehood but add that recognition is in some way *also* necessary. These are usually analysed under the heading of the constitutive theory, but they borrow features from the declaratory approach, too. I will refer to them as the 'effectiveness-plus-recognition' view. Variants of this view face a range of difficulties.

One constitutive theorist who belonged in this category was Paul Guggenheim. He accepted that 'customary international law fixes the conditions in which' an entity is considered a state—the effectiveness criteria—but argued that meeting the criteria as a matter of fact, without something more, is not sufficient for

[142] Guiding Principles Applicable to Unilateral Declarations of States Capable of Creating Legal Obligations [2006] 2(2) ILC Ybk 161, principle 8.

[143] This would infect other states too. Imagine that a treaty to invade Sparta is made between Athens (which recognizes Sparta) and Boeotia (which does not). Athens's intended conduct would clearly breach its peremptory duty to Sparta not to use force. But Sparta does not count as a state protected by this peremptory norm *for the purpose of relations between Athens and Boeotia*, because Boeotia does not recognize it. So the treaty does not derogate from a peremptory norm and is valid.

statehood: '*authoritative certification*' of the existence of a state is also 'indispensable'.[144] In the absence of an international court or organization 'charged with declaring when marks the beginning of the validity of a State order', it instead

> falls to the subjects of the law of nations (sovereign States above all) to certify themselves, as organs of the international legal order, whether they find themselves in the presence of a new State. Recognition thus takes place by unilateral act of the pre-existing State that acts as an organ of the decentralized international community . . .[145]

Kelsen, in his later writings, similarly argued that states 'alone are the authorities empowered by general international law to decide' whether an entity fulfils the criteria for statehood.[146] But this variant of the effectiveness-plus-recognition view is precarious. Crawford points out that such 'authoritative certification' is not required to resolve *other* questions of law or fact; otherwise, international law 'would be reduced to a form of imperfect communications, a system for registering the assent or dissent of individual States without any prospect of resolution'.[147] Furthermore, as Marek noted,

> if it is true that it is international law which determines *in substance* its subjects, then recognizing States do no more than state the position under international law. What if they state it obviously incorrectly? What is the result of their withholding recognition from a State fulfilling all conditions required by international law, or conversely, of their recognizing an obvious fiction? . . . Which, according to Professors Kelsen and Guggenheim, is then to prevail: international law which . . . decides the issue in substance, or the States which have disregarded this decision?[148]

If the test of effectiveness prevails, this approach collapses into the effectiveness-only view and recognition becomes irrelevant; if recognition (or a lack thereof) prevails, the approach collapses into the recognition-only view and effectiveness becomes irrelevant.

Another variant of the effectiveness-plus-recognition view was suggested by Lauterpacht. He saw recognition as constitutive of statehood but proposed that if an entity meets the effectiveness criteria then other states have a *duty* to recognize

[144] Paul Guggenheim, *Traité de droit international public: avec mention de la pratique internationale et suisse* (Librairie de l'Université, Georg & Cie 1953) vol 1, 190–1 (translation with emphasis from original).
[145] Ibid, vol 1, 191 (translation).
[146] Kelsen, 'Recognition' (n 123) 607. Compare also Lauterpacht, *Recognition* (n 105) 55.
[147] Crawford, *Creation* (n 9) 20.
[148] Marek (n 83) 137–8.

it; they 'are not entitled to serve exclusively the interests of their national policy and convenience regardless of the principles of international law in the matter'.[149] But this, too, is unconvincing. A duty to recognize hints that a person already exists with the correlative right to be recognized.[150] And if it has already been accepted that effectiveness suffices to constitute a person to *that* degree, there can be no reason of principle for requiring the extra step of recognition before this person can acquire further relations. Moreover, whatever the legal significance of recognition may be, practice and *opinio iuris* have historically tended against the existence of a duty to grant it.[151] In 1992 the Badinter Commission described recognition as 'a discretionary act that other States may perform when they choose and in a manner of their own choosing, subject only to compliance with the imperatives of general international law'.[152] Practice might eventually change. Thomas Grant argues that a 'degree of collective process by 1991–92 had entered the norm governing recognition' and that western European states, in deciding whether or not to recognize the would-be successor states of Yugoslavia, tried 'to give individual policy the appearance of originating in consensus'.[153] But at present the evidence does not support the existence of the duty to recognize proposed by Lauterpacht.

The particular difficulties faced by these earlier attempts to hybridize effectiveness and recognition are avoided by John Dugard. His variant of the effectiveness-plus-recognition view, however, suffers from a different problem. He accepts that where an entity meets certain criteria, it acquires the relations of states relative to every other such entity (rather than solely relative to other states that recognize it); but he argues, in essence, that these criteria for statehood include not only effectiveness *but also recognition*. His starting point is the formulation of the criteria for statehood that appears in the Montevideo Convention:

> The state as a person of international law should possess the following qualifications:
> (a) a permanent population;
> (b) a defined territory;
> (c) government; and
> (d) capacity to enter into relations with the other states.[154]

149 Lauterpacht, *Recognition* (n 105) 6.
150 Compare Talmon, 'Constitutive' (n 6) 103.
151 Grant, *Recognition* (n 63) 127–8; Shaw (n 20) 326.
152 *Opinion No 10* (Badinter Commission) (1992) 92 ILR 206, para 4. On 'imperatives of general international law', see this book ss 4.1.1, 4.1.2. Compare *Restatement: Foreign Relations* (n 4) pt 202.
153 Grant, *Recognition* (n 63) 197, further 218. Compare *Re Secession of Quebec* (Supreme Court, Canada) (1998) 115 ILR 536, para 143: the 'process of recognition, once considered to be an exercise of pure sovereign discretion, has come to be associated with legal norms'. In cases such as the Congo, the duty to respect self-determination may create something close to a duty to recognize: see this book s 4.2.
154 Montevideo Convention, art 1.

This adds a fourth requirement to the traditional criteria of population, territory, and government: capacity to enter into relations with other states. Dugard argues that 'without recognition on the part of at least some States', an entity will not be able to demonstrate this criterion.[155] This interpretation of the criterion is dubious. Read literally, 'capacity' suggests that an entity, for its own part, is potentially able to enter into relations, not that other states are actually *willing* to have relations with it; unwillingness on the part of other states, as Talmon observes, merely denies an entity the *opportunity* to enter into relations.[156]

This interpretation of the Montevideo Convention is not vital to Dugard's theory; recognition might instead be a free-standing requirement of statehood that is not mentioned in the Convention or other traditional formulations. But the theory is in any case paradoxical. How many recognitions are needed before an entity acquires the rights and other relations of states relative to every other state? Dugard cites *Caglar v Billingham*, in which the British special commissioners of inland revenue held that in 'view of the non-recognition of the Turkish Republic of Northern Cyprus by the whole of the international community other than Turkey . . . it cannot enter into relations with other states' and 'does not, therefore, satisfy the fourth requirement of statehood'.[157] In other words, Turkey could not singlehandedly lift Northern Cyprus over the bar set by the ostensible requirement and thereby impose duties towards it on every other state: recognition by a single other state was not enough. So it appears that, on Dugard's theory, the requirement is some critical mass of recognitions greater than one. Imagine that there is an entity that meets the other criteria for statehood but is totally unrecognized. If all existing states take Dugard's view that this entity is not a state and that a single recognition would not be enough to transform it into one, then no existing state, acting consistently with that view, will ever recognize it. To satisfy the requirement, a critical mass of states will each have to recognize an entity *that does not yet meet the requirement*.[158] That would amount to practice and *opinio iuris* contrary to the existence of the requirement. How could a customary norm emerge and survive if, in order for it to operate, the practice and *opinio iuris* of a critical mass of states had to be to contrary to its existence?

155 Dugard, 'Secession' (n 81) 58, further 56–8. For another approach sharing some features with Dugard's, see François Finck, 'The State between fact and law: The role of recognition and the conditions under which it is granted in the creation of new States' (2016) 36 Polish Yearbook of International Law 51.

156 Talmon, 'Constitutive' (n 6) 117.

157 *Caglar v Billingham (Inspector of Taxes)* (Special Commissioners, England) (1996) 108 ILR 510, para 182.

158 Perhaps a way around this would be for a critical mass of states to recognize a hitherto-unrecognized entity simultaneously. That has arguably happened in some cases. Dugard, 'Secession' (n 81) 64 notes that most states 'did not bother' to declare formally that they recognized South Sudan when it was granted independence in July 2011; they just voted—simultaneously—to admit it to the United Nations. But this does not always happen; eg, recognitions of Bangladesh trickled in over several years: this book s 4.2.2.

Dugard warns that if his theory is wrong, that 'denies the existence of Montevideo's fourth requirement for statehood'.[159] That might be no great loss. It is true that, lacking a more authoritative attempt to codify the criteria, international lawyers often reach for the Montevideo Convention. But there is no magic in it; it is a largely hortatory treaty from 1933 ratified by a handful of states in the Americas, not an authoritative statement of custom.[160] And others have observed that, on a more literal interpretation of the phrase 'capacity to enter into relations'—one not entailing recognition—it adds nothing that is not already implied by the traditional criteria, notably government; an even better view may be that it is a synonym of the criterion of independence, which I have already identified as a fourth criterion.[161]

An additional weakness of the view that *both* effectiveness *and* recognition are necessary for statehood, common to all variants of this view, is that it is no better than the effectiveness-only view at explaining cases, such as Somalia in the 1990s, in which a state fails the effectiveness criteria except on a very generous or inconsistent interpretation. If *both* factors were always necessary, then no amount of recognition could compensate for the absence of effectiveness. Dugard observes that Somalia's apparent continuous existence as a state, despite the lack of a functional government, 'proves that a State cannot "die" without the withdrawal of recognition'.[162] But logically this observation does not imply that recognition is necessary for statehood, as he infers, only that recognition can be *sufficient*. That is actually more suggestive of the final possible view that I am going to consider.

3.4 The view that either effectiveness or recognition can suffice

In explaining why the Vatican City is a state, Crawford remarks that 'recognition by other States is of considerable importance especially in marginal or borderline cases'.[163] He writes of another tiny entity, Monaco, that its statehood 'resulted not from any indisputable qualifications for statehood but [from] its widespread recognition and acceptance as a State'.[164] This was because Monaco arguably failed the criterion of independence, in that, among other things, it had agreed 'to exercise its

[159] Ibid, 57–8.

[160] Grant doubts that the Montevideo formulation of the criteria was legally binding even between parties to the Convention; he suggests it 'was at best "soft law"': Thomas D Grant, 'Defining statehood: The Montevideo Convention and its discontents' (1999) 37 Columbia Journal of Transnational Law 403, 456.

[161] Lowe (n 8) 158; Crawford, *Creation* (n 9) 62. See also Talmon, 'Constitutive' (n 6) 116–17.

[162] Dugard, 'Secession' (n 81) 60.

[163] Crawford, *Creation* (n 9) 223.

[164] Ibid, 293.

rights of sovereignty in complete conformity with the political, military, naval and economic interests of France'.[165] As a general matter, Crawford observes that

> in some cases at least, an entity that for some reason may not qualify as a State under the [effectiveness criteria] may nonetheless be recognized as such. Such recognition may be constitutive of legal obligation for the recognizing or acquiescing State; it may also tend to consolidate a general legal status at that time precarious or in the process of being constituted. . . . Recognition, while in principle declaratory, may thus be of great importance in particular cases.[166]

As this illustrates, I am not the first to speculate that, even if statehood ordinarily depends on effectiveness, recognition alone might sometimes be sufficient.[167] This, however, is seldom acknowledged for what it is. Despite Crawford's remark that recognition is 'in principle declaratory', if it is not always merely declaratory then that amounts to an abandonment of the declaratory principle in its traditional form—an abandonment of the effectiveness-only view.

I will call the idea that *either* effectiveness *or* recognition can suffice for statehood the 'effectiveness-or-recognition' view. My earlier conclusions about how effectiveness creates statehood—the most persuasive element of the declaratory theory—are not challenged by this view. I adopt them here without further discussion: there is a norm defining any entity that meets effectiveness criteria as a state (as a general rule, subject to exceptions to be considered later); there are norms granting customary rights and other relations to all the entities so defined; and there is a norm that their practice and *opinio iuris* contribute to custom, which, circularly, is how all these norms acquire their validity. But I need to consider the manner in which recognition could function as an alternative rule creating statehood. I will look first at the explanatory strengths of the effectiveness-or-recognition view in the abstract, then at the consequences of recognition between the recognized entity and states that recognize it, and finally at the consequences beyond that relationship.

[165] Treaty Establishing the Relations of France with the Principality of Monaco (17 July 1918) 981 UNTS 363, art 1; other articles further restricted Monégasque sovereignty. A new treaty that took effect in 2005 toned these restrictions down: Traité destiné à adapter et à confirmer les rapports d'amitié et de coopération entre la République Française et la Principauté de Monaco (24 October 2002) JORF no 6 du 7 janvier 2006 texte 6. Compare the protectorates and 'associated states' discussed in this book s 5.1.2.

[166] Crawford, *Creation* (n 9) 93. At 501 he adds that in some cases where 'international organizations or groups of States—especially the so-called "Great Powers"—have exercised a collective authority to supervise, regulate and condition' the creation of states, that may amount to 'a form of collective recognition'.

[167] Compare also the somewhat different approach in Vidmar, 'Explaining' (n 75); Jure Vidmar, *Democratic Statehood in International Law: The Emergence of New States in Post-Cold War Practice* (Hart 2013).

3.4.1 Explanatory strengths

There are two ways in which two alternative rules creating statehood might co-exist. Each rule might have to apply in discrete circumstances, meaning that some entities can acquire statehood by effectiveness and others by recognition but no entity can acquire it by both methods. Or it might be that both rules can apply to the same entity at the same time. Przemysław Saganek, referring to the act of granting recognition, asks whether it is redundant to 'treat as a legal transaction an act giving rise to obligations which would lie upon a state even without that act'.[168] He concludes that there is nothing to stop identical duties from arising in multiple ways.[169] It is common for the same state to have identical rights or duties under both treaty and custom—for example, under the articles of the Charter dealing with force and under the coexisting customary norm prohibiting force.[170] By analogy, the same entity might acquire an identical package of relations—the rights and other relations of a state—both by being recognized and under customary norms whose applicability depends on effectiveness. So the two rules need not have mutually exclusive spheres of application.

At the same time, their spheres of application need not overlap completely. I will find later that on the effectiveness-or-recognition view (unlike on the traditional recognition-only view), recognition cannot be used to create new states willy-nilly in derogation from the territorial integrity of existing states.[171] But this and other exceptions can be left aside until Chapter 4; for the purpose of this general discussion of the rules, I have been referring to examples—Somalia, the Vatican City, Monaco—that are unaffected by exceptions.

If entities such as these can acquire statehood *either* by effectiveness *or* by recognition *or* by both methods, then recognition can serve to repair any deficiencies in their effectiveness. This is why I foreshadowed that there is less evidence than might be thought on which to base a detailed examination of how the effectiveness criteria apply in different scenarios. Where an entity is universally recognized but there is ambiguity about whether the entity meets the effectiveness criteria, the effectiveness-or-recognition view makes it impossible to resolve the ambiguity: any deficiencies of effectiveness would in any event be repaired by recognition. In a sense this serves to make the law *more* rather than less certain, because the ambiguity does not affect the ultimate legal outcome. To explain the statehood of Somalia or the Vatican City, it is no longer necessary to interpret the criteria generously, to postulate multiple sets of criteria applicable in different scenarios, or to recalibrate the criteria in a manner inconsistent with wider practice: it is sufficient

168 Saganek (n 122) 503.
169 Ibid, 504.
170 *Nicaragua v US* [1986] ICJ Rep 14, paras 183–90.
171 This book ss 4.1.1, 4.1.2.

that these entities are recognized. The effectiveness-or-recognition view thus lacks a major weakness of the effectiveness-only view.

An additional strength of the effectiveness-or-recognition view is that it gives firm legal significance to acts that recognizing states clearly intend to imbue with some significance.

Consider Palestine's campaign for recognition as a state. It has claimed statehood since 1988,[172] but it could have met the effectiveness criteria at that time only on an idiosyncratic view: its would-be government was based in Algeria, and its would-be territory was administered by Israel. Still, many states recognized it, and some of those states explicitly affirmed that it met the criteria.[173] More recently, when Sweden recognized Palestine in 2014, it, too, explicitly affirmed that the criteria were met.[174] The argument was by then stronger than in 1988, in that Palestinians had some control over territory, though since this control was supervised by Israel it remained doubtful whether Palestine met the criterion of independence.[175] But what is clear in any case, whether or not Palestine met the criteria, is this: as a matter of politics, a decision by a state to recognize Palestine did not depend solely on how that state's officials interpreted the criteria. The Swedish foreign affairs minister gave reasons for granting recognition that were avowedly political: to lend 'support to the moderate Palestinian forces', to 'facilitate an agreement' with Israel 'by making the parties in these negotiations less unequal', and to 'contribute to more hope and optimism among young Palestinians and Israelis'.[176] Her references to decisions that had 'hampered a two-state solution' and to 'those who will manage the complex Palestinian state-building process' might even be taken as an admission that Sweden did not genuinely think that Palestine was already a full-fledged state. In short, Sweden clearly intended its recognition to have some significance beyond merely providing an interpretation of the effectiveness criteria.

Another instance in which political reasons were offered for granting recognition is the joint recognition policy that western European states tried to adhere to in the early 1990s, with mixed success. As part of this policy, they set preconditions for granting recognition. In the Guidelines on the Recognition of New States in

[172] Declaration of Independence of Palestine (18 November 1988) annex to UN doc A/43/827.

[173] Eg, Algeria, Indonesia, Mauritania, Niger, Senegal, and Yemen argued that Palestine met the criteria of population, territory, government, and independence in Explanatory Note Concerning the Request for the Admission of the State of Palestine to Unesco (12 May 1989) Unesco doc 131 EX/43.

[174] Sweden 'considers that the international law criteria for the recognition of Palestine have been satisfied': Sweden, 'Sweden recognises Palestine and increases aid' (press release, 30 October 2014).

[175] Some ambivalence is expressed in Report of the Committee on the Admission of New Members Concerning the Application of Palestine for Admission to Membership in the United Nations (11 November 2011) UN doc S/2011/705. See also *Knox v Palestine Liberation Organization*, 306 F Supp 2d 424 (SDNY, 2004); Crawford, *Creation* (n 9) 434–48; and, from among the vast literature, the selections in Victor Kattan (ed), *The Palestine Question in International Law* (British Institute of International and Comparative Law 2008).

[176] Margot Wallström, 'The Government will decide today to recognise the State of Palestine' (30 October 2014) DN Debatt.

Eastern Europe and in the Soviet Union, adopted in December 1991, the European Community and its member states affirmed

> their readiness to recognise, subject to the normal standards of international practice and the political realities in each case, those new States which, following the historic changes in the region, have constituted themselves on a democratic basis, have accepted the appropriate international obligations and have committed themselves in good faith to a peaceful process and to negotiations.[177]

They then listed the requirements of their 'common position on the process of recognition of these new States', which included—to give one example among many—'guarantees for the rights of ethnic and national groups and minorities'.[178] Talmon classifies these as 'political conditions for recognition' rather than 'criteria for statehood'.[179] They treated recognition as something more than a declaration of an already-existing status (though it was that as well: recognition by the states making the declaration remained 'subject to the normal standards'). The effectiveness-or-recognition view gives legal significance to this political reality.

These explanatory strengths of the effectiveness-or-recognition view are, of course, not a conclusive reason to accept it. In order to show that this view is correct, I will have to show that recognition can actually result in an entity having the rights and other relations of states.

3.4.2 Consequences relative to recognizing states

The effectiveness-or-recognition view offers no reason to think that recognition functions outside the ordinary rules about how norms and legal relations are created (in contrast to the recognition-only view, which treats recognition as a special contractual arrangement on which the entirety of international law is based). Ordinarily, legal relations can be created by two entities between themselves or even by one entity acting unilaterally—subject, as always, to any relevant peremptory norms. So in the first instance I will consider what consequences recognition might have solely for recognizing states and the recognized entity.

Authorities that directly concern the consequences of recognition for recognizing states and the recognized entity are elusive. Victor Rodríguez Cedeño, the special rapporteur on unilateral acts of states, reported to the International Law Commission in 2003 that he could find no references 'to the act of recognition

[177] European Community, Guidelines on the Recognition of New States in Eastern Europe and in the Soviet Union (16 December 1991) 62 BYIL 559.
[178] Ibid. See further Grant, *Recognition* (n 63) 156–60.
[179] Talmon, 'Constitutive' (n 6) 108–9.

of a State . . . being examined by the international courts with a view to determining whether it is binding or not'.[180] Some relevant practice is identified by Jean Charpentier. Most of it concerns *governments*, to which he believed the same rule applied,[181] but one of his illustrations concerns the recognition as a state of an entity whose effectiveness was in doubt. In 1920, the League of Nations appointed a committee of jurists to give an opinion on the demilitarization of the Aaland Islands, which were the subject of a dispute between Finland and Sweden. A preliminary question was whether the matter 'should, according to International Law, be entirely left to the domestic jurisdiction of Finland', which exercised sovereignty over the islands.[182] The answer was no, because the dispute had arisen during Finland's separation from Russia in 1917–18, before Finland had 'acquired the character of a definitively constituted State'.[183] Charpentier argued that if the matter had been considered under a bilateral arbitral procedure between Sweden and Finland, this solution could not have been reached, because Sweden had recognized Finland in January 1918 and hence was bound to accept Finland's sovereignty over the islands except insofar as its recognition came with reservations.[184] Charpentier thought that the committee had impliedly acknowledged this when it remarked that 'Sweden has always shown by her attitude that she was interested in the Aaland Islands question, and she has always acted as if her recognition had been given subject to reservations'.[185]

Despite the scarcity of authorities on point, there are compelling reasons of principle to conclude that recognition is binding between a recognizing state and the recognized entity. I will reach this conclusion by comparing recognition with three established mechanisms by which states can create relations: estoppel, unilateral declarations, and treaties.

Estoppel is a concept borrowed from domestic common-law systems, possibly on the basis that it is one of the 'general principles of law' referred to in the Statute of the International Court.[186] Vice-President Alfaro said of estoppel in *Temple of Preah Vihear* that 'wide divergences exist as to its meaning, its character, its scope and even its denomination'.[187] In the same case, it was defined by Judge Spender in the following terms (though he referred to the concept as 'preclusion'):

[180] Victor Rodríguez Cedeño, Sixth Report on Unilateral Acts of States [2003] 2(1) ILC Ybk 53, para 74.
[181] Jean Charpentier, *La Reconnaissance Internationale et l'Évolution du droit des gens* (Pédone 1956) 225–35.
[182] Report of the International Committee of Jurists upon the Legal Aspects of the Aaland Islands Question (1920) 3 LNOJ Sp Supp 3, 3.
[183] Ibid, 14.
[184] Charpentier (n 181) 227.
[185] Report of the Committee of Jurists on the Aaland Islands (n 182) 8.
[186] Statute of the International Court of Justice (26 June 1945) art 38(1)(c).
[187] *Temple of Preah Vihear (Cambodia v Thailand)* [1962] ICJ Rep 6, 39 (Vice-President Alfaro).

> the principle operates to prevent a State contesting before the Court a situation contrary to a clear and unequivocal representation previously made by it to another State, either expressly or impliedly, on which representation the other State was, in the circumstances, entitled to rely and in fact did rely, and as a result that other State has been prejudiced or the State making it has secured some benefit or advantage for itself.[188]

Recognition is sometimes said to create an estoppel. Antonio Cassese argued that it bars a

> recognizing State from altering its position and claiming that the new entity lacks statehood. In other words, the granting of recognition creates an *estoppel* precluding the recognizing State from contesting the legal personality of the new State. (It is widely recognized that international law upholds the common law concept of estoppel, whereby a party is barred from alleging or denying a fact or claiming a right, to the detriment of another party entitled to rely upon such conduct in consequence of previous allegation, denial, or conduct, or admission by the former party.)[189]

A difficulty with this line of thinking is the requirement that the recognized entity must have relied on the recognition to its detriment. This might mean that not every recognition can create an estoppel, especially where, beyond the act of recognition itself, no further interaction has occurred between the recognizing state and the entity, such that there can be no element of reliance. Estoppel is also limited in another respect. It might impose duties on the state that is estopped, but it does not grant any *rights* to the estopped state; it therefore cannot create the whole package of rights and other relations of states between the estopped state and the recognized entity. Charpentier made an argument about recognition that gives it a similarly limited scope (though he was not expressly invoking the concept of estoppel). He wrote that the 'recognition *of an ineffective State or government*' is surely

> *attributive of competences*, but in the sense that the recognizing State creates for itself an obligation to respect the competences that it has recognised in the entity in question. Let us be clear: the effect of the recognition is in no way to render opposable to the recognizing State a status that does not exist, only to oblige it to

[188] Ibid, 143–4 (Judge Spender dissenting). Compare *North Sea Continental Shelf* [1969] ICJ Rep 3, para 30. For further case law, see Thirlway (n 120) vol 1, 27–43; vol 2, 1121–7.

[189] Antonio Cassese, *International Law* (2nd edn, OUP 2005) 74. Georg Schwarzenberger and ED Brown, *A Manual of International Law* (6th edn, Professional Books 1976) 56 similarly argued that good faith may estop a state from denying that it has recognized an entity, though this was based on a recognition-only view.

> respect the recognised competences, only those, and only those whose operation depends on its will.[190]

The recognizing state acquires an 'obligation *not to contest*' the relations recognized in the entity, such as a treaty-making power, insofar as their operation depends on its will.[191]

There are, then, grounds for thinking that recognition can create an estoppel, but that it can do so only in certain conditions and that this creates only some of the relations of states.

The next mechanism, a unilateral declaration, will be seen to have wider potential consequences for recognition, subsuming those of estoppel. A unilateral declaration is an act of will by which the declaring state intends to create the rights and other relations in the declaration. It must be given publicly. These two requirements were cited in the seminal case, *Nuclear Tests*, in which the International Court held that France was bound by a unilateral declaration that it would cease atmospheric nuclear tests.[192] The same two requirements are codified in the Commission's Guiding Principles on Unilateral Declarations:

> Declarations publicly made and manifesting the will to be bound may have the effect of creating legal obligations. When the conditions for this are met, the binding character of such declarations is based on good faith; States concerned may then take them into consideration and rely on them; such States are entitled to require that such obligations be respected.[193]

Although detrimental reliance is not required, if an addressee of a unilateral declaration has relied on it then that may be relevant to whether the declaration can be revoked.[194]

Recognition virtually always meets one of these two requirements: it tends to be granted publicly.[195] And the remaining requirement, an intention to be bound, will unambiguously be met if the recognizing state clearly articulates an intention to create rights and other relations between itself and the recognized entity. But there may be evidence that the state's reason for granting recognition is that it

[190] Charpentier (n 181) 225 (translation with emphasis from original).
[191] Ibid, 227 (translation).
[192] *Nuclear Tests (New Zealand v France)* [1974] ICJ Rep 457, paras 45–53.
[193] Guiding Principles Applicable to Unilateral Declarations, principle 1.
[194] Ibid, principle 10.
[195] There have been secret agreements about future recognition. Antonio López de Santa Anna of Mexico secretly agreed to secure recognition of the Republic of Texas: Treaty of Velasco (14 May 1836) in Oscar J Martínez (ed), *US–Mexico Borderlands: Historical and Contemporary Perspectives* (Scholarly Resources 1996) 17. This was extracted under coercion and was not ratified by Mexico. The United Kingdom and France secretly agreed that they were prepared 'to recognize and protect an independent Arab State or a Confederation of Arab States' in the Sykes–Picot Agreement, UK–France (16 May 1916) 221 CTS 323.

believes that the recognized entity meets the effectiveness criteria and hence that the rights and other relations already exist on that basis, as with some recognitions of Palestine. This is an apparent obstacle. Can it be said, in this scenario, that the recognizing state has the intention of *creating* legal relations?

The apparent obstacle will be overcome if it is possible for unilateral declarations to serve a double function: to declare that, on the declaring state's interpretation of norms of international law, certain legal relations already exist; and at the same time, for the removal of doubt, to commit the declaring state to that interpretation. In *US—Sections 301–310 of the Trade Act of 1974* (albeit in a very different context), a panel of the World Trade Organization seemed to assume that this is possible. It suggested that a unilateral declaration can bind the declaring state to comply with an interpretation of an existing duty. The declaration was a statement of administrative action that purported to be 'an authoritative expression' by the United States 'concerning its views regarding the interpretation and application of the Uruguay Round agreements, both for purposes of US international obligations and domestic law'.[196] The panel, applying a test that it described as at least as stringent as that from *Nuclear Tests*, found that this was 'intended to express US understanding of its international obligations as incorporated in domestic US law'.[197] Although the declaration did 'not create a new international legal obligation for the US', because the relevant treaty provision was binding already, it clarified and gave 'an undertaking, at an international level, concerning aspects of domestic US law, in particular, the way the US has implemented its obligations under' the provision.[198] It may be similar where recognition is based on a belief that the recognized entity meets the effectiveness criteria. Recognition is intended to express the recognizing state's understanding of the norm giving the relations of states to effective entities. Like the declaration by the United States, this could amount to a unilateral declaration meeting the requirement of intention.

Consistent with this, recognition has been described by international lawyers in terms that echo the language of unilateral declarations and that attribute a double function to it. Eric Suy argued that recognition is a unilateral act of will by which a person 'notes an existing situation and expresses the intention of considering it as legitimate, as being the law' and that the person is from that time onward 'no longer entitled to contest the legal character' of the situation.[199] Rodríguez Cedeño, in a report to the Commission, defined 'recognition' as a 'unilateral expression of will . . . acknowledging the existence of a *de facto* or *de jure* situation or the legality of a legal claim, with the intention of producing specific legal effects, and

[196] *US—Sections 301–310 of the Trade Act of 1974* (WTO case WT/DS152/R, 22 December 1999) para 7.110.

[197] Ibid, para 7.118 n 692, para 7.121.

[198] Ibid, para 7.125.

[199] Eric Suy, *Les Actes juridiques unilatéraux en droit international public* (Librairie Générale de Droit et de Jurisprudence 1962) 191, 207 (translation).

in particular accepting its opposability'.[200] The references to the double function of recognition in these remarks are explicit: recognition is intended to *acknowledge* an existing 'situation' and at the same time to *produce* 'legal effects'. Rodríguez Cedeño was defining recognition in a wide sense, going beyond recognition as a state, but his definition was apparently meant to embrace recognition as a state.[201] He added that 'a State which has recognized a certain claim or an existing state of affairs cannot contest its legitimacy in future'.[202]

Some further caution is needed here in using the word 'recognition'. Saganek notes that it is sometimes used to refer to actions that are merely tacit—or even to silence—and concludes that 'defining recognition as a declaration of will is too risky'.[203] It may be that the requirements of a unilateral declaration are not met by all the conduct that is described, for some purpose or other, as an act of 'recognition'. Imagine, for example, that a state, in the act of granting recognition, says explicitly that if it turns out to be incorrect that the recognized entity meets the effectiveness criteria then it does not intend to commit to treating the entity as a state. That act might not qualify as a declaration with binding legal effects. Some other acts of recognition might not take the form of a declaration at all. In general, unilateral declarations 'may be formulated orally or in writing'.[204] Recognition as a state is often granted in writing, either expressly in a diplomatic note or impliedly by a message of congratulations on independence or the accreditation of diplomats.[205] But it may be that tacit recognition that is inferred from conduct does not meet the requirements for a binding unilateral declaration. Whether particular acts amount to unilateral declarations and with what consequences is in general a matter of 'their content, of all the factual circumstances in which they were made, and of the reactions to which they gave rise'.[206] The upshot of all this is that particular cases may have to be considered on their merits; it cannot be assumed that everything that is described as 'recognition' constitutes a unilateral declaration.

Subject to this, recognition as a state generally does meet the requirements for a unilateral declaration. It remains to consider what legal relations are thereby created.

According to the Commission's Guiding Principles, a unilateral declaration can give not only rights but also *duties* to its addressee insofar as the addressee has 'clearly accepted' it.[207] Applied to recognition as a state, this condition is almost certain to be met: existing states tend to recognize entities only if the entities

[200] Rodríguez Cedeño (n 180) para 67.
[201] On the variety of meanings of 'recognition' see Saganek (n 122) ch 12.
[202] Rodríguez Cedeño (n 180) paras 96, 102.
[203] Saganek (n 122) 477.
[204] Guiding Principles Applicable to Unilateral Declarations, principle 5.
[205] Saganek (n 122) 551–8 collates a number of lists of the means by which recognition may be granted.
[206] Guiding Principles Applicable to Unilateral Declarations, principle 3.
[207] Ibid, principle 9.

actually claim statehood relative to existing states. Additionally, if a unilateral declaration accepted by its addressee can create both rights and duties directly, it can presumably also create them *indirectly*—first, by creating powers, susceptibilities, and so on between the recognizing state and the entity and, second, insofar as the entity's practice and *opinio iuris* could contribute to new customary norms that apply between the recognizing state and the entity (though the contribution made to custom by a single extra entity is likely to be negligible). It follows that where an entity is recognized as a state—assuming that the requirements for a unilateral declaration are met and that the entity consents to being recognized—the entity is defined as a state relative to the recognizing state for the purposes of all the customary norms concerning states.

This is the means by which interpreting recognition as a unilateral declaration subsumes the more limited consequences of interpreting it as an act creating an estoppel.

The other mechanism of creating relations that might be compared with recognition is the power to make treaties. Recognition is, of course, not always granted by treaty. But occasionally it is. For example, the Dayton Agreement of 1995 provided that the 'Federal Republic of Yugoslavia [Serbia-Montenegro] and the Republic of Bosnia and Herzegovina recognize each other as sovereign independent States within their international borders'.[208] A treaty provision by which two treaty parties recognize each other as states, on its face, creates or confirms a legal norm that the rights and other relations of states exist between those two parties. This observation strengthens what I have concluded about unilateral declarations. If an entity can acquire the rights and other relations of states bilaterally by treaty, alongside any rights and other relations that it may possess already on the ground of meeting the effectiveness criteria, then that provides a reason to think that a similar result can be achieved by a unilateral declaration. International law operates on a principle of parallelism between treaty and non-treaty duties: they function in a similar way.[209]

Some international lawyers argue that the UN Charter is a treaty of this sort, with the result that all members of the United Nations can be deemed to recognize all other members—perhaps even those that persistently claim otherwise, such as states that do not recognize Israel.[210] It is true that the Charter describes members

[208] General Framework Agreement for Peace in Bosnia and Herzegovina, Dayton (21 November 1995) 35 ILM 89, art 10. Another example of recognition by treaty is the Thomson–Urrutia Treaty, US–Colombia (6 April 1914) 42 Stat 2122, art 3, discussed in this book s 4.1.1.

[209] Compare Articles on Responsibility of States, commentary to art 2, para 7; James Crawford, *State Responsibility: The General Part* (CUP 2013) 390 n 151.

[210] A notable example is John Dugard, *Recognition and the United Nations* (Grotius 1987) ch 4, especially 78–80; Dugard, 'Secession' (n 81) 64–8. Contrast Raič (n 38) 45–7. See further Thomas D Grant, *Admission to the United Nations: Charter Article 4 and the Rise of Universal Organization* (Nijhoff 2009) ch 7.

as 'States'.[211] This contrasts with the League of Nations, membership of which was open to any 'fully self-governing State, Dominion or Colony'.[212] But I noted in the introduction that, as with the League, a few original members of the United Nations were not states (though all these entities have now acquired statehood: the Philippines in 1946, India in 1947, and Belarus and Ukraine in 1991). Even if these are dismissed as anomalies and the argument confined to *new* UN members, which are explicitly required to be states by the Charter, there is another reason to doubt the argument that membership entails recognition. This is the fact that many states still make an effort to recognize a new state formally, even after it has been admitted to the United Nations and even if the recognizing state voted for its admission.[213] It has been suggested that 'the only definitive conclusion to be drawn from membership of the UN is that an entity is a State *for the purposes of the Charter*', which may not equate to statehood for all purposes.[214] Still, this means that at a minimum UN members agree to treat each other as states for *some* purposes and hence to give *some* of the rights and other relations of states to each other, including the duty to refrain from the threat or use of force.[215] So the Charter, even if not strictly a treaty of recognition, approximates one for important purposes.

I have found reasons for thinking that recognition can have force as a unilateral declaration, under a treaty, or (to a more limited extent) insofar as it creates an estoppel. But it may be artificial and unnecessary to attempt to squeeze every instance of recognition into one of these established categories. They are manifestations of the same basic principles. Treaties and unilateral declarations are acts of will by which states consent to rights and duties.[216] Estoppel and unilateral declarations are based on the principle of good faith; a treaty must similarly be performed and interpreted in good faith.[217] Yet another comparable mechanism by which states may create norms applicable specifically between those states is 'local' custom.[218] Recognition as a state could be seen as an additional method of creating relations that is likewise based on the underlying principles of good faith or consent: an express or tacit undertaking or agreement of a special sort that is binding

[211] Charter, art 3 (the original members in 1945) art 4 (new members); see also *Conditions of Admission of a State to Membership in the United Nations (Article 4 of the Charter) (Advisory Opinion)* [1948] ICJ Rep 57.

[212] Covenant of the League of Nations (28 June 1919) art 1(2).

[213] Rich (n 73) 64.

[214] Colin Warbrick, 'States and recognition in international law' in Malcolm D Evans (ed), *International Law* (2nd edn, OUP 2006) 217, 261 (emphasis from original). See also Crawford, *Creation* (n 9) 175–6.

[215] Charter, arts 2(4) 42, 51.

[216] An act creating an estoppel, however, is not necessarily an act of will intended to be binding: Thirlway (n 120) vol 1, 11–12; James Crawford, *Brownlie's Principles of Public International Law* (8th edn, OUP 2012) 421.

[217] *Delimitation of the Maritime Boundary in the Gulf of Maine Area (Canada/US)* [1984] ICJ Rep 246, para 130 (estoppel); *Nuclear Tests* [1974] ICJ Rep 457, para 49 (unilateral declarations); Vienna Convention on Treaties, arts 26, 31.

[218] See this book s 2.4.3.

in international law. David Raič argues in similar terms that 'on the basis of the principle of good faith' a 'recognized entity may rely on its specific legal status vis-à-vis the recognizing State'.[219]

Since there are multiple grounds on which recognition may be binding (and the same act may be binding on more than one of these grounds, for example, as a unilateral declaration and insofar as it creates an estoppel) it will be fruitful to think about recognition in the following way. What is distinctive about acts of recognition as a state is not the manner in which they are performed but the *package of legal relations* that they create: they create the relations of states between the recognizing state and the recognized entity. Recognition can thus be defined as the exercise of a Hohfeldian power to create these relations, whether it is analysed as a treaty-making power, a power to make unilateral declarations, an underlying power based on consent or good faith, or more than one of those things. When I refer to recognition from now on, I will generally mean acts meeting this definition.

The idea that recognition is an exercise of a power has an implication that is relevant to the manner in which it functions. A recognized entity might be a state anyway by virtue of meeting the effectiveness criteria. But it is also possible that the entity would not otherwise be a state—and the explanatory strengths of the effectiveness-or-recognition view all rest on that possibility. It may be, in fact, that the entity has no rights and duties at all before being recognized. Yet in principle there is something that the entity must already have before being recognized. It must, at a minimum, have a pre-existing susceptibility.[220]

Recall that saying that an entity has a Hohfeldian susceptibility is the correlate of saying that another entity has a power to change its legal relations, in this case that a state has a power to recognize it.[221] This is not saying very much about the entity: it does not have any further implications for the entity's legal status. It is primarily a way to describe the scope of the correlative power, and international lawyers will typically just speak with reference to the power. But it allows me to tie up a thread from Chapter 1, where I made the following clarification about the correlativity of Hohfeldian relations. A state's rights over its territory, though they might be described as rights in a thing (*in rem*) rather than rights against a specific other entity, can still be interpreted as correlating with duties of other entities. It is just that they correlate with duties of 'persons constituting a very large and

[219] Raič (n 38) 38 n 81.

[220] It might be thought that, in order to acquire the duties as well as the rights of a state, the entity must additionally have a pre-existing *power*—a power to consent to the recognition. Compare the requirement, codified in Guiding Principles Applicable to Unilateral Declarations, principle 9, that the addressee of a unilateral declaration must consent in order to acquire any duties; treaty duties, of course, also require consent. But the entity's power to consent to the state's act of recognition might be created *by that act*: it need not be pre-existing. All that can be said for certain is that the entity must have a pre-existing *susceptibility*. Similarly, on the susceptibility to be granted a treaty-making power, see this book s 5.1.1.

[221] See this book s 1.1.2.

indefinite class': every entity that has a duty to respect that state's territory.[222] Thus, I explained, it does not matter that the bearers of the correlative duties cannot be comprehensively listed, because they can be defined as a class. It is the same with the power of states to recognize other entities. The class of entities with the correlative susceptibility is, in this case, 'large and indefinite' in an extreme sense. Subject to any exceptions yet to be discussed, it is the class of *all entities*—of everything that might be legally constructed as a fact. That is the point of the effectiveness-or-recognition view: states can recognize an entity regardless of whether it meets the effectiveness criteria or any other particular factual criterion. I also noted in Chapter 1 that the International Court, among other authorities, has described a person as an entity that is 'capable of possessing international rights and duties'—that has the *capacity* to possess them.[223] But I omitted the term 'capable' from my definition of personality, observing that it implies that some persons may have a capacity to possess rights and duties without actually possessing any.[224] It is now clear that this omission was justified. An indefinite number of entities are 'capable' of possessing rights and duties, in the sense that a state might decide that they are so capable and recognize them. Similarly, it would be a mistake to define persons to include every entity with a Hohfeldian susceptibility. Unless the number of persons is to expand to infinity, which would render the concept useless, the definition must be confined to entities that actually possess a right or duty.

A further advantage of this definition of personality is that it helps to defend the idea that recognition can ever suffice for statehood against a common criticism. This is the criticism that 'juridical effects even of a unilateral act cannot be conceived except between entities already endowed with juridical personality'.[225] The criticism, in other words, is that an entity cannot acquire personality by recognition, because the susceptibility to being recognized is itself an element or consequence of personality. This seems to treat 'juridical personality' as a monolithic package of rights, duties, and susceptibilities that cannot be disaggregated. But there is no reason of logic why a susceptibility cannot exist separately from rights and duties. On my narrow definition of personality as the actual possession of a right or duty, it is clear that an entity—such as the potential object of an act of recognition—may lack personality in my narrow sense and yet may have a susceptibility to be granted rights and duties in the future.

I conclude that each state has a power to recognize any other entity as a state, exercisable through a unilateral declaration or a treaty or perhaps in other ways,

[222] WN Hohfeld, 'Some fundamental legal conceptions as applied in judicial reasoning [part 2]' (1917) 26 Yale Law Journal 710, 718.

[223] *Reparation for Injuries Suffered in the Service of the United Nations (Advisory Opinion)* [1949] ICJ Rep 174, 179.

[224] This book s 1.2.

[225] Lauterpacht, *Recognition* (n 105) 57. Lauterpacht did not think this criticism applied to his own effectiveness-plus-recognition view, because he saw recognition as an act 'in pursuance of a legal duty'.

regardless of whether the entity meets the effectiveness criteria (subject to exceptions yet to be discussed).

3.4.3 Consequences beyond recognizing states

The consequence of recognition is bilateral: the recognizing state and the recognized entity are defined as states relative to each other for the purposes of customary norms concerning states.[226] They thereby acquire, relative to each other, all the rights, duties, and other legal attributes of states. This applies to recognizing states only. I will speculate in Chapter 5 about one manner in which, hypothetically, widespread but less-than-universal recognition of an entity might have consequences for non-recognizing states; but for reasons to be given there, even if that hypothesis is correct, any significance it has in practice is negligible.[227] So the discussion will proceed on the basis that recognition functions as an exercise of a power with direct consequences for the recognized entity and recognizing states, but not for non-recognizing states. This accords with how international law works in other contexts; for example, states cannot impose treaty duties on non-parties without their consent.[228]

There may still be some *indirect* consequences for non-recognizing states. In 2012, the UN General Assembly gave Palestine 'non-member observer State status' and cited, among other things, the fact that '132 States Members of the United Nations' (a majority) recognized it.[229] Later, when Palestine submitted to the jurisdiction of the International Criminal Court and acceded to the Court's statute, the prosecutor observed that the UN secretary-general, when designated as the depository of a treaty that is open to accession by 'all States', will adhere to the practice of the General Assembly; since the Assembly had given Palestine 'observer State status', it followed that Palestine 'must be considered a "State" for the purposes' of the Court's statute.[230] Thus recognition may have indirect consequences for parties to the UN Charter or to an 'all States' treaty that do not recognize Palestine: Palestine may be considered a state relative to them for specific purposes. But such consequences are possible only because those parties have

[226] The entity's practice and *opinio iuris* might (albeit to a negligible extent) contribute to the formation of customary norms applicable not only between recognizing states and the entity, but also *among recognizing states*. But this still could not have any consequences for relations with non-recognizing states.

[227] This book s 5.2.

[228] Vienna Convention on Treaties, arts 34–7. A non-party must expressly accept such a duty; in contrast, it is 'presumed' to assent to a right granted to it by the treaty 'so long as the contrary is not indicated'.

[229] GA res 67/19 (29 November 2012, Palestine) preamble and para 2.

[230] International Criminal Court, 'The Prosecutor of the International Criminal Court, Fatou Bensouda, opens a preliminary examination of the situation in Palestine' (press release, 16 January 2015).

consented to a particular treaty regime that has developed in a particular way; it remains the case that recognizing states cannot bind non-recognizing states unless the non-recognizing states have consented to be bound. It will become evident in Chapter 5 that, since entities such as Taiwan can join treaties whether or not they are states, the fact that an entity such as Palestine is a party to a treaty does not necessarily indicate that the entity has statehood for all purposes relative to all other parties.[231]

I have discussed the position of both recognizing and non-recognizing states; I also need to say a few words about the consequences recognition may have for *non-states*.

Although recognizing states cannot bind other states, it is conceivable that they have some sort of control over non-states. Imagine that there is a customary norm under which all states have a duty to certain non-states, such as international organizations or individuals. Can the recognition of an entity by states ever render this customary norm applicable between the recognized entity and a non-state? And can some non-states themselves, perhaps international organizations, render the norm applicable using a power of 'recognition' analogous with that of states? Comprehensive answers to these questions are beyond the scope of this book because they would entail an analysis of the personality of international organizations and individuals. But some general observations can be made. Many of the legal relations between states and non-states flow from treaties or the exercise of other powers, such as unilateral declarations. Here an entity such as Palestine is in a position similar to that of an effective state: *neither* entity can join a human rights treaty or an international organization without the consent of other states, as expressed in the relevant treaty. So to that extent the question of whether recognition defines the recognized entity as a state relative to non-states does not matter. Instead, the question is important only to the extent that states acquire legal relations relative to non-states *merely by virtue of being defined as states*. There are not many clear examples of this[232] (and some examples may be of little help in answering the question, because the existence of relations can be explained in another way: for instance, if Palestine has a duty to respect the human rights of individuals, that duty might arise under human rights treaties rather than as a consequence of recognition). This paucity of evidence has two implications: first, it may prove practically very difficult to identify what consequences recognition has for non-states; second, any such consequences may be of limited practical importance.

[231] This book s 5.1.1.

[232] Although I will not consider the position of international organizations or individuals, in this book s 5.2 I will consider whether state-like non-states ever acquire rights and duties directly under customary norms rather than under treaties or the like. I will identify only a few cases, some of them ambiguous.

3.5 States and states-in-context

The effectiveness-or-recognition view is the most persuasive explanation of statehood. It accepts that there is a customary norm 'entities that meet effectiveness criteria are defined as states': I will call this the 'effectiveness norm'. But states also have a power of recognition that can result in a state and an entity that recognize each other being defined as states relative to each other: I will call this the 'recognition norm'. Compliance with either rule may suffice for an entity to acquire the rights and other relations of states; neither is necessary.

In most respects, the effectiveness norm is the more important of the two rules. I have concluded that this norm (custom creates states) along with another customary norm (states create custom) forms part of the self-reproducing circle of conditional statements from which other norms of international law derive their validity. That includes norms empowering states to recognize other entities as states. If no states owed their legal existence to the effectiveness norm, this system-wide concept of validity would collapse and international law would have to revert to something like the recognition-only view. So it is critical for the functioning of international law that at least some states are defined as states by the effectiveness norm. In any case, almost all are. A further respect in which effectiveness is the more important of the two rules will emerge from Chapter 4: I will show that the recognition norm defers to the territorial frontiers laid down by the effectiveness norm, such that in practice recognition plays a supplementary or gap-filling role.[233] In one respect, however, the recognition norm might be seen as the more important rule. If a lawyer is called on to establish that two entities are states relative to each other—say, before an international court—then it may be much easier to show that the entities recognize each other than it would be to conduct a detailed analysis of the effectiveness criteria. Saganek, in concluding that there is nothing to stop identical duties from arising in multiple ways, suggests that recognition, being more precise, 'will be the main point of reference': it resolves uncertainty.[234] So both rules operate, in different ways, to stabilize international law; they complement each other.

What *is* statehood according to this effectiveness-or-recognition view?

A consequence of the two rules—the effectiveness norm and the recognition norm—is that, for the sake of clarity, one must actually speak about two categories of state-like entities with personality: 'states' in the full sense and 'states-in-context'. I emphasize that the two rules do not correspond exactly with these two categories. *Either* rule is capable of creating states in the full sense; the recognition norm can additionally create states-in-context.

[233] This book s 4.1.1.
[234] Saganek (n 122) 504.

First consider the meaning of 'statehood' in the full sense. An entity that is defined as a state under the effectiveness norm acquires two attributes: it becomes subject to the numerous customary norms in the form 'any entity that is defined as a state has a particular right or other relation' and also to the norm 'the practice and *opinio iuris* of all the entities that are defined as states contribute to customary norms'. It acquires these two attributes relative to every other entity that is defined as a state in this way. There is also an alternative way to achieve the same legal outcome. An ineffective entity that is recognized universally—by every effective state—can acquire the same two attributes relative to every effective state under the recognition norm. An example may be Somalia in the 1990s. In practice, in terms of their rights and other relations, there is no difference between this ineffective state created by the recognition norm and a state created by the effectiveness norm (subject to the position of non-states, which I noted may be of limited practical importance[235]). Furthermore, since most states are both clearly effective and universally recognized, either rule can be invoked as a basis for their legal status. It is pragmatic and broadly consistent with how entities such as Somalia are described to refer to all these entities as 'states' without further qualification, whether their statehood depends on effectiveness, universal recognition, or both. Statehood, then, can be defined as the possession relative to all other states of the two attributes that I mentioned: an entity is subject to the customary norms giving particular legal relations to entities defined as states and also to the norm that states contribute to custom. I repeat that the term 'state' essentially serves as a cross-reference, in that the substance of statehood in practice depends on the changing content of customary norms.

At the start of this chapter I introduced a third attribute: states comprise a class of facts that meet effectiveness criteria. This is a feature of states under the effectiveness norm, but on the definition I have just given it is not an indispensable attribute of statehood as such. States are always facts, but they are not always facts that meet the effectiveness criteria.

The other category of entities consists of 'states-in-context'. Note that the difference between an ineffective entity that is recognized universally—a state in the full sense—and one that is recognized less-than-universally is quantitative: the universally recognized entity is defined as a state relative to a greater number of other entities. Still, it would be misleading to use the term 'state', without further qualification, to describe an ineffective entity that is recognized by just one or several states. 'State-in-context' is a more precise term for such an entity: Palestine, for example, is at a minimum a state-in-context,[236] because it is recognized by some

[235] Its importance may be especially limited where an ineffective entity is recognized universally, because of the possibility that the applicability of any relevant customary norms might be confirmed by 'recognition' by non-states and because, in practice, their applicability is unlikely to be challenged anyway.

[236] By 'at a minimum' I mean regardless of whether it is a state in the full sense on the ground of effectiveness—a factually complex question on which I have refrained from expressing a firm view in this chapter.

but not all states (and it does not fall within any of the exceptions to be discussed later[237]). An even more precise approach is to specify the relevant recognizing state: Palestine is a state-in-context relative to, among other states, Sweden. The term 'state-in-context' also embraces the possibility of such an entity being treated as a state relative to non-recognizing states for specific purposes, such as Palestine at the UN General Assembly.

Since the distinction between states and states-in-context is a quantitative rather than a sharp analytical one, the overriding consideration in deciding which term to use is convenience. Strictly, on the definitions I have given, an ineffective entity that is recognized by every state in the world except one or two is a 'state-in-context' but not a 'state' in the full sense. But in practice it is likely to be more convenient simply to call this entity a state.

In this chapter, then, I have identified two categories of state-like entities with personality: states and states-in-context. It is evident already that, as in the past eras of international law that I discussed in Chapter 2, a monolithic conception of statehood and a dichotomy between states and non-states cannot capture the diversity of state-like entities; a monolithic conception also conceals the existence of two alternative paths to statehood. The definitions of states and states-in-context I have given here are, however, only provisional, because I still have to look at exceptions to the effectiveness and recognition norms.

[237] See this book s 4.1.1.

4
States
Exceptions

I have identified two general rules. Under the effectiveness norm, an entity that meets effectiveness criteria is a state relative to all other states. Under the recognition norm, a recognizing state and a recognized entity are states or states-in-context relative to each other (it is convenient to call an entity a state where recognition is universal and a state-in-context in other cases, but for present purposes the recognition norm raises essentially the same issues whichever term applies in a particular case). Yet when officials or lawyers debate an entity's statehood, they seldom limit themselves to arguments about effectiveness and recognition. They also invoke the concepts I will consider in this chapter. The first part of it deals with the principle that no law arises from unlawfulness, which is most often invoked in cases of the use of force. I will show that this underpins three exceptions to the general rules: the 'premature-recognition' and 'collective-non-recognition' exceptions to the recognition norm and the 'unlawful-effectuation' exception to the effectiveness norm. The second part of the chapter deals with self-determination. Although this influences the creation of states in a variety of ways, its most direct impact may be as an exception to the exceptions: it may enable the general rules to operate despite the principle that no law arises from unlawfulness. Most of the norms that will lead me to these conclusions, including self-determination and the prohibition of the use of force, are peremptory norms (*ius cogens*).[1]

I will close the chapter by using the examples of Kosovo and Somaliland to illustrate that, although self-determination and the principle that no law arises from unlawfulness are sometimes decisive, the exceptions are limited in scope: statehood usually still depends on the general rules, especially effectiveness, even in some cases with atypical features.

[1] Articles on Responsibility of States for Internationally Wrongful Acts [2001] 2(2) ILC Ybk 26, commentary to art 40, para 5; *Military and Paramilitary Activities in and against Nicaragua (Nicaragua v US)* [1986] ICJ Rep 14, para 190.

Statehood and the State-Like in International Law. Rowan Nicholson, Oxford University Press (2019).
© Rowan Nicholson
DOI: 10.1093/oso/9780198851219.001.0001

4.1 The principle that no law arises from unlawfulness

The thrust of the principle that no law arises from unlawfulness (*ex iniuria ius non oritur*) is that if conduct by an entity would ordinarily have consequences for legal relations or norms, but if in the circumstances the conduct is unlawful, then those consequences are prevented from occurring.[2] But this is not a rule of general applicability that indiscriminately nullifies every legal consequence of every unlawful act or omission. On the contrary, unlawful conduct is often permitted to have major consequences for relations or norms. It generally triggers the law of state responsibility, which gives remedial rights and powers to victims of the unlawful conduct.[3] And an unlawful occupation of foreign territory imposes a variety of duties on the occupier under international humanitarian law. The principle that no law arises from unlawfulness certainly does not intervene to prevent *this* law from arising from unlawfulness. It is a loose principle that underpins a variety of more specific norms; these norms prevent specific unlawful conduct from giving rise to specific consequences, chiefly consequences that, if allowed to occur, would be to the advantage of the wrongdoer.

An example of the principle in action can be drawn from article 52 of the Vienna Convention on the Law of Treaties: a 'treaty is void if its conclusion has been procured by the threat or use of force in violation of the principles of international law embodied in the Charter of the United Nations'.[4] This touches on two legal questions that must be carefully distinguished. The first question is whether, in the course of making a treaty, one of the treaty parties breaches a duty that it owes to another entity: whether the treaty party's conduct is lawful or unlawful. The second question is whether the norms ostensibly created by the treaty genuinely are binding legal norms: whether those norms are valid or invalid in international law. These two questions are not necessarily linked, but the effect of article 52 is to link them: if a treaty party's conduct is unlawful in a particular way ('in violation of the principles . . . embodied in the Charter') then the treaty norms that would otherwise have arisen from that conduct are invalid (they are 'void', which means that the norms in the treaty 'have no legal force', subject to some savings provisions in the Convention[5]). Article 52 is a specific concrete norm that reflects the principle that no law arises from unlawfulness: Olivier Corten observes that its 'basis . . . can

[2] 'Ex iniuria ius non oritur' in Aaron X Fellmeth and Maurice Horwitz, *Guide to Latin in International Law* (OUP 2009). Compare the definition of nullity in Prosper Weil, 'Le droit international public en quête de son identité: Cours général de droit international public' (1992) 237 Recueil des cours 9, 314.

[3] Articles on Responsibility of States, arts 28–41.

[4] Vienna Convention on the Law of Treaties (23 May 1969) 1155 UNTS 331, art 52.

[5] Ibid, art 69. Further on the terms 'void' and 'invalid' as used in the Convention see Marcelo Kohen and Sarah Heathcote, 'Article 42: 1969 Vienna Convention' in Olivier Corten and Pierre Klein (eds), *The Vienna Conventions on the Law of Treaties: A Commentary* (OUP 2011) vol 2, 1015, paras 11–12.

be found in the maxim *injuria jus non oritur*, which was considered a "general principle of law"' by the drafters of the Convention.[6]

The principle can also prevent norms and relations from being terminated. In *Gabčíkovo-Nagymaros*, Hungary argued that its own failure to comply with a treaty together with the reciprocal failure by the other party, Czechoslovakia, had the consequence of repudiating the treaty; but the International Court held that 'this reciprocal wrongful conduct did not bring the Treaty to an end' and that this sustained the 'principle *ex injuria jus non oritur*'.[7]

To determine how the principle that no law arises from unlawfulness affects statehood, I will need to search for further specific, concrete manifestations of it—though some guidance can be sought from analogies with established manifestations of the principle. On my provisional definition, an entity can be described as a state (or at least a state-in-context) if it is encompassed by the numerous customary norms in the form 'any entity that is defined as a state has a particular right or other relation' and also the norm 'the practice and *opinio iuris* of all the entities that are defined as states contribute to customary norms'. So the question to be considered is this: if conduct is of a kind that would ordinarily transform an entity into a state (or state-in-context), but if in the circumstances the conduct is unlawful, then does that unlawfulness prevent statehood from being created? The conduct that leads to statehood is quite different under each of the two general rules: under the recognition norm, the conduct is the act of recognition; under the effectiveness norm, the conduct that may be relevant varies. So I will consider separately how the principle that no law arises from unlawfulness affects each of the two general rules, starting with the recognition norm.

4.1.1 The premature-recognition exception to the recognition norm

The first situation I will discuss is where recognition derogates from a state's territorial integrity. It will be seen that this is an exception to the recognition norm. I begin with some preliminary points about territorial integrity and the related notion of unilateral secession.

Territorial integrity has been defined as 'the territorial "oneness" or "wholeness" of the State'.[8] It may have a number of manifestations.[9] What is relevant here is

[6] Olivier Corten, 'Article 52: 1969 Vienna Convention' in Olivier Corten and Pierre Klein (eds), *The Vienna Conventions on the Law of Treaties: A Commentary* (OUP 2011) vol 2, 1201, para 2. Some of the other grounds for treaty invalidity (which include fraud and corruption: Vienna Convention on Treaties, arts 46–51) appear similar but may constitute defects of consent rather than manifestations of the principle that no law arises from unlawfulness.

[7] *Gabčíkovo-Nagymaros Project (Hungary/Slovakia)* [1997] ICJ Rep 7, paras 114, 133.

[8] Samuel KN Blay, 'Territorial integrity and political independence' (last updated 2010) MPEPIL.

[9] Eg, it may stand for the loose policy of preserving territorial stability that underlies the principle *uti possidetis* (as you possess). This principle applies to pre-independence boundaries, which 'might

a state's Hohfeldian right that its territorial integrity be respected. This is a right with a long pedigree. Emer de Vattel maintained in 1758 that '[w]e should not only refrain from usurping the territory of others; we should also respect it, and abstain from every act contrary to the rights of the sovereign: for a foreign nation can claim no right in it'.[10] A newer formulation appears in the Friendly Relations Declaration of 1970: '[e]very State shall refrain from any action aimed at the partial or total disruption of the national unity and territorial integrity of any other State or country'.[11] As this indicates, respecting territorial integrity is a duty of '[e]very State' that correlates, in the familiar Hohfeldian way, with a right of 'any other State'. This may be seen as part of the package of relations embraced by the term 'sovereignty', perhaps as a manifestation or implication of a state's broader right to exercise jurisdiction within its own territory, which correlates with a duty of non-intervention borne by each other state.[12]

Two things do *not* follow from this right that territorial integrity be respected.

First, it does not make attempts at unilateral secession unlawful. By 'unilateral secession' I mean the acquisition of statehood by an entity whose territory was previously part of an existing state without that parent state's consent. It is relevant in this situation that the duty to respect territorial integrity, like the correlative right, vests in states rather than in a wider class of entities. The International Court confirmed this in *Kosovo*: 'the scope of the principle of territorial integrity is confined to the sphere of relations between States'.[13] Thus an entity that is not yet a state but

be no more than delimitations between different administrative divisions or colonies all subject to the same sovereign'; it secures respect for those boundaries 'at the moment when independence is achieved': *Frontier Dispute (Burkina Faso/Mali)* [1986] ICJ Rep 554, para 23, compare para 30. It is thus a principle about territory that applies 'at the moment when' statehood is acquired. So although often invoked in debates about statehood, it is not directly relevant to the question at hand, which is not the extent of a new state's territory but *whether an entity is a state at all.* Compare *Opinion No 3* (Badinter Commission) (1992) 92 ILR 170, 171: only once the collapse of Yugoslavia had led 'to the creation of... independent States' (which depended on effectiveness) would its former internal boundaries 'become frontiers'.

---

[10] Emer de Vattel, *The Law of Nations* (first published 1758, Béla Kapossy and Richard Whatmore eds, Liberty Fund 2008) pt II.93.

[11] Declaration on Principles of International Law Concerning Friendly Relations and Co-operation Among States in Accordance with the Charter of the United Nations, annex to GA res 2625 (XXV) (24 October 1970) principle *e*. The International Court has held that consent to a General Assembly resolution such as the Friendly Relations Declaration 'expresses an *opinio juris*' and hence that it may be regarded as custom (though this is not necessarily true of all resolutions): *Nicaragua v US* [1986] ICJ Rep 14, para 188. Compare Final Act of the Conference on Security and Co-operation in Europe, Helsinki (1 August 1975) 14 ILM 1292, principle IV.

[12] This book s 2.3. See also the discussion of non-intervention in *Nicaragua v US* [1986] ICJ Rep 14, paras 202–5.

[13] *Accordance with International Law of the Unilateral Declaration of Independence in Respect of Kosovo (Advisory Opinion)* [2010] ICJ Rep 403, para 80. Compare Report of the International Committee of Jurists upon the Legal Aspects of the Aaland Islands Question (1920) 3 LNOJ Sp Supp 3, 5: 'all that has been said concerning the attributes of the sovereignty of a State, generally speaking, only applies to a nation which is definitively constituted as a sovereign State', as distinct from an entity in the process of becoming a state.

that seeks to secede unilaterally does not have a duty to respect its parent state's territorial integrity, and its attempt at unilateral secession is not unlawful on that basis.[14] This is to be expected: non-state entities do not generally bear the duties of statehood any more than they enjoy the rights of statehood; in most contexts, their conduct is not specifically regulated by norms of international law at all. (Of course, this is just the general position in international law; under the parent state's own domestic law, attempting unilateral secession might constitute sedition or another criminal offence.)

The other thing that territorial integrity does *not* do is prevent a unilateral secessionist entity from actually acquiring statehood under the effectiveness norm. On the contrary, unilateral secession has historically been a common method of acquiring statehood. A few examples among many from the 'age of revolution' from 1789 to 1848 are the republics of Latin America (which seceded from Spain), Greece (from the Ottoman Empire), and Belgium (from the Netherlands).[15] In cases such as these, the parent state resisted secession and withheld its consent for a long time. In the absence of such consent, foreign states were reluctant to accept the secessionist entity as a state. But both states and international lawyers during this period accepted that achieving statehood by unilateral secession was nonetheless possible—eventually. William Harcourt wrote in 1863 that as far

> as any practical rule can be deduced from historical examples it seems to be this—When a sovereign State, from exhaustion or any other cause, has virtually and substantially abandoned the struggle for supremacy it has no right to complain if a foreign State treat the independence of its former subjects as *de facto* established; nor can it prolong its sovereignty by a mere paper assertion of right. . . . Rebellion, until it has succeeded, is Treason; when it is successful, it becomes Independence. And thus the only real test of independence is final success.[16]

This can be interpreted in terms of the effectiveness norm. Usually, an entity cannot become sufficiently effective so long as its parent state is actively contesting its claim to statehood; if the parent state substantially gives up, the entity can consolidate its effectiveness.

There are not many recent examples of truly unilateral secessions, as distinct from cases where the parent state has eventually consented to independence, such

[14] The Court concluded, in particular, that territorial integrity does not create a 'general prohibition against unilateral declarations of independence': *Kosovo* [2010] ICJ Rep 403, para 81.

[15] This term is borrowed from Eric Hobsbawm, *The Age of Revolution: 1789–1848* (Weidenfeld & Nicolson 1962). See also Mikulas Fabry, *Recognizing States: International Society and the Establishment of New States since 1776* (OUP 2010) chs 1–3.

[16] William Vernon Harcourt, *Letters by Historicus on Some Questions of International Law* (Macmillan 1863) 9–10. For further nineteenth-century formulations of the rule, see James Crawford, *The Creation of States in International Law* (2nd edn, OUP 2006) 382–3 n 30.

as Eritrea and South Sudan.[17] The sparseness of the practice leads some scholars to doubt whether the traditional view is still correct. Jure Vidmar has suggested that nowadays (at least in the absence of self-determination, which introduces complications to be discussed later) if 'the parent State continues to exist and does not consent' then it is arguable that 'the only way' for an entity to acquire statehood 'is through international recognition':[18] In my terms, this would mean that the effectiveness norm cannot operate in unilateral secession cases but the recognition norm can. In support of this, Vidmar quotes from the Canadian Supreme Court's *Secession of Quebec* opinion. If Quebec were to try to secede unilaterally from Canada, the Court said,

> [t]he ultimate success of such a secession would be dependent on recognition by the international community, which is likely to consider the legality and legitimacy of secession having regard to, amongst other facts, the conduct of Quebec and Canada, in determining whether to grant or withhold recognition.[19]

Vidmar remarks that this 'can hardly be squared with the declaratory theory'—with the idea that effectiveness is sufficient for statehood.[20] Elsewhere in the opinion, however, the Court clarified that the effectiveness norm was ultimately decisive and recognition merely 'a practical matter':

> Although recognition by other states is not, at least as a matter of theory, necessary to achieve statehood, the viability of a would-be state in the international community depends, as a practical matter, upon recognition by other states. That process of recognition is guided by legal norms. However, international recognition is not alone constitutive of statehood... Recognition occurs only after a territorial unit has been successful, as a political fact, in achieving secession.[21]

This essentially affirms the traditional view that unilateral secession may eventually be achieved 'as a political fact'—by effectiveness—even if that is very difficult in practice.

The Badinter Commission impliedly took the same view of some of the successor states of Yugoslavia. The Commission held on 29 November 1991 that Yugoslavia, though 'in the process of dissolution', had 'until now retained its international personality'; it went on to hold that by 27 April 1992 this process was complete and the

[17] Jure Vidmar, 'Explaining the legal effects of recognition' (2012) 61 ICLQ 361, 365–70. See further Marcelo Kohen (ed), *Secession: International Law Perspectives* (CUP 2006).
[18] Vidmar, 'Explaining' (n 17) 374. See also Jure Vidmar, *Democratic Statehood in International Law: The Emergence of New States in Post-Cold War Practice* (Hart 2013) 237.
[19] *Re Secession of Quebec* (Supreme Court, Canada) (1998) 115 ILR 536, para 155.
[20] Vidmar, 'Explaining' (n 17) 375.
[21] *Quebec* (1998) 115 ILR 536, para 142, compare para 106.

old state of Yugoslavia no longer existed.[22] It also held that Slovenia and Croatia 'definitively' broke all links with the organs of Yugoslavia and became 'sovereign States in international law' on 8 October 1991 and that Macedonia did so on 17 November.[23] The significance of these dates is that they indicate that Slovenia, Croatia, and Macedonia became states during the period when Yugoslavia 'retained its international personality'. The Commission thus assumed that it was possible for entities to secede unilaterally from a still-existing parent state. Although the Commission referred to the process as 'dissolution', it implied that this dissolution involved both unilateral secession and, subsequently, the extinction of the old state.[24]

If a unilateral secessionist entity succeeds in acquiring statehood under the effectiveness norm, then from that moment onward it has its own right that its territorial integrity be respected and the scope of the parent state's equivalent right is correspondingly diminished. Reflecting this, 'the case of the emergence of the new State' is sometimes listed among the 'modes for the acquisition of territorial sovereignty'.[25] In practice, since unilateral secession is a complex and often violent process, it may be difficult to pinpoint when this happens. But in principle it happens at a particular moment; there is no period when both the parent state and the entity have incompatible rights over the same territory.[26] The Badinter Commission called the relevant date 'a question of fact that is to be assessed in each case in the light of the circumstances in which each of the States concerned was created'.[27]

In sum, then, states have a duty to respect territorial integrity that correlates with a right of other states. Since the duty does not apply to entities that are not yet states, it does not make attempts at unilateral secession unlawful, nor does it prevent them from succeeding under the effectiveness norm (although for practical

[22] *Opinion No 1* (Badinter Commission) (1991) 92 ILR 162, paras 2–3; *Opinion No 8* (Badinter Commission) (1992) 92 ILR 199, para 4; *Opinion No 11* (Badinter Commission) (1993) 96 ILR 719, para 7.

[23] *Opinion No 11* (1993) 96 ILR 719, paras 4–6. The Commission also held that Bosnia acquired statehood on 6 March 1992. This date is not only significantly later but less certain; doubts were still being expressed about Bosnia's effectiveness when it was admitted to the United Nations in May. See Roland Rich, 'Recognition of states: The collapse of Yugoslavia and the Soviet Union' (1993) 4 EJIL 36, 49–51; Thomas D Grant, *The Recognition of States: Law and Practice in Debate and Evolution* (Praeger 1999) 164–5. On the names of Yugoslavia, Macedonia, and Bosnia, see footnotes in this book s 3.1.4.

[24] See further Crawford, *Creation* (n 16) 707–14.

[25] Robert Jennings, *The Acquisition of Territory in International Law* (Manchester UP 1963) 12, further 6–12.

[26] Eg, the committee of jurists that gave an opinion on the Aaland Islands found it 'difficult to say at what exact date the Finnish Republic, in the legal sense of the term, actually became a definitively constituted State': Report of the Committee of Jurists on the Aaland Islands (n 13) 9. But it assumed that such an exact date existed in principle—it decided an issue on the ground that the issue had arisen before Finland 'acquired the character of a definitively constituted State', that is, before the relevant date: at 14. A second body held that Finland had acquired statehood earlier: Report Submitted to the Council of the League of Nations by the Commission of Rapporteurs on the Aaland Islands Question (16 April 1921) LN doc B7 21/68/106.

[27] *Opinion No 11* (1993) 96 ILR 719, para 3. See further *Opinion No 1* (1991) 92 ILR 162, 164–5.

reasons success may be very difficult). This is the traditional view and remains consistent with recent practice and authorities.

With these preliminary points established, I can move on to how territorial integrity creates an exception to the recognition norm.

Although a unilateral secessionist entity itself has no duty to respect its parent state's territorial integrity, *other existing states* certainly do; to use the formulation from the Friendly Relations Declaration, other states have a duty to 'refrain from any action aimed at the partial or total disruption of the national unity and territorial integrity' of the parent state.[28] And recognition by other states of a unilateral secessionist entity that does not yet met the effectiveness criteria—known as 'premature' recognition—is an action of precisely that kind. This is a caveat frequently given to the traditional view of unilateral secession. For instance, in 1778, France negotiated a treaty with the nascent United States, even though the parent state, Great Britain, was still resisting the secession. Harcourt observed that at the time 'it was decisively established that such conduct was unlawful, and afforded a justifiable cause of war'.[29] The US secretary of state, William Seward, made the same point in 1861 in the context of the attempted unilateral secession of the Confederate States of America:

> We freely admit that a nation may, and even ought, to recognize a new State which has absolutely and beyond question effected its independence, and permanently established its sovereignty; and that a recognition in such a case affords no just cause of offence . . . On the other hand, we insist that a nation that recognizes a revolutionary State, with a view to aid its effecting its sovereignty and independence, commits a great wrong against the nation whose integrity is thus invaded, and makes itself responsible for a just and ample redress.[30]

Hersch Lauterpacht thought that there was 'practical unanimity among international lawyers' that 'premature recognition is more than an unfriendly act; it is an act of intervention and an international delinquency'.[31] The traditional view still holds on this point, too. In 1967–70, for instance, five states recognized Biafra, which had unilaterally declared independence from Nigeria. David Ijalaye describes these recognitions as, 'in the circumstances, premature, thus "constituting a tortious act against the lawful government [of Nigeria] and thus a breach

[28] Friendly Relations Declaration, principle *e*.

[29] Harcourt (n 16) 9; compare John Bassett Moore, *A Digest of International Law* (US GPO 1906) vol 1, 73.

[30] William H Seward, Letter to Charles Francis Adams (10 April 1861) in *Message of the President of the United States to the Two Houses of Congress, at the Commencement of the Second Session of the Thirty-seventh Congress* (*Foreign Relations* series, US GPO 1861) 71, 76–7.

[31] Hersch Lauterpacht, *Recognition in International Law* (first published 1947, CUP 2013) 8, 8 n 5. See further John Dugard, 'The secession of states and their recognition in the wake of Kosovo' (2013) 357 Recueil des cours 9, 23–6.

of international law"'.[32] Christian Tomuschat concurs that premature recognition remains unlawful, calling it 'a head-on attack on the sovereign powers of the parent State which seeks to preserve its territorial integrity . . . a case of unlawful intervention'.[33]

Here one must draw the distinction (which I illustrated earlier using the law of treaties) between the unlawfulness of conduct and the invalidity of ostensible consequences of that conduct. Premature recognition is unlawful, but that does not *necessarily* lead to the conclusion that it is also invalid. A conclusion that premature recognition is 'invalid' would mean that it does not have the consequence that the recognizing state and the recognized entity are defined as states relative to each other. For premature recognition to be invalid in this sense, there must be an applicable norm that reflects the principle that no law arises from unlawfulness. Lauterpacht speculated that there was such a norm: premature recognition, being 'a denial of the sovereignty of the parent State', was 'a recognition which an international tribunal would declare not only to constitute a wrong, but probably also to be in itself invalid'.[34] As the word 'probably' hints, he could not point to any international tribunal that had actually declared this. But it will be seen that, although there is still no unambiguous authority, nowadays there is a good reason to accept this conclusion.

An unusual illustration of the problem is Panama's unilateral secession from Colombia. In August 1903, the Colombian legislature declined to ratify a treaty with the United States to build a canal across the isthmus of Panama.[35] A way around this obstacle to American commercial interests was soon found. On 3 November, Panamanian rebels, assisted by US warships, declared independence. On the 13 November, the United States recognized Panama as a new state. Only a few days later, on the 18 November, the United States and Panama concluded the Hay–Bunau-Varilla Treaty. Panama thereby transferred to the United States, within what became known as the Panama Canal Zone, 'all the rights, power and authority . . . which the United States would possess and exercise if it were the sovereign of the territory'.[36] Although transferred by a bilateral treaty, as quasi-sovereign rights over territory these were rights that might ordinarily have applied *in rem*, relative to all other states.[37] The treaty also required Panama to transfer to the

[32] David A Ijalaye, 'Was "Biafra" at any time a state in international law?' (1971) 65 AJIL 551, 559, quoting Rosalyn Higgins, *The Development of International Law Through the Political Organs of the United Nations* (OUP 1963) 138.

[33] Christian Tomuschat, 'Recognition of new States—the case of premature recognition' in Peter Hipold (ed), *Kosovo and International Law: The ICJ Advisory Opinion of 22 July 2010* (Nijhoff 2012) 31, 35.

[34] Lauterpacht (n 31) 8–9. This must be read in the context of his effectiveness-plus-recognition view, discussed in this book s 3.3.

[35] Moore (n 29) vol 3, 46–113.

[36] Hay–Bunau-Varilla Treaty, US–Panama (18 November 1903) 33 Stat 2234, art 3.

[37] On whether the rights amounted to sovereignty *as such*, rather than something more limited, see David G Hanrahan, 'Legal aspects of the Panama Canal Zone—in perspective' (1965) 45 Boston

United States 'all rights which it now has or hereafter may acquire to the property of ... the Panama Railroad Company as a result of the transfer of sovereignty from the Republic of Colombia to the Republic of Panama'.[38] The recognition and the transfer of rights were controversial. An American scholar, Theodore S Woolsey, lamented that the United States, 'by recognizing the new State of Panama within ten days of its secession, as possessed of sovereignty although *sans* a constitution, *sans* a government, *sans* a definite status, *sans* everything', had acted prematurely and unlawfully.[39]

Eventually, the United States itself began to entertain doubts about the hasty transfer of rights. In 1912, President William Taft endorsed a proposal for a treaty with Colombia under which a tribunal would adjudicate, 'taking into consideration the stipulations of the treaty between the United States and Panama, and the *status quo* of Panama, as thereby recognized', whether it was the United States or Colombia that was 'the owner of the reversionary rights of the Panama Railway'; if it was Colombia, the United States would pay an indemnity for the rights.[40] That proposal went nowhere. In 1914, however, the two states signed the Thomson–Urrutia Treaty, under which Colombia was to recognize Panama; in exchange, the United States would express 'sincere regret' about the events of 1903 and give Colombia $25 million along with certain privileges over the canal.[41] This was objected to as an implied admission that recognition had been premature.[42] Philander C Knox, formerly US secretary of state, called it 'an apology that fouls our title to Panama'.[43] Theodore Roosevelt said '[e]ither the course we took in 1903 was right' (he had been president at the time), 'in which case it is worse than an outrage now to pay blackmail, or it was wrong, in which case we have now no right to be on the Isthmus'.[44] Partly due to these objections, US ratification of the treaty was delayed until 1922. In the end, 'sincere regret' was deleted and words inserted that 'the title to' the canal and railway 'is now vested entirely and absolutely in the United States of America, without any incumbrances or indemnities whatever'.[45]

University Law Review 64. See also *SS Wimbledon (UK, France, Italy, and Japan v Germany)* (1923) PCIJ ser A 1, 25–8.

[38] Hay–Bunau-Varilla Treaty, art 8.

[39] Theodore S Woolsey, 'The recognition of Panama and its results' (1904) 3 Canadian Law Review 91, 93.

[40] William H Taft, Letter to Philander C Knox (30 November 1912), quoted in James Brown Scott, 'The treaty between Colombia and the United States' (1921) 15 AJIL 430, 438–9.

[41] The text of the treaty before its later modification can be found at 9 LNTS 301.

[42] Watt Stewart, 'The ratification of the Thomson–Urrutia Treaty' (1930) 10 Southwestern Political and Social Science Quarterly 416, especially 420.

[43] Philander C Knox, Letter to William H Taft (20 May 1914), quoted in Richard L Lael, 'Struggle for ratification: Wilson, Lodge, and the Thomson–Urrutia Treaty' (1978) 2 Diplomatic History 81, 89.

[44] Theodore Roosevelt, Letter to William J Stone (11 July 1914), quoted in ibid, 83.

[45] Thomson–Urrutia Treaty, US–Colombia (6 April 1914) 42 Stat 2122, art 1 as modified; Lael (n 43) 88.

JB Scott remarked that this insertion 'removes any cloud from that title, as far as Colombia is concerned'.[46]

Although the controversy was resolved by consent, it still provides glimmers of evidence about whether or not premature recognition is valid. The key point is that it was assumed that, *if* the recognition of Panama had been premature, then the transfer of rights to the United States—during the period when Panama's effectiveness remained in doubt—would therefore have been invalid. Roosevelt objected that the Americans would then have 'no right to be on the Isthmus'; Knox feared that it would 'foul' their 'title to Panama'. Consider this assumption in light of the two possible views about premature recognition.

The first view is that premature recognition is *invalid*. This would have made the transfer a dead letter: Panama would have been purporting to transfer rights that it did not actually have at the time, not even relative to the United States. So this view leads categorically to the assumption, made by the Americans, that if the recognition of Panama was premature then the transfer was invalid. This is also consistent with Colombia's position, though Colombia made the point in ambiguous terms (and its position is further clouded by a separate argument that it made, to the effect that the transfer of rights breached a Colombian–US treaty from 1846).[47] Its foreign minister, Luis Carlos Rico, wrote to the Americans in 1904:

> If, for the Government of the United States, the recognition of Panama as an independent Republic is an accomplished fact, and as such it considers it irrevocable, without stopping to show the illegitimacy of the theory of the accomplished facts when they are contrary to foreign right and to the engagements with third parties, I make the declaration that the recognition of the independence of the Colombian Department of Panama by the United States and other powers does not make void nor does it limit the rights of sovereignty of Colombia on the Isthmus of that name, and that this Republic does not admit, in principle, that the recognition is of an irrevocable character.[48]

This disputed the applicability of the principle that law arises from the facts (*ex factis ius oritur*) on the ground that the recognition was 'contrary to foreign right'. It impliedly relied on the opposite principle: that no law arises from unlawfulness (*ex iniuria ius non oritur*).

The alternative view is that premature recognition is *valid* between the recognizing state and the recognized entity. This raises some abstruse questions. Initially, the transfer of quasi-sovereign rights could, even on this view, have had

[46] Scott (n 40) 432.

[47] Luis Carlos Rico, Letter to Alban G Snyder (12 April 1904) in *Papers Relating to the Foreign Relations of the United States: 1904* (US GPO 1904) 206, 223–4.

[48] Ibid, 220.

force only between the United States and Panama. But when Panama eventually met the effectiveness criteria and acquired statehood relative to *all* states, could the transfer then have come into force *in rem*, relative to all states, given that the transferor and transferee had validly consented to it? Might anything else have invalidated it? Woolsey implied that premature recognition was valid but speculated that the transfer could still be invalid on the ground that 'Panama's agreement to lease territory and cede property, which Colombia still claims' was 'a contract to do an unlawful act'[49] (though it is hard to see why unlawfulness would invalidate the transfer but not the recognition). Depending on the answers to these questions, the view that premature recognition is valid *might* be consistent with the notion that the transfer was invalid, at least relative to Colombia. But equally it might not; it does not support that notion in a categorical way.

The most straightforward explanation of the episode, then, is that premature recognition—and hence any transaction that depended on it—was simply assumed to be invalid, though since other explanations may be available this does not amount to compelling evidence.

If the Panama episode offers only limited evidence of whether premature recognition is valid, most other cases cannot offer even that much. Practice in most cases will look similar whichever view is correct: since recognition lacks direct consequences for non-recognizing states anyway, the parent state and other non-recognizing states will retain the same rights and other relations no matter what; and as for recognizing states, their practice will tend to reflect their stance that recognition was not premature in the first place, whether or not that stance is legally correct.

This might lead one to doubt that the question of whether premature recognition is valid is a meaningful one. Is there a difference between saying that Panama 'had' statehood relative to the United States, on the ground that it had been validly recognized, and saying that the United States incorrectly 'treated' it as a state? One reply is as follows. It is true that, when a norm about validity clashes with what a recalcitrant state 'treats' as valid, the norm may have only a limited influence on state behaviour. But the mere fact that it is part of the language of international law gives it *some* influence; in this case, it may have influenced the Americans to clear matters up with Colombia.[50] A further reply is that, in any event, this is a logical and familiar use of the language of international law, which is a system of norms that is distinct from politics, not a mere description of state behaviour.[51] The difference

[49] Woolsey (n 39) 99–100. Woolsey thought that 'premature or wrongful recognition may violate the rights of the parent State', but still 'accomplishes its object' in that, 'so far as the recognizing State is concerned, the new body is to be allowed to exercise towards it the rights of statehood'.

[50] Another example will appear in this book s 4.1.2: apartheid South Africa's conduct in Namibia. As with Panama, the situation eventually came into line with the language of international law, and that language—which was used to put pressure on South Africa—had at least some influence on events.

[51] See this book ss 1.1.1, 1.2, 2.1.1.

between valid and invalid recognition is of the same character as the firmly established difference between a valid treaty and an invalid treaty whose parties 'treat' it as valid between themselves—as, perhaps, with the treaty between the United States and Panama. In addition, however malleable the concept of validity may have been at the time of the Panama episode, nowadays it is more robust. I concluded in Chapter 3 that, in light of the emergence of peremptory norms, there can now be no doubt that international law has a single, system-wide concept of validity; a state cannot simply decide for itself what counts as valid in international law.[52] So the emergence of peremptory norms confirms that the question under discussion—whether premature recognition is valid—is meaningful.

Peremptory norms also make it possible to answer the question with more conviction than was justifiable at the time of the Panama episode. A legal relation or norm ostensibly created by a treaty, unilateral declaration, or other exercise of power is invalid if it 'conflicts with a peremptory norm'.[53] Premature recognition, if valid, would amount to an exercise of a power to grant rights and other relations to the recognized entity that *conflict directly* with the still-existing rights of the parent state over the contested territory. This includes rights under peremptory norms, such as the parent state's right that other states not use force within the territory. Imagine, for example, that a prematurely recognized entity invites the recognizing state to deploy troops on 'its' territory (Panama did this: under the Hay–Bunau-Varilla Treaty, the United States could 'employ armed forces for the safety or protection of the Canal'[54]). The power to issue this invitation is among the customary relations of states. But putting this power in the hands of the prematurely recognized entity conflicts with the parent state's still-existing right under a peremptory norm that other states not deploy troops on the parent state's territory without its consent. Thus the act of premature recognition is invalid for the same reason that a treaty to invade the territory of a third state is invalid.

This is a reason of principle to conclude that premature recognition—recognition in breach of an existing state's territorial integrity—is invalid. The alternative view would lead to intractable conflicts with peremptory norms. This is an exception to the recognition norm that reflects the principle that no law arises from unlawfulness. I will refer to it as the 'premature-recognition exception'. My reason for referring to it in this way rather than explicitly in terms of territorial integrity will become evident later, when I look at self-determination scenarios in which an allusion to territorial integrity would be inapt.[55] Although confirmed by

[52] This book s 3.2.

[53] Vienna Convention on Treaties, art 53; Guiding Principles Applicable to Unilateral Declarations of States Capable of Creating Legal Obligations [2006] 2(2) ILC Ybk 161, principle 8. See further this book s 3.2.

[54] Hay–Bunau-Varilla Treaty, art 23.

[55] This book s 4.2.2.

a principle that has emerged only in recent decades, this exception accords with the most straightforward explanation of the earlier Panama episode.

The reasoning that has led me to confirm the existence of this exception is similar to the reasoning that led me to reject the recognition-only view of statehood (the recognition-only view excluded the possibility of a system-wide concept of validity, which is necessary for peremptory norms to exist). This is no coincidence. In both cases, the introduction into the system of the concept of peremptory norms has the consequence of subordinating recognition to effectiveness. The premature-recognition exception protects against a proliferation of recognized but ineffective states or states-in-context whose existence would derogate from the territorial integrity of effective states. In cases of direct conflict, this preserves the exclusivity of the territorial integrity of states. Bear in mind, however, that recognition is subordinated to effectiveness *only* in cases of direct conflict; the exception is not so far-reaching as to nullify the effectiveness-or-recognition view altogether. If there is no still-existing parent state with a still-existing right that its territorial integrity be respected, the exception does not apply and the recognition norm may be able to operate.

This leaves two groups of cases in which the recognition norm can operate unhindered by the premature-recognition exception. First, the recognized entity may claim territory that is not otherwise claimed by any state. That was the case with Somalia in the 1990s[56] and is true of the Vatican City, Monaco, and most other entities whose effectiveness is dubious but that have been recognized universally. Recognizing the Vatican City's sovereignty over territory that is not otherwise claimed by any state cannot derogate from any state's territorial integrity. The complex case of Palestine may also fall partially into this group: the Gaza Strip and the majority of the West Bank are not formally claimed by Israel or any other state, only by Palestine. Second, it may be that an existing state does claim the relevant territory, but the claim is legally unsound. If one state forcibly conquers another and invalidly annexes its territory, the annexed entity can still be lawfully and validly recognized. Often such an entity *is* recognized, as, for example, with Poland when it was partitioned between Germany and the Soviet Union during the Second World War and represented by a government-in-exile in London.[57] As will be seen, similar reasoning can be applied where a state invalidly claims the territory of a people with a right to external self-determination.[58] A currently existing would-be state that may fall into this category is the Saharawi Arab Democratic Republic.[59]

[56] With the caveat that part of the territory was also claimed by Somaliland, on which see this book s 4.3.

[57] This is true whether or not the annexed entity also retains statehood under the effectiveness norm, despite the suppression of its independence, on which see Crawford, *Creation* (n 16) 519–22, 689–95.

[58] See this book s 4.2.2 on Guinea-Bissau.

[59] See further Sven Simon, 'Western Sahara' in Christian Walter, Antje von Ungern-Sternberg, and Kavus Abushov (eds), *Self-Determination and Secession in International Law* (OUP 2014) 255.

Most of its ostensible territory is claimed and occupied by Morocco, whose claim is widely held to be unsound. Since it is recognized by some but not all states, and on the premise that the premature-recognition exception does not apply, it is, like Palestine, at a minimum a state-in-context relative to recognizing states, even though there is doubt about its effectiveness.

The premature-recognition exception helps to explain why unilateral secession is very difficult even though a unilateral secessionist entity does not have a duty to respect its parent state's territorial integrity. In other scenarios—such as those exemplified by Somalia, the Vatican City, Palestine, and the Saharawi Arab Democratic Republic—the recognition norm can cure defects in an entity's effectiveness. But since that is not possible in a unilateral secession scenario, the entity is *legally compelled* to meet the effectiveness criteria, strictly and incontestably. Moreover, typically it must do so in the face of military resistance by its parent state. There is hence no need to postulate a stricter set of effectiveness criteria to explain the difficulty of unilateral secession: it is just that this is the main scenario in which the effectiveness criteria operate in their purest form, uncontaminated by the recognition norm. This adds to the explanatory strength of the effectiveness-or-recognition view.

The premature-recognition exception is not the only exception to the recognition norm that reflects the principle that no law arises from unlawfulness. I now turn to another one.

4.1.2 The collective-non-recognition exception to the recognition norm

The next exception is connected to the collective duty of non-recognition. Nowadays this is a standard element of theories about statehood. But since other theories assume that there is only one general rule creating statehood, whereas I have identified two (the effectiveness norm and the recognition norm), it must be reanalysed in that light. Here I am concerned with how it creates an exception to the recognition norm; at this stage I am not entering into the separate question of whether there is a parallel exception to the effectiveness norm.

In 1931, 'Manchukuo' purported to secede unilaterally from China. According to the League of Nations, the 'Manchurian independence movement' could succeed only 'owing to the presence of Japanese troops', and political authority in Manchukuo rested 'in the hands of Japanese officials and advisers'.[60] This led to what is called the Stimson doctrine. The US secretary of state, Henry Stimson, declared that his government—to be joined by many others—would not

[60] Report Provided for in Article 15(4) of the Covenant on Manchuria (1933) 112 LNOJ Sp Supp 56, 72.

> recognize any situation, treaty or agreement which may be brought about by means contrary to the covenants and obligations of the [Kellogg–Briand Pact of 1928], to which treaty both China and Japan, as well as the United States, are parties.[61]

The parties to the Kellogg–Briand Pact had renounced war 'as an instrument of national policy'.[62] The League of Nations, referring to the Pact, described the Japanese regime as 'incompatible with fundamental principles of existing international obligations'.[63] Although the Pact came to be seen as a naïve failure, the Stimson doctrine was given new life after 1945, when a fresh attempt to prohibit force was made in the UN Charter and the concept of peremptory norms—among them the prohibition of force—crystallized into custom. It has evolved into a customary norm imposing on states a collective duty of non-recognition, which has been codified in the Articles on Responsibility of States. The duty applies to any 'serious breach by a State of an obligation arising under a peremptory norm of general international law'.[64] No state 'shall recognize as lawful a situation created by' such a serious breach, nor shall it 'render aid or assistance in maintaining that situation'.[65]

An example of an entity covered by the collective duty of non-recognition is Northern Cyprus. Turkey unlawfully occupied part of the territory of Cyprus by force in 1974; in 1983, with Turkish support, Northern Cyprus declared independence.[66] The Security Council called upon 'all States not to recognize any Cypriot State other than the Republic of Cyprus'.[67]

Some clarifications must be made about this duty of non-recognition.

First, in this context the word 'recognize' is not always used to mean recognizing an entity as a state. For instance, in *Namibia*, the International Court held that a collective duty of non-recognition applied to apartheid South Africa's continued presence in Namibia after the termination of its League of Nations mandate in 1966[68] (the Court cited a resolution of the Security Council rather than the *customary* duty of non-recognition, but the International Law Commission

[61] Henry L Stimson, Letter to William Cameron Forbes (7 January 1932) in *Foreign Relations of the United States: Japan: 1931–1941* (US GPO 1943) vol 1, 76.

[62] General Treaty for Renunciation of War as an Instrument of National Policy, Paris [Kellogg–Briand Pact] (27 August 1928) 94 LNTS 57, art 1.

[63] Report on Manchuria (n 60) 76.

[64] A breach 'is serious if it involves a gross or systematic failure by the responsible State to fulfil the obligation': Articles on Responsibility of States, art 40.

[65] Ibid, art 41(2).

[66] See further Crawford, *Creation* (n 16) 143–7.

[67] SC res 541 (18 November 1983, Cyprus) para 7.

[68] *Legal Consequences for States of the Continued Presence of South Africa in Namibia (South West Africa) notwithstanding Security Council Resolution 276 (1970) (Advisory Opinion)* [1971] ICJ Rep 16, para 119.

has commented that this resolution reflected the customary duty, on the basis that South Africa's presence was in breach of the peremptory norm of self-determination[69]). Furthermore, exactly which features of a 'situation' must not be 'recognized' in this wide sense may be complex. In *Namibia*, the Court held that the collective duty 'should not result in depriving the people of Namibia of any advantages derived from international co-operation' and 'cannot be extended to those acts, such as, for instance, the registration of births, deaths and marriages, the effects of which can be ignored only to the detriment of the inhabitants'.[70] The European Court of Human Rights has applied similar reasoning to Northern Cyprus.[71] This complexity, however, can largely be left aside here. What matters is that the duty certainly applies to the recognition of an entity *as a state*, whatever else it may or may not cover.

Second, the collective duty as codified in the Articles—no state 'shall recognize as lawful a situation created by' a serious breach of a duty under a peremptory norm[72]—seems to mean 'lawful' in a very loose sense. Conduct by particular entities can be described as lawful, but how can a 'situation' be lawful? The Security Council and the Court formulated the collective duty more clearly when they applied it to South Africa's presence in Namibia. The Security Council called on states to refrain from dealings with South Africa that were 'inconsistent' with either of two propositions: first, that South Africa's presence was 'illegal'; second, that acts by South Africa 'on behalf of or concerning Namibia' were 'illegal and invalid'.[73] The Court held that states had a duty 'to recognize' not only the 'illegality' but also the 'invalidity' of South Africa's presence.[74] This clarifies that the duty can require states to refrain from recognizing *the validity of legal relations that an entity claims to have*.[75] In Namibia, the relevant relations were the rights and powers that South Africa claimed to have in the territory. In a case where an entity claims to be a state,

[69] SC res 276 (30 January 1970, Namibia); Articles on Responsibility of States, commentary to art 40, para 8.

[70] *Namibia* [1971] ICJ Rep 16, para 125. See also para 122.

[71] *Loizidou v Turkey* (ECHR) (1996) 108 ILR 443, paras 44–5; *Cyprus v Turkey* (ECHR) (2001) 120 ILR 11, paras 89–102; *Demopoulos v Turkey* (ECHR) (2010) 158 ILR 88, para 93. Note that these decisions do not on their face attribute any rights or duties in international law to the Northern Cypriot entity *itself*. The legal relations that were directly in issue were the human rights of individuals in the territories and the duties of the entity's external military supporter, Turkey. So the existence of exclusions from the collective duty of non-recognition does not necessarily entail that entities such as this have a degree of personality falling short of 'full' statehood. Compare *Ilaşcu v Moldova and Russia* (ECHR app 48787/99, 8 July 2004).

[72] Articles on Responsibility of States, arts 40–1.

[73] SC res 276 (30 January 1970, Namibia) paras 2, 5.

[74] *Namibia* [1971] ICJ Rep 16, para 119.

[75] Compare Martin Dawidowicz, 'The obligation of non-recognition of an unlawful situation' in James Crawford, Alain Pellet, and Simon Olleson (eds), *The Law of International Responsibility* (OUP 2010) 677, 683: 'the unlawful situation flowing from the breach of [a peremptory] norm results in a *legal* claim to status or rights by the wrongdoing State which is capable of being denied by other States'. See also *Legal Consequences of the Construction of a Wall in the Occupied Palestinian Territory (Advisory Opinion)* [2004] ICJ Rep 136, 232 (Judge Kooijmans).

the relevant relations are the customary rights and other relations of a state that the entity claims to have.

So the collective duty of non-recognition, so far as it is relevant to the present discussion, entails the following: if an entity claims to have the rights and other relations of a state, and if that 'situation' is created by a serious breach of a duty under a peremptory norm, it is unlawful for existing states to recognize the ostensible relations as valid.

Despite the inclusion of a reference to validity, this norm deals directly only with the question of whether conduct is unlawful: it is *unlawful* for states to recognize relations as valid; the act of recognizing an entity as a state is *unlawful*. This does not say anything explicit about whether or not the act of recognition, despite being unlawful, can still validly transform the entity into a state relative to the recognizing state. That is the question to be discussed here. A conclusion that the unlawful recognition is *invalid*—meaning that it cannot make the entity a state even relative to the recognizing state—would accord with the broad principle that no law arises from unlawfulness.

That conclusion can be reached by way of an analogy.

In *Namibia*, one of the acts that were prohibited by the collective duty of non-recognition was making a treaty in which 'South Africa purports to act on behalf of or concerning Namibia'.[76] Like an unlawful act of recognition, this is unlawful conduct of a kind that would ordinarily create legal relations between the parties. So were the relations ostensibly created by such a treaty invalid? The Court said they were: 'official acts performed by the Government of South Africa on behalf of or concerning Namibia' were 'invalid'.[77] In *Kasikili/Sedudu Island*, it applied this to an ostensible treaty between South Africa, acting on Namibia's behalf, and Botswana.[78] The Court did not explain *why* such a treaty was invalid. The grounds for invalidity listed in the Vienna Convention—which are said to be exhaustive[79]—do not specifically refer to collective non-recognition. Yaël Ronen suggests that one of the established grounds for invalidity must apply, and she identifies which one: under the Convention, a treaty is invalid if 'it conflicts with a peremptory norm'.[80]

This ground could apply in two different ways.

First, some treaties made by South Africa might have been invalid because the norms and relations that the treaties purported to create would conflict with

[76] *Namibia* [1971] ICJ Rep 16, para 122; see also paras 123–4.

[77] Ibid, para 125.

[78] *Kasikili/Sedudu Island (Botswana/Namibia)* [1999] ICJ Rep 1045, para 69.

[79] Vienna Convention on Treaties, art 42(1): the 'validity of a treaty . . . may be impeached only through the application of the present Convention'. Kohen and Heathcote (n 5) paras 15, 22–37 consider whether there are, nonetheless, any additional grounds for treaty invalidity; they conclude that there are not.

[80] Yaël Ronen, *Transition from Illegal Regimes under International Law* (CUP 2010) 110–11; Vienna Convention on Treaties, art 53.

peremptory norms. But Ronen observes that if this were 'the exclusive yardstick' for conflicts between treaties and peremptory norms, then 'not every treaty of an illegal regime would be invalid'.[81] For example, in 1969 South Africa, on Namibia's behalf, made a treaty with Portugal about the development of a river basin, the provisions of which were not in themselves objectionable.[82] After independence, Namibia and Angola (Portugal's successor) treated this treaty as if it were valid. However, they did so only on the basis that 'the Namibian and Angolan ministers of agriculture "validated" the agreement'—which amounted to 'the conclusion of a new agreement, with terms identical to the 1969 one'.[83] The *original* treaty was invalid. This is not a unique case. Ronen surveys practice concerning the Bantustans (which I will discuss shortly), the unlawful annexations of the Baltic states and East Timor, and other cases in which the duty of non-recognition has made it unlawful to recognize an 'illegal regime', and she concludes that what the Court said about Namibia is true generally: '[t]reaties concluded by an illegal regime are invalid *ab initio*'.[84] This practice cannot be explained on the basis of a narrow view of what qualifies as a conflict with peremptory norms.

Alternatively, perhaps the act of making a treaty is *as such* in conflict with a peremptory norm, even if the provisions of the treaty are not objectionable. The conflict would arise because, by making the treaty, a state unlawfully recognizes a 'situation created by' a breach of a peremptory norm. This view is articulated by Alexander Orakhelashvili:

> An agreement . . . to ignore the effects of [a peremptory] norm in *inter se* relations is itself an attempt to make a peremptory norm *inter se* inoperable and to deprive it of its legal force. A consequential derogation undermines the primary prohibition, and it is difficult not to qualify this as a conflict with *jus cogens*.[85]

This can explain the Court's approach in *Namibia* and *Kasikili/Sedudu* and the wider practice.

In any case, whatever exact explanation is given for the invalidity of treaties made in breach of the collective duty of non-recognition, it is clear from the practice that the breach invalidates the treaties. It is a short leap to the conclusion that recognition in breach of the collective duty of non-recognition, by analogy, is invalid. Like an invalid treaty, it is an ostensible exercise of a power by a state to create norms and relations in defiance of a peremptory norm. Here, then, is another exception to the

[81] Ronen (n 80) 111.
[82] Agreement on the First Phase of Development of the Water Resources of the Cunene River Basin, South Africa–Portugal (21 January 1969) SATS 1/1969.
[83] Ronen (n 80) 120, 131.
[84] Ibid, 157, further 110–58.
[85] Alexander Orakhelashvili, *Peremptory Norms in International Law* (OUP 2008) 139.

recognition norm, based on the collective duty of non-recognition: the 'collective-non-recognition' exception.

4.1.3 The unlawful-effectuation exception to the effectiveness norm

I have identified two exceptions to the recognition norm. If recognition is unlawful because it breaches a state's territorial integrity (the premature-recognition exception) or a collective duty of non-recognition (the collective-non-recognition exception), then that unlawfulness renders it invalid. These are straightforward applications of the principle that no law arises from unlawfulness. It is more complicated to apply the principle to the effectiveness norm. Unlawfulness is a characteristic of certain *conduct*. Under the recognition norm, statehood arises directly *from* conduct—from the act of recognition—whereas, under the effectiveness norm, it arises not from conduct as such but automatically under a customary norm setting out factual criteria. But there are still circumstances in which statehood might be said to 'arise' from unlawfulness: the fact that an entity meets the effectiveness criteria may be a consequence of conduct that breaches a peremptory norm.

These are more or less the same circumstances as those in which the collective-non-recognition exception applies to the recognition norm: a breach of a peremptory norm triggers a duty not to recognize the 'situation' created by the breach. This may not *necessarily* entail a parallel exception to the effectiveness norm (even if that seems likely for the sake of consistency); the possibility must be considered on its own merits. But there are reasons to conclude, albeit somewhat tentatively, that there is an exception to the effectiveness norm that parallels at least some instances of the collective-non-recognition exception.

The possibility has arisen in three scenarios.

The first and most common scenario involves the breach of the peremptory norm prohibiting the use of force. An aggressor state uses force in another state's territory; an entity in the territory unilaterally declares independence and tries to meet the effectiveness criteria; insofar as it succeeds in meeting the criteria, its success is a consequence of the use of force. This is the scenario in Northern Cyprus. It would have been the scenario in Manchukuo (and perhaps even Panama), but the concept of peremptory norms did not yet exist at that time.

The scenario raises some evidential difficulties. There is plenty of evidence that states refrain from treating entities such as Northern Cyprus as states. But the *opinio iuris* accompanying this practice is somewhat ambiguous, because it tends to take the form of exhortations not to *recognize* the entity—and these cannot necessarily be interpreted as statements about the applicability of the effectiveness norm. In addition, the practice generally cannot confirm whether or not there is an exception to the effectiveness norm, because it is usually unclear whether entities of this kind meet the effectiveness criteria in the first place, on the ground that they may not be independent of their external military supporters. In *Cyprus v Turkey*, the European Court of Human Rights held that Turkey had 'effective overall control over northern Cyprus'.[86] It is true that many states, such as Soviet and US 'client states' during the Cold War, have had links to external military supporters, and this has not cast doubt on their independence. But perhaps the test for independence is stricter here. James Crawford argues that 'there is a presumption'—predating the prohibition of the use of force that existed from 1945—'against the independence of entities created by the use of force or during a period of belligerent occupation'.[87] He cites Manchukuo and the puppet entities created by the Axis states during the Second World War.

Still, even if an entity created by an unlawful use of force fails the effectiveness criteria, that is what Crawford elsewhere calls 'a contingent judgement'.[88] What if it later becomes genuinely independent? The question of whether there is an exception to the effectiveness norm still demands an answer, despite the ambiguity of the practice and *opinio iuris*. There are reasons to think the entity would not be a state *even if* it met the criteria.[89]

Consider an established customary norm concerning the annexation of territory that is another manifestation of the principle that no law arises from unlawfulness. In *Wall in the Occupied Palestinian Territory*, the International Court remarked that there is a norm 'entailing the illegality of territorial acquisition resulting from the threat or use of force'.[90] Security Council practice confirms that such a forcible annexation is not only unlawful but also *invalid*; for example, in 1990, it declared that 'annexation of Kuwait by Iraq under any form and whatever pretext has no legal validity, and is considered null and void'.[91] If the effectiveness norm could apply in these circumstances, it might offer aggressor states a tempting means of evading this established norm about annexation. Instead of directly annexing foreign territory, an aggressor state could persuade an entity on the territory to

[86] *Cyprus v Turkey* (2001) 120 ILR 11, para 77. There are a few other would-be states whose independence might be doubted on this ground. Transdniestria (generally treated as part of Moldova) and Abkhazia and South Ossetia (generally treated as part of Georgia) are supported by Russia. Artsakh (also known as Nagorno-Karabakh and generally treated as part of Azerbaijan) is supported by Armenia. See further Christian Walter, Antje von Ungern-Sternberg, and Kavus Abushov (eds), *Self-Determination and Secession in International Law* (OUP 2014), especially chs 7–11. The European Court of Human Rights has held that Transdniestria 'remains under the effective authority, or at the very least under the decisive influence, of the Russian Federation, and in any event that it survives by virtue of the military, economic, financial and political support given to it by the Russian Federation': *Ilaşcu v Moldova and Russia* (ECHR app 48787/99, 8 July 2004) para 392.

[87] Crawford, *Creation* (n 16) 132–3; compare *Knox v Palestine Liberation Organization*, 306 F Supp 2d 424 (SDNY, 2004) 437–8.

[88] Crawford, *Creation* (n 16) 344.

[89] Compare ibid, 148.

[90] *Wall* [2004] ICJ Rep 136, para 87, citing Friendly Relations Declaration, principle *a*.

[91] SC res 662 (9 August 1990, Iraq and Kuwait) para 1.

declare independence, militarily assist the entity to meet the effectiveness criteria and become a new state, and finally annex the territory with the friendly new state's consent. The aggressor state would breach any number of norms along the way, and yet—*if* there were no exception to the effectiveness norm—international law would have to validate the result. This would undermine the norm that the annexation of territory by force is invalid.

This is close to what Russia tried to do in Ukraine. On 16 March 2014, an entity calling itself the 'Republic of Crimea' unilaterally declared independence from Ukraine; on 18 March, it signed a treaty with Russia in which it consented to Russian annexation.[92] This mayfly republic, which spent a matter of hours attempting to secure its existence as an effective entity before abandoning its claim to independence, plainly did not meet the effectiveness criteria in the first place.[93] But other states, in denying that it had ever been a state, did not primarily rely on the argument that it failed the effectiveness criteria. The General Assembly affirmed that 'the territory of a State shall not be the object of acquisition by another State resulting from the threat or use of force' and called on states 'to desist and refrain from . . . any attempts to modify Ukraine's borders through the threat or use of force or other unlawful means'.[94] The implication is that it was beside the point whether or not the Republic of Crimea met the effectiveness criteria. Russia could not use force 'to modify Ukraine's borders'. This covered both attempts to annex Ukrainian territory directly (in accordance with the established norm about annexation) *and* attempts to create a friendly new state on the territory (suggesting that the effectiveness norm could not be used to evade the norm about annexation). This analysis has intuitive appeal. The established customary norm that annexation by force is invalid reflects the principle that no law arises from unlawfulness; the same principle supports the conclusion that the effectiveness norm will not validate the creation of a state by force.

The example also shows that, even if an entity fails the effectiveness criteria anyway, an exception to the effectiveness norm can still have a rhetorical value. Ukraine did not need to present arguments about whether the Republic of Crimea met the effectiveness criteria; it was enough that, in any event, that would have resulted from Russia's use of force.

This leaves at least three questions of scope unanswered. First, it may be logical to extend the reasoning to an unlawful *threat* of force that scares a state into relinquishing territory: such a threat, like an unlawful use of force, is a breach of a peremptory norm. Second, the norm that the annexation of territory is invalid possibly also extends to *lawful* uses of force.[95] In 1967, Israel occupied East Jerusalem

[92] Thomas D Grant, *Aggression against Ukraine: Territory, Responsibility, and International Law* (Palgrave Macmillan 2015), especially 13–21.
[93] Ibid, 39–40.
[94] GA res 68/262 (27 March 2014, Ukraine) preamble, para 2.
[95] Rainer Hofmann, 'Annexation' (last updated 2013) MPEPIL, paras 23–4; John Dugard, *Recognition and the United Nations* (Grotius 1987) 113.

and other territories as a result of a use of force that Israel characterized as lawful self-defence against Arab states.[96] Shortly after the war, without expressing a view on the accuracy of that characterization, the Security Council emphasized 'the inadmissibility of the acquisition of territory by war'; in 1980, after Israel proclaimed Jerusalem its complete and unified capital, the Council reaffirmed 'that the acquisition of territory by force is inadmissible' and that measures to change the status of the city were 'null and void'.[97] This raises the question of whether the exception to the effectiveness norm similarly extends to an entity created by a lawful use of force. Third, it is uncertain what would happen if the external military supporter withdrew all support. Would that clean away the taint of unlawfulness, so that, provided the entity could cling on to its independence despite objections by the parent state, it could eventually acquire statehood after all?

Before I draw a conclusion about the scope of the exception to the effectiveness norm, I need to consider the two other scenarios that have arisen. These involve unlawful conduct other than force—breaches of the peremptory norms prohibiting racial discrimination and genocide. One scenario arose between 1976 and 1981, when South Africa ostensibly granted independence to four 'Bantustans': Transkei, Bophuthatswana, Venda, and Ciskei.[98] The Bantustans were supposedly 'homelands' for parts of South Africa's black population but in fact were transparently instruments of the policy of apartheid; their creation breached the norm prohibiting racial discrimination.[99] The other scenario concerned Republika Srpska, an entity whose independence was declared unilaterally by Bosnian Serbs in 1992 on territory also claimed by Bosnia.[100] In the *Genocide (Bosnia)* case, Bosnia argued that this entity was not a state, among other reasons, because its 'purported' statehood

> came about as a result . . . of the genocidal practice of ethnic cleansing. As the United Nations Security Council has made clear in numerous other cases, the creation or maintenance of an entity purporting to be a state in violation of the prohibition of the use of force, or all other rules of *jus cogens*, such as the prohibition of apartheid, and it is submitted, the obligation not to perpetrate genocide, cannot have legal consequences.[101]

[96] See further Christine Gray, *International Law and the Use of Force* (3rd edn, OUP 2008) 161.

[97] SC res 242 (22 November 1967, Middle East) preamble; SC res 478 (20 August 1980, Israel) para 3. Other resolutions were to similar effect. See also *Wall* [2004] ICJ Rep 136, paras 75, 78.

[98] Crawford, *Creation* (n 16) 338–48; Dugard, *Recognition* (n 95) 98–108.

[99] This is described as peremptory in Articles on Responsibility of States, commentary to art 40, para 4; see also *Armed Activities on the Territory of the Congo (New Application: 2002) (Democratic Republic of the Congo v Rwanda) (Jurisdiction and Admissibility)* [2006] ICJ Rep 6, paras 73–8.

[100] *Application of the Convention on the Prevention and Punishment of the Crime of Genocide (Bosnia and Herzegovina v Serbia and Montenegro)* [2007] ICJ Rep 43, para 233.

[101] Bosnia and Herzegovina, Memorial (15 April 1994) ICJ Pleadings: *Application of the Convention on the Prevention and Punishment of the Crime of Genocide (Bosnia and Herzegovina v Yugoslavia (Serbia and Montenegro))*, para 6.3.2.8. The prohibition of genocide is described as peremptory in Articles on Responsibility of States, commentary to art 40, para 4; see also *Application of the Convention on the*

Bosnia's argument that the creation of the entity was 'a result' of genocide was not certain of success.[102] But it at least suggests a possibility. So the Bantustans and Republika Srpska represent possible scenarios in which, as with the scenario involving force, an entity might meet the effectiveness criteria as a consequence of a breach of a peremptory norm.

It is, however, difficult to draw firm inferences from these cases. In both of them the familiar evidential difficulty reappears: the Bantustans and Republika Srpska were not generally treated as states by other states, but this does not confirm that there is an exception to the effectiveness norm, because it is not certain that they met the criterion of independence in the first place. The Bantustans were puppets of South Africa.[103] After South Africa democratized in 1994, they were not invited to sign treaties of annexation as if they were genuinely independent states; they were just reintegrated into South Africa by domestic legislation, and resistance by authorities in Ciskei and Bophuthatswana was suppressed.[104] As for Republika Srpska, the International Criminal Tribunal for the former Yugoslavia later observed that an external supporter, Serbia-Montenegro, 'had the final say regarding the undertaking of international commitments by' the entity and 'in addition pledged, at the end of the conflict, to ensure respect for those international commitments'; this confirmed that it 'exercised control over that entity . . . until the end of the conflict'.[105]

The most that can be said is that it is plausible that there is an exception to the effectiveness norm where an entity is created by a breach of *any* peremptory norm, including the norms prohibiting racial discrimination and genocide. That would mirror the scope of the collective-non-recognition exception to the recognition norm. This illustrates the adaptability of the principle that no law arises from

Prevention and Punishment of the Crime of Genocide (Bosnia and Herzegovina v Yugoslavia (Serbia and Montenegro)) (Provisional Measures) [1993] ICJ Rep 325, 440 (Judge *ad hoc* Lauterpacht).

[102] Dawidowicz (n 75) 683 doubts that genocide can, 'in principle, result in any legal consequences which are capable of being denied'. See further Stefan Talmon, 'The duty not to "recognize as lawful" a situation created by the unlawful use of force or other serious breaches of a *jus cogens* obligation: An obligation without real substance?' in Christian Tomuschat and Jean-Marc Thouvenin (eds), *The Fundamental Rules of the International Legal Order: Jus Cogens and Obligations Erga Omnes* (Brill 2005) 99, 117–20.

[103] Vaughan Lowe, *International Law* (OUP 2007) 158.

[104] Crawford, *Creation* (n 16) 346–7.

[105] *Prosecutor v Tadić (Appeal against Conviction)* (ICTY) (1999) 124 ILR 61, para 160. Compare *Application of the Convention on the Prevention and Punishment of the Crime of Genocide (Bosnia and Herzegovina v Serbia and Montenegro)* [2007] ICJ Rep 43, para 241, further paras 237–40. The International Court clarified that Republika Srpska's dependence on Serbia-Montenegro was not 'total': para 394, further paras 385–95. But it was considering on what ground state responsibility could be attributed to Serbia-Montenegro, which is a different question from compliance with the effectiveness criteria. The relevant point, in any event, is that the evidence that Republika Srpska fell short of the criteria is at least sufficient to prevent a clear inference from being drawn about whether an exception to the effectiveness norm applied in this case. Further on Serbia-Montenegro and my use of that name for it, see this book s 3.1.4, including footnotes.

unlawfulness: there may be novel scenarios, not yet thought of by scholars or manifest in practice, in which the scope of the exceptions that I have identified might be stretched further or in which new analogies might be drawn. The values protected by peremptory norms are given so much weight that they might justify quite rapid legal developments in response to new situations.

I conclude that there is an exception to the effectiveness norm where the fact that an entity meets the effectiveness criteria is a consequence of a use of force by an external supporter. This applies at a minimum where the supporter's conduct is unlawful and at a minimum while the entity is sustained by the conduct; it probably extends to a threat of force. The exception may also extend to an entity that meets the criteria as a consequence of a breach of any other peremptory norm. This is the 'unlawful-effectuation' exception.

A side-effect of this exception to the effectiveness norm is to create an overlap between the two exceptions to the recognition norm. Imagine that an external supporter unlawfully uses force to detach a unilateral secessionist entity from its parent state (the Northern Cyprus or Crimea scenario). The unlawful-effectuation exception to the effectiveness norm applies. Since the secession cannot succeed, the parent state retains its right that its territorial integrity be respected, and the premature-recognition exception to the recognition norm applies. And since the situation is created by a breach of a peremptory norm, the collective-non-recognition exception to the recognition norm *also* applies. But although the two exceptions to the recognition norm both apply in this scenario, the overlap between them is not absolute. The premature-recognition exception applies to *all* cases of premature recognition, even if there has previously been no breach of a peremptory norm to trigger the collective-non-recognition exception; for instance, it would also apply if a state tried to recognize Quebec. The opposite occurred in the case of the Bantustans: South Africa had waived its right that its territorial integrity be respected, so the premature-recognition exception did not apply, but the collective-non-recognition exception *did* apply: the General Assembly and Security Council called on states not to recognize the Bantustans.[106] Thus, although the exceptions all reinforce each other, each has something separate to do.

There is also one idiosyncratic case—Rhodesia—in which there are reasons to think that the effectiveness norm was not hindered by an exception and so could create a state, yet at the same time that state could not be recognized. But I will consider this case in the course of discussing the second principle to be dealt with in this chapter: self-determination.

[106] GA res 31/6A (26 October 1976, South Africa) para 3; SC res 402 (22 December 1976, Lesotho and South Africa) para 1.

4.2 Self-determination

Self-determination has many meanings. Sometimes it is a hortatory or political idea: in the past that may have been all it was, until it took on a concrete role in international law during the wave of decolonization after 1945.[107] Sometimes it is spoken of as a specific right, sometimes as a broad principle, and sometimes in such fuzzy terms that one cannot tell exactly what it is supposed to be. Since it is a far-reaching idea whose role continues to evolve, my discussion of it here cannot be exhaustive or definitive. I will focus on the least controversial manifestation of self-determination, which is also the one with the clearest impact on the creation of states: the duty to respect a people's external self-determination. I will begin by drawing out how this duty is generally relevant to statehood.

'Internal' self-determination means 'a people's pursuit of its political, economic, social and cultural development within the framework of an existing state'.[108] 'External' self-determination, in contrast, is a principle that allows a 'people' to choose other options, including the 'establishment of a sovereign and independent State', 'free association or integration with an independent State', and 'emergence into any other political status freely determined by a people'.[109] This choice is available only in certain circumstances. According to the Canadian Supreme Court in *Quebec*, it is available

> where 'a people' is governed as part of a colonial empire; where 'a people' is subject to alien subjugation, domination or exploitation; and possibly where 'a people' is denied any meaningful exercise of its right to self-determination within the state of which it forms a part. In other circumstances, peoples are expected to achieve self-determination within the framework of their existing state.[110]

Beyond this, there is not much guidance to be found about what counts as a 'people'.[111] Most cases of self-determination involve peoples of 'non-self-governing territories', which mainly means colonized territories. The United Nations maintains a list of these territories.[112]

[107] Antonio Cassese, *Self-Determination of Peoples: A Legal Reappraisal* (CUP 1995) 11–33; Arnulf Becker Lorca, 'Petitioning the international: A "pre-history" of self-determination' (2014) 25 EJIL 497; Report of the Committee of Jurists on the Aaland Islands (n 13) 5.

[108] *Quebec* (1998) 115 ILR 536, para 126.

[109] Friendly Relations Declaration, principle e, quoted in *Quebec* (1998) 115 ILR 536, para 126. See also the earlier Declaration on the Granting of Independence to Colonial Countries and Peoples, GA res 1514 (XV) (14 December 1960); *Western Sahara (Advisory Opinion)* [1975] ICJ Rep 12, para 57.

[110] *Quebec* (1998) 115 ILR 536, para 154.

[111] Compare ibid, paras 123–5. One attempt at 'a description (but not a definition) of a "people"' can be found in International Meeting of Experts on Further Study of the Concept of the Rights of Peoples, Final Report and Recommendations (22 February 1990) Unesco doc SNS-89/CONF.602/7, para 22.

[112] Charter of the United Nations (26 June 1945) ch XI. This does not refer expressly to self-determination, only to a duty accepted by administering states 'to develop self-government, to take due account of the political aspirations of the peoples, and to assist them in the progressive

Respecting external self-determination is a *duty*. As the Friendly Relations Declaration puts it:

> Every State has the duty to promote, through joint and separate action, realization of the principle of equal rights and self-determination of peoples, in accordance with the provisions of the Charter, and to render assistance to the United Nations in carrying out the responsibilities entrusted to it by the Charter regarding the implementation of the principle, in order:
> (*a*) To promote friendly relations and co-operation among States; and
> (*b*) To bring a speedy end to colonialism, having due regard to the freely expressed will of the peoples concerned;
>
> and bearing in mind that subjection of peoples to alien subjugation, domination and exploitation constitutes a violation of the principle, as well as a denial of fundamental human rights, and is contrary to the Charter.[113]

It is clear which entities bear this duty: it is a duty of '[e]very state', although in practice it falls more heavily on states that govern non-self-governing territories. There is some debate about which entities bear the correlative Hohfeldian right. The International Court has indicated that 'respect for the right to self-determination is an obligation *erga omnes*'.[114] This means that the duty is owed, at least in part, to the international community as a whole.[115] In addition, language such as that in the Friendly Relations Declaration suggests that the duty correlates with a right of peoples themselves: '[b]y virtue of the principle of equal rights and self-determination of peoples . . . all peoples have the right freely to determine . . . their political status' and 'every State has the duty to respect this right'.[116] Doubts have been raised about whether an entity as nebulous as a 'people' can strictly be said to bear a 'right'.[117] Against this is the fact that the language of rights is used universally and unambiguously, including by the General Assembly and the International Court. But in any event, this debate will not affect the arguments that I will make here, which rely

development of their free political institutions'. But this came to be interpreted as a reference to self-determination: Ulrich Fastenrath, 'Article 73' in Bruno Simma and others (eds), *The Charter of the United Nations: A Commentary* (3rd edn, OUP 2012) 1829, para 13. Articles 1(2) and 55 do refer expressly to self-determination, albeit only in general terms.

113 Friendly Relations Declaration, principle *e*.

114 *Legal Consequences of the Separation of the Chagos Archipelago from Mauritius in 1965 (Advisory Opinion)* [2019] ICJ Rep, para 180. Compare *East Timor (Portugal v Australia)* [1995] ICJ Rep 90, para 29.

115 On what it means for a duty to be owed to the international community as a whole, see this book s 1.1.2.

116 Friendly Relations Declaration, principle *e*.

117 See further Cassese, *Self-Determination* (n 107) 141–58; Bart L Smit Duijzentkunst, *The Concept of Rights in International Law* (doctoral thesis, University of Cambridge, 2015) ch 7.

on the premise that the *duty* is borne by states but do not require me to commit to a position on the bearer of the correlative right. For the sake of simplicity, I will speak as if peoples do have a right to external self-determination, but this is on the understanding that it would not matter for my purposes if they did not have a right in a strict sense.

How is statehood affected by the duty of states to respect external self-determination?

The Friendly Relations Declaration says that territories retain non-self-governing status until peoples have 'exercised their right of self-determination'.[118] If 'exercising' the right meant merely choosing a new status, that might imply that the change of status—potentially, the creation of a new state—could happen at the moment of choice. Self-determination by itself would then be enough to create a new state, seemingly without regard to effectiveness *or* recognition. But this is not the case. Sometimes there *is* no identifiable moment of choice: in *Western Sahara* the Court noted that a consultation may be 'totally unnecessary, in view of special circumstances'.[119] Even where there is a plebiscite or other consultation, the people may be invited to vote for a status that is scheduled to begin on a specified future date.[120] As the General Assembly has indicated in a related context, there is no change of status until the new status has actually been 'attained'; the people's choice must be *implemented*.[121] For example, in February 1961, plebiscites were held in the British-administered trust territory of the Northern and Southern Cameroons.[122] The north voted to join Nigeria;[123] the south voted to join Cameroun (a separate territory that was already a state[124]). But the borders did not change overnight. The General Assembly resolved that 'the decisions . . . should be immediately implemented': in the north that meant by June; in the south it meant by October, after necessary arrangements could be made.[125] It is similar where the status chosen is statehood. The administering state is not expected to organize a vote and then just walk away from the territory; it usually tries to implement the people's choice

118 Friendly Relations Declaration, principle *e*.

119 *Western Sahara* [1975] ICJ Rep 12, para 59. Compare Cassese, *Self-Determination* (n 107) 74, further 76–8.

120 Eg, GA res 1569 (XV) (18 December 1960, Western Samoa); GA res 1626 (XVI) (18 October 1961, Western Samoa).

121 The General Assembly has indicated that an administering state retains its duty to report on a non-self-governing territory until the territory has actually 'attained a full measure of self-government', which may entail '[e]mergence as a sovereign independent State': Principles Which Should Guide Members in Determining Whether or Not an Obligation Exists to Transmit the Information Called for in Article 73 e of the Charter of the United Nations, annex to GA res 1541 (XV) (15 December 1960) principles I, II, VI.

122 GA res 1608 (XV) (21 April 1961, Cameroons).

123 In an earlier plebiscite in 1959, the people of the Northern Cameroons had voted to postpone the decision about joining Nigeria: GA res 1473 (XIV) (12 December 1959, Cameroons). See further *Northern Cameroons (Cameroon v UK) (Preliminary Objections)* [1963] ICJ Rep 15.

124 The former French Cameroun. The enlarged state is now spelled *Cameroon* in English.

125 GA res 1608 (XV) (21 April 1961, Cameroons) paras 3–5.

through negotiations with the people's representatives and may help to build new institutions.

Since changes of status are usually implemented in this manner, most cases of state creation involving external self-determination can be explained by the ordinary effectiveness norm: a new entity is created that meets the criteria of territory, population, government, and independence.

Even if implementation fails, there is usually still no need to look beyond the ordinary general rules in order to explain how an entity acquires statehood: the ordinary recognition norm can suffice. An example is the Congo.[126] When Belgium granted the Congo independence in 1960, it collapsed into chaos. It was riven by movements for secession, one of which led to a civil war in Katanga; two factions emerged claiming to be the government; and Belgian troops were soon reintroduced, followed by a UN force.[127] The Congo was the Somalia of its day: despite being widely recognized and admitted to the United Nations, it did not appear to meet the effectiveness criteria. An explanation of the Congo that has been given by others is that the effectiveness criterion 'of "government" is less stringent than has been thought, at least in particular contexts'.[128] Thus it 'is to be presumed that a new State granted full formal independence by a former sovereign has the international right to govern its territory' and 'the principle of self-determination will operate to reinforce the effectiveness of territorial units created with the consent of the former sovereign'.[129] But I have already made the point that the existence of the recognition norm makes it unnecessary to postulate that the effectiveness criteria are different in cases of different types.[130] That applies here: recognition by other states is enough to explain how the Congo became a state, regardless of whether the effectiveness criteria were met (the premature-recognition exception could not preclude recognition, Belgium having relinquished any rights over the territory[131]).

In all these scenarios, the duty of external self-determination indirectly influences how and when a state is created. Administering states are enjoined to fulfil the duty by creating a new entity that meets the effectiveness criteria, in particular by granting it independence. In cases such as the Congo, the duty encourages other

[126] Officially what is here called the Congo was, in 1960, the Republic of the Congo (capital: Léopoldville) and after multiple name changes is now the Democratic Republic of the Congo (capital: Kinshasa). It is to be distinguished from the current Republic of the Congo (capital: Brazzaville), also called Congo-Brazzaville.

[127] Crawford, *Creation* (n 16) 56–7. See further Thomas Kanza, *Conflict in the Congo: The Rise and Fall of Lumumba* (Penguin 1972).

[128] Crawford, *Creation* (n 16) 57.

[129] Ibid, 58, 128. Compare Malcolm N Shaw, *International Law* (7th edn, CUP 2014) 149; David Raič, *Statehood and the Law of Self-Determination* (Kluwer 2002) 104.

[130] This book ss 3.1.5, 3.4.1.

[131] Compare Crawford, *Creation* (n 16) 57–8: 'Belgium was precluded from denying the consequences of its own conduct', so 'there was no international person against whom recognition of the Congo could be unlawful'. Generally on the applicability of the premature-recognition exception in a non-self-governing territory, see this book s 4.2.2.

states—perhaps even legally obliges them[132]—to be generous in deciding whether to recognize an entity. But the influence is at most indirect. Self-determination does not replace or modify the effectiveness and recognition norms; those norms are still sufficient to explain the entity's statehood.

That is the general situation. What I am now going to consider is whether, in atypical cases, self-determination *directly* determines whether an entity acquires statehood. I will look first at the possibility that it creates a free-standing exception to the effectiveness norm, distinct from the exception based on unlawfulness that I have already identified; then I will look at whether self-determination creates an exception *to the exceptions*, enabling statehood to be acquired regardless of unlawfulness. I will find support for this second possibility.

4.2.1 A self-determination exception to the effectiveness norm?

Arguments that self-determination creates a free-standing exception to the effectiveness norm tend to rely on the case of the British colony of Southern Rhodesia. On 11 November 1965, the white minority in this colony unilaterally declared it independent as 'Rhodesia'.[133] The United Kingdom, hesitant to use force against its own 'kith and kin', did not resist the attempt at unilateral secession militarily.[134] The result of this absence of military resistance by the parent state was that Rhodesia probably met the effectiveness criteria.[135] It existed until December 1979, when its government agreed to a resumption of British rule; shortly afterward, the United Kingdom granted the territory independence as Zimbabwe.[136]

Rhodesia systematically discriminated against its black majority. JES Fawcett argued that it could not be a state on the ground that a new requirement had emerged that a state 'not be based upon a systematic denial in its territory of certain civil and political rights, including in particular the right of every citizen to participate in the government of his country'.[137] This seems to put the argument too ambitiously. As Stefan Talmon observes, plenty of undemocratic or illiberal states would fail such a requirement.[138] Nor was the systematic racial discrimination in Rhodesia

[132] Compare *Quebec* (1998) 115 ILR 536, para 111: the Canadian Supreme Court alluded to attempts 'to found [an] argument . . . on the implied duty of states to recognize the legitimacy of secession brought about by the exercise of the well-established international law right of "a people" to self-determination'.

[133] Dugard, *Recognition* (n 95) 90–8.

[134] Vera Gowlland-Debbas, *Collective Responses to Illegal Acts in International Law: United Nations Action in the Question of Southern Rhodesia* (Nijhoff 1990) 70. The United Kingdom had been urged to resist a secession militarily in GA res 2022 (XX) (5 November 1965, Southern Rhodesia) paras 7, 8, 11.

[135] Crawford, *Creation* (n 16) 129; JES Fawcett, 'Note' (1971) 34 Modern Law Review 417.

[136] Agreements Concluded at Lancaster House Conference (September–December 1979) 19 ILM 387.

[137] JES Fawcett, 'Security Council resolutions on Rhodesia' (1965–66) 41 BYIL 103, 112.

[138] Stefan Talmon, 'The constitutive versus the declaratory theory of recognition: *Tertium non datur*?' (2005) 75 BYIL 101, 121–2.

unique; it was of a piece with apartheid South Africa, whose statehood was not doubted. Crawford reformulates the argument in less ambiguous terms: the 'principle of self-determination . . . operates as a peremptory requirement, suspending statehood until the constitutional and governmental structure of the territory is brought into line with the principle'.[139] The problem, on this formulation, was specifically that the discriminatory structure of Rhodesia was out of line with its people's right to a choice of status. Fawcett and Crawford's argument thus postulates an exception to the effectiveness norm in certain circumstances where there is a people with a right to external self-determination.

It must be emphasized how fundamentally different this argument is from the three exceptions that I identified earlier. All the other exceptions follow the same basic pattern: statehood cannot be created because its creation would be a *consequence of unlawful conduct*, reflecting the principle that no law arises from unlawfulness. But on the Rhodesia argument, the fact that justifies 'suspending' statehood does not appear to be unlawfulness under the norm—self-determination—on which the argument relies. This is because the whole point of the argument is to show that Rhodesia was not a state, and yet the duty to respect external self-determination is a duty *of states*—non-states do not have it and cannot breach it. It would be paradoxical to argue that an entity is prevented from acquiring the duties and other relations of states on the ground that the entity has breached one of those very duties. As a matter of logic, then, the argument must be interpreted as saying that Rhodesia's 'structure' was in conflict with the right or principle of self-determination in some looser way that did not as such constitute a breach of the duty to respect external self-determination.

This is not a reason to reject the argument. It just restricts the possibility of leaning on analogies; the argument must stand on its own feet, as an argument about a consequence *specifically* of self-determination, not about breaches of peremptory norms generally.

There are two types of evidence to consider, both of which are elements of the collective response to Rhodesia by states acting through organs of the United Nations.

First, there are the resolutions condemning the unilateral declaration of independence and calling for the non-recognition of Rhodesia. The Security Council alluded to the right of 'the people of Southern Rhodesia to determine their own future' as formulated in the Colonial Declaration issued by the General Assembly in 1960—that is, the right to external self-determination.[140] It also described the declaration of independence as 'having no legal validity',[141] although this does not

[139] Crawford, *Creation* (n 16) 388, further 129–31.
[140] SC res 217 (20 November 1965, Southern Rhodesia) para 7. Compare SC res 232 (16 December 1966, Southern Rhodesia) para 4.
[141] SC res 217 (20 November 1965, Southern Rhodesia) para 3.

signify much. The declaration was certainly not valid in British *domestic* law. And in international law, a declaration of independence never has 'legal validity' in the sense that in itself it is enough to create a state; if it results in the creation of a state, that is because it contributes to the circumstances in which the effectiveness norm or the recognition norm applies.[142] More significant was the Security Council's decision, universally heeded, to call on 'all States not to recognize this illegal racist minority regime'.[143]

The International Law Commission has cited the non-recognition of Rhodesia as an example of the collective duty of non-recognition (from which I derived the collective-non-recognition exception to the recognition norm).[144] The collective duty is usually triggered by a 'serious breach' of a peremptory norm.[145] Language used by the Security Council implies that there had been a breach of the peremptory norm requiring respect for external self-determination: in 1970, it described the abolition of the monarchy by Rhodesia as 'aimed at repressing the African people in violation of [the Colonial Declaration]'.[146] In *Kosovo*, the International Court cited Rhodesia as one of several cases in which declarations of independence 'were, or would have been, connected with . . . egregious violations of norms of general international law, in particular those of a peremptory character'.[147] There is no reason to think that these breaches were attributable to a state other than Rhodesia. Yet as I have stressed, the duty to respect external self-determination is a duty borne and potentially breached *by states*, so the apparent applicability of the collective duty might imply that Rhodesia *was* a state. This inference cannot be drawn categorically. Perhaps the customary duty of non-recognition does not always require a 'serious breach' of a peremptory norm and the formulation in the Articles on the Responsibility of States is too narrow. Or perhaps the Security Council decided to call for non-recognition of Rhodesia as an exercise of discretion, even if the *customary* duty did not already apply.[148] The Security Council's decision might then have been binding on states under article 25 of the Charter.[149] In 1970, the Security Council confirmed the binding force of its call for non-recognition: 'acting under Chapter VII of the Charter', it '[*decided*] that Member States shall refrain from

142 Compare the distinct proposition that a unilateral declaration of independence is not generally *unlawful*, which was confirmed by the International Court in *Kosovo* [2010] ICJ Rep 403, para 84.

143 SC res 216 (12 November 1965, Southern Rhodesia) para 2; SC res 217 (20 November 1965, Southern Rhodesia) para 6.

144 Articles on Responsibility of States, commentary to art 41, para 8.

145 Ibid, art 40.

146 SC res 277 (18 March 1970, Southern Rhodesia) preamble.

147 *Kosovo* [2010] ICJ Rep 403, para 81.

148 In 1978, when the Rhodesian government organized elections in which the black majority would be allowed to participate, some states ceased to rule out recognition, though the Security Council stood firm: Talmon, 'Duty not to "recognize"' (n 102) 123 n 102; SC res 423 (14 March 1978, Southern Rhodesia).

149 On the binding force of resolutions under Charter art 25, see *Namibia* [1971] ICJ Rep 16, paras 111–16.

recognizing this illegal régime'.[150] On any of these grounds, it is possible that the customary duty as formulated in the Articles did not apply, in which case the non-recognition of Rhodesia does not have any implications either way about whether Rhodesia was a state under the effectiveness norm.

In short, on one possible interpretation this evidence contradicts the postulated exception to the effectiveness norm, and on any other view it is inconclusive.

The second type of evidence is the condemnation of Rhodesia for breaching other duties that are borne by states. According to a resolution of 1979, the Security Council was

> *Gravely concerned* at the numerous hostile and unprovoked acts of aggression committed by the illegal minority regime in Southern Rhodesia violating the sovereignty, air space and territorial integrity of the Republic of Zambia . . .[151]

It called for

> the payment of full and adequate compensation to the Republic of Zambia by the responsible authorities for the damage to life and property resulting from the acts of aggression . . .[152]

As Talmon remarks, this indicates that it was 'possible for the international community to ascribe responsibility to Rhodesia for acts of aggression [and] other violations of international law'.[153] This strongly implies that Rhodesia was a state. I have already observed, quoting the International Court, that 'territorial integrity is confined to the sphere of relations between States'.[154] So acts 'violating the . . . territorial integrity' of Zambia could have been committed *only* by a state. The Security Council similarly accused Rhodesia of breaching 'the sovereignty and territorial integrity' of Angola and Mozambique.[155]

This highlights a troubling implication of the argument that there is an exception to the effectiveness norm in cases such as Rhodesia. The exception to the effectiveness norm that I identified earlier—the unlawful-effectuation exception—does not tend to leave territory in a complete legal vacuum. It is true that in a case involving the use of force, such as Northern Cyprus, the parent state has lost all effective control over the territory, and the unilateral secessionist entity, not being a state, may not have the duties that a state would have. But the entity does have an

[150] SC res 277 (18 March 1970, Southern Rhodesia) para 2.
[151] SC res 455 (23 November 1979, Southern Rhodesia and Zambia) preamble.
[152] Ibid, para 5.
[153] Talmon, 'Constitutive' (n 138) 103 n 10.
[154] *Kosovo* [2010] ICJ Rep 403, para 80.
[155] SC res 445 (8 March 1979, Southern Rhodesia) para 1. Also compare SC res 424 (17 March 1978, Southern Rhodesia and Zambia).

external military supporter that can be held responsible for conduct in the territory in at least some circumstances.[156] In the Rhodesia scenario, in contrast, there is no external supporter to be held responsible. Nor will responsibility tend to fall on the ostensible administering state, in this case the United Kingdom; a state is not responsible for conduct by a rebellion that is outside its control (which is what Rhodesia would presumably be if not a state).[157] Perhaps Rhodesian officials might be held responsible for breaches of international criminal or humanitarian law in their capacity as individuals or a non-state armed group.[158] But, except for Rhodesia itself, there is no entity with control on the ground that might have, for example, duties to respect the territorial integrity of neighbouring states. The possibility of a vacuum is a reason of policy for *not* precluding an entity such as Rhodesia from acquiring statehood—and hence the duties of states—under the effectiveness norm.

Ways around this have been suggested. Crawford's solution is that '[r]elevant' norms of international law can 'apply to *de facto* entities' in order to avoid an 'undesirable legal vacuum'.[159] Jochen Frowein proposed a concept of '*de facto* regimes' that are 'partial subjects of international law' and 'will be held responsible' and yet may not be states.[160] But the idea of a *de facto* status that falls short of statehood introduces an unnecessary complication and raises any number of questions about precisely which 'relevant' rights and duties the status entails, if it is to be assumed that they are somehow different from the ordinary rights and duties of states. And anyway, as Talmon observes, 'there is no State practice to support it': most of the entities pointed to by Frowein, such as East Germany and North Korea, were later confirmed to be states.[161] A much simpler explanation is available. An entity such as Rhodesia *is* a state—under the effectiveness norm. But this is consistent with the idea that, because of the entity's racially discriminatory structure, the entity

156 Eg, Turkey's responsibility for Northern Cyprus in *Loizidou v Turkey* (1996) 108 ILR 443 paras 49–57; *Cyprus v Turkey* (2001) 120 ILR 11, paras 69–81. Compare *Ilaşcu v Moldova and Russia* (ECHR app 48787/99, 8 July 2004) para 382: Russia had responsibility 'in respect of the unlawful acts committed by the Transdniestrian separatists, regard being had to the military and political support it gave them to help them set up the separatist regime and the participation of its military personnel in the fighting'. Moldova (as the 'legitimate' sovereign) had a duty to take limited measures that were 'in its power' and 'in accordance with international law to secure to the applicants the rights guaranteed by the Convention': at paras 330–1.

157 Articles on Responsibility of States, commentary to art 10, para 2.

158 See this book s 5.2.

159 Crawford, *Creation* (n 16) 99. Compare Antonio Cassese, *International Law* (2nd edn, OUP 2005) 76. A potentially narrower suggestion, that the customary norm prohibiting the use of force applies not only to states but also to '*de facto* governments', is made in Ian Brownlie, *International Law and the Use of Force by States* (Clarendon 1963) 380–1. Talmon, 'Constitutive' (n 138) 180 takes a different approach: collective non-recognition does not have 'a *status-destroying* effect' on statehood, so an entity may be responsible for unlawful conduct as if it were a state, but other states can, through non-recognition, 'withhold the rights inherent in statehood from a new State'—a '*status-denying*' effect or 'sanction'.

160 Jochen A Frowein, 'De facto regime' (last updated 2013) MPEPIL, paras 2–3.

161 Talmon, 'Constitutive' (n 138) 103–4. Compare Christian Hillgruber, 'The admission of new states to the international community' (1998) 9 EJIL 491, 498.

cannot be *recognized* as a state: on the effectiveness-or-recognition view, evidence of collective non-recognition is not necessarily connected with the question of effective statehood. The result is that Rhodesia could be accused of suppressing external self-determination and could be held responsible for breaches of Zambia's territorial integrity, but at the same time it was diplomatically and economically isolated and given no opportunity to enter into treaties or other optional relations with other states.

I conclude that there is not enough evidence to show that self-determination creates a free-standing exception to the effectiveness norm in cases such as Rhodesia; on the contrary, there are reasons to think Rhodesia was a state, albeit one that could not be recognized.

4.2.2 A self-determination exception to the exceptions

There is another way in which self-determination could directly determine whether an entity acquires statehood (or statehood-in-context). The exceptions to the general rules that reflect the principle that no law arises from unlawfulness (the premature-recognition and collective-non-recognition exceptions to the recognition norm, and the unlawful-effectuation exception to the effectiveness norm) are underpinned or reinforced by peremptory norms. But a peremptory norm is not totally invulnerable to other norms; its scope may be limited by *other* peremptory norms, and, after it has emerged, it may be 'modified . . . by a subsequent norm of general international law having the same [peremptory] character'.[162] Self-determination is a peremptory norm. And there are indications that self-determination creates an exception to the exceptions to the general rules; that is, it enables the effectiveness and recognition norms to operate in the ordinary way, regardless of the exceptions based on unlawfulness.

I begin with the impact on the premature-recognition exception to the recognition norm.

It may be wondered whether the premature-recognition exception, which I derived from the duty of states to respect each other's territorial integrity, can even apply in principle in the usual scenario involving external self-determination—namely, in a non-self-governing territory. This is because the 'territory of a colony or other Non-Self-Governing Territory has, under the Charter, a status separate and distinct from the territory of the State administering it'.[163] It may be inapt to

[162] Vienna Convention on Treaties, art 53.

[163] Friendly Relations Declaration, principle *e*. This is despite the fact that in some cases an administering state has treated a non-self-governing territory as an integral part of its metropolitan territory under its domestic constitution—notably France with respect to Algeria, on which see Raič (n 129) 96–7.

speak as if the duty to respect the 'integrity' of the administering state's territory extended to such a 'separate and distinct' territory.

However, so long as a territory remains non-self-governing, the administering state does have rights over the territory. After Indonesia invaded East Timor in 1975, the Security Council continued to describe the former colonizer, Portugal, as 'administering Power in the Territory under Chapter XI of the Charter' (the chapter on non-self-governing territories).[164] In the later *East Timor* case, Portugal argued that its 'duties, powers and rights . . . as the administering Power' were 'opposable to Australia' and that, by making and applying a treaty premised on recognizing East Timor as Indonesian territory, Australia was 'in breach of the obligation not to disregard but to respect' some of those duties, powers, and rights.[165] By analogy with Portugal's argument, premature recognition of an entity as a state might breach the administering state's rights over a non-self-governing territory. And this, by analogy with recognition in breach of a state's territorial integrity, might trigger the premature-recognition exception to the recognition norm. It would be surprising were this not so, because a unilateral secessionist entity could then be recognized prematurely in defiance of a consultative and orderly independence process that complied with the UN Charter. I will proceed on the basis that the scenarios are analogous—that even if, strictly, an administering state's territorial integrity does not extend to a non-self-governing territory, its rights over the territory have the same result for relevant purposes. But partly since this is hard to confirm, my conclusions about self-determination will be expressed with some hesitation.

Even if the right to external self-determination does not as such completely override the premature-recognition exception, there are indications that it creates an exception to the exception in more limited circumstances. Consider what the Friendly Relations Declaration says about territorial integrity. After introducing and elaborating on the principle of self-determination, it adds that nothing in the paragraphs dealing with the principle

> shall be construed as authorizing or encouraging any action which would dismember or impair, totally or in part, the territorial integrity or political unity of sovereign and independent States conducting themselves in compliance with the principles of equal rights and self-determination of peoples as described above and possessed of a government representing the whole people belonging to the territory without distinction as to race, creed or colour.[166]

The Canadian Supreme Court said something similar in *Quebec*, adding that a state that complies with 'self-determination in its internal arrangements' is entitled to

[164] SC res 384 (22 December 1975, East Timor) preamble.
[165] *East Timor* [1995] ICJ Rep 90, para 10. The Court held that it could not exercise jurisdiction.
[166] Friendly Relations Declaration, principle *e*.

have its 'territorial integrity recognized by other states'.[167] These are reaffirmations of the duty to respect territorial integrity. But the duty is loaded up with qualifications. The implication is that a state that does *not* conduct itself 'in compliance with . . . self-determination' may *not* retain to the full extent its right that its territorial integrity be respected. Since I have raised doubts about whether a state's territorial integrity strictly even extends to a non-self-governing territory, in that scenario there is even more reason to think that, by analogy, an administering state that denies self-determination may no longer have rights over the territory for certain purposes. This broad idea is taken up by Crawford. If a state 'forcibly denies self-determination' to a people, which then attempts to secede unilaterally,

> self-determination operates in favour of the statehood of the seceding territory, provided that the seceding government can properly be regarded as representative of the people of the territory. In such a case recognition may be extended even though the independence of the territory is not 'disputed without rational hope of success'. . . . [S]elf-determination may legitimize recognition that would otherwise be premature.[168]

Crawford backs away from the implication that recognition itself creates statehood in this scenario: 'it is difficult to accept that the normal requirement of effective government has been entirely displaced'.[169] But on the effectiveness-or-recognition view, it follows naturally that the recognition norm creates statehood-in-context relative to recognizing states.

In sum, a state that denies a people's right to external self-determination—certainly where it resists the fulfilment of the right violently—may 'lose' its rights over the territory, at least for relevant purposes; since recognition no longer breaches such rights, the premature-recognition exception does not apply and the recognition norm can operate unhindered.

There is practice consistent with this. Algeria, for instance, was recognized by a number of states while France was still resisting its independence in the period 1958–62.[170] The clearest case is Portugal's refusal to relinquish its African colonies. In a resolution in December 1973, the General Assembly approved 'the credentials of the representatives of Portugal, on the clear understanding . . . that they do not represent the Portuguese-dominated Territories of Angola and Mozambique nor could they represent Guinea-Bissau, which is an independent State'.[171] This

[167] *Quebec* (1998) 115 ILR 536, para 154.

[168] Crawford, *Creation* (n 16) 387, paraphrasing John Quincy Adams, Letter to Richard Rush (18 August 1823) in *British and Foreign State Papers: 1823–1824* (Ridgway & Sons 1843) 299, 300.

[169] Crawford, *Creation* (n 16) 387.

[170] Ibid, 385. See further Raič (n 129) 95–105.

[171] GA res 3181 (XXVIII) (17 December 1973, Portugal) para 1. See further Dugard, *Recognition* (n 95) 73–4.

implies that Angola and Mozambique, although not yet states and still 'Portuguese-dominated', fell outside the territory over which Portugal had either a right that its territorial integrity be respected or any relevant rights as administering state. The resolution explicitly affirms that Guinea-Bissau, where an insurgent entity had won partial control against military resistance by Portugal, had actually acquired statehood. About forty states—among them China, India, and the Soviet Union—had recognized Guinea-Bissau by the date of the resolution; by the end of May 1974, eighty-four states had.[172] Its statehood relative to those states can be explained on the basis that Portugal no longer had rights over the territory that might be breached by premature recognition and hence the recognitions were valid.

Note that the General Assembly assumed that Guinea-Bissau also had statehood relative to *Portugal* (which would not recognize it until August 1974[173]). In November 1973, it condemned Portugal for being in 'violation of the sovereignty and territorial integrity' of Guinea-Bissau.[174] This assertion could be made compellingly only on the basis that Guinea-Bissau met the effectiveness criteria, which is open to doubt.[175] But there is room for some speculation here. Depriving Portugal of its rights over the territory might have made the effectiveness criteria much easier to meet. The criteria traditionally require a parent state to have 'virtually and substantially abandoned the struggle' to defend its territory.[176] Portugal would not have accepted that it had abandoned the struggle, but in a legal sense it no longer *was* a parent state defending its own territory; its position was more akin to that of a foreign aggressor.[177] So Portugal's resistance did not operate to preclude the criteria from being met. In any event, doubts about whether Guinea-Bissau had statehood relative to Portugal do not affect my narrower conclusion that it could be validly recognized by other states.

By depriving a recalcitrant state such as Portugal of its rights over territory (and thereby cancelling out the premature-recognition exception to the recognition norm), the principle of self-determination gains some teeth. Earlier, I noted that if an administering state tries to implement a people's choice to create a new state, statehood tends to be created by the ordinary effectiveness norm or, if not, at least by the recognition norm. It is now clear that, even if the administering state *refuses* to implement the people's choice or wish, self-determination can eventually

[172] Charles Rousseau, 'Chronique des faits internationaux' (1974) 78 Revue générale de droit international public 1096, 1168, further 1166–71.

[173] Joint Declaration of Portugal and the African Party for the Independence of Guinea-Bissau (26 August 1974) 13 ILM 1244.

[174] GA res 3061 (XXVIII) (2 November 1973, Guinea-Bissau) paras 2–3.

[175] Bunyan Bryant and others, 'Recognition of Guinea (Bissau)' (1974) 15 Harvard International Law Journal 482, 491–3.

[176] Harcourt (n 16) 9.

[177] Compare Friendly Relations Declaration, principle *e*: every 'State has a duty to refrain from any forcible action which deprives peoples . . . of their right to self-determination and freedom and independence'.

enable the emergence of a new state. As Antonio Cassese put it, the duties that self-determination imposes on the administering state

> do not produce the immediate legal effect of rendering the legal title over colonial territories null and void. Rather . . . they envisage a temporary legal regime that must of necessity lead to the eventual *extinction* of legal title. In a way, these obligations act as a sort of time-bomb: the holder of the sovereign title has to fulfil them knowing that by this action it will eventually have to relinquish its title.[178]

It is hard to find evidence in practice of whether this 'time-bomb' affects the other exceptions to the general rules about statehood as well as the premature-recognition exception. This is another reason my conclusions about self-determination will be somewhat hesitant. But some hints, albeit of very ambiguous relevance, can be extracted from the independence of Bangladesh, and these are reinforced by broader considerations of principle.

Bangladesh, until then known as East Pakistan, unilaterally declared independence from Pakistan in April 1971. India forcibly intervened in support of the secessionist entity. In December, the Pakistani army surrendered to Indian troops.[179] India's use of force, since it was not in clear self-defence or authorized by the Security Council, was on its face unlawful. So insofar as Bangladesh met the effectiveness criteria, its effectiveness may have been a consequence of a breach of the peremptory norm prohibiting force. I have found that ordinarily in such a situation the collective-non-recognition exception prevents the recognition norm from applying and the unlawful-effectuation exception prevents the effectiveness norm from applying. Yet no call for non-recognition came from the United Nations. On the contrary, many states, including India, the Soviet Union, the United Kingdom, France, and the United States, recognized Bangladesh during 1972, despite Pakistani objections.[180]

The reason this episode can provide only very ambiguous hints is that it is far from clear that self-determination was at all relevant. East Pakistan was never on the UN list of non-self-governing territories. Treating it as a self-determination case (as do some scholars I will cite) is a largely after-the-fact explanation of an event that might be explicable in some other way.[181] Still, the episode has commonalities with clearer cases of self-determination. In 1960, the General Assembly had resolved to treat as '[*p*]*rima facie*' non-self-governing 'a territory which is

[178] Cassese, *Self-Determination* (n 107) 186–7.

[179] Crawford, *Creation* (n 16) 140–3; Dugard, *Recognition* (n 95) 75–6.

[180] Ved P Nanda, 'Self-determination in international law: The tragic tale of two cities—Islamabad (West Pakistan) and Dacca (East Pakistan)' (1972) 66 AJIL 321, 336.

[181] One alternative explanation is that India's use of force for some reason did not trigger the collective-non-recognition or the unlawful-effectuation exception; another is that Bangladesh was not really a state on any basis (or even a state-in-context) until Pakistan eventually acquiesced in its independence.

geographically separate and is distinct ethnically and/or culturally from the country administering it'.[182] East Pakistan was all those things. It had a mostly Bengali population and was separated from the rest of Pakistan, from which it was administered, by about 1800 kilometres of Indian territory. In the Security Council, India described Pakistan's actions in East Pakistan as an 'attempt to hold under colonial rule 75 million persons whom they have exploited for 23 years' and argued that if the General Assembly's indicators were applied 'we could declare East Pakistan a non-self-governing territory' (although this view was not endorsed by other states).[183] So perhaps the people of East Pakistan had a customary right to external self-determination based on commonalities with the non-self-governing territories on the UN list. An even more controversial basis for this hypothesis is the possibility, speculated about in *Quebec*, that such a right comes into being where a people 'is denied any meaningful exercise of its right to self-determination within the state of which it forms a part': Pakistan was accused not only of exploiting the territory but also of genocide.[184]

The hypothesis that external self-determination applied has been invoked to explain how Bangladesh could have acquired statehood despite India's use of force. Jean Salmon has argued that 'if the act of force creating Bangladesh was unlawful, the result is not', because it followed acts of violence by Pakistan that impeded the fulfilment of external self-determination.[185] Crawford makes a similar argument, observing that if East Pakistan was *not* 'a self-determination unit' then, faced with the widespread recognition of Bangladesh, it would be difficult to sustain the view that there is a 'criterion of legality regulating the creation of States by the use of external illegal force'.[186] In my terms, the argument is that, where a people's right to external self-determination is being forcibly denied, the collective-non-recognition exception does not prevent an entity from acquiring statehood under the recognition norm, nor does the unlawful-effectuation exception prevent it from acquiring statehood under the effectiveness norm. This is despite an unlawful use of force: law, in this scenario, *can* arise from unlawfulness—to vindicate self-determination. This argument is of limited scope in that it does not apply where (as, for instance, in Crimea[187]) there does not exist a people with a right to external self-determination that is being forcibly denied.

Since Bangladesh, not being a clear case of self-determination, offers only a shaky foundation for this conclusion, it will be helpful to turn to more abstract principles.

[182] Principles Which Should Guide Members under Article 73 e, principle IV.
[183] Samar Sen, India, in SC 1606th mtg (4 December 1971) UN doc S/PV.1606, paras 168, 185.
[184] *Quebec* (1998) 115 ILR 536, para 154; Nanda (n 180), especially 336.
[185] Jean Salmon, 'Naissance et reconnaissance du Bangla-Desh' in Josef Tittel (ed), *Multitudo legum ius unum: Festschrift für Wilhelm Wengler* (Interrecht 1973) vol 1, 467, 490 (translation).
[186] Crawford, *Creation* (n 16) 142, further 140–3.
[187] Grant, *Aggression* (n 92) 23–33, 54–8.

The existence of an exception to the collective-non-recognition exception accords with the usual functioning of the collective duty of non-recognition. In *Namibia*, in discussing which acts are and are not prohibited by the collective duty, Judge Dillard remarked that 'the maxim *ex injuria jus non oritur* is not so severe as to deny that any source of right whatever can accrue to third persons acting in good faith'.[188] Imagine a case similar to the Bangladesh episode save that external self-determination unambiguously applies. The third entity 'acting in good faith' is the would-be new state (equivalent to Bangladesh) as distinct from the perpetrator of the unlawful use of force (equivalent to India) and its victim, the recalcitrant administering state (equivalent to Pakistan). The rights that 'can accrue' to the would-be new state are the rights inherent in statehood. It would be perverse if unlawful conduct by a foreign state could deprive a blameless entity of rights that would fulfil a people's right to external self-determination. This reinforces the conclusion that the collective duty of non-recognition does not make recognition unlawful or invalid in these circumstances.

Similar reasoning suggests that self-determination creates a limited exception to the unlawful-effectuation exception to the effectiveness norm: it would be perverse if a foreign state's unlawful conduct could prevent the fulfilment of a people's right to external self-determination through the creation of an effective state. This is further reinforced by the definition of 'aggression' adopted by the General Assembly in 1974, which was intended to clarify aspects of the prohibition of the use of force. It provides that '[n]othing in this Definition', in particular not the provision defining which acts constitute aggression,

> could in any way prejudice the right to self-determination, freedom and independence, as derived from the Charter, of peoples forcibly deprived of that right and referred to in the [Friendly Relations Declaration], particularly peoples under colonial and racist régimes or other forms of alien domination; nor the right of these peoples to struggle to that end and to seek and receive support, in accordance with the principles of the Charter and in conformity with the abovementioned Declaration.[189]

Note that it does not necessarily follow, from the existence of a people's right to 'receive support', that a forcible intervention by a foreign state is actually *lawful* (it is hard to see how the explicit prohibition of force in the Charter could be overcome).[190] But it appears that such unlawful conduct cannot 'prejudice the right to

[188] *Namibia* [1971] ICJ Rep 16, 167 (Judge Dillard).

[189] Definition of Aggression, annex to GA res 3314 (XXIX) (14 December 1974) art 7.

[190] Friendly Relations Declaration, principle *e* similarly provides that if a state takes 'forcible action which deprives peoples . . . of their right to self-determination' then 'such peoples are entitled to seek and to receive support in accordance with the purposes and principles of the Charter'. See further Gray (n 96) 59–64. A relevant case, not involving the creation of a new state, may be India's annexation by force of the Portuguese-administered enclave of Goa in 1961 in purported vindication of a right to

self-determination'; the result is that, if an entity emerges that meets the effectiveness criteria, it can become a state.

I draw the following conclusion—with some hesitation, given the uncertainties I have mentioned, but consistent with broad principles and with what evidence does exist. Where a people has a right to external self-determination, at least where a recalcitrant administering state is violently resisting the fulfilment of that right, there is an exception to all the exceptions to the general rules. Statehood is determined by the ordinary effectiveness and recognition norms, regardless of the principle that no law arises from unlawfulness. To this must be added a reminder that I am speaking only about very atypical scenarios in which unlawfulness appears to preclude statehood: if there is no unlawfulness, an entity can always acquire statehood in fulfilment of self-determination in the ordinary way.

4.3 The limited scope of the exceptions

My conclusions point to a three-stage test of statehood, in which the recognition norm and the effectiveness norm must be considered in parallel at each stage. Stage one is to apply those two general rules. Stage two is to apply any relevant exceptions to the recognition norm (the premature-recognition and collective-nonrecognition exceptions) and the effectiveness norm (the unlawful-effectuation exception). These exceptions all reflect the principle that no law arises from unlawfulness. Stage three is, if relevant, to apply the exception to the exceptions (self-determination). A state for the purposes of international law can be defined as an entity that passes this test on the basis of effectiveness or universal recognition or both and thereby acquires, relative to all other states, the attributes I discussed in Chapter 3: it is covered by the customary norms in the form 'any entity that is defined as a state has a particular right or other relation' and is also covered by the norm 'the practice and *opinio iuris* of all the entities that are defined as states contribute to customary norms'. A state-in-context is an entity that, on the basis of the same test, acquires these attributes relative to one or some recognizing states but not necessarily relative to all states for all purposes.

A critical observer might worry that the existence and complexity of the exceptions—not to mention the exception to the exceptions—complicates statehood so much that it becomes doubtful whether there remain any truly 'general' rules at all. My response to this is to emphasize that the exceptions are limited in scope: statehood *usually* still depends on the general rules that I introduced in the previous chapter, especially effectiveness.

external self-determination that was being suppressed. Doubts about whether this annexation was valid were eventually resolved by Portuguese acquiescence: Treaty on Recognition of India's Sovereignty over Goa, Daman, Diu, Dadra and Nagar Haveli, India–Portugal (31 December 1974) 982 UNTS 158, art 1.

The limited scope of the exceptions can be illustrated by applying the three-stage test I have outlined to Kosovo, which unilaterally declared independence from Serbia in 2008.

Stage one of the test is to apply the recognition and effectiveness norms. Kosovo was soon recognized by more than one hundred states, though not by Serbia or numerous others.[191] As for effectiveness, the question of whether Kosovo met the criterion of independence is muddied by the fact that the territory remained for several years under administration by the United Nations, which exercised a number of governmental functions; moreover, without the presence of a UN-mandated military organization, it is unlikely that Kosovo 'would have been able to defend itself against the Serbian armed forces if these had been instructed to quell the secession'.[192] But Kosovo ceased to be under international supervision in 2012.[193] From that time, despite some ongoing doubts, there was at least a strong argument to be made that it met the effectiveness criteria, and some scholars have expressed that view.[194]

Stage two is to apply the exceptions to the general rules. Serbia might have asserted—although for political reasons it did not—that Kosovo's attempted unilateral secession was enabled by an unlawful use of force: the 1999 bombing campaign, led by the United States, to end Serbian persecution of Kosovars.[195] The International Court did not explicitly deal with this point in the *Kosovo* opinion (it evaded deciding whether Kosovo's declaration of independence 'led to the creation of a State'[196]). But the little that it did say has clear implications. It distinguished Kosovo from cases such as Rhodesia, Northern Cyprus, and Republika Srpska. In those other cases, it said, the Security Council made

> a determination as regards the concrete situation existing at the time that those declarations of independence were made; the illegality attached to the declarations of independence thus stemmed . . . from the fact that they were, or would have been, connected with the unlawful use of force or other egregious violations of norms of general international law, in particular those of a peremptory

[191] Alain Pellet, 'Kosovo—the questions not asked: Self-determination, secession, and recognition' in Marko Milanović and Michael Wood (eds) *The Law and Politics of the Kosovo Advisory Opinion* (OUP 2015) 268, 277.

[192] Tomuschat (n 33) 39.

[193] Report of the Secretary-General on the United Nations Interim Administration Mission in Kosovo (8 November 2012) UN doc S/2012/818, para 6.

[194] For the view that Kosovo meets the criteria, see Tomuschat (n 33) 36–40, 45 and James Crawford, 'Kosovo and the criteria for statehood in international law' in Marko Milanović and Michael Wood (eds), *The Law and Politics of the Kosovo Advisory Opinion* (OUP 2015) 280, 290. Contrast the earlier view of Colin Warbrick, 'Kosovo: the declaration of independence' (2008) 57 ICLQ 675, 689.

[195] Serbia, Written Statement (15 April 2009) ICJ Pleadings, *Accordance with International Law of the Unilateral Declaration of Independence in Respect of Kosovo*, paras 412–524; Marko Milanović, 'Arguing the Kosovo case' in Marko Milanović and Michael Wood (eds), *The Law and Politics of the Kosovo Advisory Opinion* (OUP 2015) 21, 34.

[196] *Kosovo* [2010] ICJ Rep 403, paras 51, 56.

character (*jus cogens*). In the context of Kosovo, the Security Council has never taken this position.[197]

The Court implied that Kosovo's attempted secession was not 'connected with' an unlawful use of force. There is reasoning to support this. Even if the 1999 campaign was unlawful, the aggressors did not unlawfully occupy the territory; instead, the Security Council created the UN administration.[198] And almost nine years passed between the use of force and Kosovo's attempted secession. The Court's remarks suggest that, since there was no relevant unlawful conduct, the collective-non-recognition and unlawful-effectuation exceptions did not apply.

Whether the premature-recognition exception applied depends on effectiveness: so long as Kosovo was not effective, recognition breached Serbia's right that its territorial integrity be respected and was invalid (and this is still the position if Kosovo remains ineffective).

It is striking that up to this stage of the test, since recognition is neutralized and since the other exceptions did not apply, *all that matters* is whether Kosovo was effective.

Stage three is to apply the exception to the exceptions. Although Kosovo was not listed as a non-self-governing territory, the principle of self-determination was invoked by some of its supporters.[199] *If* its people had a right to external self-determination whose fulfilment was being violently resisted by Serbia—a claim that many international lawyers would contest—that might have made a marginal difference to the outcome. It might have cancelled out the premature-recognition exception: states could then have recognized Kosovo, which would have thereby become a state-in-context, during a period when Kosovo was not yet effective. The difference to the outcome would only be marginal because whether Kosovo was a state in the full sense would still depend on whether it met the effectiveness criteria.

My aim here is not to stake out a categorical position on the controversies raised by Kosovo (including whether it meets the effectiveness criteria; if so, when it first did so; and the role of external self-determination). That would require a more detailed and speculative analysis of the criteria, the facts, and the very contentious question of how self-determination operates outside the context of non-self-governing territories. My aim is just to observe that even a case as politically messy

[197] Ibid, para 81.

[198] SC res 1244 (10 June 1999, Kosovo). But contrast suggestions that the 1999 use of force nonetheless enabled Kosovo's declaration of independence, triggering a collective duty of non-recognition: Alexander Orakhelashvili, 'Statehood, recognition and the United Nations system: A unilateral declaration of independence in Kosovo' (2008) 12 Max Planck Yearbook of United Nations Law 1, 30–1; Olivier Corten, 'Déclarations unilatérales d'indépendance et reconnaissances prématurées: Du Kosovo à l'Ossétie du sud et à l'Abkhazie' (2008) 112 Revue générale de droit international public 721, 747–9.

[199] Eg, Netherlands, Written Statement (17 April 2009) ICJ Pleadings: *Accordance with International Law of the Unilateral Declaration of Independence in Respect of Kosovo*, paras 3.1–3.22.

as Kosovo may ultimately come down to the ordinary general rules, in this case the effectiveness norm, rather than depending on exceptions. The case is certainly *factually* exceptional. Traditionally, a state could crush an attempt at secession by force (and that basically remains the law, absent self-determination), whereas with Kosovo other states engineered factual circumstances in which Serbia could not practicably do this, in particular by creating the UN administration. But however controversial the result of this collective action may be, the case does not appear to be *legally* exceptional in the same sense as other cases I have discussed in this chapter, such as Northern Cyprus or the Bantustans; it appears to come down to the effectiveness criteria. Apart from the premature-recognition norm, which plays a frequent and important role in subordinating the recognition norm to the effectiveness norm, the exceptions tend to apply only in a few special scenarios.

Another example will serve to illustrate the limited scope of exceptions to the general rules in a different way: the 'Republic of Somaliland'. A former British protectorate, it was fleetingly independent before being incorporated into the larger state of Somalia in 1960; it purported to secede unilaterally in 1991, when Somalia collapsed into anarchy, and has governed itself autonomously ever since.[200] It is difficult to see what more Somaliland could do to meet the effectiveness criteria. Its parent state 'virtually and substantially abandoned the struggle for supremacy' (which generally indicates that a unilateral secessionist entity has become effective)[201] in the radical sense that it ceased to have a government capable of being supreme anywhere. Yet Somaliland is universally unrecognized and largely ignored.

This case might look as if it must fall within an exception to the general rules.

But the exceptions I have identified are irrelevant. And unlike in some of the cases from which I derived those exceptions, states do not tend to justify their treatment of Somaliland by reference to unlawfulness or other exceptional features: there is no clear *opinio iuris* to support an exception. On closer inspection, even the practice is inconclusive about whether Somaliland is a state. I have found (and in this respect I am in accord with the prevailing 'declaratory' view) that effectiveness can be sufficient for statehood, without a need for recognition; in addition, states have no general duty to recognize another state or to invite it to participate in treaties or international organizations.[202] If one takes this seriously—if one takes seriously the idea that statehood depends on rules that operate in a broadly predictable manner, not just on *ad hoc* decisions—then one must be prepared, very occasionally, to encounter a state that is universally unrecognized. In the past, consistent with this, some effective entities have been ignored for very long periods for

[200] Scott Pegg, *International Society and the De Facto State* (Ashgate 1998) 85–97; Scott Pegg and Pål Kolstø, 'Somaliland: Dynamics of internal legitimacy and (lack of) external sovereignty' (2015) 66 Geoforum 193.

[201] Harcourt (n 16) 9; this book s 4.1.1.

[202] On whether there is a duty to recognize, see this book s 3.3 and the caveat about the Congo in s 4.2.

political reasons. For example, Haiti declared independence in 1804 after expelling the French, but, being the product of a revolt by black slaves, it was ostracized for decades: the United Kingdom recognized it in 1825, France in 1838, and the United States as late as the 1860s.[203] And earlier I cited evidence that Rhodesia was an effective but universally unrecognized state.[204] In the case of Somaliland, other states may not wish to grant recognition because that might encourage secessionists elsewhere or might undermine efforts to reconstruct the larger Somalia; it has also been suggested that the current situation suits the political and economic interests of some neighbouring states.[205] The situation might continue to evolve: states such as the United Arab Emirates, although they still do not recognize Somaliland, have shown a willingness to co-operate pragmatically with it. In 2018, a company owned by the emirate of Dubai signed a contract with Somaliland to develop the port of Berbera; Ethiopia is also involved. Somalia responded that the contract was void and 'a violation of Somalia's sovereignty'. Somaliland, in turn, described the response by Somalia as 'a declaration of war'.[206]

A lesson here is that not every case in which practice appears to diverge from the general rules about statehood is necessarily evidence of an exception to those rules. This holds true even if Somaliland is not a state. International lawyers who have sought explanations of why it may not be a state have not tended to postulate a further exception, to be added to the short list that I have produced; instead, they have speculated that Somaliland may not be effective after all[207] or else (contrary to the prevailing view) that effectiveness is not sufficient.[208]

I will go a little further: not every case of apparently divergent practice is necessarily evidence of anything. Today, the practice relevant to statehood is comparatively stable and consistent, certainly if the comparison is with the pre-twentieth-century practice that I discussed in Chapter 2, from which I could not extract a settled rule.[209] Yet in an area of law as politicized as statehood, some divergent or potentially misleading practice might still emerge. The scholar of statehood cannot always assume that the practice of all states is invariably consistent with international law, then form a conclusion from that practice about whether a particular entity is a state, and then work backward to an explanation. An attempt to resolve every anomaly by that method might lengthen the list of exceptions and caveats until it really is doubtful whether any 'general' rules remain. In

[203] Charles H Wesley, 'The struggle for the recognition of Haiti and Liberia as independent republics' (1917) 2 Journal of Negro History 369, 376.

[204] If Haiti was ostracized because the government was controlled by members of a black majority, compare how Rhodesia was ostracized for basically the opposite reason: this book s 4.2.1.

[205] Pegg and Kolstø (n 200) 198.

[206] International Crisis Group, Somalia and the Gulf Crisis (Africa Report No 260, 5 June 2018) 17–18.

[207] Crawford, *Creation* (n 16) 412–15.

[208] Dugard, 'Secession' (n 31) 58–9. On the evidence that effectiveness *is* sufficient see this book s 3.1.4.

[209] This book ss 2.4.3, 2.6.

cases such as Kosovo in which the practice is divided, that method would be of no use at all. What the scholar can do is to identify general rules and exceptions that are evidenced by clear practice and *opinio iuris* (cautiously supplemented by broad principles that are themselves derived from practice and *opinio iuris*); the scholar can then use those norms to form views about cases in which practice and *opinio iuris* are not clear. That is the approach I just took to Kosovo. Forming an unshakable conclusion about Somaliland is equally difficult. But the norms I have identified at least leave open the possibility that it is a state despite—like Haiti—being ostracized.

This largely brings to end my analysis of states and states-in-context. I will summarize the three-stage test I have developed in the conclusion to this book as a whole. But still to be discussed, before I can form that conclusion, is the personality of other state-like entities; and that discussion will corroborate and clarify some points relevant to statehood.

5

Other state-like entities in a world of states

I found in Chapter 2 that, before the twentieth century, the state-like entities that had a degree of personality in international law were very diverse. That was the age of the Ottoman Empire with its regime of consular jurisdiction, of imperial China with its universalist tribute system, of treaty-making African entities, and of Japan with its aspiration to join the 'civilized' West. I even doubted whether the term 'state' could be given a technical legal meaning in that context. International law today does not come close to replicating the diversity of the past. It is dominated by entities of the type I discussed in Chapters 3 and 4: states in the full, technical legal sense. To a lesser extent it is also concerned with states-in-context. I am nonetheless going to consider statehood in the light of the rules that exist today about how *other* state-like entities can acquire personality. I have two purposes in doing this. The first is to corroborate and clarify some of my conclusions about statehood. In particular, the discussion in this chapter will provide extra support for the recognition norm—for the idea that, when an existing state recognizes an entity as a state, that can function as an exercise of power to create bilateral legal relations. It will also provide evidence about whether states are entities of a unique type or just the dominant members of a family of entities. Second, the discussion will draw out some further implications of my conclusion that there are two general rules about statehood: the recognition and effectiveness norms.

The structure of this chapter will reflect the distinction between those two general rules. I will look at how state-like entities other than states and states-in-context acquire personality in a manner analogous to the recognition norm, which I will call 'volitional' personality. Then I will look at how they might acquire 'automatic' personality, a term I have already used in discussing the effectiveness norm.[1] The entities to be discussed include autonomous territories and other subentities of states, such as Hong Kong and Quebec; entities whose precise status is contested, such as Taiwan; protectorates; and entities in 'free association'. But I am not seeking to catalogue all the state-like entities that may have personality. On the contrary, it will become evident that the rules are too flexible for that to be done comprehensively; it will prove possible to draw general conclusions only at a fairly high level of abstraction. Nor will I analyse international organizations, individuals, or other non-state-like entities that lie outside the scope of this book, though I will refer to some of them by way of illustration.

[1] This book s 3.1.1.

Statehood and the State-Like in International Law. Rowan Nicholson, Oxford University Press (2019).
© Rowan Nicholson
DOI: 10.1093/oso/9780198851219.001.0001

5.1 Personality acquired volitionally

Recall WN Hohfeld's definition of a power, which I introduced in Chapter 1: an entity's ability to create or change rights, duties, or other legal relations.[2] And recall that in his scheme, which I have adopted, these relations are always correlative: a right of one entity correlates with a duty of another entity, and so on with the other pairs of Hohfeldian relations. When I describe a legal relation as 'volitional', I mean that its validity primarily depends on the exercise of a power. Typically in international law, the power is exercised by the entity that receives the relation *or* by the entity that receives the correlative relation *or* by both of those entities: in these cases it might be called a power to consent.[3] This volitional category encompasses any relations created by treaties and unilateral declarations; and it extends to relations whose validity primarily but indirectly depends on those things, such as duties to comply with judgments by an international court whose jurisdiction derives from consent. When I first introduced Hohfeldian powers, I doubted whether the creation of custom could be analysed in terms of powers; in any event I will not analyse it in that way for the purpose of this chapter. So the volitional category does not generally include customary relations as such. But it does include relations created by the recognition norm: although their content is derived from customary norms concerning states, the validity of the relations primarily depends on the exercise of powers of recognition by the recognized entity and recognizing states.

The word 'primarily' is important, because it is never the case in international law, at least not nowadays, that the validity of relations depends *solely* on an exercise of a power. The power must in turn be derived from somewhere, for example, from the customary norms about unilateral declarations. Thus the term 'volitional' and its opposite, 'automatic', do not represent two totally disconnected methods of constructing a legal system; the distinction is just a pragmatic one designed to help to identify how entities acquire personality.

I defined personality as the possession, by an entity that is constructed as a fact by norms of international law, of rights or duties given to it by such norms.[4] So insofar as an entity has volitional rights and duties, its personality can also be said to be volitional. The question to be considered is how a state-like entity might end up with a degree of volitional personality and yet not be a state.

[2] WN Hohfeld, 'Some fundamental legal conceptions as applied in judicial reasoning [part 1]' (1913) 23 Yale Law Journal 16, 44; this book s 1.1.2.

[3] The other possibility is that the power is exercised by an entity or entities to create volitional relations between *two other entities*, neither of which has exercised a power to consent. I will not consider here whether this ever occurs in situations involving international organizations or individuals. But it is not typical in international law and will not arise in the discussion of state-like entities in this chapter.

[4] This book s 1.2.

Statehood provides the standard against which to measure the degree of such personality. States are often described as 'full' international legal persons.[5] In *Reparation for Injuries*, the International Court remarked that a state 'possesses the totality of the international rights and duties recognized by international law', whereas international organizations (and by implication persons of other types) have a more tightly circumscribed package of relations.[6] 'Full' and 'totality' are not strictly accurate: there exist rights and duties in international law that are obviously not possessed by states, such as the human rights of individuals. But it is true that the rights and duties that states bear under customary norms are greater in number and in consequence than those borne by any other entity. This suggests two volitional ways in which a state-like entity might end up with a degree of personality falling short of that of states: it might start with statehood and then *lose* some rights or duties; or it might start with no personality at all and then *gain* rights or duties. In other words, a position lying between no personality and 'full' personality might be reached from either direction.

5.1.1 An entity gains rights or duties short of statehood

The scenario in which the entity starts from a position of having no personality at all might occur where a state makes a treaty with a state-like entity that lacks statehood.

States and international organizations can certainly make treaties. But states have also made agreements that may appear to be treaties with a miscellany of other entities, including state-like non-states (examples of which I will discuss) and even companies.[7] Whether these are explicitly *called* treaties is not necessarily legally significant; the important legal question is whether these agreements create relations that are valid within the internal framework of international law, as distinct from relations governed solely by domestic law or a non-legally-binding political bargain. The Vienna Conventions on treaty law are of little help here. They apply solely to treaties whose parties are states or international organizations; they say that this restriction 'shall not affect . . . the legal force' of agreements to which other 'subjects of international law' are parties, but they leave unanswered the question

[5] Eg, Michael Byers, *Custom, Power and the Power of Rules: International Relations and Customary International Law* (CUP 1999) 75.

[6] *Reparation for Injuries Suffered in the Service of the United Nations (Advisory Opinion)* [1949] ICJ Rep 174, 180, further 178. See also *Legality of the Use by a State of Nuclear Weapons in Armed Conflict (Advisory Opinion Requested by the World Health Organization)* [1996] ICJ Rep 66, para 25.

[7] Thomas D Grant, 'Who can make treaties? Other subjects of international law' in Duncan B Hollis (ed), *The Oxford Guide to Treaties* (OUP 2012) 125. A striking example, which Grant (at 142–3) describes as 'a treaty granting private rights directly' is Agreement with a View to the Administrative and Technical Re-organization of the Southern Railway Company's System, Austria–Hungary–Italy–Kingdom of the Serbs, Croats and Slovenes–Southern Railway Company (Südbahn) (29 March 1923) 23 LNTS 255.

of what such agreements may exist.[8] Scholars sometimes try to answer the question by searching for norms giving treaty-making powers to specific classes of non-states. For example, Christine Bell considers whether non-state parties to peace agreements might be 'subjects of international law' by virtue of being non-state armed groups, indigenous peoples, or representatives of secessionist minorities.[9] This search turns out to be

> a tautological exercise. . . . The tautology arises because a claim to international subjectivity . . . involves examining what rights, powers, duties, and immunities the actors in question are accorded on the international plane, including whether they are permitted to sign treaties or international agreements. Moreover, the main evidence of such permission may be the existence of an internationalized peace agreement itself. Recognizing peace agreements as international agreements therefore seems to require the nonstate group and the agreement to 'bootstrap' each other into the international legal realm.[10]

This approach to non-states, however, seems to assume that in order to make a treaty an entity must already have 'subjectivity' in some wider sense. An advantage of my narrow definition of personality—which requires an entity actually to possess at least one Hohfeldian right or duty, rather than merely a 'capacity' to acquire one by treaty or otherwise—is that it avoids embedding assumptions such as this in basic terminology. It can distinguish between the actual possession of rights or duties and an ability to acquire them by treaty.

So what are the theoretical preconditions for acquiring rights and duties by treaty? As a matter of *fact* (or to be precise, as a matter of how norms of international law construct or apprehend the facts), there may have to be an identifiable entity that is capable of performing the conduct involved in making a treaty. Compare *Cameroon v Nigeria*: in expressing doubts about whether the Kings and Chiefs of Old Calabar could make a treaty, the International Court remarked that there was not 'convincing evidence of a central federal power' that was capable of acting on behalf of 'individual townships'.[11] But this factual precondition is distinct from whether an entity must already have a degree of 'subjectivity' before it can

[8] Vienna Convention on the Law of Treaties (23 May 1969) 1155 UNTS 331, arts 1, 3; Vienna Convention on the Law of Treaties between States and International Organizations or between International Organizations (21 March 1986, not yet in force) UN doc A/CONF.129/15, arts 1, 3.

[9] Christine Bell, 'Peace agreements: Their nature and legal status' (2006) 100 AJIL 373, 381–3.

[10] Ibid, 383–4. She goes on to discuss in detail why it matters whether such agreements are legally binding. If there is no enforcement mechanism anyway, there may not seem much practical difference between a treaty within the framework of international law and a political bargain. But legal bindingness might, among other things, dissuade a non-state party from treating an agreement as a mere 'piece of paper': at 387.

[11] *Land and Maritime Boundary between Cameroon and Nigeria (Cameroon v Nigeria: Equatorial Guinea Intervening)* [2002] ICJ Rep 303, para 207. See further this book s 2.6.

make a treaty, if that is taken to mean that it must already possess a treaty-making power or some other legal relation. Theoretically, the minimum *legal relation* that an entity must initially possess in order to acquire rights and duties by treaty is a Hohfeldian susceptibility. It is true that both parties must exercise contractual powers to make a treaty. The situation in which the only legal relation that an entity initially possesses is a susceptibility will occur where the other prospective treaty party has a *power to give the entity a treaty-making power* (which is equivalent to saying that the entity has a correlative susceptibility).

I made very similar observations in Chapter 3 in arguing that an entity may have a susceptibility to be recognized as a state even if it does not yet have any rights or duties.[12] Under the recognition norm, a state has a power to give such an entity, relative to itself, the whole gamut of rights, powers, and other relations that customary norms give to states, which of course include a treaty-making power. If a state can give an entity all those things, that implies (*a fortiori*) that it can give an entity just *one* of those things: a state has a power to recognize an entity as a treaty-maker and thereby empower the entity to make a treaty with that particular state. This extrapolation from the recognition norm may actually have firmer support among international lawyers than the idea that recognition can create statehood. William Worster observes that the 'debate over the law of recognition, while contentious in the case of states, is largely uncontroversial for non-state actors', which participate in international law not 'by inherent right, as states do, but rather as a result of states admitting them', a process 'analogous to the constitutive theory of state recognition'.[13]

If the default position or general rule is that states can make treaties with a non-state, even one that otherwise lacks personality, there is no need to search for specific norms giving a treaty-making power to specific classes of non-states. There may be major exceptions to the general rule, as I will discuss; but it is then the exceptions that must be specifically identified. Moreover, as far as *state-like* non-states are concerned, the existence of such a general rule is consistent with practice. Oliver Lissitzyn, writing in 1962, doubted that there were

> any objective criteria of international personality or treaty-making capacity. The very act or practice of entering into international agreements is sometimes the only test that can be applied . . . For example, India had come to be regarded as an international person possessed of treaty-making capacity long before independence because, beginning with the Treaty of Versailles in 1919, there had developed a practice of India's becoming a separate party to international agreements. . . .

[12] This book s 3.4.2. On arguments that a treaty-making power is an element of personality, see also s 1.2.

[13] William Thomas Worster, 'Relative international legal personality of non-state actors' (2016) 42 Brooklyn Journal of International Law 207, 212.

> The very exercise of treaty-making capacity by a subordinate entity endows it with legal personality under international law.[14]

I noted in the introduction that colonial India was a member of the League of Nations and went on to join the United Nations in its own right before independence. I also noted that Australia and the other dominions began to make treaties before they became states.[15]

In fact, there are many examples of treaties between states and a 'subentity' of a foreign state (I will use this term broadly to cover an entity with its own governmental institutions in a metropolitan, non-self-governing, or other territory for which a state has responsibility in international law). Some scholars have expressed doubt about this possibility on theoretical grounds. Alf Ross argued in 1947 that 'self-governing communities alone are by nature suited to be subject to international duties' because they, unlike subentities, can 'control the conduct, that is to say, the internal legal act, required of them as subjects' of international law.[16] This is far too inflexible an assumption: the government of a subentity may have a high level of 'control' over certain areas of domestic law, especially within a federation. But equally, the fact that treaties with subentities are possible in theory does not mean that every agreement with a subentity must be a treaty. It is a question of practice, in particular of how subentities are perceived by the states with which they make agreements.

On one hand, it is often doubtful that states *intend* to recognize a subentity as a treaty-maker in international law. The regions and communities of Belgium—like Swiss cantons, German *Länder*, and some other subentities—have treaty-making powers according to domestic constitutional law.[17] In 1994, on signing a treaty to admit new members to the European Union, Belgium declared that both it and its regions and communities had 'entered into an undertaking at the international level'.[18] But Belgium then accepted a counter-declaration by other treaty parties that this was just an explanation of its domestic law and that it alone was responsible under the treaty. Even where a treaty is made directly with the government of a subentity of a state rather than with the state's central government, this may be on the understanding that the subentity's government is acting as an organ or agent of the whole state.[19] If so, the subentity itself does not acquire any rights or duties.

[14] Oliver J Lissitzyn, 'Efforts to codify or restate the law of treaties' (1962) 62 Columbia Law Review 1166, 1183–4.

[15] See also this book s 3.1.1 on the dominions and s 3.4.2 on UN membership.

[16] Alf Ross, *A Textbook of International Law: General Part* (Annie I Fausbøll tr, Longmans, Green, & Co 1947) 26 (emphasis removed).

[17] Constitution fédérale de la Confédération suisse, art 56; Basic Law for the Federal Republic of Germany, art 32(3); Constitution Belge, art 167(3). For further examples see Grant (n 7) 127–33; Duncan B Hollis, 'Why state consent still matters—non-state actors, treaties, and the changing sources of international law' (2005) 23 Berkeley Journal of International Law 137, 146–55.

[18] Minutes of the Signing [1994] OJEC C241, 402.

[19] Anthony Aust, *Modern Treaty Law and Practice* (CUP 2000) 49.

On the other hand, there are cases in which the more natural inference is that a subentity does acquire rights and duties and hence personality in international law. Hong Kong is perhaps the clearest current example of this. It is a special autonomous region of China but performs a number of state-like functions, such as issuing its own passports; Macau has a similar status within China.[20] The Basic Law of Hong Kong provides that it 'may on its own, using the name "Hong Kong, China", maintain and develop relations and conclude and implement agreements with foreign states and regions and relevant international organizations in the appropriate fields'.[21] James Crawford observes that under this provision 'treaties are entered into by Hong Kong "on its own": evidently they are to be counted . . . as treaties to which Hong Kong is a party as such'.[22] Yet there is no doubt that Hong Kong remains a subentity of China and certainly not a separate state. China has significant powers over its affairs, including a residual power to make treaties on its behalf.[23]

Two other cases suggesting that subentities can sometimes make treaties involve France. It lobbied for its territory of New Caledonia to be allowed to join a treaty on fish stocks in the Pacific; other states resisted this on the ground that, since France itself also intended to join, together they would have two votes.[24] France has also made agreements with the Canadian province of Quebec that it considered to be binding in international law.[25]

In addition to a subentity, another state-like entity that may benefit from the possibility that non-states can make treaties is one whose status is uncertain or contested. In Chapter 3, I highlighted a reason for thinking that Taiwan is not a separate state from China, but this leaves open the question of what *else* Taiwan could be—for instance, whether it is a subentity of China that, like Hong Kong, is ultimately subordinate to the central government in Beijing or, alternatively, a part of China 'under separate administration' that is not subordinate to the other part.[26] Other states are evasive about Taiwan's status, as is the government of Taiwan itself. Within the World Trade Organization regime, which is based on a treaty, it is referred to obliquely as the 'Separate Customs Territory of Taiwan, Penghu, Kinmen and Matsu'.[27] What makes this evasiveness feasible is the possibility that an entity

[20] Basic Law of the Hong Kong Special Administrative Region of the People's Republic of China, arts 13, 154.

[21] Ibid, art 151.

[22] James Crawford, *The Creation of States in International Law* (2nd edn, OUP 2006) 249.

[23] Basic Law of the Hong Kong Special Administrative Region of the People's Republic of China, art 153.

[24] Convention on the Conservation and Management of Highly Migratory Fish Stocks in the Western and Central Pacific Ocean (5 September 2000) 2275 UNTS 43; Hollis (n 17) 153.

[25] Babak Nikravesh, 'Quebec and Tatarstan in international law' (1999) 23 Fletcher Forum of World Affairs 227, 242.

[26] Crawford (n 22) 211; this book s 3.1.1.

[27] Membership is open to any 'State or separate customs territory possessing full autonomy in the conduct of its external commercial relations and of the other matters provided for' in the agreements: Marrakesh Agreement Establishing the World Trade Organization (15 April 1994) 1867 UNTS

such as Taiwan can acquire treaty rights and duties *regardless* of what other status it has. This also makes possible binding treaties between, for example, the Palestine Liberation Organization or the Palestinian Authority and states that do not recognize Palestine as a state.[28]

The possibility that states can, in theory, make treaties with state-like entities such as Hong Kong and Taiwan is an extrapolation from the recognition norm, reinforced by practice. One might equally extrapolate from the exceptions to the recognition norm.[29] Worster remarks that 'it is not entirely clear whether the limitations on nonrecognition for purported states, such as *jus cogens* violations or *ex injuria jus non oritur* considerations' (which underpin what I called the collective-non-recognition exception) apply to the personality of non-states, though this may just reflect a lack of practice.[30] But there are signs of something like the premature-recognition exception to the recognition norm (which applies where recognition breaches a state's right that its territorial integrity be respected and possibly an administering state's rights over a non-self-governing territory). Lissitzyn thought that '[p]erhaps the only limitation on the possession and exercise of treaty-making capacity by a political subdivision is lack of consent to the exercise of such capacity by the dominant (or "sovereign") entity to which the subdivision is subordinate'.[31] Thomas Grant draws a similar conclusion.[32] In the case of Hong Kong, China's consent is reinforced by a declaration made jointly with the United Kingdom.[33] There is evidence that consent is required even if the subentity is a non-self-governing territory; for instance, the United Kingdom authorizes Bermuda and the British Virgin Islands to make treaties using an 'Instrument of Entrustment'.[34] The hesitation of states to make treaties with a subentity of another state without that other state's consent may partly reflect a concern that such treaties would breach the other state's rights and might be invalid on that ground (though it may also partly

154, art XII(1). Not only Taiwan but also Hong Kong and Macau have membership separate from that of China.

---

[28] Eg, agreements with Israel in the 1990s, on which see John Quigley, 'The Israel–PLO interim agreements: are they treaties?' (1997) 30 Cornell International Law Journal 717. He concludes that they are treaties.

[29] This book ss 4.1.1, 4.1.2.

[30] Worster (n 13) 212–13.

[31] Lissitzyn (n 14) 1184.

[32] The two usual requirements are 'authorization of the responsible State and acceptance of that competence by potential treaty-partners', though in the case of a treaty with a non-self-governing territory or other external territory 'there may also be a third criterion—the responsible State's international commitments to third States vis-à-vis its external territories': Grant (n 7) 136, further 131–2, 148. Compare Humphrey Waldock, First Report on the Law of Treaties [1962] 2 ILC Ybk 27, 36; Hollis (n 17) 146–55.

[33] Joint Declaration on the Question of Hong Kong, China–UK (19 December 1984) 1399 UNTS 61.

[34] Grant (n 7) 137; Aust (n 19) 52. Compare United Nations Convention on the Law of the Sea (10 December 1982) 1833 UNTS 3: under art 305(1)(e), it is open to 'all territories which enjoy full internal self-government, recognized as such by the United Nations, but have not attained full independence' in accordance with the Colonial Declaration and 'which have competence' over relevant matters.

reflect concerns about whether the subentity has enough authority in practice to fulfil the treaty). Duncan Hollis identifies a 'trend by which some sub-state actors are concluding international agreements outside the conditions laid down by their states', though he queries whether these are binding. [35]

Possibly with exceptions, it seems that a state-like entity, even one that otherwise lacks personality, can gain rights or duties falling short of statehood under a treaty with a state.

5.1.2 A state loses some of the rights or duties of states

The first scenario I have discussed can be compared with a second one: where an entity starts with statehood but then *loses* some of the rights and duties inherent in statehood while retaining others. It is a commonplace that states can relinquish their rights by consent. For example, a coastal state has an 'exclusive right to authorize and regulate drilling' on its own continental shelf, but it can relinquish this right relative to a neighbouring state by giving its 'express consent' by treaty.[36] No one would suggest that by doing so it ceases to be a state in the full sense.[37] Of interest here is the scenario, different in degree if not in kind, where an entity relinquishes *so much* of what makes it a state as to raise doubts about whether it still *is* one. That might result in a state-like entity whose personality falls short of statehood.

Historically, a state-like entity that gave a foreign state rights or powers connected with its sovereignty was known as a protectorate. In 1892, for instance, Abu Dhabi and other Trucial Sheikhdoms (now the United Arab Emirates) agreed not to 'enter into any agreement or correspondence with any Power' except the United Kingdom, nor to 'consent to the residence' in their territories of 'the agent of any other Government' without British assent, nor to 'cede, sell, mortgage or otherwise give for occupation any part of' their territories except to the United Kingdom.[38] Some arrangements of this sort even empowered the protector to cede territory on the protectorate's behalf.[39] Other types of dependency arrangement exist today,

[35] Hollis (n 17) 155.

[36] Convention on the Law of the Sea, arts 81 (the right), 77(2) (relinquishment by 'express consent').

[37] Compare *SS Wimbledon (UK, France, Italy, and Japan v Germany)* (1923) PCIJ ser A 1, 25: the Permanent Court declined 'to see in the conclusion of any Treaty by which a State undertakes to perform or refrain from performing a particular act an abandonment of its sovereignty'.

[38] Treaties between the UK and Abu Dhabi, Ajman, Debai, Shargah, Ras-el-Khaimah, and Umm-al-Kawain (6–8 March 1892) 176 CTS 457. Examples of other treaties that gave the United Kingdom some control over external affairs are Treaty of Peace, Afghanistan–UK (26 May 1879) 155 CTS 105, art 2; Treaty of Amity, UK–Tonga (18 May 1900) 107 BFSP 521. See further Crawford (n 22) ch 7. Protectorates before the twentieth century must be seen in light of my conclusions in Chapter 2 that non-Western entities may not have been 'states' in a technical legal sense but may still have had sovereignty.

[39] But if the protectorate arrangement was silent, such a power was not implied: Crawford (n 22) 310.

though the term 'protectorate' tends to be replaced with a less-colonial-sounding term such as 'associated state'. The Marshall Islands and the Federated States of Micronesia have given the United States 'full authority and responsibility for security and defense matters in or relating to' them.[40] Among other things, these entities have agreed to 'consult, in the conduct of their foreign affairs', with the United States; they have agreed 'to refrain from actions that the Government of the United States determines, after appropriate consultation' with the relevant entity's government, 'to be incompatible with its authority and responsibility for security and defense matters'; and they have agreed that 'the United States may invite members of the armed forces of other countries to use military areas and facilities' in their territories.[41] This could be interpreted as a partial relinquishment of their sovereignty: they do not have a right to exclude the United States or its invitees from acting on their territories within the terms of the association agreements. In itself such a partial relinquishment of sovereignty poses no problem of principle. As Lassa Oppenheim put it, 'sovereignty is divisible, so that the powers connected with sovereignty need not necessarily be united in one hand'; generally, statehood (on my definition) entails a package of rights and other relations that can be disaggregated into components.[42]

There is still a potential problem, however. Statehood under the effectiveness norm requires independence, so relinquishing functions connected with sovereignty might raise doubts about whether an entity still *is* a state.[43] It clashes with Judge Anzilotti's definition of independence in *Austro-German Customs Régime*. On his definition, independence entails that an entity exist 'as a separate State and not subject to the authority of any other State or group of States'. The opposite, dependence, 'necessarily implies a relation between a superior State (suzerain, protector, etc.) and an inferior or subject State (vassal, *protégé*, etc.)'—a 'relation between the State which can legally impose its will and the State which is legally compelled to submit to that will'.[44] If independence requires that an entity not be dependent on a superior state, then might the result of a protection or association arrangement be not merely to divide or subordinate the entity's statehood but to

[40] Compact of Free Association (1 October 1982 and 25 June 1983) Pub L No 99–239, 99 Stat 1800, s 311(a). See also 48 USC 1921. Along with Palau, which entered into a similar arrangement with the United States in 1994, these entities were parts of the US-administered Trust Territory of the Pacific Islands. See further Masahiro Igarashi, *Associated Statehood in International Law* (Kluwer 2002) ch 6.

[41] Compact of Free Association, ss 123(a), 313(a), 315.

[42] LFL Oppenheim, *International Law* (Longmans, Green, & Co 1905–6) vol 1, pt 66. The remark survives in Robert Jennings and Arthur Watts, *Oppenheim's International Law* (9th edn, Longman 1996) vol 1, pt 36 with the comment that although this is 'practical' and evidenced by 'partially independent states', it is 'abnormal and possibly illogical'. But it would be illogical only if a state were perceived as a monolithic thing that could not be disaggregated into distinct attributes, an idea that I rejected in this book s 3.2.

[43] Compare Vaughan Lowe, *International Law* (OUP 2007) 158–9.

[44] *Customs Régime between Germany and Austria (Advisory Opinion)* (1931) PCIJ ser A/B 41, 57 (Judge Anzilotti).

end it altogether? Whether any particular arrangement had this result would depend on the details of that arrangement rather than on the terms used to describe it: arrangements form a spectrum 'from virtually complete independence to loss of actual independence such that statehood is in question'.[45]

The effectiveness-or-recognition view of statehood, according to which recognition can suffice for statehood regardless of the criterion of independence, is of great use in resolving this problem. If states universally recognize that an entity such as the Marshall Islands has the relations of a state, albeit a state that is subject to an association arrangement, that suffices to sustain it as an entity that has statehood *minus* any rights or other relations that the entity has given away. Its personality can be explained by the exercise of powers of two types: treaty-making powers and recognition. The same is true of the rights and powers of the superior state; a protectorate or association arrangement created by a bilateral treaty, as with any other bilateral treaty provision, does not generally have force for non-parties. The Permanent Court observed in *Nationality Decrees Issued in Tunis and Morocco* that the

> extent of the powers of a protecting State in the territory of a protected State depends, first, upon the Treaties between the protecting State and the protected State . . . and, secondly, upon the conditions under which the Protectorate has been recognized by third Powers as against whom there is an intention to rely on the provisions of these Treaties.[46]

Here, then, is another volitional way in which a state-like entity might end up with a degree of personality falling short of that ordinarily inherent in statehood. It is true that the Marshall Islands and Micronesia are described as states and have separate membership of the United Nations; in 2014, the Marshall Islands even filed an application in the International Court against its 'protector' the United States.[47] But the mere use of the term 'state' in this context is not necessarily indicative of the degree of an entity's personality. The International Court has held that even Morocco, during a period when France and Spain had far-reaching rights and powers over not only external but even domestic affairs, could be described as 'a sovereign State'.[48] As Crawford puts it, when 'States become subject to protectorates

[45] Crawford (n 22) 289.

[46] *Nationality Decrees Issued in Tunis and Morocco (Advisory Opinion)* (1923) PCIJ ser B 4, 27. Crawford (n 22) 307 writes that this view was always taken of true 'international' protectorates, but he adds that 'colonial' protectorates, the kind imposed on African entities in the nineteenth century (on which see this book s 2.5.1), were 'types of territorial arrangement—matters of status, not contract'.

[47] International Court of Justice, 'The Republic of the Marshall Islands files Applications against nine States for their alleged failure to fulfil their obligations with respect to the cessation of the nuclear arms race at an early date and to nuclear disarmament' (press release, 25 April 2014). The case against the United States did not proceed, because it did not accept jurisdiction.

[48] *Rights of Nationals of the United States of America in Morocco (France v US)* [1952] ICJ Rep 176, 188.

which substantially restrict their independence, they are nevertheless, by a sort of convention, regarded as continuing as States for at least some purposes.'[49]

The scenarios I have identified blur into each other. I have cited the Marshall Islands and Micronesia as examples of states that lost some of their rights as states. But there was in reality no period of time when these were 'full' states; they went straight from being administered by the United States to being in association with it.[50] So they might instead be analysed as entities that, like Hong Kong, have gained some but never quite all of the rights and duties of 'full' statehood through treaties or recognition. The scenarios hint at a general power of states to determine the extent of a state-like non-state's personality relative to themselves. This power may be exercisable not only by treaty or recognition but by other volitional means that accord with principles of consent and good faith, such as a unilateral declaration.[51] The limits of this general power and the exceptions to it have not clearly been tested in practice. But it has potentially very wide implications: recognition might be able to sustain any number of arrangements that divide the rights and duties ordinarily inherent in statehood between multiple entities.

The analogy with the recognition norm goes both ways. If states have a general power to give an entity rights and other relations relative to themselves, then those relations might include all the relations inherent in statehood. So the evidence for this power provides some extra corroboration of the recognition norm: when an existing state recognizes an entity as a state, that can function as an exercise of a power to create legal relations bilaterally.

5.2 Personality acquired automatically

The remaining type of relations and personality that may be acquired by state-like non-states is what I am describing as 'automatic'. It may be wondered why I am using the term instead of a similar term that has been used before in international law: 'objective'.

One reason is that the term 'objective' is potentially very misleading. It might be read as implying that there is an 'objective' test of whether relations are valid. But that is true of all international legal relations, however they come into being;

[49] Crawford (n 22) 296.

[50] Ibid, 581–4.

[51] The International Law Commission has suggested that unilateral declarations may be addressed to non-states, citing Jordan's 1988 declaration waiving claims to the West Bank, 'which was addressed simultaneously to the international community, to another State (Israel) and to another entity, the Palestine Liberation Organization: Guiding Principles Applicable to Unilateral Declarations of States Capable of Creating Legal Obligations [2006] 2(2) ILC Ybk 161, commentary to principle 6, para 2. See also Victor Rodríguez Cedeño, Sixth Report on Unilateral Acts of States [2003] 2(1) ILC Ybk 53, para 94; Worster (n 13).

for one thing, even volitional relations may be invalidated by peremptory norms.[52] Or the term might be read as implying that an entity has personality relative to all states rather than just one or several. But that is not necessarily determined by the distinction drawn in this chapter: an entity that acquires personality under the effectiveness norm (automatically) and one that acquires it by being universally recognized (volitionally) may both have personality relative to all states.

Another reason for avoiding the term 'objective' is the way it was used in *Reparation for Injuries*. The International Court called the United Nations 'an entity possessing objective international personality, and not merely personality recognized by [member states] alone'.[53] Recall that the Court's definition of personality emphasized a capacity to bring 'international claims' and did not emphasize the actual possession of rights or duties.[54] Accordingly, the Court highlighted the capacity of the United Nations to bring a 'functional protection' claim if a UN agent is injured in a way that 'involves the responsibility' of a non-member state; but it did not discuss how 'that responsibility might be engaged'—that is, it did not identify any relevant substantive rights borne by the United Nations that might be breached by a non-member state.[55] CF Amerasinghe argues that functional protection might be based on a breach of an agreement but that a 'non-member state does not owe specific duties to the organization under [customary international] law'.[56] So the Court's use of the term 'objective' may be compatible with a hypothesis that the substantive[57] rights and duties of the United Nations are all volitional in that they all exist relative to entities that become members of it, make treaties with it, or exercise other powers (though since the United Nations is not a state-like

[52] Compare the discussion of whether international law is an 'objective system of law' in this book s 3.2, quoting Krystyna Marek, *Identity and Continuity of States in Public International Law* (2nd edn, Librairie Droz 1968) 136. See also the discussion of the system-wide concept of validity in this book s 3.1.3.

[53] *Reparation for Injuries* [1949] ICJ Rep 174, 185.

[54] Ibid, 179.

[55] Ibid, 185. The question had been raised by the assassinations in Israel (then not yet a member state) of UN agents, among them Folke Bernadotte: Yuen-Li Liang, 'Reparation for injuries suffered in the service of the United Nations' (1949) 43 AJIL 460, 460–1. The United Nations later brought a claim against Israel respecting Bernadotte 'based upon three elements of responsibility: failure to exercise due diligence and to take all reasonable measures for the prevention of the murder; liability of [Israel] for actions committed by irregular forces in territory under [its control]; and failure to take all the measures required by international law and by the Security Council resolution of 19 October 1948 [SC res 59] to bring the culprits to justice': Annual Report of the Secretary-General on the Work of the Organization (1 July 1949–30 June 1950) UN doc A/1287, 125. Israel did not admit these contentions but made reparation anyway.

[56] CF Amerasinghe, *Principles of the Institutional Law of International Organizations* (2nd edn, CUP 2004) 392–3.

[57] The Court's conclusions about functional protection might suggest that the United Nations has a *remedial* right relative to all states. But a remedial right is purely abstract or dormant unless it can be brought into operation by breach of a substantive right—it must be a remedy *for* something—and if that requires the creation of a volitional substantive right, perhaps the remedial right could be described as volitional as well, certainly for practical purposes. Further on remedial and substantive rights, see this book s 1.1.2.

entity, I will not seek to resolve the point here).[58] In any case, this use of 'objective' reflects concerns quite different from mine: I rejected a requirement of a capacity to bring claims as inapt and arbitrary; and my definition of personality requires the actual possession of a right or duty.[59]

When I refer to 'automatic' relations, then, I am not adopting the distinction used by the Court; nor am I invoking any other meaning of 'objective'. What I mean is that a right, duty, or other relation—and hence potentially an entity's personality—does not primarily depend on the exercise of a Hohfeldian power. Since the volitional and automatic categories are defined by exclusion of each other, together they cover any conceivable means of acquiring relations. Thus the automatic category includes customary relations created by the effectiveness norm but would also include relations derived from natural law, in the event any exist.

I found that explaining the automatic personality of states was greatly complicated by the circularity of saying that states, the creators of customary norms, are themselves created *by* such norms.[60] In theory, other state-like entities might acquire automatic personality in a less complex way: states create customary norms in the form 'any entity that meets certain criteria has a particular right or duty'; those norms then give personality to the relevant entities. But it turns out to be difficult to identify state-like entities to which such norms apply.

One possibility is a non-state armed group, which may control territory or perform some state-like functions. A non-state party to an 'armed conflict not of an international character occurring in the territory' of a state has certain humanitarian duties listed in common article 3 of the Geneva Conventions.[61] Although this is a treaty provision, it reflects a customary norm that applies without any of the parties to the conflict having to exercise a power to consent.[62] Another possibility is a 'people', if it is correct that peoples themselves are bearers of rights to external self-determination under a customary norm.[63] But peoples and non-state

[58] There is also a debate about whether the type of personality enjoyed by the United Nations is shared by all international organizations or only by those 'of a universal character': see Henry G Schermers and Niels M Blokker, *International Institutional Law: Unity within Diversity* (5th rev, Nijhoff 2011) pt 1568.

[59] This book s 1.2.

[60] This book s 3.1.3.

[61] Geneva Conventions [I, II, III, and IV] (12 August 1949) 75 UNTS 31, 85, 135, 287, art 3.

[62] *Military and Paramilitary Activities in and against Nicaragua (Nicaragua v US)* [1986] ICJ Rep 14, para 218; further Sandesh Sivakumaran, 'The addressees of Common Article 3' in Andrew Clapham, Paola Gaeta, and Marco Sassòli (eds), *The 1949 Geneva Conventions: a Commentary* (OUP 2015) 415, especially paras 35–8. Contrast Protocol [I] Additional to the Geneva Conventions of 12 August 1949, and Relating to the Protection of Victims of International Armed Conflicts (8 June 1977) 1125 UNTS 3, arts 1(4), 96(3): an authority representing a 'people' that is fighting in the exercise of its right to self-determination may 'undertake to apply' the Geneva Conventions and Protocol I 'by means of a unilateral declaration'. This creates volitional personality, because it primarily depends on an exercise of a power. In earlier periods, the personality of non-state armed groups was said to depend on recognition by states: eg, WE Hall, *A Treatise on International Law* (4th edn, Clarendon 1895) 35; further Tiqiang Chen, *The International Law of Recognition with Special Reference to Practice in Great Britain and the United States* (Praeger 1951) 303–6. See also Daragh Murray, *Human Rights Obligations of Non-State Armed Groups* (Hart 2016).

[63] This book s 4.2.

armed groups are state-like only in a borderline sense, and the automatic personality that they may have is in any case very small in degree and exists for very narrow purposes.

A more clearly state-like possibility is an entity in '[f]ree association with an independent State'.[64] Niue and the Cook Islands are in free association with New Zealand; Puerto Rico's arrangement with the United States has comparable features.[65] Free association is similar to—and may even be equated with—the associated statehood of the likes of the Marshall Islands. If the entities I have just mentioned differ, the difference is only that their status, certainly that of Puerto Rico, is contrasted more sharply with '[e]mergence as a sovereign independent state'; unlike the Marshall Islands, none of them has become a UN member, and in 1960 the General Assembly listed free association as a means other than statehood by which a people 'can be said to have reached a full measure of self-government'.[66] The General Assembly added that free association 'should be the result' of a choice that 'retains for the peoples of the territory . . . the freedom to modify the status of that territory through the expression of their will by democratic means and through constitutional processes'; and the 'territory should have the right to determine its internal constitution without outside interference, in accordance with due constitutional processes and the freely expressed wishes of the people'.[67] These *might* amount not to mere suggestions but to actual rights held by an entity, either relative to a state involved in an association arrangement or perhaps even—like the closely related right to external self-determination—relative to all states.[68] They *might* be underpinned by customary norms. And even if their applicability is triggered by an undertaking by the state involved (an exercise of a power), the ongoing validity of the rights *might* be sustained by the customary norms rather than primarily by the undertaking. If these suppositions are correct, free association gives an entity a degree of automatic personality. But that is speculative.

[64] Principles Which Should Guide Members in Determining Whether or Not an Obligation Exists to Transmit the Information Called for in Article 73 e of the Charter of the United Nations, annex to GA res 1541 (XV) (15 December 1960) principle VI.

[65] GA res 2064 (XX) (16 December 1965, Cook Islands); GA res 3285 (XXIX) (13 December 1974, Niue). Puerto Rico is known as a 'Commonwealth'. But the General Assembly accepted that this status amounted to 'a mutually agreed association' and that on this basis Puerto Rico's people had 'effectively exercised their right to self-determination': GA res 748 (VIII) (27 November 1953, Puerto Rico) paras 3–4. Further on the complexities of the status of Puerto Rico, see Igarashi (n 40) 44–62.

[66] Principles Which Should Guide Members under Article 73 e, principle VI. See further Igarashi (n 40).

[67] Principles Which Should Guide Members under Article 73 e, principle VII. See also Factors Indicative of the Attainment of Independence or of Other Separate Systems of Self-Government, annex to GA res 742 (VIII) (27 November 1953) third part ('Factors indicative of the free association of a Territory').

[68] Compare Crawford (n 22) 633: 'given that association arrangements are accepted in practice as satisfying the principle of self-determination, and are accepted on the basis of undertakings to which the metropolitan State is committed, in principle those arrangements are . . . binding in international law'.

In fact, except for states under the effectiveness norm, there is no clear instance of a class of state-like entities with automatic personality.[69] Crawford draws a similar conclusion:

> while statehood is a legal concept with a determinate, though flexible, content it is probably the only such concept in the field of legal personality. Other general terms (protectorate, suzerain, confederation, internationalized territory, and so on) may be more or less convenient *classifications* of common forms of organization; but they are classifications without legal consequences beyond those arising from the specific agreements or instruments in question.[70]

In my terms, state-like non-states of most types have no more than volitional personality.

There remains one other possibility that belongs under the automatic heading. Instead of giving personality to multiple state-like entities that form a class defined by certain criteria, a customary norm could give personality to a single, specific entity—a class of one.

Imagine if statehood could be created in this way. There might be a customary norm that Palestine, specifically, is a state, regardless of effectiveness *and* regardless of recognition by any particular state. Widespread but less-than-universal recognition might be interpreted as state practice and *opinio iuris* supporting such a norm. I omitted this possibility from earlier chapters because it would be largely inconsequential and unverifiable. Non-recognizing states, especially those that deny vociferously that Palestine is a state, would qualify as persistent objectors: if a state objects to a norm while it is 'in the process of formation' and maintains the objection persistently, the norm 'is not opposable' to that state.[71] The norm that Palestine is a state might still apply relative to *new* states that emerged *after* the formation of the norm, because they would not have had an opportunity to object. But with that negligible exception, it would apply solely relative to recognizing states and so would have no consequences for states beyond the consequences that already follow from the recognition norm.

In contrast, there might be scope for custom to give a lesser degree of personality to a specific entity, especially one that has been around for so long that it is too late to object. The clearest candidate for this is the Holy See. This is composed of the central institutions of the Roman Catholic Church and has existed for centuries; it

69 If there is room for argument or for future development of the law on the status of '*de facto* regimes' or '*de facto* governments', as Rhodesia was said by some scholars to be, that is another possible class of state-like entities with automatic personality—though I expressed doubt about this idea in this book s 4.2.1.

70 Crawford (n 22) 718–19.

71 Conclusions on Identification of Customary International Law [2018] 2(2) ILC Ybk, UN doc A/73/10, conclusion 15; further this book s 2.3.

is not necessarily the same thing as the newer entity I discussed in Chapter 3, the Vatican City, which is considered to be a state with a tiny territory in Rome.[72] It raises two questions concerning personality.

The first is whether the Holy See has any international legal personality that cannot be explained on the basis of the statehood of the Vatican City. Confusingly, it is the Holy See, not the Vatican City, that is described as 'a Permanent Observer State' in the United Nations; the Holy See is also party to numerous multilateral treaties, including human rights treaties and the Vienna Convention on Diplomatic Relations.[73] States conduct diplomatic relations with the Holy See, not with the Vatican City.[74] One explanation of all this is that the Holy See operates as the 'government' of the Vatican City but 'has an additional non-territorial status which is much more significant in practice'.[75] In other words, there are two legally distinct but institutionally intertwined entities: a state (the Vatican City) and a non-state with personality of its own (the Holy See). An alternative explanation is that there is a single compound person. But even some proponents of this explanation, such as Ioana Cismas, accept that the Holy See's personality is not wholly contingent on the statehood of the Vatican City.[76] Evidence for this is that it continued to conduct diplomatic relations and to make 'concordats' (tantamount to treaties) in the period when it did not on any view have sovereignty over any territory—between Italy's annexation of the old Papal States in 1870 and the creation of the Vatican City in 1929.[77] On either of these explanations, then, the Holy See appears to be a state-like entity with personality that cannot be explained on the basis of statehood. That is also its own view: it has described itself as 'a sovereign subject of international law having an original, non-derived legal personality independent of any territorial authority or jurisdiction'.[78]

The second question is whether this personality is to any extent automatic. The Holy See's description of its personality as 'original' and 'non-derived' suggests that it does not depend on recognition or the exercise of another power by a particular state. Some scholars accept this.[79] On this view, custom may extend to the Holy

72 This book s 3.1.5.

73 GA res 58/314 (1 July 2003, Holy See), confirming the Holy See's status and listing a number of treaties.

74 For examples see Kurt Martens, 'The position of the Holy See and Vatican City State in international relations' (2006) 83 University of Detroit Mercy Law Review 729, 755–8.

75 Crawford (n 22) 230; compare Martens (n 74) 760.

76 Ioana Cismas, *Religious Actors and International Law* (OUP 2014) 238: 'the Holy See had a degree of personality after 1870, as a *sui generis* entity by virtue of historical circumstances drawing on its religious legitimacy'; nowadays 'the Holy See and the Vatican share a single international personality' that derives both from those historical circumstances and from 'the state-like resemblance conferred on the construct by the Lateran Treaty in 1929'. Her detailed analysis of this compound person is at 153–238.

77 Crawford (n 22) 226. See also Cismas (n 76) 160–6; John R Morss, 'The international legal status of the Vatican/Holy See complex' (2015) 26 EJIL 927, 939–41.

78 Committee on the Rights of the Child: Replies of the Holy See to the List of Issues (2 December 2013) UN doc CRC/C/VAT/Q/2/Add.1, para 6.

79 Finn Seyersted, *The Common Law of International Organizations* (Nijhoff 2008) 92–6, 387–8 n 83.

See the automatic applicability of certain rights or duties, such as a right that a state's domestic courts accord it sovereign immunity (which domestic courts tend to do[80]). But here, once again, there is uncertainty. Other scholars liken the Holy See to the Sovereign Military Hospitaller Order of St John of Jerusalem, of Rhodes, and of Malta. An Italian court observed in 1957 that 'the status of the Order as a subject of international law, at any rate *vis-à-vis* the Italian State, cannot be doubted because the Italian State, by establishing a legation, has recognized the sovereignty of the Order within its own territory' and that 'it is within the exclusive competence of each individual State to accord to an entity the status of a sovereign body and to regard it as a subject of international law'.[81] It has been suggested that such entities have personality relative solely to states that willingly have relations with them.[82] If the Holy See lacks automatic personality, its example—along with that of the Sovereign Order of Malta—reinforces my earlier conclusion that states are generally empowered to recognize entities and thereby give them a degree of volitional personality.

I conclude that it is possible for state-like entities other than states to acquire automatic personality under a customary norm, either a norm about a specific entity or one defining a class of entities; but there are only ambiguous indications of this in practice.

5.3 A world of states

Although I have identified some state-like entities that have volitional personality falling short of statehood—at least in the 'full' degree—their status tends in one way or another to be connected with statehood: they include subentities of states (Hong Kong), possible subentities of states whose status is uncertain (Taiwan), and associated states (the Marshall Islands). Their personality also depends on the exercise of powers *by* states. The theoretical possibility that a state-like non-state might acquire automatic personality equally relies on customary norms created *by* states. Moreover, statehood provides the clearest example of each category of personality: under the recognition norm, states create personality volitionally relative to themselves; under the effectiveness norm, custom creates it automatically. Thus this chapter, although not directly concerned with statehood, has served to demonstrate its dominance over other legal forms that might be taken by state-like entities. One explanation of this is that, even if there is room for more diversity theoretically, there is not much room geographically: today, unlike in the nineteenth

[80] Eg, *O'Bryan v Holy See*, 556 F 3d 361 (6th Cir, 2009).
[81] *Scarfò v Sovereign Order of Malta* (Tribunal of Rome, Italy) (1957) 24 ILR 1, 2.
[82] Crawford (n 22) 30, 226–33. Compare Seyersted (n 79) 54–5, who puts this forward as a fallback explanation for an entity's apparent personality if it fails general criteria for personality.

century or earlier eras, states in the technical legal sense cover virtually the whole inhabitable surface of the Earth. What diversity exists among state-like entities is now mostly to be found among states and states-in-context.[83] Still, the existence of other possibilities means that this homogeneity might not be permanent.

[83] In addition to differences deriving from the coexistence of the effectiveness and recognition norms, there may also be other legally relevant differences among states. See especially Gerry Simpson, *Great Powers and Outlaw States: Unequal Sovereigns in the International Legal Order* (CUP 2004).

Conclusion

The extended family of nations

Which state-like entities have personality in international law? My choice to answer this wider question rather than analysing states alone has proven rewarding in three respects.

First, it has drawn attention to the different types and degrees of personality that might coexist within the same system of law. I defined personality as the possession, by an entity that is constructed as a fact by norms of international law, of Hohfeldian rights or duties given to it by such norms. Since every right or duty is borne by an entity relative to another entity (which bears the correlative duty or right), and since personality is a function of rights and duties, an entity's personality is always relative to certain other entities. It is ultimately about conduct that is *by* one entity and *towards* another entity. This is true regardless of whether personality is acquired by one or both of the methods I discussed in the last chapter: volitionally (meaning that the validity of rights or duties depends primarily on the exercise of a power, such as an act of recognition) and automatically (meaning that their validity does not primarily depend on the exercise of a power). What these methods of acquiring personality often *do* determine is the *entities relative to which personality exists*. Thus, in the old Western tradition of universalist natural law, it was believed that state-like entities acquired rights automatically from nature even relative to non-Western entities, such as the Mongol Empire, that neither knew nor cared about them. In contrast, according to the strictest versions of positivism—as reflected in the contractual view of custom and the recognition-only view of statehood, which were both prominent in the nineteenth century—an entity could acquire rights solely relative to other entities that volitionally consented. At the same time my conception of personality leaves open the possibility that, in the right conditions, volitional personality can amount to much the same thing as automatic personality, a possibility that has shaped my analysis of statehood.

Nudging that analysis of statehood in a particular direction is the second consequence of the wide approach that I have taken. My approach has led me to question whether states have always been a legally distinct class and the extent to which they are homogenous today.

I found that before the early twentieth century the rules about which state-like entities had personality and to what extent were unstable. This instability was caused in part by tension between the allowance for automatic personality made by

Statehood and the State-Like in International Law. Rowan Nicholson, Oxford University Press (2019).
© Rowan Nicholson
DOI: 10.1093/oso/9780198851219.001.0001

the declining naturalist tradition and the positivist insistence that personality had to be acquired volitionally by consent. I argued that a coherent technical concept of statehood could not emerge until this instability was resolved. This became possible after non-Western state-like entities were colonized or, as with Japan and the Ottoman Empire, integrated into Western international law, so that the remaining state-like entities of the world were more homogenous in form; it was assisted by the triumph of the legislative view of custom, under which these entities all acquired the same package of rights and other relations even if they did not specifically consent to each relation.

That was how I made the point in Chapter 2; in light of subsequent chapters it can be taken further. Competing volitional and automatic approaches *continued* to destabilize the rules about the personality of state-like entities in the twentieth century, though the competition was now narrowed to a debate about how statehood was acquired. At one extreme was the view that it depended solely on automatically applicable criteria of effectiveness (the effectiveness-only view); at the other was the view that it depended solely on volitional acts of recognition by other states (the recognition-only view). I found that the recognition-only view—which amounts to a denial that international law had any automatically applicable component or even a single, system-wide concept of validity—was confirmed definitively to be incorrect by the emergence of peremptory norms in the mid-twentieth century. This is not because of the substance of the particular peremptory norms that emerged.[1] Their significance was that, since they were norms that states could never contract out of, they took for granted the existence of norms that were valid system-wide, regardless of consent by any particular state.

International law today has both volitional and automatic elements, and the theory of statehood that I have formulated (the effectiveness-or-recognition view plus exceptions) is a synthesis of elements of both types. It can now be summarized as follows.

1. There are two coexisting general rules under which an entity may be defined as a state.
    (a) The effectiveness norm: there is a customary norm 'entities that meet effectiveness criteria are defined as states'. The criteria relate to territory, population, government, and independence. They thus relate to how an entity is constructed as a fact by norms of international law (they do not include prior possession of a right or duty) and apply automatically (they do not require an entity to exercise a power).
    (b) The recognition norm: an existing state has a power to recognize an entity as a state with the result that the existing state and the entity are

[1] The emergence of a peremptory norm prohibiting the use of force also helped, in a different way, to stabilize international law as a system: by affirming that it was not subordinate to raw power politics.

defined as states relative to each other. This power is exercisable by unilateral declaration, treaty, or perhaps other volitional means that accord with principles of consent and good faith.

2. There are exceptions to these general rules that reflect the principle that no law arises from unlawfulness. To some extent—though not necessarily in all circumstances—they bring the two general rules into alignment. They include at least the following.
   (a) The premature-recognition exception to the recognition norm: recognition is invalid if it amounts to a breach of the duty to respect a state's territorial integrity (and probably, by analogy, an administering state's rights over a non-self-governing territory). This tends to occur where an entity attempts to secede unilaterally from its parent state and is recognized prematurely, before it meets the effectiveness criteria.
   (b) The collective-non-recognition exception to the recognition norm: recognition is invalid if it breaches a collective duty not to recognize a situation created by a serious breach of a duty arising under a peremptory norm, such as an unlawful use of force.
   (c) The unlawful-effectuation exception to the effectiveness norm: meeting the effectiveness criteria does not create statehood where the fact that an entity meets the criteria is a consequence of a use of force by an external supporter, at a minimum if the supporter's conduct is unlawful and at a minimum while the entity's effectiveness is sustained by the conduct. This exception may extend to an entity that meets the criteria as a consequence of a breach of another peremptory norm.
3. If a people has a right to external self-determination, at least where a recalcitrant administering state is violently resisting the fulfilment of that right, there is probably an exception to some or all of the exceptions: statehood can be acquired under the effectiveness or recognition norm despite arising from unlawfulness. Self-determination also tends to shape the operation of the general rules in less direct ways.
4. There are customary norms in the form 'any entity that is defined as a state has a particular right or other relation'. This creates a package of relations. Since all these relations are acquired by the same means, none of them is analytically more 'fundamental' than the others, though sovereignty has historically been at the core of them.
   (a) An entity that *either* qualifies under the effectiveness norm *or* is validly recognized as a state by all other existing states has the package of relations relative to all other such entities. Either way, it can be described as a state without further qualification.
   (b) An entity that does not qualify under the effectiveness norm and that nonetheless is validly recognized by some but not all other existing states

has the package of relations relative solely to recognizing states. It can be described as a state-in-context.

5. There is a customary norm 'the practice and *opinio iuris* of all the entities that are defined as states contribute to customary norms'. This norm gives rise to the customary norms that create states, but at the same time it arises *from* states created by those norms: together, all these norms form a self-reproducing circle. To call a norm of international law 'valid' means that it can be derived directly or indirectly from this circle.

In arriving at this theory I have not pursued every line of enquiry as far as possible; notably, I have not looked at the effectiveness criteria in as much detail as some scholars (though this is partly because the existence of an alternative path to statehood—the recognition norm—makes it harder be certain when the criteria are being applied). The theory challenges conventional wisdom insofar as it emphasizes that states are not as homogenous as they may appear but have diverse legal underpinnings: effectiveness, recognition, or both. In other ways the theory serves to confirm conventional wisdom. It defends the idea that meaningful 'objective' statements can be made, within the internal framework of international law, about whether an ostensible norm is valid or about whether an entity is a state. It also confirms that the dominant state-like entities with personality in international law today are states in a technical sense.

There is a caveat to the last point—and this is the third respect in which my choice of state-like entities as the category for analysis, rather than states alone, has been rewarding.

Before the twentieth century there is no question that a great variety of state-like entities had personality in international law, including precolonial entities in Africa and elsewhere that were seldom or never described as 'states'. Since then, despite the dominance of states in the strict sense, international law has continued to attribute personality to other state-like entities. This can occur by volitional means—primarily through the power of states to recognize or make treaties with non-states—and, in principle at least, by automatic means. The general rules about statehood can be seen as special applications of the even-more-general principles by which state-like entities of all kinds can acquire personality. States-in-context, of which Palestine and the Saharawi Arab Democratic Republic are possible examples, form an often overlooked category of state-like entities. Others include the likes of the Holy See.

Contrasting these entities with states provides a further insight into what statehood means. In this book I have alluded to two ways in which state-like entities may have something less than 'full' personality. States-in-context have the same package of rights and other relations as states, but their personality is not 'full', in the sense that they have this package solely relative to some existing states, not relative to all of them. Various other state-like entities—subentities of states such as Hong Kong, entities in free association, and so on—have personality that is less than 'full' in a different sense: they lack the whole package. Only states have personality that is 'full' in both senses. I have likened the term 'state' to a cross-reference, because the actual content of the package of relations that is inherent in statehood depends on the changing content of the customary norms that refer to states. But statehood could also be understood, by contrast with the status of the other state-like entities that I have discussed, as the 'fullest' degree of personality and related attributes that is presently available in international law.

I began the book by observing that there is a vagueness to the word 'nation', as incorporated into the term 'international law'. But it may be no worse than any other single word at describing the state-like entities between which international law applies. It might be interpreted broadly and loosely to encapsulate the diversity and instability of the past, the present primacy of states—which themselves have diverse legal underpinnings—and the potential for diversity today. In the nineteenth century, scholars spoke of a family of nations comprising an exclusive inner group of Western states. It would be more accurate, speaking either of their time or of ours, to say that international law applies within a wider 'extended family' of nations.

Bibliography

Ago, Roberto, Second Report on State Responsibility [1970] 2 ILC Ybk 177

Akashi, Kinji, 'Japan–Europe' in Bardo Fassbender and Anne Peters (eds), *The Oxford Handbook of the History of International Law* (OUP 2012) 724

Albert, Hans, *Treatise on Critical Reason* (first published 1968, Mary Varney Rorty tr, Princeton UP 1985)

Alexandrowicz, CH, 'Theory of recognition *in fieri*' (1958) 34 BYIL 176

Alexandrowicz, CH, 'Treaty and diplomatic relations between European and South Asian powers in the seventeenth and eighteenth centuries' (1960) 100 Recueil des cours 203

Alexandrowicz, CH, 'Doctrinal aspects of the universality of the law of nations' (1961) 37 BYIL 506

Alexandrowicz, CH, 'The Afro-Asian world and the law of nations (historical aspects)' (1968) 123 Recueil des cours 117

Alexandrowicz, CH, *The European–African Confrontation: A Study in Treaty Making* (Sijthoff 1973)

Alfonso Martínez, Miguel, Final Report on Treaties, Agreements and Other Constructive Arrangements between States and Indigenous Populations (22 June 1999) UN doc E/CN.4/Sub.2/1999/20

Alfredsson, Gudmundur, 'Indigenous peoples, treaties with' (last updated 2011) MPEPIL

Amerasinghe, CF, *Principles of the Institutional Law of International Organizations* (2nd edn, CUP 2004)

Anderson, Benedict, *Imagined Communities: Reflections on the Origin and Spread of Nationalism* (first published 1983, rev edn, Verso 2006)

Andrews, JA, 'The concept of statehood and the acquisition of territory in the nineteenth century' (1978) 94 Law Quarterly Review 408

Anghie, Antony, *Imperialism, Sovereignty and the Making of International Law* (CUP 2004)

Annacker, Claudia, 'The legal régime of *erga omnes* obligations in international law' (1994) 46 Austrian Journal of Public and International Law 131

Annual Report of the Secretary-General on the Work of the Organization (1 July 1949–30 June 1950) UN doc A/1287

Anonymous, 'Government recognition in Somalia and regional political stability in the Horn of Africa' (2002) 40 Journal of Modern African Studies 247

Anzilotti, Dionisio, *Cours de droit international* (3rd edn, Gilbert Gidel tr, Recueil Sirey 1929)

Applicabilité du droit des gens européen aux nations orientales—questionnaire (1877) 1 Annuaire IDI 141

Arias-Salgado, Fernando, Oral Statement for Spain (18 July 1975) ICJ Pleadings: *Western Sahara*, vol 5, 51

Aspremont, Jean d', *Epistemic Forces in International Law: Foundational Doctrines and Techniques of International Legal Argumentation* (Elgar 2015)

Aust, Anthony, *Modern Treaty Law and Practice* (CUP 2000)

Banner, Stuart, *Possessing the Pacific: Land, Settlers, and Indigenous People from Australia to Alaska* (Harvard UP 2009)

Statehood and the State-Like in International Law. Rowan Nicholson, Oxford University Press (2019).

© Rowan Nicholson

DOI: 10.1093/oso/9780198851219.001.0001

Becker Lorca, Arnulf, *Mestizo International Law: A Global Intellectual History 1842–1933* (CUP 2014)

Becker Lorca, Arnulf, 'Petitioning the international: A "pre-history" of self-determination' (2014) 25 EJIL 497

Bedjaoui, Mohammed, Oral Statement for Algeria (15 July 1975) ICJ Pleadings: *Western Sahara*, vol 4, 467

Bell, Christine, 'Peace agreements: Their nature and legal status' (2006) 100 AJIL 373

Bentham, Jeremy, *Introduction to the Principles of Morals and Legislation* (first published 1789, OUP 1996)

Bernstorff, Jochen von, *The Public International Law Theory of Hans Kelsen* (CUP 2010)

Besson, Samantha, 'Sovereignty' (last updated 2011) MPEPIL

Blay, Samuel KN, 'Territorial integrity and political independence' (last updated 2010) MPEPIL

Bonfils, Henri, and Paul Fauchille, *Manuel de droit international public* (4th edn, Rousseau 1905)

Borchard, Edwin M, *The Diplomatic Protection of Citizens Abroad* (Banks Law 1916)

Bosnia and Herzegovina, Memorial (15 April 1994) ICJ Pleadings: *Application of the Convention on the Prevention and Punishment of the Crime of Genocide (Bosnia and Herzegovina v Yugoslavia (Serbia and Montenegro))*

Bowden, Brett, 'The colonial origins of international law: European expansion and the classical standard of civilization' (2005) 7 Journal of the History of International Law 1

Bowden, Brett, *The Empire of Civilization: The Evolution of an Imperial Idea* (University of Chicago Press 2009)

British and Foreign State Papers: 1823–1824 (Ridgway & Sons 1843)

Brölmann, Catherine, and Janne Elisabeth Nijman, 'Personality' in Jean d'Aspremont and Sahib Singh (eds), *Concepts for International Law: Contributions to Disciplinary Thought* (Elgar 2019) 678

Brown, Philip Marshall, 'The Aaland Islands question' (1921) 15 AJIL 268

Brownlie, Ian, *International Law and the Use of Force by States* (Clarendon 1963)

Brownlie, Ian, 'The expansion of international society: The consequences for the law of nations' in Hedley Bull and Adam Watson (eds), *The Expansion of International Society* (Clarendon 1984) 357

Bryant, Bunyan, and others, 'Recognition of Guinea (Bissau)' (1974) 15 Harvard International Law Journal 482

Bull, Hedley, *The Anarchical Society: A Study of Order in World Politics* (4th edn, Palgrave Macmillan 2012)

Burrell, William (ed), *Reports of Cases Determined by the High Court of Admiralty and Upon Appeal Therefrom* (William Clowes & Sons 1885)

Buzan, Barry, *An Introduction to the English School of International Relations* (Polity 2014)

Byers, Michael, *Custom, Power and the Power of Rules: International Relations and Customary International Law* (CUP 1999)

Calvo, Carlos, *Dictionnaire de droit international public et privé* (Puttkammer & Muhlbrecht 1885)

Campbell, Tom, *Rights: A Critical Introduction* (Routledge 2006)

Cassese, Antonio, *Self-Determination of Peoples: A Legal Reappraisal* (CUP 1995)

Cassese, Antonio, *International Law* (2nd edn, OUP 2005)

Cassese, Antonio, 'States: Rise and decline of the primary subjects of the international community' in Bardo Fassbender and Anne Peters (eds), *The Oxford Handbook of the History of International Law* (OUP 2012) 49

Charpentier, Jean, *La Reconnaissance Internationale et l'Évolution du droit des gens* (Pédone 1956)
Chen, Tiqiang, *The International Law of Recognition with Special Reference to Practice in Great Britain and the United States* (Praeger 1951)
Chiang, Frank, *The One-China Policy: State, Sovereignty, and Taiwan's International Legal Status* (Elsevier 2018)
Cismas, Ioana, *Religious Actors and International Law* (OUP 2014)
Coates, Ken, 'North American Indigenous peoples' encounters' in Bardo Fassbender and Anne Peters (eds), *The Oxford Handbook of the History of International Law* (OUP 2012) 787
Cohen, Jean L, 'Sovereignty in the context of globalization: A constitutional pluralist perspective' in Samantha Besson and John Tasioulas (eds), *The Philosophy of International Law* (OUP 2010) 261
Cohen, Raymond, and Raymond Westbrook (eds), *Amarna Diplomacy: The Beginnings of International Relations* (Johns Hopkins UP 2000)
Combacau, Jean, *Le Droit des traités* (Presses Universitaires de France 1991)
Committee on the Rights of the Child: Replies of the Holy See to the List of Issues (2 December 2013) UN doc CRC/C/VAT/Q/2/Add.1
Corten, Olivier, 'Déclarations unilatérales d'indépendance et reconnaissances prématurées: Du Kosovo à l'Ossétie du sud et à l'Abkhazie' (2008) 112 Revue générale de droit international public 721
Corten, Olivier, 'Article 52: 1969 Vienna Convention' in Olivier Corten and Pierre Klein (eds), *The Vienna Conventions on the Law of Treaties: A Commentary* (OUP 2011) vol 2, 1201
Craven, Matthew, 'What's in a name? The former Yugoslav Republic of Macedonia and issues of statehood' (1995) 16 Australian Yearbook of International Law 199
Crawford, James, *The Creation of States in International Law* (2nd edn, OUP 2006)
Crawford, James, Oral Statement for the UK (10 December 2009) ICJ Pleadings: *Accordance with International Law of the Unilateral Declaration of Independence in Respect of Kosovo*, CR 2009/32, 46
Crawford, James, *Brownlie's Principles of Public International Law* (8th edn, OUP 2012)
Crawford, James, 'Chance, order, change: The course of international law' (2013) 365 Recueil des cours 9
Crawford, James, *State Responsibility: The General Part* (CUP 2013)
Crawford, James, 'Kosovo and the criteria for statehood in international law' in Marko Milanović and Michael Wood (eds), *The Law and Politics of the Kosovo Advisory Opinion* (OUP 2015) 280
Crawford, James, and Rowan Nicholson, 'The continued relevance of established rules and institutions regarding the use of force' in Marc Weller (ed), *The Oxford Handbook of the Use of Force in International Law* (OUP 2015) 96
'The crisis in Korea' (1968) 58 US Department of State Bulletin 188
Dawidowicz, Martin, 'The obligation of non-recognition of an unlawful situation' in James Crawford, Alain Pellet, and Simon Olleson (eds), *The Law of International Responsibility* (OUP 2010) 677
Dawson, Christopher (ed), *The Mongol Mission: Narratives and Letters of the Franciscan Missionaries in Mongolia and China in the Thirteenth and Fourteenth Centuries* (Sheed & Ward 1955)
Dickinson, Edwin DeWitt, *The Equality of States in International Law* (Harvard UP 1920)
Documents relatifs à la session de La Haye, 25–31 Août 1875 (1877) 1 Annuaire IDI 36

Dugard, John, *Recognition and the United Nations* (Grotius 1987)
Dugard, John, 'The secession of states and their recognition in the wake of Kosovo' (2013) 357 Recueil des cours 9
Dworkin, Ronald, *Law's Empire* (Hart 1986)
Edmundson, William A, *Introduction to Rights* (CUP 2004)
Explanatory Note Concerning the Request for the Admission of the State of Palestine to Unesco (12 May 1989) Unesco doc 131 EX/43
Fabry, Mikulas, *Recognizing States: International Society and the Establishment of New States since 1776* (OUP 2010)
Fairbank, JK, 'The early treaty system in the Chinese world order' in JK Fairbank and Ta-tuan Ch'en (eds), *The Chinese World Order: Traditional China's Foreign Relations* (Harvard UP 1968) 257
Fassbender, Bardo, and Anne Peters (eds), *The Oxford Handbook of the History of International Law* (OUP 2012)
Fastenrath, Ulrich, 'Article 3' in Bruno Simma and others (eds), *The Charter of the United Nations: A Commentary* (3rd edn, OUP 2012) 335
Fastenrath, Ulrich, 'Article 73' in Bruno Simma and others (eds), *The Charter of the United Nations: A Commentary* (3rd edn, OUP 2012) 1829
Fawcett, JES, 'Security Council resolutions on Rhodesia' (1965–66) 41 BYIL 103
Fawcett, JES, 'Note' (1971) 34 Modern Law Review 417
Fellmeth, Aaron X, and Maurice Horwitz, *Guide to Latin in International Law* (OUP 2009)
Ferguson, Yale H, 'Governance, global' in Bertrand Badie, Dirk Berg-Schlosser, and Leonardo Morlino (eds), *International Encyclopedia of Political Science* (SAGE 2011) vol 4, 1010
Ferguson, Yale H, and Richard W Mansbach, *Polities: Authority, Identities and Change* (South Carolina Press 1996)
Finck, François, 'The State between fact and law: The role of recognition and the conditions under which it is granted in the creation of new States' (2016) 36 Polish Yearbook of International Law 51
Fisch, Jörg, 'Peoples and nations' in Bardo Fassbender and Anne Peters (eds), *The Oxford Handbook of the History of International Law* (OUP 2012) 27
Fitzmaurice, Andrew, 'Discovery, conquest, and occupation of territory' in Bardo Fassbender and Anne Peters (eds), *The Oxford Handbook of the History of International Law* (OUP 2012) 840
Fitzmaurice, Andrew, 'Equality of non-European nations in international law' in Randall Lesaffer and Inge van Hulle (eds), *International Law in the Long Nineteenth Century* (Brill 2018)
Foreign Relations of the United States: Japan: 1931–1941 (US GPO 1943)
Frowein, Jochen A, 'De facto regime' (last updated 2013) MPEPIL
Gathii, James Thuo, 'Imperialism, colonialism, and international law' (2007) 54 Buffalo Law Review 1013
Gong, Gerrit W, *The Standard of 'Civilization' in International Society* (Clarendon 1984)
Gowlland-Debbas, Vera, *Collective Responses to Illegal Acts in International Law: United Nations Action in the Question of Southern Rhodesia* (Nijhoff 1990)
Grant, Thomas D, 'Defining statehood: The Montevideo Convention and its discontents' (1999) 37 Columbia Journal of Transnational Law 403
Grant, Thomas D, *The Recognition of States: Law and Practice in Debate and Evolution* (Praeger 1999)

Grant, Thomas D, *Admission to the United Nations: Charter Article 4 and the Rise of Universal Organization* (Nijhoff 2009)

Grant, Thomas D, 'Who can make treaties? Other subjects of international law' in Duncan B Hollis (ed), *The Oxford Guide to Treaties* (OUP 2012) 125

Grant, Thomas D, *Aggression against Ukraine: Territory, Responsibility, and International Law* (Palgrave Macmillan 2015)

Gray, Christine, *International Law and the Use of Force* (3rd edn, OUP 2008)

Grewe, Wilhelm G, *The Epochs of the Law of Nations* (first published 1984, Michael Byers tr, de Gruyter 2000)

Grotius, Hugo, *The Rights of War and Peace* (first published 1625, Richard Tuck ed, Liberty Fund 2005)

Guggenheim, Paul, *Traité de droit international public: Avec mention de la pratique internationale et suisse* (Librairie de l'Université, Georg & Cie 1953)

Hall, WE, *A Treatise on International Law* (4th edn, Clarendon 1895)

Hanrahan, David G, 'Legal aspects of the Panama Canal Zone—in perspective' (1965) 45 Boston University Law Review 64

Harcourt, William Vernon, *Letters by Historicus on Some Questions of International Law* (Macmillan 1863)

Hart, HLA, *The Concept of Law* (first published 1961, 3rd edn, OUP 2012)

Hazard, John N, 'Cleansing Soviet international law of anti-Marxist theories' (1938) 32 AJIL 244

Hazard, John N, 'Socialism and international public law' (1985) 23 Columbia Journal of Transnational Law 251

Hébié, Mamadou, 'The role of the agreements concluded with local political entities in the course of French colonial expansion in West Africa' (2015) 85 BYIL 21

Hegel, GWF, *Elements of the Philosophy of Right* (first published 1821, HB Nisbet tr, CUP 1991)

Heldrich, Andreas, and Anton F Steiner, 'Legal personality' in Alex Chloros, Max Rheinstein, and Mary Ann Glendon (eds), *International Encyclopedia of Comparative Law*, vol 4: *Persons and Family* (Mohr 2007) 3

Higgins, Rosalyn, *The Development of International Law Through the Political Organs of the United Nations* (OUP 1963)

Higgins, Rosalyn, 'Conceptual thinking about the individual in international law' (1978) 4 British Journal of International Studies 1

Hillgruber, Christian, 'The admission of new states to the international community' (1998) 9 EJIL 491

Hillsborough, Romulus, *Samurai Revolution: The Dawn of Modern Japan Seen through the Eyes of the Shogun's Last Samurai* (Tuttle 2014)

Hobbes, Thomas, *Leviathan* (first published 1651, Richard Tuck ed, CUP 1996)

Hobsbawm, Eric, *The Age of Revolution: 1789–1848* (Weidenfeld & Nicolson 1962)

Hochschild, Adam, *King Leopold's Ghost: A Story of Greed, Terror, and Heroism in Colonial Africa* (Houghton Mifflin 1998)

Hoffmeister, Frank, 'Litigating against the European Union and its Member States—who responds under the ILC's Draft Articles on international responsibility of international organizations?' (2010) 21 EJIL 723

Hofmann, Rainer, 'Annexation' (last updated 2013) MPEPIL

Hohfeld, WN, 'Nature of stockholders' individual liability for corporation debts' (1909) 9 Columbia Law Review 285

Hohfeld, WN, 'Some fundamental legal conceptions as applied in judicial reasoning [part 1]' (1913) 23 Yale Law Journal 16

Hohfeld, WN, 'Some fundamental legal conceptions as applied in judicial reasoning [part 2]' (1917) 26 Yale Law Journal 710

Holland, TE, *Studies in International Law* (Clarendon 1898)

Holland, TE, *Lectures on International Law* (Sweet & Maxwell 1933)

Hollis, Duncan B, 'Why state consent still matters—non-state actors, treaties, and the changing sources of international law' (2005) 23 Berkeley Journal of International Law 137

Holsti, KJ, *Taming the Sovereigns: Institutional Change in International Politics* (CUP 2004)

Hsü, Immanuel CY, *China's Entrance into the Family of Nations* (Harvard UP 1960)

Hui, Victoria Tin-bor, *War and State Formation in Ancient China and Early Modern Europe* (CUP 2005)

Identification of Customary Law: Comments and Observations Received from Governments (14 February 2018) UN doc A/CN.4/716

Igarashi, Masahiro, *Associated Statehood in International Law* (Kluwer 2002)

Ijalaye, David A, 'Was "Biafra" at any time a state in international law?' (1971) 65 AJIL 551

Independent International Commission on Kosovo, *The Kosovo Report: Conflict, International Response, Lessons Learned* (OUP 2000)

International Criminal Court, 'The Prosecutor of the International Criminal Court, Fatou Bensouda, opens a preliminary examination of the situation in Palestine' (press release, 16 January 2015)

International Court of Justice, 'The Republic of the Marshall Islands files Applications against nine States for their alleged failure to fulfil their obligations with respect to the cessation of the nuclear arms race at an early date and to nuclear disarmament' (press release, 25 April 2014)

International Crisis Group, Somalia and the Gulf Crisis (Africa Report No 260, 5 June 2018)

International Meeting of Experts on Further Study of the Concept of the Rights of Peoples, Final Report and Recommendations (22 February 1990) Unesco doc SNS-89/CONF.602/7

Jennings, Robert, *The Acquisition of Territory in International Law* (Manchester UP 1963)

Jennings, Robert, and Arthur Watts, *Oppenheim's International Law* (9th edn, Longman 1996)

Jessup, Philip C, 'The Palmas Island arbitration' (1928) 22 AJIL 735

Kanza, Thomas, *Conflict in the Congo: The Rise and Fall of Lumumba* (Penguin 1972)

Kattan, Victor (ed), *The Palestine Question in International Law* (British Institute of International and Comparative Law 2008)

Keeton, GW, *The Development of Extraterritoriality in China* (Longmans, Green, & Co 1928)

Kelsen, Hans, 'Recognition in international law: Theoretical observations' (1941) 35 AJIL 605

Kelsen, Hans, *General Theory of Law and State* (Anders Wedberg tr, Harvard UP 1949)

Kelsen, Hans, 'The draft Declaration on Rights and Duties of States: Critical remarks' (1950) 44 AJIL 259

Kelsen, Hans, *Principles of International Law* (Rinehart 1952)

Kelsen, Hans, 'Théorie du droit international public' (1953) 84 Recueil des cours 1

King, Michael, and Chris Thornhill, *Niklas Luhmann's Theory of Politics and Law* (Palgrave Macmillan 2003)

Kohen, Marcelo (ed), *Secession: International Law Perspectives* (CUP 2006)

Kohen, Marcelo, and Sarah Heathcote, 'Article 42: 1969 Vienna Convention' in Olivier Corten and Pierre Klein (eds), *The Vienna Conventions on the Law of Treaties: A Commentary* (OUP 2011) vol 2, 1015

Korovin, Evgeny, 'La République des Soviets et le droit international' [1925] Revue générale de droit international public 292

Koskenniemi, Martti, *The Gentle Civilizer of Nations: The Rise and Fall of International Law 1870–1960* (CUP 2001)

Kramer, Matthew H, 'Rights without trimmings' in Matthew H Kramer, NE Simmonds, and Hillel Steiner, *A Debate over Rights: Philosophical Enquiries* (Clarendon 1998) 7

Kreijen, Gerard, *State Failure, Sovereignty and Effectiveness: Legal Lessons from the Decolonization of Sub-Saharan Africa* (Nijhoff 2004)

Lael, Richard L, 'Struggle for ratification: Wilson, Lodge, and the Thomson–Urrutia Treaty' (1978) 2 Diplomatic History 81

Lauterpacht, Hersch, 'Règles générales du droit de la paix' (1937) 62 Recueil des cours 95

Lauterpacht, Hersch, *Recognition in International Law* (first published 1947, CUP 2013)

Lauterpacht, Hersch, 'The subjects of the law of nations [part 1]' (1947) 63 Law Quarterly Review 438

Lauterpacht, Hersch, 'The subjects of the law of nations [part 2]' (1948) 64 Law Quarterly Review 97

Lauterpacht, Hersch, Report on the Law of Treaties [1953] 2 ILC Ybk 90

Lawson, FH, 'The creative use of legal concepts' (1957) 32 New York University Law Review 909

Liang, Yuen-Li, 'Reparation for Injuries Suffered in the Service of the United Nations' (1949) 43 AJIL 460

Lindley, MF, *The Acquisition and Government of Backward Territory in International Law* (Longmans, Green, & Co 1926)

Lissitzyn, Oliver J, 'Efforts to codify or restate the law of treaties' (1962) 62 Columbia Law Review 1166

Liszt, Franz von, *Le droit international* (first published 1913, Gilbert Gidel tr, Pédone 1927)

Longobardo, Marco, 'The self-proclaimed statehood of the Islamic State between 2014 and 2017 and international law' (2017) 33 Anuario Español de Derecho Internacional 205

Lorimer, James, *The Institutes of the Law of Nations: A Treatise of the Jural Relations of Separate Political Communities* (William Blackwood & Sons 1883–84)

Lowe, Vaughan, *International Law* (OUP 2007)

Luhmann, Niklas, 'The self-reproduction of law and its limits' in Gunther Teubner (ed), *Dilemmas of Law in the Welfare State* (de Gruyter 1988) 111

Luhmann, Niklas, *Law as a Social System* (first published 1993, Klaus Ziegert tr, OUP 2004)

MacCormick, Neil, *Institutions of Law: An Essay in Legal Theory* (OUP 2007)

Mälksoo, Lauri, 'Russia–Europe' in Bardo Fassbender and Anne Peters (eds), *The Oxford Handbook of the History of International Law* (OUP 2012) 764

Manning, William R (ed), *Diplomatic Correspondence of the United States Concerning the Independence of the Latin American Nations* (OUP 1925)

Marek, Krystyna, *Identity and Continuity of States in Public International Law* (2nd edn, Librairie Droz 1968)

Martens, Georg Friedrich von, *Précis du droit des gens moderne de l'Europe* (new edn, Aillaud 1831)

Martens, Kurt, 'The position of the Holy See and Vatican City State in international relations' (2006) 83 University of Detroit Mercy Law Review 729

McNair, Arnold Duncan (ed), *International Law Opinions* (CUP 1956)

Message of the President of the United States to the Two Houses of Congress, at the Commencement of the Second Session of the Thirty-seventh Congress (Foreign Relations series, US GPO 1861)

Michaels, Ralf, 'What is non-state law? A primer' in Michael A Helfand (ed), *Negotiating State and Non-State Law: The Challenge of Global and Local Legal Pluralism* (CUP 2015) 41
Milanović, Marko, 'Arguing the Kosovo case' in Marko Milanović and Michael Wood (eds), *The Law and Politics of the Kosovo Advisory Opinion* (OUP 2015) 21
Miller, David Hunter, *The Drafting of the Covenant* (GP Putnam's Sons 1928)
Moore, John Bassett, *A Digest of International Law* (US GPO 1906)
Morgenthau, Hans, 'Positivism, functionalism, and international law' (1940) 34 AJIL 260
Morgenthau, Hans, *Politics among Nations: The Struggle for Power and Peace* (2nd edn, Knopf 1954)
Morss, John R, 'The legal relations of collectives: Belated insights from Hohfeld' (2009) 22 Leiden Journal of International Law 289
Morss, John R, 'The international legal status of the Vatican/Holy See complex' (2015) 26 EJIL 927
Muldoon, James (ed), *The Expansion of Europe: The First Phase* (University of Pennsylvania Press 1977)
Murray, Daragh, *Human Rights Obligations of Non-State Armed Groups* (Hart 2016)
Naff, Thomas, 'The Ottoman Empire and the European states system' in Hedley Bull and Adam Watson (eds), *The Expansion of International Society* (Clarendon 1984) 143
Naffine, Ngaire, 'Who are law's persons? From Cheshire Cats to responsible subjects' (2003) 66 Modern Law Review 346
Nanda, Ved P, 'Self-determination in international law: The tragic tale of two cities—Islamabad (West Pakistan) and Dacca (East Pakistan)' (1972) 66 AJIL 321
Neff, Stephen C, *Justice among Nations: A History of International Law* (Harvard UP 2014)
Neff, Stephen C, 'The dormancy, rise and decline of fundamental liberties of states' (2015) 4 Cambridge Journal of International and Comparative Law 482
Netherlands, Written Statement (17 April 2009) ICJ Pleadings: *Accordance with International Law of the Unilateral Declaration of Independence in Respect of Kosovo*
Nijman, Janne Elisabeth, *The Concept of International Legal Personality: An Inquiry into the History and Theory of International Law* (Asser 2004)
Nikravesh, Babak, 'Quebec and Tatarstan in international law' (1999) 23 Fletcher Forum of World Affairs 227
Nobles, Richard, and David Schiff, 'Introduction' in Niklas Luhmann, *Law as a Social System* (first published 1993, Klaus Ziegert tr, OUP 2004) 1
Nobles, Richard, and David Schiff, *A Sociology of Jurisprudence* (Hart 2006)
Nobles, Richard, and David Schiff, *Observing Law through Systems Theory* (Hart 2013)
Nordquist, Myron, Satya N Nandan, and Shabtai Rosenne (eds), *United Nations Convention on the Law of the Sea, 1982: A Commentary* (first published 1985, Brill 2013)
Nys, Ernest, *Les origines du droit international* (Castaigne 1894)
Obregón Tarazona, Liliana, 'The civilized and the uncivilized' in Bardo Fassbender and Anne Peters (eds), *The Oxford Handbook of the History of International Law* (OUP 2012) 917
O'Connell, DP, 'International law and boundary disputes' (1960) 54 ASIL Proc 77
O'Connell, DP, *State Succession in Municipal Law and International Law* (CUP 1967)
Oeter, Stefan, 'International law and general systems theory' (2001) 44 German Yearbook of International Law 72
Onuma, Yasuaki, 'When was the law of international society born? An inquiry of the history of international law from an intercivilizational perspective' (2000) 2 Journal of the History of International Law 1

Oppenheim, LFL, *International Law* (Longmans, Green, & Co 1905–6)
Oppenheim, LFL, *International Law* (3rd edn, Ronald F Roxburgh ed, Longmans, Green, & Co 1920)
Orakhelashvili, Alexander, 'The idea of European international law' (2006) 17 EJIL 315
Orakhelashvili, Alexander, *Peremptory Norms in International Law* (OUP 2008)
Orakhelashvili, Alexander, 'Statehood, recognition and the United Nations system: A unilateral declaration of independence in Kosovo' (2008) 12 Max Planck Yearbook of United Nations Law 1
Özsu, Umut, 'The Ottoman Empire' in Bardo Fassbender and Anne Peters (eds), *The Oxford Handbook of the History of International Law* (OUP 2012) 429
Paparinskis, Martins, 'Regulating treaties: A comparative perspective' in Christian J Tams, Antonios Tzanakopoulos, and Andreas Zimmermann (eds), *Research Handbook on the Law of Treaties* (Elgar 2014) 39
Papers Relating to the Foreign Relations of the United States: 1904 (US GPO 1904)
Parfitt, Rose, '*Empire des nègres blancs*: The hybridity of international personality and the Abyssinia crisis of 1935–36' (2011) 24 Leiden Journal of International Law 849
Parfitt, Rose, 'The spectre of sources' (2014) 25 EJIL 297
Parfitt, Rose, 'Theorizing recognition and international personality' in Florian Hoffmann and Anne Orford (eds), *The Oxford Handbook of the Theory of International Law* (OUP 2016) 583
Parlett, Kate, *The Individual in the International Legal System: Continuity and Change in International Law* (CUP 2011)
Parry, Clive, and Charity Hopkins (eds), *Index to British Treaties 1101–1968* (Her Majesty's Stationery Office 1970)
Patel, Bimal N, 'India' in Bardo Fassbender and Anne Peters (eds), *The Oxford Handbook of the History of International Law* (OUP 2012) 500
Pegg, Scott, *International Society and the De Facto State* (Ashgate 1998)
Pegg, Scott, and Pål Kolstø, 'Somaliland: Dynamics of internal legitimacy and (lack of) external sovereignty' (2015) 66 Geoforum 193
Pellet, Alain, 'Article 38' in Andreas Zimmermann and others (eds), *The Statute of the International Court of Justice: A Commentary* (OUP 2012) 731
Pellet, Alain, 'Kosovo—the questions not asked: Self-determination, secession, and recognition' in Marko Milanović and Michael Wood (eds), *The Law and Politics of the Kosovo Advisory Opinion* (OUP 2015) 268
Peters, Anne, 'Treaty making power' (last updated 2009) MPEPIL
Peyrefitte, Alain, *The Collision of Two Civilisations: The British Expedition to China in 1792–4* (Jon Rothschild tr, Harper Collins 1993)
Piggott, Francis, *Extraterritoriality: The Law Relating to Consular Jurisdiction* (Butterworth 1907)
Pitts, Jennifer, 'Empire and legal universalisms in the eighteenth century' (2012) 117 American Historical Review 92
Portmann, Roland, *Legal Personality in International Law* (CUP 2010)
Pufendorf, Samuel von, *De jure naturae et gentium* (first published 1672, CH Oldfather tr, Clarendon 1934)
Quatrième commission d'étude—application aux nations orientales du droit des gens coutumier de l'Europe (1879) 3–4(1) Annuaire IDI 298
Quigley, John, 'The Israel–PLO interim agreements: Are they treaties?' (1997) 30 Cornell International Law Journal 717
Raič, David, *Statehood and the Law of Self-Determination* (Kluwer 2002)

Rasilla del Moral, Ignacio de la, 'The shifting origins of international law' (2015) 28 Leiden Journal of International Law 419

Redslob, Robert, 'La reconnaissance de l'état comme sujet de droit international' (1934) 13 Revue de droit international 429

Report of the Committee on the Admission of New Members Concerning the Application of Palestine for Admission to Membership in the United Nations (11 November 2011) UN doc S/2011/705

Report of the International Committee of Jurists upon the Legal Aspects of the Aaland Islands Question (1920) 3 LNOJ Sp Supp 3

Report Provided for in Article 15(4) of the Covenant on Manchuria (1933) 112 LNOJ Sp Supp 56

Report of the Secretary-General on the United Nations Interim Administration Mission in Kosovo (8 November 2012) UN doc S/2012/818

Report Submitted to the Council of the League of Nations by the Commission of Rapporteurs on the Aaland Islands Question (16 April 1921) LN doc B7 21/68/106

Republic of China (Taiwan) Mainland Affairs Council, 'The official position of the Republic of China (Taiwan) on the People's Republic of China's Anti-Secession (Anti-Separation) Law' (press release, 29 March 2005)

Restatement of the Law: The Foreign Relations Law of the United States (3rd edn, American Law Institute 1987)

Reynolds, Henry, *Aboriginal Sovereignty: Reflections on Race, State and Nation* (Allen & Unwin 1996)

Rich, Roland, 'Recognition of states: The collapse of Yugoslavia and the Soviet Union' (1993) 4 EJIL 36

Rodríguez Cedeño, Victor, Sixth Report on Unilateral Acts of States [2003] 2(1) ILC Ybk 53

Ronen, Yaël, *Transition from Illegal Regimes under International Law* (CUP 2010)

Ross, Alf, *A Textbook of International Law: General Part* (Annie I Fausbøll tr, Longmans, Green, & Co 1947)

Rousseau, Charles, 'Chronique des faits internationaux' (1974) 78 Revue générale de droit international public 1096

Saganek, Przemysław, *Unilateral Acts of States in International Law* (Brill 2016)

Sahli, Fatiha, and Abdelmalek El Ouazzani, 'Africa north of the Sahara and Arab countries' in Bardo Fassbender and Anne Peters (eds), *The Oxford Handbook of the History of International Law* (OUP 2012) 385

Salmon, Jean, 'Naissance et reconnaissance du Bangla-Desh' in Josef Tittel (ed), *Multitudo legum ius unum: Festschrift für Wilhelm Wengler* (Interrecht 1973) vol 1, 467

Salmond, John, *Jurisprudence* (7th edn, Sweet & Maxwell 1924)

Sari, Aurel, 'The conclusion of international agreements by the European Union in the context of the ESDP' (2008) 57 ICLQ 53

Scharf, Michael P, 'Musical chairs: The dissolution of States and membership in the United Nations' (1995) 28 Cornell International Law Journal 29

Schermers, Henry G, and Niels M Blokker, *International Institutional Law: Unity within Diversity* (5th rev, Nijhoff 2011)

Schlag, Pierre, 'How to do things with Hohfeld' (2015) 78 Law and Contemporary Problems 185

Schlesinger, Rudolf, *Soviet Legal Theory* (2nd edn, Routledge 1951)

Schwarzenberger, Georg, 'The standard of civilisation in international law' (1955) 8 Current Legal Problems 212

Schwarzenberger, Georg, and ED Brown, *A Manual of International Law* (6th edn, Professional Books 1976)

Scott, James Brown, 'The treaty between Colombia and the United States' (1921) 15 AJIL 430
Searle, John R, *Speech Acts: An Essay in the Philosophy of Language* (CUP 1969)
Serbia, Written Statement (15 April 2009) ICJ Pleadings, *Accordance with International Law of the Unilateral Declaration of Independence in Respect of Kosovo*
Serge, Victor, and Natalia Sedova-Trotsky, *The Life and Death of Leon Trotsky* (Arnold J Pomerans tr, Wildwood House 1975)
Sextus Empiricus, *Outlines of Scepticism* (first published late 2nd century, Julia Annas and Jonathan Barnes trs, rev edn, CUP 2000)
Seyersted, Finn, *The Common Law of International Organizations* (Nijhoff 2008)
Shaw, Malcolm N, *Title to Territory in Africa: International Legal Issues* (Clarendon 1986)
Shaw, Malcolm N, *International Law* (7th edn, CUP 2014)
Simma, Bruno, 'NATO, the UN and the use of force: Legal aspects' (1999) 10 EJIL 1
Simon, Sven, 'Western Sahara' in Christian Walter, Antje von Ungern-Sternberg, and Kavus Abushov (eds), *Self-Determination and Secession in International Law* (OUP 2014) 255
Simpson, Gerry, *Great Powers and Outlaw States: Unequal Sovereigns in the International Legal Order* (CUP 2004)
Sinha, S Prakash, 'Perspective of the newly independent states on the binding quality of international law' (1965) 14 ICLQ 121
Sivakumaran, Sandesh, 'The addressees of Common Article 3' in Andrew Clapham, Paola Gaeta, and Marco Sassòli (eds), *The 1949 Geneva Conventions: A Commentary* (OUP 2015) 415
Smit Duijzentkunst, Bart L, *The Concept of Rights in International Law* (doctoral thesis, University of Cambridge, 2015)
Smith, Bryant, 'Legal personality' (1928) 37 Yale Law Journal 283
Smith, Herbert Arthur (ed), *Great Britain and the Law of Nations*, vol 1: *States* (PS King & Son 1932)
Stark, Francis R, *The Abolition of Privateering and the Declaration of Paris* (Columbia University 1897)
Stewart, Watt, 'The ratification of the Thomson–Urrutia Treaty' (1930) 10 Southwestern Political and Social Science Quarterly 416
Suy, Eric, *Les Actes juridiques unilatéraux en droit international public* (Librairie Générale de Droit et de Jurisprudence 1962)
Svarverud, Rune, *International Law as World Order in Late Imperial China: Translation, Reception and Discourse, 1847–1911* (Brill 2007)
Sweden, 'Sweden recognises Palestine and increases aid' (press release, 30 October 2014)
Talmon, Stefan, *Recognition of Governments in International Law with Particular Reference to Governments in Exile* (OUP 1998)
Talmon, Stefan, 'The constitutive versus the declaratory theory of recognition: *Tertium non datur*?' (2005) 75 BYIL 101
Talmon, Stefan, 'The duty not to "recognize as lawful" a situation created by the unlawful use of force or other serious breaches of a *jus cogens* obligation: An obligation without real substance?' in Christian Tomuschat and Jean-Marc Thouvenin (eds), *The Fundamental Rules of the International Legal Order: Jus Cogens and Obligations Erga Omnes* (Brill 2005) 99
Tams, Christian J, *Enforcing Obligations Erga Omnes in International Law* (CUP 2005)
Tang, Chi-Hua, 'China–Europe' in Bardo Fassbender and Anne Peters (eds), *The Oxford Handbook of the History of International Law* (OUP 2012) 701
Teubner, Gunther, 'Autopoiesis in law and society: A rejoinder to Blankenburg' (1984) 18 Law and Society Review 291
Teubner, Gunther, *Law as an Autopoietic System* (Anne Bankowska and Ruth Adler trs, Blackwell 1993)

Thirlway, Hugh, *The Law and Procedure of the International Court of Justice: Fifty Years of Jurisprudence* (first published 1989–2011, OUP 2013)
Thirlway, Hugh, *The Sources of International Law* (OUP 2014)
Tomuschat, Christian, 'Recognition of new States—the case of premature recognition' in Peter Hipold (ed), *Kosovo and International Law: The ICJ Advisory Opinion of 22 July 2010* (Nijhoff 2012) 31
Tur, Richard, 'The "person" in law' in Arthur Peacocke and Grant Gillett (eds), *Persons and Personality: A Contemporary Inquiry* (Blackwell 1987) 116
Twiss, Travers, 'Applicability of the European Law of Nations to African Slave States' (1876) 1 Law Magazine and Review 409
US Department of State, 'Somalia President Hassan Sheikh Mohamud's visit to Washington, DC' (press release, 17 January 2013)
Vattel, Emer de, *The Law of Nations* (first published 1758, Béla Kapossy and Richard Whatmore eds, Liberty Fund 2008)
Vidmar, Jure, 'Explaining the legal effects of recognition' (2012) 61 ICLQ 361
Vidmar, Jure, *Democratic Statehood in International Law: The Emergence of New States in Post-Cold War Practice* (Hart 2013)
Vitoria, Francisco de, *De Indis et de jure belli* (first published 1557, John Pawley Bate tr, Carnegie Institution of Washington 1917)
Waldock, Humphrey, First Report on the Law of Treaties [1962] 2 ILC Ybk 27
Wallström, Margot, 'The Government will decide today to recognise the State of Palestine' (30 October 2014) DN Debatt
Walter, Christian, Antje von Ungern-Sternberg, and Kavus Abushov (eds), *Self-Determination and Secession in International Law* (OUP 2014)
Warbrick, Colin, 'States and recognition in international law' in Malcolm D Evans (ed), *International Law* (2nd edn, OUP 2006) 217
Warbrick, Colin, 'Kosovo: The declaration of independence' (2008) 57 ICLQ 675
Ward, Robert, *An Enquiry into the Foundation and History of the Law of Nations in Europe from the Time of the Greeks and Romans to the Age of Grotius* (first published 1795, Garland 1973)
Weil, Prosper, 'Le droit international public en quête de son identité: Cours général de droit international public' (1992) 237 Recueil des cours 9
Wesley, Charles H, 'The struggle for the recognition of Haiti and Liberia as independent republics' (1917) 2 Journal of Negro History 369
Westlake, John, *Chapters on the Principles of International Law* (CUP 1894)
Wheaton, Henry, *Elements of International Law* (3rd edn, Lea & Blanchard 1846)
Wheeler, Gerald C, *The Tribe, and Intertribal Relations in Australia* (J Murray 1910)
Whyte, Frederick, *China and Foreign Powers: An Historical Review of their Relations* (OUP 1927)
Wight, Martin, *Systems of States* (Leicester UP 1977)
Wight, Martin, *Power Politics* (2nd edn, Penguin 1979)
Woolsey, Theodore S, 'The recognition of Panama and its results' (1904) 3 Canadian Law Review 91
Worster, William Thomas, 'Relative international legal personality of non-state actors' (2016) 42 Brooklyn Journal of International Law 207
Yamauchi, Susumu, 'Civilization and international law in Japan during the Meiji era (1868–1912)' (1994) 24 Hitotsubashi Journal of Law and Politics 1

Index

Note: *For the benefit of digital users, indexed terms that span two pages (e.g., 52–53) may, on occasion, appear on only one of those pages.*

Statehood and the State-Like in International Law. Rowan Nicholson, Oxford University Press (2019).

© Rowan Nicholson

DOI: 10.1093/oso/9780198851219.001.0001